Global Stage

Teacher's Book 4

Dave Tucker

macmillan education

Macmillan Education
4 Crinan Street
London N1 9XW
A division of Springer Nature Limited

Companies and representatives throughout the world

Teacher's Book ISBN 978-1-380-00248-8
Teacher's Blended Pack ISBN 978-1-380-00246-4

Written by Dave Tucker

First published 2019

Designed by emc design ltd
Front cover design and concept by 3CD
Cover adaptation by Roberto Martinez

The authors and publishers would like to thank the following for permission to reproduce their photographs: Matthew Hayes (p. 16), Lina Acosta Sandaal (p. 18)

The authors and publishers are grateful for permission to reprint the following copyright material: p. 11 Extract from 'Framework for 21st Century Learning' © 2017 Partnership for 21st Century Skills. Reprinted with permission; p. 17 Extract from 'Collaborative for Academic, Social, and Emotional Learning' © 2017 CASEL. Reprinted with permission.

Full acknowledgements for illustrations and photographs in the facsimile pages can be found in the **Language Book** ISBN: 978-1-380-00247-1 and **Literacy Book** ISBN: 978-1-786-32593-8.

Printed and bound in Mexico

This book was printed in November 2018 by:
Editorial Impresora Apolo, S.A. de C.V.
Centeno 150-6, Granjas Esmeralda,
Iztapalapa, C.P. 09810,
Ciudad de México, México.

2023 2022 2021 2020 2019
10 9 8 7 6 5 4 3 2 1

Contents

macmillan education

Unit	Vocabulary	Explore Language	Global Citizenship
Language Review	**Vocabulary** *Performance, Time, Money, Math, Patterns, Materials, Illnesses, Cures, Machines* **Grammar** *Have to, Don't Have to, Should, Shouldn't, Present Progressive, Comparatives, Superlatives, Going to*		
1 Let's Start with Art page 10	**Types of Art** *collage, installation, landscape, mobile, mural, photography, portrait, sculpture, sketch, still life* **Describing Art** *background, bright, dark, detailed, foreground, light, pale, shadow, simple* **Song** *Art is for Everyone*	Quantifiers: *A Little, A Few, All, Most* *Too* and *Enough* with adjectives	Why is art important to peop **Listening Skills** Listening for gist and details
2 How Long Is It? page 22	**Experiments** *experiment, float, height, length, measure, pour, scale, thermometer, weight, width* **Time** *calendar, century, decade, hour, millennium, minute, month, second, year* **Song** *Measure It!*	Future Predictions: *Going to* and *Will* Future Plans: Present Progressive	Why do we measure time? **Listening Skills** Listening for gist and details
Put It Together	**Review Units 1 and 2** *Give a Reason!*		
3 Be My Friend page 36	**Emotions** *calm, confident, embarrassed, grateful, lonely, nervous, proud, relaxed, stressed, upset* **Friendships** *break a promise, forgive, get along well with, have a falling out with, keep in touch with, laugh at, make a promise, make friends with, tell a secret* **Song** *You'll Be Fine*	First Conditional: Statements First Conditional: Questions	What does it mean to be a friend? **Listening Skills** Listening for gist and details
4 What's Up There? page 48	**Space** *astronaut, astronomer, comet, galaxy, observatory, planet, shooting star, solar system, spaceship, telescope* **Mars** *crater, Earth, ice cap, iron, Mars, rock, sand dune, satellite, soil* **Song** *The Astronomer's Song*	Modal Verbs of Obligation: *Have to* and *Must* Modal Verbs of Possibility and Advice: *Might* and *Should*	Why is it important to learn about space? **Listening Skills** Listening for gist and details
Put It Together	**Review Units 3 and 4** *Race Around the Galaxy*		
5 So That's How They Did It page 62	**Vikings** *crops, fight, helmet, hunt, shield, stew, sword, village, warrior, weave* **Trade and Travel** *coins, fur, honey, jewelry, leather, necklace, pottery, silk, spices, wheat, wood* **Song** *The Viking Life*	*Used to*: Statements *Used to*: Questions	Why did people trade and explore in the past? **Listening Skills** Listening for gist and details

peaking	Writing	International English	Literacy Book
			Literacy: *Scanning, Making Inferences and Predictions, Identifying Perspective, Identifying Facts and Opinions, Author's Purpose, Cause and Effect* **Spelling:** *–ough, –ight, or, ar*
onversation iving opinions **ronunciation** lent *gh* 1	**Sentence Building** Reviewing parts of speech **Product** Cinquain Poems	**US** *I kind of like it.* **UK** *I quite like it.*	**Fantasy** *True Colors* **Instructional Text** *My Guide to Photography* **Reading Skill** Understanding facts and opinions
resentation iving advice **ronunciation** Vord stress 1	**Word Building** Nouns to adjectives **Product** The Process of an Experiment	**US** *scale; schedule* **UK** *scales; diary*	**Fantasy** *A World Without Time* **Informational Text** *Timelines* **Reading Skill** Visualizing
resentation alking about your friend **ronunciation** ilent *l*	**Sentence Building** Conjunctions: *and, because, but, or, so* **Product** An Email to a Friend	**US** *get along well with, have a falling out with* **UK** *get on well with, fall out with*	**Informational Text** *A Friendly Message* **Story** *Trust Me* **Reading Skill** Describing and understanding characters
onversation Making offers, showing enthusiasm, aying what you know **ronunciation** Vord stress 2	**Sentence Building** Reviewing question words **Product** A Magazine Interview	**US** *Never give up!* **UK** *You mustn't give up!*	**Story** *Hope You Like Fish* **Biography** *First Man in Space* **Reading Skill** Scanning for specific information
Conversation Negotiating **Pronunciation** Silent *c*	**Sentence Building** Giving examples **Product** A Character Profile	**US** *figure out* **UK** *work out*	**Informational Text** *The Silk Road* **Folk Tale** *Sinbad's First Voyage* **Reading Skill** Identifying points of view

;peaking	Writing	International English	Literacy Book
;onversation ;iving reasons, disagreeing politely, eciding together **'ronunciation** *h* as /f/	**Sentence Building** Adding information **Product** A Postcard	**US** *flashlight, bug spray, sunscreen* **UK** *torch, insect repellent, sun cream*	**Instructional Text** *SOS* **Story** *Panic or Calm?* **Reading skill** Understanding sequence of events
'resentation)escribing pictures **'ronunciation** ʤ/ and /g/	**Paragraph Building** Pronouns **Product** A Fact File	**US** *faucet; hose* **UK** *tap; hosepipe*	**Informational Text** *Clean Water for All* **Story** *The New Dam* **Reading Skill** Understanding inferences
'resentation)escribing movies, giving ecommendations **'ronunciation** *;chwa* /ə/	**Text Type** Features of a script **Product** A Movie Script	**US** *movie star* **UK** *film star*	**Informational Text** *Action Stars* **Play** *Actors on Set!* **Reading Skill** Understanding cause and effect
Presentation Predictions, giving opinions **Pronunciation** Silent *gh* 2	**Punctuation** Reviewing dialogues **Product** A Story	**US** *take out the trash, wash the dishes; I already did the laundry; railroad, apartment building* **UK** *take out the rubbish, do the washing up; I've already done the laundry; railway, block of flats*	**Fiction** *Pinocchia* **Informational Text** *Fast Forward* **Reading Skill** Comparing and contrasting
Conversation Discussing an object **Pronunciation** *gh* as /f/	**Sentence Building** Interesting adjectives **Product** A Description	**US** *savory* **UK** *savoury*	**Informational Text** *Sense Superstore* **Poem** *The Wrinklecrinkle Man* **Reading Skill** Identifying literal and figurative language

Unit	Reading 1	Reading 2	Reading Skill	Content Area	Social and Emotional Learning	Key Concept	Language Book
Literacy Review	Scanning; Making Inferences and Predictions; Identifying Perspective; Spelling final *ough* and *ight*; Scanning; Identifying Facts and Opinions; Author's Purpose; Cause and Effect; Spelling *or* and *ar*						
1 Let's Start With Art page 8	**Fiction** *True Colors* Fantasy	**Nonfiction** *My Guide to Photography* Instructional Text **Spelling** final *ent*	Understanding facts and opinions	Arts and Humanities: Photography	Relationship Skills: Provide help to those who need it	Why do people make art?	**Vocabulary** types of art and describing art **Grammar** quantifiers *a little, a few, all, most; too* and *enough* with adjectives
2 How Long Is It? page 24	**Fiction** *A World Without Time* Fantasy **Spelling** final *le*	**Nonfiction** *Timelines* Informational Text	Visualizing	Math: Measuring Time	Self-Management: Set plans and work towards goals	How do things change over time?	**Vocabulary** experiments and time **Grammar** future predictions: *going to* and *will* future plans: present progressive
3 Be My Friend page 40	**Nonfiction** *A Friendly Message* Informational Text **Spelling** final *ed*	**Fiction** *Trust Me* Story	Describing and understanding characters	Science: Sociology and Technology	Social Awareness: Evaluate others' emotional reactions	What makes a good friend?	**Vocabulary** emotions and friendships **Grammar** first conditional
4 What's Up There? page 56	**Fiction** *Hope You Like Fish* Story **Spelling** long *i*	**Nonfiction** *First Man in Space* Biography	Scanning for specific information	Science: Space Exploration	Self-Management: Attention control, maintain optimal work performance	How do we explore space?	**Vocabulary** space and Mars **Grammar** modal verbs: *have to, must; might, should*
5 So That's How They Did It page 72	**Nonfiction** *The Silk Road* Informational Text	**Fiction** *Sinbad's First Voyage* Folk Tale **Spelling** soft *c*	Identifying points of view	History: Important Places	Self-Management: Overcome obstacles and create strategies for more long-term goals	How has travel changed from ancient times?	**Vocabulary** Vikings, trade, and travel **Grammar** *used to*

Unit	Reading 1	Reading 2	Reading Skill	Content Area	Social and Emotional Learning	Key Concept	Language Book
6 Ready for Anything page 88	**Nonfiction** *SOS* Instructional Text **Spelling** initial *st*	**Fiction** *Panic or Calm?* Story	Understanding sequence of events	Science: Emergency Management	Self-Management: Exhibit positive motivation, hope, and optimism	What can you do to survive in an emergency?	**Vocabulary** actions, survival, and camping equipment **Grammar** present perfect simple
7 Every Last Drop page 104	**Nonfiction** *Clean Water for All* Informational Text	**Fiction** *The New Dam* Story **Spelling** final *ful and* fully	Understanding inferences	Science: Environmental Studies	Relationship Skills: Demonstrate leadership skills when necessary, being assertive and persuasive	How do you use water every day?	**Vocabulary** the water cycle and water **Grammar** gerunds as subjects prepositions: after adjectives
8 Lights, Camera, Action page 120	**Nonfiction** *Action Stars* Informational Text **Spelling** final *ing*	**Fiction** *Actors on Set!* Play	Understanding cause and effect	Arts and Humanities: Drama	Relationship Skills: Exhibit cooperative learning and working towards group goals	Why do movies need a team?	**Vocabulary** physical characteristics and movies; movie genres and features **Grammar** defining relative clauses: *who, that, where* adjectives: *-ing* or *-ed*
9 The World of Tomorrow page 136	**Fiction** *Pinocchia* Science Fiction	**Nonfiction** *Fast Forward* Informational Text **Spelling** soft *g*	Comparing and contrasting	Science: Engineering	Relationship Skills: Provide help to those who need it	How will family life change 100 years from now?	**Vocabulary** household chores, towns, and cities **Grammar** present perfect simple: *ever, never,* and *already* present perfect simple and simple past
10 Use Your Senses page 152	**Nonfiction** *Sense Superstore* Informational Text	**Fiction** *The Wrinklecrinkle Man* Poem **Spelling** long e	Identifying literal and figurative language	Science: Biology	Responsible Decision-Making: Become self-reflective and self-evaluative	Why are our senses so important?	**Vocabulary** sense verbs and adjectives **Grammar** tag questions: *do, did, be, should, will, have*

Welcome to *Global Stage*

You have in your hands a complete language and literacy course that will support you and your students in developing their English skills, and their love of reading and the English language.

The **Language Book** contains the building blocks of language skills and systems. Students will focus on learning the language and how it works. Beautiful picture dictionary scenes, lively songs, and contextualized grammar sections support them in figuring out and learning new language. Photos and texts about children around the world will inspire them to explore thought-provoking questions about what it means to be a Global Citizen. Live-action videos will expose learners to other children using the language they are learning before they take their turn.

The **Literacy Book** contains a variety of fictional and nonfictional texts, as well as activities for learners to explore literacy concepts, develop reading skills, and respond to the texts they have read. As they work through the course, students will further develop their thinking skills, and they will build self-reflection skills, which will allow them to become increasingly more effective and independent learners.

Together, the **Language** and **Literacy Books** explore topics across the curriculum while exposing students to differences in American and British English through the International English feature.

How to Use the Books Together

The **Language Book** and **Literacy Book** units are designed to provide a complete English language learning experience. There is no prescribed order for teaching the books: You may start with either book. You can choose to work through a whole unit and then move to the other book. Alternatively, you can start with the first **Literacy Book** reading, then move to the **Language Book**, then back to the second **Literacy Book** reading.

Used together, the two books cover the four skills, provide a solid foundation in vocabulary and grammar, and help train your learners to become competent users of English and independent thinkers.

Pedagogical Philosophy

The goal of ***Global Stage*** is to support children in becoming competent and confident English speakers while also developing as self-directed, inquisitive learners and responsible global citizens.

Global Stage starts with the child and looks out towards the world.

Global Stage assumes that every learner comes to school with a wealth of knowledge, thoughts, and opinions about their lives and the world, and that this is the starting point for their continued learning. All units include moments for students to consider and share their experiences, as well as consider others' points of view. This not only validates their thoughts, priming them to be open to learning, but is also the basis for learning empathy, which is one of the goals of our Global Citizenship lesson.

We know that children learn best when they feel safe to express their emotions. This is why we have carefully interwoven a social and emotional learning strand into the course. When you read the texts with your class, you will find opportunities to pause and reflect on how the characters feel and why, as well as opportunities for the students to think about how they feel in their lives when they encounter similar situations. Building and strengthening the ability to reflect will support students in becoming considerate, thoughtful citizens of the world.

Global Stage encourages self-reflection and a growth mindset to support children in increasing their academic achievement.

Every child has strengths they can build on, as well as areas they should develop and strengthen. We also know that what students and their teachers believe about intelligence influences academic achievement. A growth mindset is the belief that intelligence is not fixed, but rather can grow and continue to develop. Carol Dweck, who coined this term, and her colleagues demonstrated that a growth mindset empowers children to increase their academic achievement.

Global Stage supports students by helping them learn to reflect on their learning. Teachers can further support their students by focusing their praise on children's effort and improvement from where they start on their learning journey. This kind of feedback that focuses on growth reinforces the notion that children have the power to make progress by working toward it, encouraging students to view their progress and skills as something they can improve, rather than purely the result of their static abilities.

Global Stage includes various forms of review to support children in improving self-reflection skills: Our **Language Book** reviews, the Think It Over pages, are always open-ended, prompting students to think about what they have learned, how they have learned it, how they think they might learn better, and what they think they should continue to work on. When you do these lessons in class, you can take advantage of this social moment for students to hear from each other. One child may mention that they learned the most with the unit song, while another might recall a game or a story. Children will benefit from considering what has worked for them and for others, while also planning for how to continue to learn. These are also moments for you to praise the class for their effort, pointing out where they've made progress.

Our **Literacy Book** includes Think Together pages, a space for students to get used to reflecting on how they respond to texts, and how working with those texts might have enriched what they think about the Key Concept questions at the top of the page.

Finally, our **Student's App** on **Navio** allows learners to review the language and skills they have studied and receive instant feedback, as well as increasing challenges as they progress. Students will be supported in learning and improving their English, while having fun and working at their own pace.

Helping children notice where they are making progress will help them build their self-reflection skills and also encourage them to seek further challenge.

Global Stage helps you teach beyond the test.

In ***Global Stage*** you will find a robust and engaging course. With its dual-book approach to language and literacy, and its focus on engaging the students and allowing them to develop their thinking and self-management skills, ***Global Stage*** supports children in learning beyond the language needed for doing well on tests.

Students are challenged to learn at a stimulating pace. They encounter a variety of topics and language points, as well as texts and ideas. But you and they have strong support every step of the way. Whether it is the way the **Language Book** sets up a speaking or writing task in incremental steps so the learner knows what to work on and the teacher can see where they need help, or the way thinking opportunities are woven into the two books, encouraging children not only to learn information but also get better at analyzing it, ***Global Stage*** supports students' long-term development. For example, throughout the six levels of ***Global Stage***, learners will be developing the ability to figure out the meaning of Words in Context. They will learn that words have many layers of meaning, and they will learn to develop strategies to figure out aspects of the meaning themselves, from the context in each text. Their goal won't be to learn the word, but rather to understand the overall meaning of the text, and to make an educated guess about what the word may mean in that context. This skill will help them become better readers, learners, and test takers throughout their academic lives in English and in whatever other language they happen to be studying.

Global Stage supports children in developing 21st Century Skills.

In their widely accepted *Framework for 21st Century Learning*, which outlines their vision for student success in the new global economy, the Partnership for 21st Century Skills says that:

> *Learning and innovation skills increasingly are being recognized as the skills that separate students who are prepared for increasingly complex life and work environments in the 21st century, and those who are not. A focus on creativity, critical thinking, communication, and collaboration is essential to prepare students for the future.*

Global Stage infuses these important skills into every unit in a way that challenges the children and enhances the learning objective in each lesson. Students are consistently given opportunities to think and discuss everything from readings and skills to grammar points and writing mechanics. This ensures they are actively communicating to form a solid and personalized understanding of English. Our Think Together lesson, in the **Literacy Book**, includes a cooperative learning activity where learners can practice collaborating in a structured way, building the skills to listen to others, participating responsibly, and contributing equally to the activity outcome. Finally, lessons like Take the Stage and Write About It encourage creativity as students plan and produce individual presentations, conversation role-plays, and texts and critical thinking as they are supported to organize their thoughts.

Course Components

Language Book

The **Language Book** contains seven lessons per unit:

- Two Vocabulary lessons. One includes a song and the other is linked to Global Citizenship themes and includes listening activities.
- Two Explore Language lessons with grammar presentation and practice.
- A speaking lesson (Take the Stage / Talk About It) that presents either a presentation or conversational skill and includes pronunciation practice. In Level 4, students explore not only individual sounds but also word stress patterns.
- A writing lesson (Write About It) that explores writing mechanisms such as spelling and punctuation.
- A Think It Over lesson that focuses on self-reflection and getting students to think about how they learn.

Inductive Approach

Throughout ***Global Stage***, students are exposed to a simplified inductive approach to grammar, vocabulary, and skills. They are guided to look at language in context so that they can discover concrete patterns. When students are given an opportunity to figure out a concept for themselves, they are much more likely to develop a deeper understanding, appreciation, and retention of knowledge.

Recycling

In addition, opportunities to review and recycle what they have learned are built into the course with the review lessons (Put It Together) after every two units. These communicative games help students enjoy revisiting and practicing target language. There is also a mid-year and an end-of-year play, so students can use the language they've learned in a practical context. The first play, *Time Traveler*, uses vocabulary and grammar structures from Units 1–5. The second play, *The Missing Ring*, recycles vocabulary and grammar structures from Units 6–10.

Literacy Book

There are two texts in each unit of the **Literacy Book**, which are fully explored in a series of lessons:

- A Get Ready to Read lesson introduces the unit topic and creates interest. It also includes the reading skill focus.
- A Reading lesson presents a fictional or nonfictional text.
- An Explore the Reading lesson includes post-reading comprehension and analysis activities as well as a spelling activity.
- Each unit ends with a Think Together lesson that draws the two readings together and explores the Key Concept for each unit.

In each unit, students encounter a reading skill and learn the use of the skill through practice in context. Learning these skills helps students read more quickly and effectively and gives them greater confidence, which in turn means they get more enjoyment from reading.

Each text includes a Words in Context feature where students are encouraged to figure out the meaning of words from their context, rather than learn the words as vocabulary.

The **Literacy Book** develops Social and Emotional Learning (SEL) and Content and Language Integrated Learning (CLIL), while also including Visible Thinking Routines (VTR) and opportunities for Critical Literacy. Students are encouraged to work collaboratively by discussing and exploring ideas through Cooperative Learning Routines.

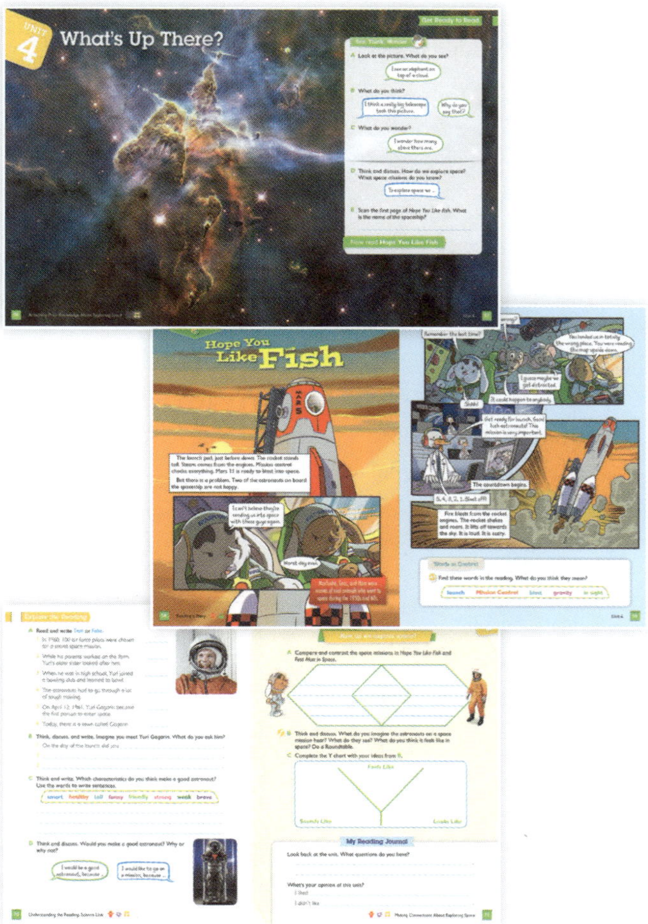

Three-Stage Reading Approach

The goal of the reading lessons is to get students reading for pleasure and to absorb information, rather than focusing on the mechanics of language in the text. The teaching notes suggest a three-stage approach to achieve this:

- Stage 1 **Engage with the Text.** This stage should be purely about reading for enjoyment and might include a prediction question to keep students motivated to find the answer.
- Stage 2 **Analyze the Text and Features.** In this stage, students read the text once again, while you help them analyze the text through the embedded callout questions. These questions will strengthen students' ability to make sense of the text and encourage them to begin thinking critically about what they are reading.
- Stage 3 **Interact with the Text.** This stage is about encouraging students to become actively involved in the learning process. They may be asked to act out the reading or to do reconstruction or analysis activities. When students interact more deeply with the text, their reading comprehension and writing skills improve, as they develop a greater understanding of how texts are constructed.

Spelling Patterns

Research shows that recognition and understanding of spelling patterns leads to improved reading. This is because both spelling and reading require students to make connections between how a word looks, how it sounds, and what it means. Knowing the spelling of a word helps students to create a more definite mental image, which supports them to read the word fluently.

The **Literacy Book** focuses on one letter combination in each unit, providing a logical framework for students to begin recognizing spelling patterns in words. Each pattern has been selected from curricula used in US schools. This structured approach to spelling has been shown to be far more effective in the long-term than the traditional practice of getting students to learn long lists of words for a test. Spelling pattern work in the **Literacy Book** is linked to one reading in each unit as part of the Explore the Reading lessons with further practice in the **Student's App** on **Navio**. Extension activities in the digital **ETB** encourage students to analyze the similarities and differences between words e.g. in word families.

Once students begin to recognize spelling patterns, they have a strategy to approach spelling and reading new words with a similar structure.

Spelling Pattern long *i*

Listen and write. Then check your answers.

1 l______ 2 l______ 3 q______ 4 g______ 5 m______

Now find more words with a long *i* in the reading.

Together, the two books lay the foundation for an inductive approach to learning, encouraging students to recognize patterns and think critically through ordering, analysis, and categorization tasks.

The Unit 1 Walkthrough notes give more in-depth information about the purpose and learning outcomes for each activity, as well as further guidance on addressing core features such as visualization, inductive grammar, international English, reading skills, the reading strategy, Words in Context, and learning reflections.

Student's App on Navio

The **Student's App** on **Navio** is where children find their practice activities for the course. It expands on the topic and objectives found in the **Language Book** and **Literacy Book**. It includes automatically graded interactive exercises for each unit, which can be done in class or for homework, so that children receive immediate feedback. These exercises cover reading and listening skills, spelling practice, speaking skill and pronunciation practice, extended writing practice, as well as grammar and vocabulary.

The **Student's App** on **Navio** world also provides support and guidance for more introspective objectives such as reading comprehension, SEL and CLIL activities.

The **Student's App** on **Navio** transforms the classroom-based lessons found in the **Language Book** and **Literacy Book** into an immersive, self-directed, game-like experience that students can do alone.

Using the **Student's App** on **Navio** with your students can take different forms:

Classroom study with **Language** and **Literacy Books** and Tap & Teach lessons. →

- Study and practice alone in a computer lab with **Student's App**.
- Study and practice alone at home with **Student's App**.
- Study and practice with parents with **Student's App**.

Each gameplay produces data which is then sent to the teacher's gradebook, providing deeper insight into each student's strengths and weaknesses, and concrete data that can be quickly accessed to create more insightful feedback.

The activities on the **Student's App** on **Navio** are benchmarked to Cambridge English online practice, ranging from *Starters* for the lower levels to *Preliminary for Schools* for Level 6. This benchmarking covers both content and web app functionality, preparing students academically and equipping them for the practical experience of online testing.

Teacher's Book

This Teacher's Book provides all the steps you need to bring each lesson of the **Language** and **Literacy Books** to life, including lesson objectives, warm up and cool down activities, and full answer keys. Audio and video scripts are at the back of the book, and Unit 1 contains a comprehensive walkthough, with clear explanations of the purpose of each activity and tips on how to make the most of them in class. The notes also remind the teacher of the additional support available through the Tap & Teach Lessons (TTL) for heads-up learning, the supplementary printouts in the Resource Bank, and extra practice students can do in class or at home.

Teacher's App on Navio

The **Teacher's App** on **Navio** is your primary source for classroom resources and supplements, and is designed to work on both laptops and tablets. It includes Tap & Teach Lessons (projectable classroom lessons), the Resource Bank, the Test Generator, Student's Progress Tracker, the **Enhanced Teacher's eBook** as well as access to the **Student's App**.

Tap & Teach Lessons (TTL)

Tap & Teach Lessons (TTL) are the course projectables. They contain tools for delivering dynamic and stimulating lessons, including class audio, videos, and interactive activities.

If you use the TTL with an interactive whiteboard, you will be able to use all the standard features, such as highlighting and hiding content.

There are three different types of video in ***Global Stage***:

- **Song Videos** (optional). These appear in Lesson 1 of the **Language Book** and may be used to practice some of the set 1 vocabulary as well as features of rhythm and stress patterns in English.
- **Speaking Videos** (essential). These appear in Lesson 5 of the **Language Book** and feature a child or children modelling a presentation or conversation, which includes functional language. Students will analyze the language and use the video as a model when planning and preparing for their own presentation or conversation.
- **Reading Videos** (optional). These accompany one reading text of the **Literacy Book** per unit to engage students in the text visually and aurally. This method of digital storytelling helps students make connections to past experiences and apply critical thinking to the new information they are being given.

Videos at Home: The Flipped Classroom Approach

If you are unable to watch the videos in class or you want to provide students with additional support, consider asking them to watch the videos at home before the lesson. This allows students to engage with the content in a way that suits them and allows them to pause and rewatch as many times as they want. It also offers parents the opportunity to watch the video with their child and support their learning.

If they watch the song or reading videos at home, give students a question or task to think about while they are watching. They will come to class feeling relaxed, confident, and prepared with ideas and observations to share. If students watch the speaking video at home, you could also have them do activities A and B from Take the Stage / Talk About It before the lesson. Watching the videos at home also frees up class time for collaborative and communicative activities.

Resource Bank

The Resource Bank is where you can find:

- **Spelling Printouts**. Extra practice of the letter combinations covered in each unit of the **Literacy Book**.
- **Differentiated Writing Support**. Attractive writing templates for the Write About It pages in the **Language Book**. These include "Support" and "Challenge" options for students that need them.
- **Review Unit Support**. Extra practice for the review units at the start of each student book. These cover grammar, vocabulary, and literacy activities.
- **Grammar Printouts**. Extra practice for each grammar lesson in the **Language Book**.
- **Tests**. Unit, mid-year, and end-of-year tests.
- **Cambridge English Exam Materials**. Practice for students preparing for *Starters*, *Movers*, or *Flyers*.
- **Letters to Parents**.
- **Other Printouts**. Graphic organizers to aid Visible Thinking Routines and reading skills in the **Literacy Book**, as well as extra materials for Put It Together games and extension activities in the **Language Book**.
- **Videos and audio tracks** to support the course.
- **Curricula and Framework mapping documents.**

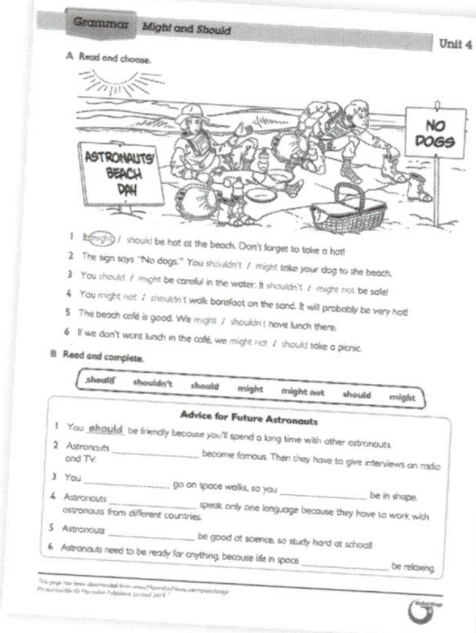

Grammar *Might and Should* Unit 4

A Read and choose.

1 It might / should be hot at the beach. Don't forget to take a hat!
2 The sign says "No dogs." You shouldn't / might take your dog to the beach.
3 You should / might be careful in the water. It shouldn't / might not be safe!
4 You might not / shouldn't walk barefoot on the sand. It will probably be very hot!
5 The beach café is good. We might / shouldn't have lunch there.
6 If we don't want lunch in the café, we might not / should take a picnic.

B Read and complete.

should shouldn't should might might not should might

Advice for Future Astronauts

1 You should be friendly because you'll spend a long time with other astronauts.
2 Astronauts ______ become famous. Then they have to give interviews on radio and TV.
3 You ______ go on space walks, so you ______ be in shape.
4 Astronauts ______ speak only one language because they have to work with astronauts from different countries.
5 Astronauts ______ be good at science, so study hard at school!
6 Astronauts need to be ready for anything, because life in space ______ be relaxing.

Test Generator

The Test Generator contains the pre-written unit, mid-year, and end-of-year test activities, as well as extra activities that allow teachers to generate and edit new tests.

Student's Progress Tracker

The Progress Tracker is an interactive gradebook that allows you to track your students' progress within ***Global Stage*** and the **Student's App** on **Navio**.

Student's App on Navio

As the teacher, you have full access to the **Student's App** on **Navio** so you can assign homework and activities for your students, and explore the digital world yourself.

Enhanced Teacher's eBook (ETB)

The digital **ETB** is an extended version of this **Teacher's Book**. In addition to teaching notes, it provides classroom management tips; ideas for differentiating activities; projects to support the Global Citizenship lessons, plus a range of activity and lesson extension features. These features include Social and Emotional Learning (SEL), Discussion, Genre, Video Focus, Critical Thinking, Creative Thinking, and Collaboration. The **ETB** also highlights key links between the **Language Book** and the **Literacy Book**.

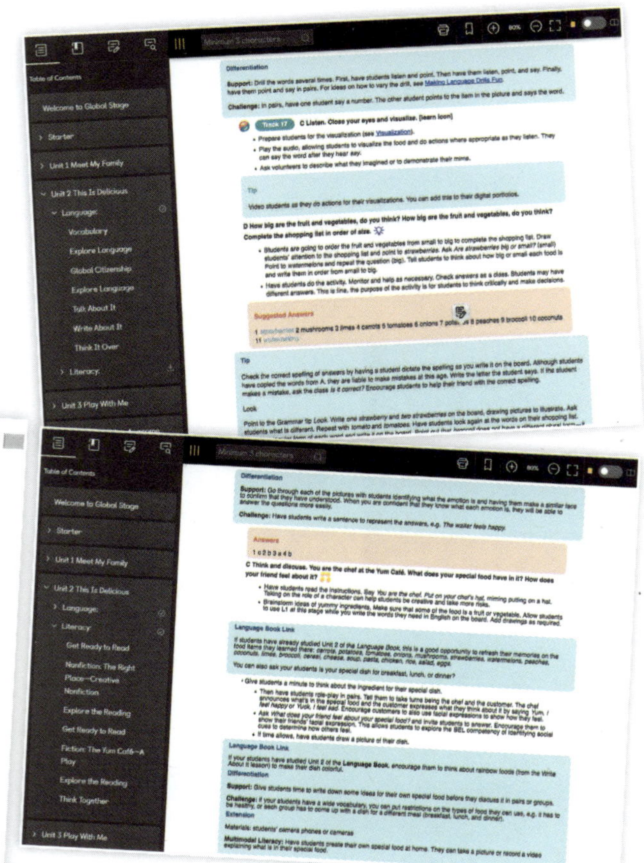

Holistic Learning

While the success of students and schools may be measured in terms of tests and grades, ***Global Stage*** believes in taking a holistic approach by developing the whole child and preparing him/her to take on the challenges of global living. Through its subject matter and in its activity types, the course encourages students to develop thinking skills, engage in cooperative learning activities, develop social and emotional learning (SEL) skills, and gain an awareness of global citizenship.

Global Citizenship Education

> *Global Citizenship Education (GCE) aims to empower learners to assume active roles, to face and resolve global challenges, and to become proactive contributors to a more peaceful, tolerant, inclusive and secure world.*
>
> —United Nations Educational, Scientific and Cultural Organization

The **Language Book** includes a Global Citizenship lesson in each unit, which has been designed to teach students about the lives of other children through the context of a listening activity. Discussion questions help them explore ideas and make connections to their own lives. The long-term objective is to prepare students for experiences outside of their everyday world and to fulfil aspirations to travel and study abroad.

In Level 4, lessons raise awareness about global issues through interesting and engaging topics designed to get students thinking about the things they can do as global citizens within their own communities. Key questions raised include: Why is art important to people?; What does it mean to be a friend?; How can communities save water? and How do cities bring people together? The Unit 1 Walkthrough notes for the **Language Book** provide guidance for teaching Global Citizenship lessons.

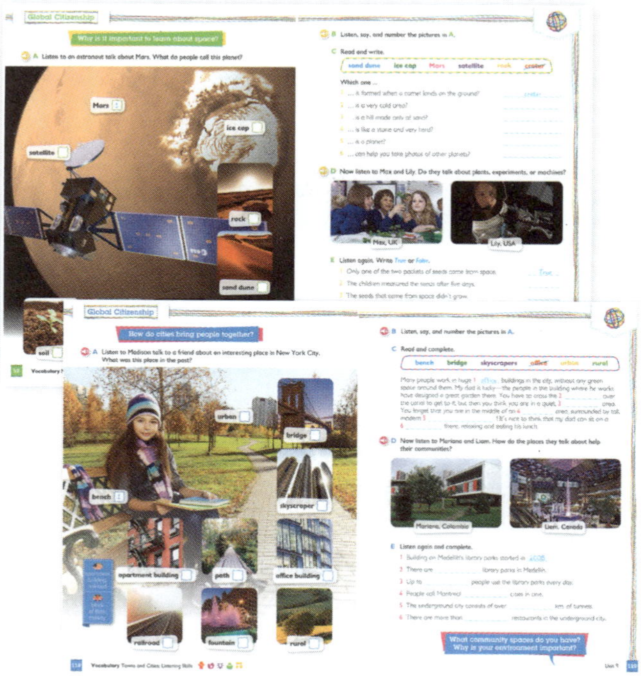

Matthew Hayes is a doctoral researcher at the Institute of Education in London under Douglas Bourn, Professor of Development Education. His research concerns Global Citizenship Education in English language textbooks.

What is GCE?

What does the future hold for your students, many of whom will graduate well into the 2030s? From the environment to the economy, poverty to jobs, challenges abound. But whatever the future holds, there is one thing we can be certain of: the biggest challenges facing humanity are not constrained by national borders or language but are truly global in scale and character. These are global problems requiring global solutions, and those of us working in education have a unique responsibility and opportunity to prepare the next generation for these challenges. GCE offers a solution to these challenges and has emerged in recent years as a high-profile policy agenda in education systems all over the world.

With this in mind, GCE can be an effective toolkit for teachers wishing to prepare their students for the challenges and opportunities of the 21st century. The skills and values it espouses are essential if our students are to successfully navigate all the future holds. GCE is too important to languish on the fringes of the curriculum, competing for space as an arbitrary additional subject in an already overcrowded timetable or sandwiched into one-off school events. Just as Digital Literacy is moving beyond ICT and into every corner of the curriculum, GCE thrives best where it is embedded in mainstream curriculum subjects. Few subjects better provide the context and aspiration called for by GCE than the teaching of English as a second language.

There is much scope for creativity too. Although GCE is a declared target of the United Nations' Sustainable Development Goals, one of its virtues is that it is not owned or prescribed by any supranational organisation. There is no mandated curriculum and no accreditation body. The core concepts underpinning GCE have been traced back to some of our earliest history and are not only to be found in Western culture and philosophy. Arab scholars, for example, have written of the influence of medieval Muslim thinkers on GCE theory.

This democratic quality to GCE enables a wide variety of policy and practice, as GCE can be adapted to local contexts and cultures, and to your classroom. There are three broad themes in current GCE thinking and practice and as you work through this textbook, you will see these throughout the exercises and subject matter.

Global orientation: Often referred to as cosmopolitanism, this area of GCE cultivates a student's awareness of the world—its structures, cultures and politics—with a positive "orientation". Its focus is on tolerance and understanding, developing citizens that can comfortably and successfully navigate the world in all its variety.

Global skills: This area is about the competencies aspired to by global citizens. You may recognize it as closely related to "21st Century Skills" and "Life Skills", and it cultivates skills such as collaboration, creativity, critical literacy, and communication. This not only prepares students for success in a competitive global knowledge economy, but for lives as contributing global citizens able to identify and solve problems that are both local and global.

Global conscientiousness: This third theme runs through all aspects of GCE and is its most distinguishing feature. It is signalled through the word "citizenship", denoting an individual's legal status as a member of a given community, with this status granting them certain rights and responsibilities. While historically this community has been restricted to the nation-state, *global* citizenship looks beyond the national to the global community of which we are all a part. Its rights and responsibilities are global in nature, calling each of us to action. This can take many forms and there should be no universal prescription of actions to be taken. It is being an *active* global citizen which is required of us. This means listening to our conscience and, when it identifies global injustice, being motivated by this to act.

Your selection of this high-level English language textbook means English is a leading subject in your curriculum and timetable. No doubt you acknowledge the English language as the *lingua franca* of the modern era, enabling your students to participate on a global scale—whether in work or life. As educators, then, what better context in which to use GCE to encourage your students to think beyond their immediate community, and be globally oriented, competent and conscientious. The English language may have an historical affinity to the West, but GCE recognises that it should not be a pedestal to promote one culture and education above any other. On the contrary, through embedding GCE in English language teaching we can encourage our students to question an unjust world and its imbalanced perspectives.

By using this textbook to teach English in a creative, forward-thinking and global way you will be providing your students with the skills and values to go out into the world and be truly active global citizens.

Social and Emotional Learning (SEL)

> *Social and emotional learning (SEL) is the process through which children and adults acquire and effectively apply the knowledge, attitudes, and skills necessary to understand and manage emotions, set and achieve positive goals, feel and show empathy for others, establish and maintain positive relationships, and make responsible decisions.*
>
> —Collaborative for Academic, Social, and Emotional Learning

Research shows that SEL can positively affect students' connection to school, promote positive behavior, and lead to academic achievement. Helping students develop social and emotional skills lays the foundation for behaviors that will lead to positive personal development and professional success.

The five SEL areas are shown below.

Self-Management
The ability to recognize emotions, thoughts, strengths and weaknesses. This includes having confidence and optimism.
Self-Awareness
The ability to regulate emotions, thoughts and behaviors in different situations. This includes managing stress and working toward goals.
Responsible Decision-Making
The ability to empathize with others, to understand social norms, and to recognize resources and support in family, schools, and community.
Relationship Skills
The ability to establish and maintain healthy relationships. This includes active listening, cooperating, and handling conflict well.
Social Awareness
The ability to make good choices based on ethics, safety, and social norms. This includes considering the well-being of oneself and others.

SEL is integrated into the **Literacy Book**, and a key concept area is addressed throughout the fictional text in each unit. As part of the reading strategy, students are guided to make connections between the SEL concept and the people and events in the text and, ultimately, to their own lives.

Lina Acosta Sandaal, MA, LMFT is the founder of Stop Parenting Alone, a parenting and therapy center in Miami in the USA. She is the parenting expert of a national morning show, and consults for MomsRising, a lobbying organization for family rights.

What is SEL?

Your mouth is dry, and your heart is in your ears. Some of your students look frozen, while others wriggle in their chairs. No one is truly into the day's well-planned discussion. What is happening? Why is the lesson failing? The lesson is suffering the effect of emotions, social awareness, and self-judgment in the classroom. In every moment of a teacher's day, the mind, brain, and body flow through the interactions between the external information and the internal understanding and reflecting of the environment. So when I am asked what is SEL and why do we need it, my response is whether you intentionally teach it or not, you have been a model for SEL from the first day you stepped into a classroom.

The goal of integrating and implementing social and emotional learning into the curriculum is to build students' ability for self-awareness, self-management, social awareness, relationship skills, and decision making. Students attain these competencies by practicing ways to understand and manage emotions, build and manage relationships, and show care and concern for others. The Fetzer Group coined the term, and the word "learning" was intentional. Social emotional skills and development are not stagnant; they continue to grow and expand with each experience students have with caregivers, teachers, friends, and the culture/community at large. If you hold this in mind, that your students are learning through repetition how to be self-aware, how to manage emotions and focus, how to continue to build and manage relationships and practice decision making, then the task of social and emotional learning in your curriculum will not feel so difficult.

Why SEL Is Important to Your Classroom

It is an absurd task to attempt to separate what happens socially and emotionally to a student from what they are cognitively learning from your lesson. When you ignore how SEL and academic achievement work together you are only teaching a percentage of your student, and not the whole child. A majority of teachers understand that their students walk into the classroom full of emotions, thoughts, and experiences that hinder their academic achievement. Deficits in social and emotional development hamper students' ability to learn, which leads to them disrupting the classroom. A student who cannot manage their emotional state will become overwhelmed with fear and embarrassment if you ask them to speak to you in a language in which they are not fluent. Focus, cognitive flexibility, and decision-making are impacted when we have low self-awareness and management of our emotional states.

Recall the difficulty of writing emails at work when you have just had a fight with a loved one on the phone. When we have a strong emotional and social response, it is hard to focus on the task at hand. If it is difficult for an adult, imagine a young student. If your curriculum includes social and emotional learning, your students will be practicing skills to make those daily stressors less intrusive to their learning. Research supports this. Children in the HighScope Perry Preschool Study showed how social and emotional skills attained in preschool continued to bring positive outcomes to those students through age 40. HighScope moved "non-cognitive" skills to the forefront of their curriculum. Conversely, the Adverse Childhood Experiences Study (ACEs) showed that children who suffer adverse experiences and do not process those emotions fare poorly both in their mental and physical health. Social and emotional learning helps students thrive throughout their entire lives.

What Well-Accomplished SEL Looks Like

Now, stop and imagine your classroom in a group discussion: one of the students is playing with his lip while rocking slightly, another student is raising her hand as high as possible, hoping you will see that she wants to speak next, and another student is mumbling in response to the story you just read together. In a classroom that prioritizes SEL, all of these examples of self-management and relationship skills are accepted. Why? Because you understand that the student who is playing with his lips and rocking regulates his emotional and physical states this way, instead of standing up and disrupting the class. The student who knows to raise her hand and contain her emotions is making a responsible, self-aware decision in managing her excitement as to not interrupt her friend who is speaking.

Finally the student who is speaking slowly, quietly and under his breath is at last risking to discuss in a group because you have spoken to your students about what it means to feel scared, how to tolerate that fear, and how to work through it. Today you reap the benefit of that continued social-emotional message. How amazing that your quiet, observant student has made the decision to speak, experiences the safety to manage his fear and the opportunity to strengthen his relationships with his friends and you, his teacher.

Content and Language Integrated Learning (CLIL)

Research has shown that content-based learning increases motivation as students see language being used in real-life contexts. The nonfictional texts in the **Literacy Book** include content from a range of different subject areas. They feature engaging topics and provide opportunities for thinking and discussion.

In Level 4, students will learn through art and humanities, math, science, and history.

Competencies

Global Stage incorporates five competencies that have been identified and linked to outcomes such as better academic performance and positive peer relationships. Relevant icons appear in the footers of each lesson, and the teaching notes in the **TB** and **ETB** highlight which activities are connected to each competency to allow for further exploration in the classroom.

Me	
Activities that develop social and creative skills and consider lifestyle choices.	
Act	
Activities that help develop a sense of social responsibility, mutual understanding, tolerance and ethical behavior.	
Think	
Activities that develop thinking skills to explain, infer, classify, discuss, notice, and discover.	
Learn	
Activities that foster learning autonomy and help develop learning strategies.	
Communicate	
Activities that promote interpersonal and collaborative skills to develop teamwork, leadership, empathy, and responsibility.	

Self-Reflection

Self-reflection is an important part of any learning process. Research shows that without regular review and reflection time, much of a lesson can be forgotten. Self-reflection increases students' understanding of how they learn best, making future learning more effective and leading to improvements in achievement.

Self-reflection is a critical feature of *Global Stage*. Students are asked to reflect on their performances and written work in the Speaking and Writing lessons in the **Language Book** and to reflect more deeply about their learning in the end-of-unit lessons in the **Language Book** and **Literacy Book**.

The Think It Over lesson in the **Language Book** provides graphic organizers for students to respond to questions such as *What did I do? How did I learn?* and *What did I learn?* The purpose of these questions is to get students into the habit of self-reflection from an early age, helping them begin to learn how to learn.

In the My Reading Journal section of the Think Together lesson in the **Literacy Book**, students are asked to give a personalized response to the readings and reflect on the unit as a whole. They are encouraged to think critically about what they enjoyed and why, what they would like to learn more about, and to identify strengths and weaknesses.

In Level 4, both the **Language Book** and **Literacy Book** ask students to start making connections between what they enjoyed and what they learned. This prepares them for higher levels where they will be expected to understand how successes were achieved, how less successful experiences can be turned into learning experiences, and to find strategies for working through activities they find less enjoyable.

The Unit 1 Walkthrough notes for both books provide more information on making these lessons a valuable and successful experience.

Learning Techniques

Visible Thinking

Visible Thinking is a flexible research-based framework developed out of Harvard University for enriching classroom learning and fostering students' intellectual development. Some of its key goals are:

- To develop deeper understanding of content.
- To encourage greater motivation for learning.
- To develop learners' thinking and learning abilities.
- To develop learners' attitudes toward thinking and learning and their alertness to opportunities for thinking and learning.
- To create a shift in classroom culture toward a community of enthusiastically engaged thinkers and learners.

Visible Thinking employs thinking routines—short, easy-to-learn strategies that help extend and deepen students' thinking. These routines make it easier for you to see how the students are thinking and interpreting content: *Are students explaining things to one another? Are they offering creative ideas? Are they brainstorming and debating plans?* Visible Thinking encourages students to develop discussion skills and to find personal meaning in the content. This stimulates their continued interest and commitment to their own learning in the classroom.

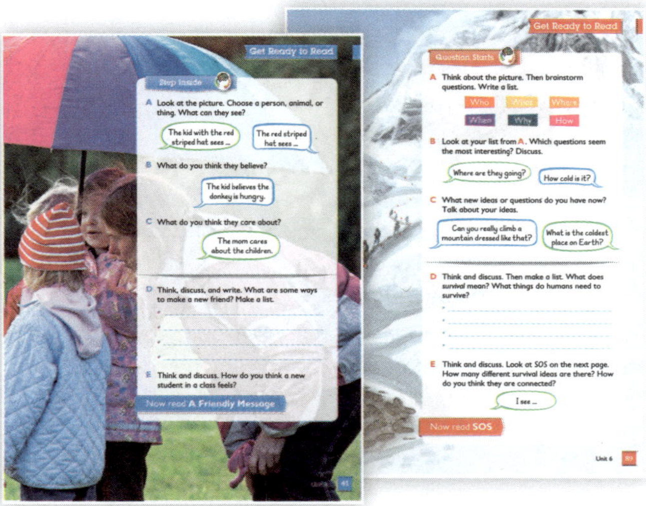

In Level 4, each opening lesson in the **Literacy Book** features one of four Visible Thinking Routines (VTR): See, Think, Wonder; Think, Pair, Share; Question Starts; or Step Inside. These routines stimulate students' curiosity and encourage them to make predictions, observations, and interpretations about the picture. They provide an opportunity for students to think about the overarching theme/topic of each **Literacy Book** unit and tie into a pre-reading activity to prepare students cognitively for what they are about to read.

See, Think, Wonder

Students are asked what they see in the picture, then what they think about it, and finally what they wonder (or what questions they have) about it. This routine works best when students are given time to think of ideas individually before sharing them with the class. In this way, students begin to use English meaningfully, although it is acceptable for them to use L1 to express more complex ideas.

Think, Pair, Share

This routine encourages individual participation and can be used with all abilities and class sizes.

Think. Students are given time to think independently about the question that has been posed, forming ideas and questions of their own.

Pair. Students are grouped in pairs to discuss their thoughts. This step allows students to articulate their ideas and to consider those of others. They are encouraged to listen to each other and use phrases like *I agree/disagree* and *Me, too.*

Share. Student pairs share their ideas with the whole class and give their reasons.

The benefit of using this routine for discussion questions is that students get to practice and learn through repetition, their ideas become more refined at each stage of the process, and they often feel more comfortable presenting ideas to a group with the support of a partner.

Think, Pair, Share is also used as a cooperative learning routine.

Question Starts

Students look at the picture and think of some questions they would like to ask about it, using the prompts Who? What? Where? When? Why? How? They then practice negotiation skills by working in groups (and then as a class), sharing their questions, and deciding on the three they think are the most interesting or that they would most like to know the answer to. The third part of the routine asks students to discuss the picture again in pairs and to come up with new questions or ideas they have about the picture or the concepts it shows. They should be encouraged to move beyond what they see and to start thinking of ideas connected to some of the themes suggested by the picture.

The purpose of this routine is that it encourages students to think more deeply about a topic and gets them into the habit of questioning beyond what they see on the page.

Step Inside

Students are asked to explore different perspectives and viewpoints as they try to imagine what a person, animal, or object in the picture can see, what they believe, and what they care about. As well as developing social and emotional skills, this routine encourages creative thinking.

For all four routines, it is important to scaffold student responses by asking follow-up questions, e.g. *What makes you say that?* and to encourage students to do the same, so that they begin to lead the discussion. Example dialogues have been provided in the teaching notes to help you do this. Make sure you keep students' thinking visible by noting down and displaying their ideas to return to in the Think Together lesson.

VTRs provide a great way to engage learners at the start of a topic, but they can also be used at different points in the unit to keep students connected to the topic or as a way to reflect on what they have learned in a meaningful way.

Cooperative Learning Routines

Teachers who use Cooperative Learning Routines can make a huge difference in achievement and engagement by providing opportunities for multiple students to participate and answer a question, instead of calling on just one student for the answer. Along with higher academic achievement, you will see a reduction in the gap between high- and low-achieving students, improved social skills, higher self-esteem, more enthusiasm for learning, a happier classroom climate, and decreased discipline problems. You will also see the emergence of leadership and conflict-resolution skills.

The following routines are used in Level 4 in both the **Literacy Book** and **Language Book**:

A **Round Robin** is where groups of four students have a limited time to take turns orally brainstorming as many different answers to a discussion question as they can within a limited time frame (e.g. one minute). A **Rally Robin** is the same but with pairs. A **Roundtable** is similar to a **Round Robin**, but students are encouraged to take turns writing down or drawing their ideas on a piece of paper, within their groups.

The **Three-Step Interview** takes the place of the traditional group discussion because each person in a group must produce and receive information. In the first two steps of this routine, students work with a student from a different group. They interview each other about a topic. Then, in the third step, students return to their original groups and take turns sharing what they have learned from their partners. You can also have them share ideas with the class.

Numbered Heads Together is a cooperative learning strategy that holds each student accountable for learning some material. Students are placed in groups and each person is given a number (from one to the maximum number in each group). The teacher poses a question and students "put their heads together" to figure out the answer. The teacher calls out a specific number to respond as spokesperson for the group. This strategy ensures that each member of a group knows the answer to a problem or question asked by the teacher. Because no one knows which number will be called, all team members must be prepared.

Inside–Outside Circle. You will need to make some space in the classroom for this routine. Students stand in concentric circles facing each other. Students in the outside circle ask questions, and those who are inside answer the question. On a signal, students rotate to create new partnerships. On another signal, students trade inside/outside roles. Talking one-on-one with a variety of partners gives extensive practice in speaking and active listening skills. Interactions can be structured to focus on specific skills and/or target language.

Option Explosion. Students discuss and share ideas to think of solutions to a problem or to generate new ideas for a plot line, e.g. *Adam and Lorna are lost in a dark forest. They see a building. What happens next? What other characters are there in this part of the play? What happens in the end?* Have students discuss each question in groups of four. Encourage them to think of problems for their characters to overcome and to suggest how they can resolve each problem. Each group can appoint a scribe. Then have students work in pairs and think again. This time they should try to use their imaginations to think beyond the more obvious plot lines and think of ideas that didn't come up during the first discussion. They can combine their earlier ideas, or use them as a platform to jump off and explore new options. Remind students that this play can be a fantasy, so crazy ideas are welcome! Monitor and ask questions to prompt students; for example, What happens if they drop their flashlight? What can they use to see?

Tips for Setting Up Class Discussions

- Write the question(s) on the board, and give students a minute to reflect in silence.
- If there is more than one discussion question, deal with each in turn, giving students time to think and discuss in pairs or small groups. Help with new words and allow the use of L1 for more complex ideas.
- Help students structure their discussions by providing appropriate graphic organizers on the board or handing out templates for the groups to fill in.
- You will not always be able to ask everyone for their ideas. Be sure you choose different students each time, so no one feels left out.
- Have students share their ideas in teams, e.g. a team per table. Have each team choose a name or color. During each lesson or activity, one person will give the team's answers and responses. Record who the speaker is for each activity so everyone gets a turn.
- Give the speaker an object, such as a cardboard microphone, to remind students who will speak.
- Use the Cooperative Learning Routines to structure the discussions and share information discussed.
- When sharing ideas as a class, Group Time can provide a relaxed atmosphere, which may encourage students to contribute more. See the **Group Time** box for more suggestions.

Group Time

Designate a particular area of the classroom for Group Time, free from distractions. Set out a circle of chairs, with no desks, so students can see each other clearly. You should also sit on a chair as part of this circle, so that it is clear your role is to encourage and facilitate discussion, rather than to lead it. At the beginning of the year have students discuss and agree on some rules for Group Time, e.g. one person speaks at a time; everyone listens to each other; students can disagree with each other, but must do so respectfully; Group Time is fun! Nominate a student to be the scribe and write up the rules the class decides on.

During Group Time, ask open-ended questions and encourage students to give reasons for their answers. Pass an object, such as a toy or a cushion, around so it is clear who is speaking. Encourage everyone to join in the discussion, but give students a safe word to use, such as "pass", if they need more thinking time. Let them know it's OK to need time to think and that you will come back to them. At the end of the Group Time discussion, praise students for their ideas.

Visualization

Visualizations are used in the vocabulary lessons of each unit to encourage students to create mental images of the new words, using their senses combined with previous experiences. Visualizations provide a different way for students to engage personally with the language and help them learn new words.

Set up a visualization activity as follows:

- Take several deep breaths with students, slowly saying *breathe in, breathe out.*
- Count down slowly from ten to one using a calm voice.
- Say *Close your eyes and visualize*, pointing to your temples with both hands to demonstrate *imagining*. If students prefer to keep their eyes open, that's fine, too. The key is for them to feel calm and relaxed, so avoid using phrases like *You must keep your eyes closed* or *Don't Look!* which will restrict students.
- Play the audio track and encourage students to imagine or act out as prompted. Pauses have been included in the audio to give students time for reflection. They then repeat the word.
- After the visualization activity, give students time to share their images. They can do this through drawing, miming, or by describing their thoughts to a partner using L1.
- Emphasize that everyone's visualizations will be different and that all ideas are valuable.

Students may need additional support the first time you do this. Pause after each word or play the audio track through twice to give them a second chance to create images in their mind. When they share images, students will learn from one another and get ideas for the next time you do this activity. The more regularly you do this, the more students will understand what is expected and the more they will get out of the activity. An optional visualization track is available in the TTL for the vocabulary in the Global Citizenship lesson.

Words in Context

The Words in Context feature focuses on helping students apply strategies for dealing with words they do not know. The goal is not for students to learn the full meaning of a word, but rather to understand what the word means in that particular context. Students discover that words have many layers of meaning, and that they will build knowledge of words over time. Every time they encounter a word, they learn one aspect of the meaning of the word.

It can be helpful to introduce the following strategies into lessons:

- Look at each sentence containing a target word, encouraging students to **look at the pictures to guess the meaning**.
- **Use the words around the new words to guess their meaning.** Tell students to look for words that they know in the sentence that contains the new word and to use these to build a context for the sentence. They should be logical when figuring out the meaning of the new word by thinking about what would make sense in this context, e.g. students may be able to identify other words in the sentence that mean the same thing, or that are connected to the new word in some way.
- **Read the next words or sentence to get clues** to explain the meaning of a new words. Encourage students to read on whenever they encounter a word they don't know, as sometimes what comes after can provide clues such as definitions, examples, or context to help them understand the word.
- **Use the sentence or paragraph before to guess the meaning of the new words.** Remind students that they can sometimes look back to get useful information and a context that will help them to figure out the meaning of the new word.
- **Think about whether the word is an object, a person, a place, or an action to figure out the meaning.** Encourage students to look at the other words around the word to help them do this, e.g. in the sentence *In a basketball game, ten players are on the court*, the preposition *on* may give students a clue that a *court* is a place.
- **Use pictures/actions/events in the video to help discover meaning.** Have students look for pictures in the text or pause the video, and encourage students to look at the image on screen to figure out the meaning of the new word.
- **Think about how the two things are similar to help understand the words.** Tell students that sometimes a writer compares two things using the word *like*, e.g. in the sentence *The famous composer lifts his arms high, and brings them down like an eagle that flies*, students can try out the action and think about what type of creature makes a similar action (a bird), in order to understand what an eagle is.
- **Use negative sentences nearby to help decode the meaning of a new word.** Explain that negative sentences can sometimes help us to figure out the meaning of a new word by stating what it isn't.
- **Use L1 knowledge to establish meaning.** Have students try to find similar words in their own language.

Multimodal Literacy

To become fully literate in today's world, students must become as proficient with the new literacies of search engines, web pages, email, instant messages, blogs, podcasts, e-books, wiki pages, digital photos, videos, and apps as they are with the traditional literacies of paper, pencil, and books.

However, students also need to learn new skills to enable them to use each of these technologies effectively, e.g. searching for key words and navigating a nonlinear reading pathway via hyperlinks. Students also need to develop and utilize critical-thinking skills for online reading. In an age when anyone may publish anything on the internet, it is more important than ever to equip students with the tools to evaluate source material.

Both the **Language Book** and the **Literacy Book** provide opportunities for developing higher-order thinking skills through activities that teach students to analyze, question, and to foster thoughtful discussion. In addition, the digital **ETB** includes Multimodal Literacy ideas for taking lessons beyond the book and integrating them with the students' own technologies. An example of this is a research project, where students are asked to find more information about a topic using both print and digital resources. Projects can be researched at home with parental support, or teachers can provide opportunities for small groups to collaborate together, culminating in a class presentation.

Students can also be encouraged to create using different technologies (including digital cameras, videos, apps) and to choose work to upload to their digital portfolios, which can be shared with parents.

Ideas for Introducing Multimodal Literacy Skills and Concepts

- **Encourage students to use *Global Stage's* digital resources.** The **Student's App** provides important early experiences of navigating an online interface in a controlled and safe environment.
- **Show how putting precise keywords into search engines can help you find better information.** If you have access to computers and are able to get online in school, give students a question to answer in pairs, but tell them they can only use one keyword. Discuss how successful

they were, then have them repeat the activity with two and then multiple keywords. Elicit that using more keywords helps you be more specific and gives you better information to answer the question.

- **Highlight the importance of scanning for key information.** When you're teaching students how to scan reading texts for relevant information, explain how this is also a useful skill for finding key information online. Every time you ask students to research something online, elicit what they need to look out for to scan effectively.
- **Have struggling readers teach more-confident readers.** When you introduce a new technology or skill in class, differentiate by teaching it to struggling readers first so that they become the experts, and then empower them to teach more-confident readers. That way, everyone is given the chance to be good at something and no one gets left behind.
- **Use digital portfolios.** Digital portfolios replace traditional folders as a way to capture and store students' work. You can put students in charge of what gets included in their portfolio as a way to encourage independence, responsibility, and reflection. They enable you to:
  - Demonstrate oral skills through videos and audio recordings, alongside on-paper tasks.
  - Empower students struggling with writing and reading by giving them alternative ways to express themselves and demonstrate learning.
  - Share students' learning easily and frequently with parents, without organizing a time for them to come into class, and without risk of the work getting mislaid at home.

Digital portfolios also allow students to view their learning journey and become a valuable tool for self-reflection. The digital **ETB** provides suggestions for digital portfolios.

Classroom Management

Making Language Drills Fun

The **Language Book** audio contains language drills to practice the new language presented in each Vocabulary and Explore Language lesson. Drilling helps familiarize students with the language and encourages them to notice the correct pronunciation and rhythm. It also allows you to see which words or phrases will need further practice.

Drilling works by being repetitive, so it is important to add some variations to make it fun and keep students engaged. You can do this by having students say the words or phrases in different ways:

- **Volume**. Have students whisper and then get progressively louder, and then quieter again.
- **Emotion**. Have students use a happy voice and then repeat with sad, angry, tired, and excited voices.
- **Speed**. Have students speak very slowly, then get progressively faster, and then slower again.
- **Voices**. Have students imagine they are a lion, then have them repeat by imagining they are a mouse, a robot, a bird, and a frog. Even when speaking in these different styles, students should be encouraged to use the correct pronunciation and intonation.

Try not to overload students by asking too much at once. The first time you play the audio, have them focus on pronunciation. When you feel they are comfortable with this, encourage them to notice and replicate the correct intonation.

For grammar drills, focus on rhythm and chunks of language, not just individual words. After practicing the recorded sentences, encourage students to make new ones with the target structure. Have the students build a substitution drill on the board starting with the original questions or sentences. Write them on the board, leaving a line for the words you want to change and encourage them to call out suggestions, e.g. *I'm* ____________ *in the morning.* Students could suggest *going swimming, catching a train*, etc. Then have them practice saying the new sentences in pairs.

Role-play in the Classroom

Performing role-plays in class is a great way for students to interact with the new language or stories and gain confidence using the language in a more informal way. Both the **Language** and **Literacy Books** offer many opportunities for role-play. For example, students can role-play the presentation dialogues in the Explore Language lessons, and they can role-play the stories in the **Literacy Book**. Some of the Talk About It lessons in the **Language Book** require students to plan and write a role-play conversation.

Five Stepping Stones to Performance

- **Step 1** Put students into groups according to how many parts there are in the dialogue or story you are going to role-play. Vary the groups and encourage students to work with classmates they don't normally work with. Pair confident students with less-confident classmates. Allow students to assign themselves roles within their groups, as this will practice negotiating skills.
- **Step 2** If the conversation or story you wish to role-play is on audio or video, then play it first for students to follow. Discuss how the characters' voices differ, and encourage them to think about how the characters are feeling at key moments in the story. Have students notice sound effects and ask them what these add to the overall effect.

  Play it again, this time encouraging students to say their lines out loud along with the audio/video. Then have students focus on reproducing the intonation.
- **Step 3** Now, give students time to practice their role-play without multimedia. They can use the dialogue or the story in the book to help them remember their part. Encourage students to speak with expression and to try to think about intonation. Where appropriate, have them think about the type of voice their character has, e.g. a deep voice or a high, squeaky voice. Tell them to think about how their character is feeling and to include some suitable facial expressions and actions.

You can challenge stronger students to continue the conversation or add embellishments to their character.

- **Step 4** When they are ready, pairs or groups can come to the front and perform their role-play for the class. Make sure everyone gets a chance to perform at some point during the course. Encourage students to video record each other's performances. These videos can be uploaded to their digital portfolios.
- **Step 5** You could organize an open event at the end of the term for parents. Have groups of students prepare and act out different stories from the **Literacy Book** or the plays from the **Language Book**. Give students extra practice time to give them confidence to perform in front of an audience. Encourage them to think about suitable sound effects to use in their performance (e.g. rustling paper for rain), or to source these through sound-effect apps. You could also get students and families involved in providing costumes and making props.

Tip Get students to vote on their favorite song from the **Language Book** and have them perform it together at the beginning of the open event. This will help dispel a lot of nerves and ensure a smoother performance when students come to act out the stories.

Differentiated Learning

Even across one class, students differ in many ways; from age, energy, interests, adaptability, experience, and familiarity with the world outside the home, to emotional maturity, linguistic aptitude, and physical development. As a way of targeting learning to meet individual students' needs, the **ETB** lesson notes include below-level *Support* differentiation ideas to help students achieve the activity goal and above-level *Challenge* ideas to extend activities. For print users, the following are ways you can differentiate activity types:

Vocabulary

Support: Check the meaning of each word by asking questions to confirm or help with understanding.

Challenge: Have students personalize the vocabulary by saying a sentence with one of the words.

Language Drills

Support: Give students enough time to process each item on the recording. Break down the phrases into smaller chunks and build them up until students have the full sentence.

Challenge: Have students substitute words in the drill to make new questions and statements. Ask them to come up with wild and funny ideas!

Conversations

Support: Give students plenty of time to prepare and allow them to write the phrases they want to use from B in their notebooks. They can read their dialogues several times until they feel comfortable enough to have a conversation without using their notebooks.

Challenge: Encourage students to add more turns in their conversation and to change the phrases they use each time.

Writing

Support: Have students discuss their ideas with a partner before completing their plan. This will help them organize their thoughts into writing.

Challenge: Give out the *Challenge* printouts to encourage students to add more information.

Question Starts Visible Thinking Routine

Support: Students may find it hard to think of a variety of questions. Suggest example questions using each question word and write them on the board. Alternatively, ask students what they think they know about the picture. This will lead into an interesting discussion and should generate more questions.

Challenge: For every question generated, encourage students to provide a secondary question that links to the previous one; e.g. *Who's the girl? And where's she from?*

Step Inside Visible Thinking Routine

Support: Write sentence beginnings on the board to help less-confident students phrase their answers and be able to contribute more easily; for example, *I think he/she/it can see … / I think he/she/it believes that … / He/she/it probably cares about ….*

Challenge: Encourage more-confident students to link their ideas for what they care about to what they are looking at and what they believe; for example, *I think he cares about (x) because he's looking at (y), and I think he believes that (z).* or *He's looking at (y), and I think he believes (z), so I think he cares about (x).*

Reading Comprehension

Support: Have students work in pairs to answer questions. They can take turns to read a question aloud. Both students in the pair should look back at the reading to find the answer. They can then compare their answers before writing them in their books.

Challenge: Have students answer the questions without looking back at the reading. They can use the reading to check their answers once they've finished.

Discussion

Support: Give students a list of questions to think about and answer before they talk. Writing notes or answers first can help shy students or those lacking confidence.

Challenge: Encourage more-confident students to voice their opinions and ask them to report back to the class without any notes in front of them.

Role-plays (in the **Literacy Book**)

Support: Play the audio while students perform the story. This way, students don't have to worry about their lines and can focus on interpreting each scene.

Challenge: Have students improvise the story, making their own changes to the dialogue.

Games Bank

Backs to the Board

Have one student sit in a chair at the front of the classroom with their back to the board so they can't see it. Write a word on the board, and have the class give clues and definitions to help the students guess the word. Write some sentence prompts on the board to help students phrase their ideas, e.g. *It's something that you use… It's a person who…*

Board Race

Divide the class into two teams and divide the board vertically in two halves. Give a board pen to one of the students on each team. Tell them the theme and give them two minutes to write as many words connected to that theme as they can. Each word must be written by a different student and only one student is allowed to be standing from each team at any time. When finished, have the teams check each other's spelling and count how many correct words each team had.

Chain Game

Use chain memory games to practice, e.g. the target language or lesson concepts. Have students sit in a circle. One student says a sentence about one of the characters in a story: *I think Ooleck is silly.* The next student adds another adjective to the sentence, e.g. Student B: *I think Ooleck is silly and determined.* This continues until someone gets mixed up or can't remember what the last person said. That student says a new sentence and starts the chain again.

You can vary this game to suit the grammar structures you wish to practice, e.g. the third person in grammar lessons. Student A: *After the lesson, I'm going to watch a video in English.* Student B: *After the lesson, he's going to watch a video in English and I'm going to sing a song in English.* Make sure students know that sentences don't have to be true!

You can play this game in teams. The team that continues one chain for the longest time, wins!

Change It Round

Write some sentences on the board, e.g. from one of the speaking videos. Underline key phrases and encourage students to suggest alternative phrases that could be used, e.g. in the sentence *I think it's very important to <u>plan your time</u>, plan your time* could be changed to *make your breakfast.* Model an example first.

Change Places

Have students place their chairs in a big circle and sit down. Remove one chair so that one student is standing. Call out yes/no questions and have students stand up and change places with another student if the answer is *yes*. The student who doesn't find a chair, stands in the middle and asks the next question (if the answer is *yes* for them, they should also move).

Correct the Teacher

Call out lines from songs, stories, or dialogues, but make mistakes. When students hear a mistake, they raise their hands and call out *No!* Choose a student to correct the mistake. You can vary this game by playing *Correct the Student*: students write and say sentences where one word is incorrect. Other students in their group listen for the mistake and provide the correction.

Disappearing Sentences

Choose four reasonably simple sentences from the text. Write the sentences on the board and have students read them aloud. Then erase two or three words from each sentence and have students say them again, including the missing words. Erase more words and repeat until students are saying the complete sentences from a (nearly) empty board.

Disappearing Words

Ask students to choose what they consider to be the most important words in a text and write them on the board (up to about 15 words). Have them turn away and then erase one word from the board. Have students turn back and identify which word is missing. Ask them how the word was used in the text. Continue until you have an empty board.

You can also play this game with key vocabulary words from a unit. Each time a word disappears, ask students to remember why it was important in the unit.

Draw It!

Have a volunteer come to the front, and show him/her a word from the vocabulary set you wish to practice, or whisper it into his/her ear. The student draws the word on the board. Have students raise their hands and guess.

Find Someone Who

Write prompts on the board and have students copy them into their notebooks, e.g. *Find someone who … went on vacation / … has more than two brothers and sisters / … wants to be a doctor when they grow up.* Then tell students to stand up and ask questions to find one person for each prompt and write down his/her name. Do one or two examples with students first, e.g. *Did you go on vacation? How many brothers and sisters do you have?* The first person to find a match for all their questions is the winner!

You can vary this by having students write the prompts themselves on a particular topic, e.g. by writing sentences about what they were doing this morning and having them ask questions to find other students who were doing the same things as them at the same time.

How Many Letters?

Read out some words and have students race to count how many letters there are in the word you have said. When students think they know the number of letters, they raise their hands. Invite a student to say the number and spell the word. Write the letters on the board and ask if the others agree the spelling is correct, then count the letters together to see if the number is also correct. You could play this game in teams, with each team getting a point for a correct number and for a correct spelling.

How Many Words?

Read out some sentences for the students to write down, like a dictation. Then, have students count the words in each sentence. (Tell them that contractions, e.g. *wasn't*, count as one word in this game.) When they think they know the number of words, they raise their hands. Invite a student to say the number, ask if the others agree, and then count the words together to see if they were correct.

I Spy

You can play *I Spy* with objects around the classroom or within the pages of the **Language Book** and **Literacy Book** (ideally projected onto the board). Say *I spy with my little eye something beginning with (A)*, and have students guess what you are looking at, then have them continue the game. Alternatively, play with adjectives: *I spy with my little eye something (rough)*. Point out they may find something that matches your description, but if it isn't the object you're thinking of, they have to continue guessing!

Mime It!

The same as *Draw It!* but students act out the word you give them.

Never-Ending Sentence

Have students make up a story using one very long sentence in a chain. Demonstrate first with a few students. Give them a story starter and have them continue the story, each saying *and, but,* or *so* before adding a new sentence, e.g.

Teacher: *Last summer I wanted a skateboard …*
Student A: *so I walked to the shop*
Student B: *and looked at the skateboards in the window*
Student C: *but I didn't like the colors*
Student D: *so I went in the shop …*

Have students play again in groups. They can do this orally, or you could have them write down their sentences. Challenge the groups to see who can keep going to make the longest sentence.

Pass the Ball

Have students sit in a circle. Throw a ball to a student and have that student give an idea/opinion, or make a sentence or prediction using the target language, when he/she catches the ball. That student then throws the ball to another student and the game continues.

Pass the Whisper!

Have students stand in a line. Whisper a sentence or question using the target language to one student and have him/her pass it on until it reaches the student nearest the door. That student must say the sentence or question aloud. Repeat as required.

Physical Spelling

Read out a key word. Have students spell out the word and do actions at the same time: they should raise their arms for letters with stalks going up (e.g. b); fold arms for words with no stalk (e.g. c), and lower arms to sides for letters with stalks going down (e.g. p).

Running Sentences

Divide the class into two teams. Give a board pen to the first student in each team. Read out a sentence that either uses target language from the lesson or is from or about the readings. After hearing the sentence *twice*, the students with the pens run to the board and write the first word of the sentence on the board and then pass the pen to the next student, who writes the next word. Both teams stop writing when one team finishes the sentence. Check the sentence to see how many correct words they had. Then play again with a different sentence. The team with the most correct sentences at the end of the game, wins.

Running Spelling

Divide the class into two teams and give one student in each team a board pen. Divide the board in two. Say a word twice. The students with the pens then run to the board and write the first letter of the word. They then hand the pen to the next student in their team who writes the next letter. Both teams stop writing when one team finishes the word. Check the spelling. Then play again with a different word. The team with the most correctly spelled words at the end of the game, wins.

Shark

Before the game starts, draw on the board a simple series of 10 steps leading down to water. On the top step, draw a stick figure. In the water draw a shark waiting with open mouth.

Use words from the lesson and draw a series of lines on the board, one for each letter. Have students raise their hands to guess the letters. For each correct guess, write the letter on the line. For each incorrect guess, erase the stick figure and draw it again one step nearer the shark. Write the wrong letters on the board so they are not repeated.

Students win if the word is completed before the stick figure reaches the shark—but they must continue saying letters, not shout out the word!

Simon Says

Use this game to practice actions and imperatives. Give an instruction. If you say *Simon says* before the instruction, students should do it. If you don't say *Simons says*, students should stay still. You can vary this game to practice grammar structures, e.g. if you say an action using the modals *You have to* or *You must (look through a telescope)*, students do the action. If you don't use the modals, students should stay still.

Spelling Bee

Say a word and have students spell it out around the class, saying one letter each. Encourage students to notice if there are any mistakes and to self-correct where possible.

Stand Up, Sit Down

Call out statements that practice the target language, e.g. *My mom is tall.* If the statement is true for students, they stand up. If it is not true, they stay sitting down. Alternatively, you can have students put their hands on their heads for true statements and keep their hands by their sides for false ones. You can play this game for any true/false statements. Have students take turns to come to the front and call out a statement.

Unscramble

Write the target vocabulary on the board with all the letters scrambled. Have students work in pairs to unscramble them. You could turn this into a race or provide a time limit. If students find it difficult, give them the first letter of each word.

What's the Next Word?

Divide the class into small groups. Read out sentences from a story, dialogue, or presentation and stop before key words. Have students decide in their groups what the next word is and raise their hands to answer.

What's the Scene?

Divide students into groups and have them mime one scene from the story. The other students must guess which scene they are miming.

What Was the Last Word?

Divide the class into two teams and give each team a board pen. Play the audio or video and stop after key vocabulary. One member of each team runs to the board and writes the last word heard.

Who Said It?

Review dialogue and characters from readings. Make handwritten cards with a quotation from the reading. First, check that students remember the names of the characters in the target reading. Then hold up one of the cards, saying *What does it say?* and have the students read it aloud all together. Say *Who said it?* When they have answered for each sign, play the reading video or audio again to check answers. Alternatively, say the quotations aloud without writing them down.

Word Tennis

In this game, pairs of students will pass words or sentences between them. Encourage them to say the words quickly, like a ball passing between tennis players. Have students take turns to say words connected to a particular topic, e.g. *friendship*:

Student A: *break*
Student B: *a promise*
Student A: *get along*
Student B: *well with*

Word Tree

Make a word tree starting with a word at the base, e.g. *space*. Draw two branches coming out of the base word, and write in two words that are connected to *space*. From each of those words, draw two more branches, each of which will have two more words connected with them. Do a quick example on the board and then have students make their own word tree in their notebooks. Then have them show and explain it to a friend.

Yes/No Game

Write a big *Yes* on the left of the board and a big *No* on the right. Tell the students you will say sentences. If they agree with the sentence or think it is true, they point left and say *Yes!* If they disagree or think it is false, they point right and say *No!*

Alternatively, make the game into a TPR (Total Physical Response) game by assigning *Yes* to one side of the room and *No* to the other and having students move from one side to the other as you say each item.

Vocabulary

Lesson Objectives

- to review vocabulary of performance, time, money, math, patterns, materials, illnesses, cures, and machines

Materials
Audio Track 1

A TRACK 1 TB p. 213 **Listen and write. Where's Lucas?**

- Have students look at the picture on p. 6. Encourage them to talk about it. If necessary, write prompts on the board (e.g. *people*, *clothes*, *place*).
- Tell students they are going to listen to some children talking. Ask a gist question: *What are they doing?* Elicit some suggestions, then play the audio and have students point to the pictures as they listen. Then check the answer (practicing for a school play).
- Refer students to the scrambled words on the page. Point out the example *noon* and explain that all the words are from the dialogue. Give students a few minutes to unscramble as many of the other words as possible in pairs. Then play the audio and tell students to write any words they missed. Play the audio again and have students raise their hands when they hear the words they've written. Display the answers on the board for students to check.
- Ask the comprehension question *Where's Lucas?* and elicit answers. Play the audio again to check.

Answers
1 *noon* 2 early 3 rehearsal 4 stage 5 late
6 costume 7 backstage 8 curtain
Lucas is under the curtain.

B **Look and write. What is Lucas's hat made of?**

- Refer students to the example answer and point out the image that provides the clue. Tell them that the other images also provide clues. Have students look at the images and complete the crossword in pairs. You may need to give them an extra clue for number 7. Can they think of a type of material used for making clothes that grows on a plant?
- Project the crossword onto the board or write numbers 1–7. Ask students to spell out their answers, and write them on the board.
- Ask students what the "hidden word" is (it is shown vertically in the middle of the crossword). Can they now answer the question *What is Lucas's hat made of?*

Answers
1 striped 2 dollar 3 add 4 coins (or cents)
5 subtract 6 silver 7 cotton It's made of plastic.

C **Read and choose.**

- Have students look at the picture. Ask them *What's happening? What do you think the problem is?* Have students read the dialogue quickly and see if they were correct.
- Refer students to the example answer and ask how they know the answer is *sneezing*. (Pete says *Achoo!*) Have students complete the activity individually and then compare answers with a partner.
- To check answers, invite students to read a sentence each and ask if the others agree.

Answers
1 *sneezing* 2 sore 3 fever 4 a cold 5 medicine
6 broken 7 cast

D **Look and complete.**

- Have students say what they can see in the image. Ask *What do you think the machine does?*
- Refer students to the example. Explain that the text describes how the machine works. Have students work in pairs to choose the correct verb phrases from the box to complete the rest of the description.
- Check the answers and write or project them onto the board.

Answers
1 *flip the switch* 2 turn the wheel 3 Pull the lever
4 push the button

Practice **Resource Bank:** Language Review Vocabulary Printouts
Student's App: Language Review Vocabulary Practice

Explore Language

Lesson Objectives

- to review *have to, don't have to, should, shouldn't,* present progressive, comparatives, superlatives, and *going to*

Materials

Audio Track 2

A Look and read. Then complete with *have to, don't have to, should,* or *shouldn't.*

- Have students look at the picture and say what they can see happening and where the people are. Ask what activities they can see people doing. Point out that this lesson continues the story of putting on a play and that there are other activities on the same day.
- Refer students to the example answer. Ask why it is *should* (it's advice on the best place to sit). Ask students which option—*have to, don't have to, should,* or *shouldn't*—means something isn't necessary (don't have to), which means something is necessary (have to), and which means something isn't a good idea (shouldn't). Have students complete the activity and compare their answers with a partner.
- Check answers and ask if everyone agrees.

Answers

1 *should* 2 have to 3 don't have to 4 should
5 shouldn't 6 shouldn't

B TRACK 2 TB p. 213 **Read and complete the dialogue. Then listen and check.**

- Have students read the dialogue quickly and say what is happening. Ask if students recognize any of the characters in the picture (they can see Ruben, Min, Mariam, and Lucas from the previous lesson).
- Refer students to the example and ask why it is *Are you enjoying* (present progressive for something happening now). Point out that all the sentences are about things happening now.
- Have students complete the dialogue. Then play the audio and have them check their answers. Ask them to check if they always have the verb *be* and the *–ing* form of the verb.
- To check answers, invite students to read a line of the dialogue each.

Answers

1 *Are you enjoying* 2 I'm waiting 3 are you doing
4 We're selling 5 's he doing 6 He's playing
7 he isn't using 8 He's catching

C Complete with the comparative or the superlative forms.

- Have students read the text quickly and say what the play is about (children having adventures at sea).
- Refer students to the example answer and ask why it is *the heaviest.* (It is superlative because the whale is number one of all the heavy sea animals and there are no other animals mentioned to make a comparison with). Remind students that longer adjectives use *more* and *most* for the comparative and superlative. Have students complete the activity individually and then compare answers with a partner.
- To check answers, invite students to read a sentence each.

Answers

1 *the heaviest* 2 the most beautiful 3 as strong
4 more dangerous 5 the biggest 6 the smallest

D The play is over. What are the children going to do next? Write.

- Refer students to the example answer. Ask *Why is it "going to"?* (It's talking about plans.) Ask students what verb they always need when they use *going to* (verb *be*).
- Have students complete the activity and compare with a friend. Invite students to come and write one sentence on the board. Ask if everyone agrees.

Answers

1 *What are you going to do now?*
2 I'm going to buy a cake.
3 Mariam's going to play a game.
4 Then we're going to watch TV at home.
5 My parents are going to take me to a restaurant.
6 And I'm not going to take off my costume.

Practice **Resource Bank:** Language Review Grammar Printouts
Student's App: Language Review Grammar Practice

Fiction

Lesson Objectives

- to review the reading skills of scanning, making inferences and predictions, and identifying perspective
- to review spelling patterns with *–ough* and *–ight*

Materials

Audio Tracks 1 and 2

A TRACK 1 TB p. 227 **Scan the story. Complete the graphic organizer. Then read.**

- Project or draw the graphic organizer on the board.
- Ask students to talk in pairs about the last good story they read: what it was about, where it happened, and who the characters were. Elicit some ideas and have students say where the information would go in the graphic: setting, characters, or the story.
- Have students scan the text in A quickly and find the information to complete the graphic organizer, then compare answers with a friend.
- Play the audio for students to read and check their answers.
- Discuss the question in the green box: *What can you tell about the character of Dad from his dialogue?* Ask the class *What do you think about Dad's character? Why?* (He seems patient—he doesn't get angry with Chris. He is optimistic—he is sure they will find the prize. He is positive—he encourages Chris with kind words.)

Answers
Setting: *morning*, desert
Characters: Chris, Dad
What Are They Doing?: digging for treasure / a prize

B **Read and answer.**

- Refer students to the example answer. Ask if students can find something in the text to justify the answer (the map says we are in the right place).
- Have students complete the activity individually and then compare with a partner. Check answers.

Answers
1 *The map shows where the prize is.* 2 Chris deals with the scorpion by pushing it away with his boot. 3 Chris tries to cool down by drinking water. 4 Chris wants to stop digging because he is tired / doesn't think they will find what they are looking for. 5 The prize is worth enough to buy a house.

C **Think and discuss. Then write. What are Dad and Chris looking for? What clues are there in the text? Make an inference.**

- Have students look at the text again for clues about what Dad and Chris are looking for. Have them discuss in pairs, then choose one idea to write in their notebooks. Remind them to include a reason for their answer.

Suggested Answer
I think Dad and Chris are looking for something valuable that comes in a box. I know this because Chris asks how much it is worth. This tells me that the prize is not money. I also know that it comes in a box because when Chris's shovel hits it, he hears a "thump."

D **Think and discuss. Then write. Look at the story dialogue. What different perspectives do Dad and Chris have?**

- Draw students' attention to the images and have them look back at the dialogue in A. Ask *How do you think Chris feels? How do you think Dad feels?* Have students discuss in pairs and then write short sentences in their notebooks.
- Invite a few students to read out their sentences.

Suggested Answers
Chris is tired. He doesn't think they will find the prize.
Dad is hopeful. He thinks they should keep looking.

E **Write and draw. What happens next? Imagine how the story ends.**

- Give student's time to think about what happens next in the story in A and how it ends. Have them write some sentences and draw a picture to illustrate. Have them share their story ideas in pairs.

Answer
Students' own answers.

TRACK 2 TB p. 227 **Spelling Patterns *–ought* and *–ight***

Listen and repeat. Then complete the words with *ough* or *ight*.

- With books closed, write *ough* and *ight* on the board and elicit ways to pronounce them. Remind students that usually the *gh* is not pronounced, but sometimes the *gh* in *ough* is pronounced with an /f/.
- With books open, play the first part of the audio and have students repeat the words. Point out the example.
- Play the first part of the audio again and have students complete as many words as they can. Then play the second part of the audio for students to check their spelling and complete any missing words. Have them underline *ight* and *ough* in each word.
- Have students look for words ending in *ight* and *ough* in the story in A and raise their hands when they find one. Elicit answers and write them on the board.

Answers
1 *knight* 2 cough 3 night 4 dough 5 delight
6 tonight 7 rough 8 light 9 tough 10 fight
11 though 12 enough
In the reading: though; enough; right; all right

Practice **Resource Bank:** Literacy Review Reading Skills Printouts
Student's App: Reading Skills Practice; Spelling Pattern Practice

Nonfiction

Lesson Objectives

- to review the reading skills of scanning and identifying facts and opinions, author's purpose, cause and effect
- Spelling with *or* and *ar*

Materials

Audio Tracks 3 and 4

A TRACK 3 TB p. 227 **Scan the text. Complete the table. Then read.**

- Ask students to make a list of the largest animals they can think of, e.g. whales, elephants, rhinos, etc. Then have them look quickly at the text and see if it includes an animal on their list. Have students complete the table with information from the text.
- Play the audio and have students read the text and check their answers.

Answers

Name of Country: Egypt
Number of Whale Skeletons: 400
Age of the Skeletons: 40 million years
Year UNESCO Recognized Wadi Al-Hitan: 2005

B Read and write *Fact* or *Opinion*.

- Refer students to the example sentence and answer. Elicit the difference between a fact and an opinion (a fact is true, while an opinion is something that someone thinks is true).
- Have students complete the activity, checking to see if the text mentions the information.
- Read the sentences and have students raise their arms for a fact and fold their arms for an opinion.

Answers

1 *Opinion* 2 Fact 3 Opinion 4 Fact 5 Fact

C Think and discuss. What is the author's purpose in writing this article? What makes you think that?

- Ask students *Does the author want people to go to Whale Valley on vacation?* (probably not) Have students discuss with a friend what the purpose might be. Then ask for ideas from the class.

Suggested Answer

I think the author's purpose is to help readers learn about Wadi Al-Hitan. I think this because the author includes a lot of facts about Whale Valley.

D Match the cause to the effect.

- Write on the board *The desert is very hot. The sun shines a lot.* Ask students which is the cause (sun) and which is the effect (hot).
- Have students match the causes and the effects, then check answers.

Answers

1 b 2 c 3 a

My Reading Journal

What was one thing that surprised you from the reading?

Have students look back at the reading and think about what they found surprising.

Then have students choose one of the ideas and write a sentence about it. To help students get started, write a prompt on the board (e.g. *It surprised me that …*).

Have students share their ideas with a friend and then ask pairs to share their ideas with the class.

Example Answer

It surprised me that they were in the middle of a desert.

TRACK 4 TB p. 227 **Spelling Patterns *ar* and *or***

Listen and repeat. Then complete the words with *ar* or *or*.

- Play the first two words of the audio. Ask students to repeat them and write them on the board. Underline the letters *ar* and *or* and elicit the pronunciation of these letters (/ɑː(r)/, /ɔː(r)/).
- Play the first part of the audio and have students repeat the words. Play the first part of the audio again and have them complete as many of the words as they can.
- Play the second part of the audio for students to check spelling and complete any missing words.
- Have students look for more words in the text with *ar* or *or* and write them in two lists. Invite students to read a word from their lists. Ask *Which words sound the same?* (*ar*: large, are; *or*: more, important, anymore, for) *Which words sound different?* (*ar*: years, area; *or*: world (/wɜː(r)ld/).

Answers

1 storm 2 alarm 3 fork 4 polar 5 cartoon
6 artist 7 torn 8 star 9 shark 10 sport
11 torch 12 world
In the reading: years, large, are, area; more, important, story, anymore, or, world, for

Practice **Resource Bank:** Literacy Review Reading Skills Printouts
Student's App: Reading Skills Practice; Spelling Pattern Practice

UNIT 1

Let's Start with Art

Unit Overview

Themes

Different types of art

The purpose of art

Synopsis

In this unit students will learn about different types of art and ways to describe art. They will find out about how art can help in communities and how to compose a good picture. They will plan and prepare a conversation to describe a piece of art and write a cinquain poem using target language from the unit.

Language Book

Vocabulary

collage, installation, landscape, mobile, mural, photography, portrait, sculpture, sketch, still life

p. 35

Explore Language

Quantifiers: *A Little, A Few, All, Most*

p. 37

Global Citizenship

Why is art important to people?

background, bright, dark, detailed, foreground, light, pale, shadow, simple

p. 39

Explore Language

Too and *Enough* with Adjectives

p. 41

Talk About It

Conversation: giving opinions

p. 43

Write About It

Cinquain Poems

Sentence Building: reviewing parts of speech

p. 45

Think It Over

Review and Reflection

p. 47

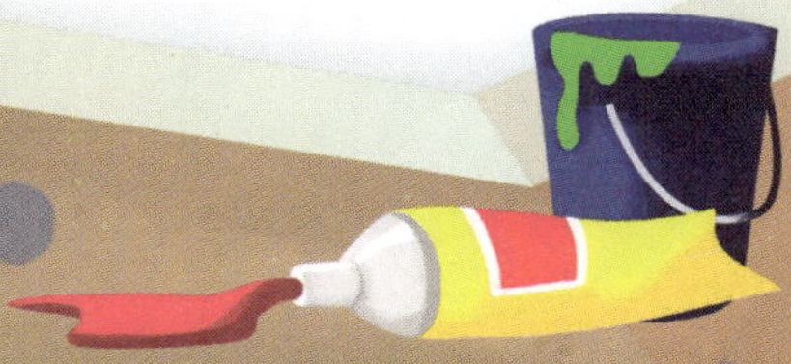

Literacy Book

Think Together
Why do people make art?
p. 61

Visible Thinking
See, Think, Wonder
p. 49

Nonfiction
Instructional Text: *My Guide to Photography*

Words in Context: *frame, element, zoom in, horizontal, vertical*
p. 57

Fiction
Fantasy: *True Colors*

Words in Context: *owner, run out of, choice, croissant, exclaims*
p. 51

Reading Skill
Understanding facts and opinions
p. 55

Spelling Pattern
–ent
p. 59

Language and Literacy Connections

The connecting theme in Unit 1 is art and why it is important.

	Language	Literacy
Vocabulary	**Set 1:** types of art **Set 2:** describing art	**Fiction:** portrait, still life **Nonfiction:** landscape(s), photography, portrait, background, foreground, simple
Grammar	**Quantifiers: *A Little, A Few, All, Most*** He only has a little hair. I know a few parents. All the paintings are by our students. Most of his hair is white. **Adjectives and Adverbs of Manner** This one's too dark. It's not big enough.	**Fiction** This still life isn't good enough! The fruit and vegetables look real, but they're too boring. Can you show us all of your paintings? **Nonfiction** I only include a few elements in the photo.
Skills	**Pronunciation:** silent *gh* l	**Reading:** understanding facts and opinions **Spelling Pattern:** *–ent*
International English	I kind of like it. / I quite like it.	apartment/flat

Lesson 1 Walkthrough: Vocabulary

This lesson introduces the theme of the unit and presents and practices the first vocabulary set.

Warm Up

Warm Up activities are either language or topic-based. Their purpose is not to pre-teach new vocabulary, but to engage students, activate prior knowledge, and prepare students cognitively for the lesson ahead. The digital **Enhanced Teacher's Book (ETB)** also contains Two-Minute Review activities to recall previously taught language or skills. These activities are quick to do, so time is not taken away from the rest of the lesson, and are easy to integrate into a classroom routine. You can choose to do both the Two-Minute Review and the Warm Up or just one or the other, to suit the needs of your class.

Activity A Contextualized Presentation: Picture Dictionary Scene

Activity A presents the first lexical set (eight to twelve words) through a picture dictionary scene. This scene is designed to support learning by providing word-picture association. Alongside this, its purpose is to get students thinking about the unit topic, reviewing language, and making connections to their own world. The scene includes key characters from the corresponding **Literacy Book** unit and the previous unit of the **Language Book** for students to identify. This is to help students make connections between the two books, between units, and between the topics and characters, to show how communities work.

The new language is contextualized aurally in a dialogue. The audio includes at least some of the target vocabulary to encourage students to explore the image and develop discrimination skills. Students should be encouraged to point to the pictures or words as they hear them mentioned. The process of listening, searching for, and finding vocabulary items helps students to engage with the target language. **Literacy Book** Links are highlighted in the digital **Enhanced Teacher's Book** (ETB).

There is always a gist or comprehension question to focus students and help them understand the general meaning of the dialogue. The digital **ETB** provides further comprehension check questions to explore the picture and audio in more detail.

Activity B Drill & Controlled Vocabulary Practice

Activity B is a drill and provides initial practice of all the target vocabulary. Pausing the audio will give all students enough time to say the words and enable you to give immediate feedback on pronunciation. For ideas on how to make drills fun, see **TB p. 23**.

The listen and number task asks students to write numbers next to the vocabulary items in the picture in the order in which they hear them mentioned. This gets students thinking about the target language, which will help them to learn it.

Activity C Visualization

Activity C is a visualization activity and offers a different pathway for students to interact with the target language. The audio prompts students to create their own mental images of the vocabulary and to do actions where appropriate. This personalized approach makes learning more meaningful and therefore more memorable. Students are not expected to articulate (in English) what they have visualized because sometimes this may be harder than the target word. However, a variety of pair-/class-work activities for exchanging ideas have been provided to give students a means for creative output.

Activity D Controlled Practice & Critical Thinking

Activity D provides further language practice by getting students to interact with the picture dictionary. Critical thinking skills are developed as students complete a categorization task such as a Venn diagram, table, or graphic organizer, and sometimes more than one answer is possible.

Activity E Song

Activity E is always a **song** connected to a unit theme and provides additional context for the target language: any words not in the dialogue in A will be included here. There is a fill-in-the-blank activity, where students are encouraged to predict the answers before listening to check. The song allows students to have fun with the language and helps them to learn through rhythm, rhyme, and repetition. There is usually a link to a Social and Emotional Learning (SEL) competency.

The song is supported by an animated video with the lyrics displayed to encourage heads-up participation. When the song lends itself to it, encourage students to invent actions or movements to do while singing: a Total Physical Response (TPR) approach will help them to learn and retain the new language. Additional Video Focus ideas are provided in the digital **ETB**.

Cool Down

The Cool Down is a final game or activity that provides an opportunity to wrap up the lesson. It reviews and reinforces the lesson objectives.

Vocabulary

Lesson Objectives

- to learn vocabulary to describe art: *collage, installation, landscape, mobile, mural, photography, portrait, sculpture, sketch, still life*
- to sing a song that explores making different types of art

Materials

Audio Tracks 3 to 6; Video

Warm Up

Ask students to think of all the places in their town or country where they can see art. Elicit suggestions and write them on the board. In pairs have students talk about different pieces of art they have seen; do they have a favorite piece? They can talk about art they have seen on TV or pictures in books.

A TRACK 3 TB p. 213 **Listen and find. What does Lucas add to some artwork?**

- Have students look at the picture on pp. 10–11 and say what they can see and where it is happening. Ask what the people are doing in the picture (looking at art and making art).
- Play the audio and have students point to the words or pictures as they listen.
- Ask the comprehension question *What does Lucas add to some artwork?* and elicit answers. Play the audio again for students to check.

Answer

Lucas adds his bus ticket to the collage.

B TRACK 4 TB p. 213 **Listen, say, and number the pictures in A.**

- Play the audio. Have students point to the pictures and say the words.
- Tell students to listen again and write numbers next to the words in the picture. Do the example together (sculpture).
- Check answers by calling out a number and having students call out the word.

Answers

1 *sculpture* 2 portrait 3 landscape 4 still life
5 collage 6 installation 7 mobile 8 mural
9 sketch 10 photography

C TRACK 5 TB p. 213 **Close your eyes. Listen, visualize, and say.**

- Prepare students for the visualization (see TB p. 21).
- Play the audio, allowing students to visualize the objects as they listen. Make sure students know not to speak until they hear the word *say*.
- Have students draw what they imagined for their partner, who then guesses the word.

D Look and write.

- Students are going to categorize the vocabulary. This encourages critical thinking because students must group words in a logical or meaningful way. Draw a Venn diagram on the board to remind students how they work. Elicit why *portrait* goes in the 2D circle and *sculpture* goes in the 3D circle.
- Give students time to complete the activity. Then check answers. You may wish to discuss why a collage can be both 2D and 3D (it depends which materials are used to make it). Can students suggest some materials for 2D and 3D collages?

Answers

2D artworks: *portrait*; landscape; still life; mural; photography; sketch
3D artworks: *sculpture*; mobile; installation
Both: collage

E TRACK 6 TB p. 213 **Listen and complete. Then watch and sing.**

- Have students turn their books over so they can't see the song lyrics. Tell them the title of the song is *Art Is for Everyone* and ask them what they think the song will be about and which words will be included. If necessary, prompt students by asking students *What kinds of art do you know?*
- Play the audio and have students raise their hands every time they hear one of their predicted words in the song.
- Have students turn their books back over. Ask *Can you guess what's missing?* Play the song again, this time pausing where necessary for students to write their answers. Point out that all the words they need are on pp. 10–11, so they can check their spelling.
- Play the song video and encourage students to sing along. Then replay the song video and have students sing and do actions for the different types of art as they hear them in the song.

Answers

1 *photography* 2 sculpture 3 collage 4 mural
5 sketch 6 still life 7 landscape 8 portrait

Cool Down

Play *Physical Spelling* (see TB p. 26) with the vocabulary from this lesson.

Practice **Student's App:** Vocabulary Practice; Song Video

Lesson 2 Walkthrough: Explore Language

The grammar lessons present and practice the target structures using a simplified inductive approach. This encourages the students to think about the patterns of language and to make and test assumptions through carefully staged and scaffolded activities. By laying the groundwork for the kinds of tasks they will do in higher levels, they are supported to become independent thinkers from the very beginning.

Activity A Contextualized Presentation

Activity A presents the lesson's grammar focus through the context of a dialogue or story. Students listen and read, but the target language is not highlighted at this point. The gist or comprehension question gives students a reason to listen and supports them to understand the story. The digital **ETB** provides questions to check students' comprehension. If you don't use the **ETB**, ask simple comprehension questions to help students make connections with prior knowledge and personalize the scenario.

Activity B Grammar Analysis Table

Activity B is a grammar table with sections for students to fill out, focusing on form. Most of the sentences come from the dialogue in Activity A; if they are not there, the answers will be filled in, with the key word(s) highlighted to provide a model. Students need to identify the sentences and copy the missing words, thereby drawing their attention to the grammar structure and to language patterns. The teacher's notes help you to scaffold the discussion for the first four units. In later units, students are encouraged to take the lead in identifying and discussing the grammar patterns and completing the table. However, the **ETB** provides additional support notes, should you prefer to continue leading the grammar discussion.

Attached to the table is a language tip, pointing out additional information related to the grammar point that needs further support. There are three types of tip:

- **Remember:** when students have most likely already seen this language feature, e.g. contractions.
- **Look:** a new, additional piece of information about the grammar, e.g. a spelling pattern or anomaly.
- **Watch Out:** highlights typical mistakes learners make.

Activity C Inductive Analysis

Activity C is a continuation of the language analysis, as students are asked to focus on the meaning and usage of the grammar structure. Concise concept statements are given to explain how the language is used. Students have to think critically to choose between different options, which helps them to interact with the language. Encourage students to discuss their ideas in pairs before checking answers as a class. First Language (L1) can be used to support this task when language in the concept statements is above level.

Activity D Drill: Sentence Level

See **TB p. 40**.

Activity E Controlled Practice: Written

See **TB p. 40**.

Activity F Freer Practice: Communication

See **TB p. 40**.

Explore Language

Lesson Objectives

- to learn how to talk about quantity using *a little*, *a few*, *all*, *most*
- to practice art vocabulary

Materials
Audio Tracks 7 and 8

Warm Up

Ask students to visualize a picture they have on display at home. Have them tell a friend who or what is in their picture.

A TRACK 7 TB p. 213 **Listen and Read. Who's Larry drawing?**

- Have students look at the pictures on p. 12. Ask them *What can you see? What do you think the people are talking about?*
- Play the audio and have students follow in their books.
- Ask the comprehension question *Who is Larry drawing?* and elicit the answer.

Answer
Larry is drawing his grandpa.

B **Look at A. Complete.**

- Write or project the table onto the board. Tell students that the sentences they need are all in the story.
- Refer students to the first sentence in the table and have them find it in the story (picture 2). Have students complete the first sentence in the table. Then have them work in pairs to complete the rest of the table.
- Complete the table on the board so that students can check their answers. Ask what kinds of words *hair*, *parents*, and *grandparents* are (nouns). Review the difference between count and noncount nouns (noncount nouns refer to things that cannot be counted, they do not have a plural form, and they are not used with *a*/*an*).
- Look at the bottom row of the table. Ask which word we use after *Most* (of). Point out that we can also use *of* after *all* but that it is not essential.
- Have students look at the Grammar tip *Remember*. Write on the board *I have a lot of apples. I have some apples. I don't have any apples.* Invite students to draw apples next to the sentences to represent the different quantifiers. Elicit that *any* can also be used for questions.

Answers
a little; a few; All; of

C **Think and discuss. Then choose.**

- Have students work in pairs to read and discuss the sentences. Tell them they can look at the table and at the story to help them circle the correct options. Then check the answers as a class.
- Elicit that we use *a little* with noncount nouns and *a few* with count nouns. Ask students *Is "some" more or less than "a little" or "a few"?* (usually more) *Is "a lot of" more or less than "all"?* (less)

Answers
1 small 2 big 3 all

D TRACK 8 TB p. 213 **Listen and say.**

- Play the audio and have students listen and repeat. For ideas on how to vary the drill, see TB p. 23.

E **Choose a picture. Look and write.**

- Ask two students to read aloud the example sentences. Have the others listen and point to the activity in the picture.
- Tell students they are going to write some sentences about one of the pictures. Have them choose one picture and write sentences about it—encourage them to use *a little*, *a few*, *all*, or *most* when they can.

Suggested Answers
Picture A: A few children are painting a mural. There are a few paint jars. There isn't any yellow paint. There is some green paint and a little red paint. Most of the objects in the collage are pictures. There are a few stars in the collage. There are a few pictures on the wall. Most of the pictures on the wall are landscapes. There is a lot of water in the vase.
Picture B: A lot of children are painting a mural. There are a few paint jars. There is some yellow paint, a little green paint, and a lot of red paint. There aren't any pictures in the collage. There are a few stars in the collage. There are a lot of pictures on the walls. There is a little water in the vase.

F **Look at E. Compare and find the differences.**

- Put students into pairs or groups, making sure there is at least one student who wrote about picture A and one who wrote about picture B in each group.
- Have students compare their sentences. Ask them how many differences they found. Invite students to share their sentences with the class.

Cool Down

Play *Correct the Teacher* with sentences about the pictures in E (see TB p. 25); for example, *In picture A, there are a few stars in the collage* (True); *In picture B, there is a lot of water in the vase* (False).

Practice **Resource Bank:** Grammar Printout
Student's App: Grammar Practice

Lesson 3 Walkthrough: Global Citizenship

This lesson presents and practices the second vocabulary set, practices listening for gist and specific details, and gives students the opportunity to learn about the lives of other children around the world and to make connections with their own lives.

Opening Question

The **opening question** takes the place of the Warm Up and is designed to activate interest and curiosity in the *Global Citizenship* topic by helping students to make connections to prior knowledge. Don't correct students at this point or give too much feedback, as the lesson is structured so that they develop ideas to discuss at the end of the class.

Activity A Contextualized Vocabulary

Activity A presents the new vocabulary through eye-catching photos or pictures, to provide a real-world context. There is a contextualized listening activity which presents some of the target language through a dialogue or monologue. This listening activity provides an introduction to the *Global Citizenship* part of the lesson on the facing page. Students will be able to make connections between this audio and the audio for D and E.

Activity B Drill & Controlled Vocabulary Practice

See **TB p. 34**.

Visualization

There is a visualization audio track for this vocabulary set on the TTL. See **TB p. 34**.

Activity C Controlled Vocabulary Practice: Written

Activity C is a read and circle or complete activity to encourage students to think critically about the new vocabulary and to use it through controlled practice.

Activity D Listening for Gist & Main Idea

Activity D provides input for the Global Citizenship discussion at the end of the lesson. There are usually two speakers who explore the Global Citizenship theme in connection to different countries around the world. Students listen for the main idea of the audio topic and answer a gist question.

Before they listen, give students some time to explore the pictures. You could let them find the countries mentioned on a world map and ask them what they already know about these countries to activate prior knowledge. Tell students to listen out for key vocabulary they recognize. Explain that thinking about these words in order will help them to understand what the listening is about and answer the gist question. Some of the new vocabulary from Activity A is always recycled here.

Activity E Listening for Details

Activity E encourages students to listen out for specific details. Ask them how many of the questions they can answer from information they have remembered from D, but reassure them that this is not a memory test and that it doesn't matter if they don't remember. Then play the audio again, so they can listen and check their answers and answer any questions they missed.

Encourage further discussion and personal response to what they heard by analyzing the answers (e.g. why something was false) and having students talk about what they found interesting or surprising.

Discussion Questions

The **Discussion Questions** address the key holistic learning concepts that run through the unit. Ultimately, the discussion can be done in pairs with some whole-class input at the end, although you may wish to have a whole-class discussion for the initial units to allow students to become familiar with the activity. The *Global Citizenship* strand at this level encourages students to think about how they can get involved in their community, and how their community can have an impact on the wider world, and on them.

There is usually one personalization question and one question that asks students to look further and see the bigger picture. Deal with each one in turn, giving students time to think and discuss in their pairs or small groups. Allow use of L1 for new words and more complex ideas as this will enable students to express themselves and develop a clearer understanding of the key concepts. You can also challenge students to provide sentences beyond their ability by translating words and phrases from L1 into English.

Bring the class back together to discuss the conclusions they have reached. Use graphic organizers on the board to present students' ideas. Revisit the opening question and see if students answer it differently now. In-depth ideas to help you structure each discussion as well as project ideas can be found in the **ETB**.

Competencies

Icons in the teaching notes highlight which activities in the **Language Book** are connected to one of the five competencies: Me, Act, Think, Learn, and Communicate. For more information, see **TB p. 19**.

Global Citizenship

Lesson Objectives

- to learn vocabulary for describing art: *background, bright, dark, detailed, foreground, light, pale, shadow, simple*
- to explore why art is important to people
- to practice listening for gist and details

Materials

Audio Tracks 9 to 11; Audio Track A; a world map (Activity D)

Opening Question

This question activates students' prior knowledge. Ask students the opening question: *Why is art important to people?* Give students time to think and elicit ideas. You could prompt students by asking *How might art be important to people in our community? but don't give students much feedback at this point. They will find out more during the lesson.*

A TRACK 9 TB p. 213 **Listen to Jane talk to her art teacher about shadow boxes. Why do people make shadow boxes?**

- Ask students if they know what Jane is holding in the picture. Tell students that it is called a shadow box.
- Play the audio and have students point to the words or pictures as they listen.
- Ask the gist question *Why do people make shadow boxes?* Elicit answers, then play the audio again for students to check.

Answer

to tell a story

B TRACK 10 TB p. 214 **Listen, say, and number the pictures in A.**

- Play the audio and have students point to the pictures and say the words.
- Tell students to listen again and number the pictures in the order they hear them. Do the example together (simple).
- Check answers by asking volunteers to call out the numbers and asking others to respond. Alternately, project the answers using the TTL.

Answers

1 *simple* 2 detailed 3 foreground 4 background
5 dark 6 light 7 shadow 8 bright 9 pale

TRACK A TB p. 214 **Visualization**

The Tap & Teach Lessons (TTL) have a visualization audio track for this vocabulary set. (See TB p. 21.)

C Read and choose.

- Project the activity onto the board and look at the example answer. Ask students what words tell us that the answer is *foreground* (in front of the castle).
- Have students complete the activity and then compare answers with a friend. Invite students to come to the board and circle the correct answer.

Answers

1 *foreground* 2 background 3 dark 4 shadow
5 bright 6 light

D TRACK 11 TB p. 214 **Now listen to Yoko and Juan. Why do people make these artworks?**

- To generate interest, have students look at the two pictures and notice where each child is from. Ask students *Where are these countries?* Use a map to find them.
- Have students look at the pictures and ask them what they can see. Ask if they have ever made something like this.
- Listening for gist: Play the audio and have students listen for the answer to the gist question *Why do people make these artworks?* Elicit answers.

Answers

Yoko: To relax, to decorate for the Star Festival
Juan: To express themselves, to make decorations for festivals

E Listen again. Write *True* or *False*.

- Listening for details: have students look at the questions and remember what they heard. Ask them to answer as many question as they can. Play the audio and stop after *... traditional Japanese art*. Ask why number 1 is false (origami is not Mexican—it's Japanese).
- Play the rest of the audio and have students complete the activity. To check answers, ask individual students to read a sentence aloud and say *True* or *False*. If the answer is false, ask one student to say why it is false.

Answers

1 *False* 2 False 3 True 4 True 5 True 6 False

Discussion Questions

- Draw students' attention to the discussion questions: *Is art important to you? Why? How does art help us understand each other?* Discuss the questions as a class (see **ETB**).
- Return to the original opening question: *Why is art important to people?* Recap ideas discussed at the beginning of the class and encourage students to share any new ideas.

Cool Down

Put students into teams. Describe the vocabulary items from A and have teams take turns to guess the word; for example, *the front of a picture* (foreground), *when there is no light* (dark). If they guess incorrectly, the other team has the chance to guess and win the point.

Practice **Student's App:** Vocabulary Practice; Listening Practice

Lesson 4 Walkthrough: Explore Language

This lesson presents and practices the second grammar structure(s) and has the same structure and purpose as Lesson 2.

Activity A Contextualized Presentation

See **TB p. 36**.

Activity B Grammar Analysis Table

See **TB p. 36**.

Activity C Inductive Analysis

See **TB p. 36**.

Throughout the digital **ETB** there are ideas to differentiate lesson content in a mixed-ability class. Support ideas suggest a simpler pathway for completing an activity or provide scaffolding to enable less-confident students to complete the activity. Challenge ideas encourage more-confident students to use additional language to take activities further. For more activity-specific differentiation ideas, see **TB p. 24**.

Activity D Drill: Sentence Level

Activity D is a drill of four to five sentences/questions to allow students to familiarize themselves with the new language. Drills give students intensive practice in hearing and saying new phrases.

The first time you play the audio, focus on pronunciation. Then play it again, this time encouraging students to concentrate on intonation. Using different activities will help you to keep drills fun and stop them from becoming repetitive. For ideas on how to vary the drill, see **TB p. 23**.

Activity E Controlled Practice: Written

Activity E is a controlled practice activity and gives students some heads-down time to use the new grammar structure. Encourage students to do this as independently as possible, using the table in Activity B, so that they can process what they have learned and you can assess their level of understanding.

Activity F Free Practice: Communication

Activity F allows students to practice the target language through a freer, more communicative activity or game. Where there is text inside speech bubbles, this provides a model, but make sure students understand that they can choose what to say. This is a chance for students to communicate and collaborate while using and practicing the target language. Students learn more by working with different people, rather than the same friend each time. One way to achieve this is by giving students a word or picture card and asking them to find another student with the same card. Students with matching cards will work together in the activity.

Explore Language

Lesson Objectives

- to learn how to use *too* and *enough*
- to practice vocabulary to describe art

Materials

Audio Tracks 12 and 13; three or four pictures to show students (Warm Up, WU)

Warm Up

Show students three or four different kinds of picture (e.g. a portrait, a wildlife picture, and a landscape). Ask students *Do you like the pictures? Why or why not?* Then have students vote for their favorite picture.

A TRACK 12 TB p. 214 **Listen and read. Which picture do Larry and Poppy like best?**

- Ask students what they can see in the picture and what they think the children are doing (comparing different versions of the same picture on the computer). Establish that one of the children is from p. 12. Play the audio and have students follow the dialogue in their books.
- Ask the gist question *Which picture do Larry and Poppy like best?* and elicit the answer.

Answer

the last picture (bottom right)

B **Look at A. Complete.**

- Write or project the table onto the board. Tell students that the sentences are all in the dialogue.
- Refer students to the first incomplete sentence in the table and have them find it in the dialogue. Elicit the answer and write it on the board.
- Have students work in pairs to complete the rest of the table.
- Invite students to come to the board to write one word each. Ask *What kinds of words are "dark," "big," and "good"?* (adjectives)
- Refer students to the Grammar tip *Remember.* Point out that *too* + adjective means the same as *not* + *adjective* + *enough*. Write a sentence on the board and ask students for another sentence with the same meaning, using either *too* or *enough*; for example, *It's not big enough.* (It's too small.) / *I'm too short.* (I'm not tall enough.)

Answers

too; big; enough; close

C **Think and discuss. Then choose.**

- Give students time to read the sentences, think about their answers, and compare ideas with a friend. Tell them they can look at the table and at the dialogue to help them circle the correct options. Then check answers as a class.

Answers

1 more 2 less

D TRACK 13 TB p. 214 **Listen and say.**

- Play the audio and have students raise their hands when they hear *too* and *enough*.
- Play the audio again, pausing after each sentence, and have students listen and repeat. For ideas on how to vary drills, see TB p. 23.

E **Read and choose.**

- Refer students to the first sentence and the example answer. Ask students if *too dirty* means more or less dirty than they want (more—so they need to wash it).
- Have students complete the activity individually and then compare their answers in pairs.
- Check answers as a class.

Answers

1 *too dirty* 2 isn't big enough 3 's too small
4 's too expensive 5 not thin enough

F **Are the objects right for the mobile? Look, choose, and say.**

- Ask students to say what they can see in the pictures and elicit the numbered items.
- Give students time to think and then have them discuss their ideas with a partner. Encourage them to use *too* and *enough* and the words in the box to express their ideas.
- Ask for ideas from the class.

Suggested Answers

1 *It's too heavy.* / It's not light enough. 2 It's too small. / *It isn't big enough.* 3 It's small enough. / It isn't too big. (It's a good choice.) 4 It's too big. / It isn't small enough. 5 It's light enough. / It isn't too heavy. (It's a good choice.) 6 It's too wet. / It isn't dry enough. 7 It's too dirty. / It isn't clean enough. 8 It's small/dry enough. / It isn't too big/wet. (It's a good choice.)

Cool Down

Ask students to imagine making a mobile with objects or items they can find in the classroom, in nature, or in their home. Write each place on the board as the center of a different spidergram. Invite students to come to the board and write the name of an object around each place.

Ask students if they think any of the items are not suitable, and encourage them to explain, using *too* or *enough*.

Practice **Resource Bank:** Grammar Printout
Student's App: Grammar Practice

Lesson 5 Walkthrough: Take the Stage / Talk About It

The first productive skills lesson is dedicated to speaking and functional language. *Take the Stage* lessons present and practice a presentation. Talk About It lessons present and practice a conversation. The productive task is modeled by a child or children in a video, which shows the students what they are going to do themselves and helps to bring the language alive. Ideally the video should be watched in class. However, if this isn't possible, use the Flipped Classroom Approach (see **TB p. 15**).

Building students' confidence in speaking is a key part of the language-learning classroom and the activities are carefully staged to help them analyze the language, brainstorm their own ideas, and plan what they will say. Performing successfully, in a conversation or a presentation, helps ensure learners are receptive to future learning.

Activity A Video Showcase

The video models the spoken practice students will do later on in the lesson. There is a gist question on the page and additional comprehension questions can be found in the digital **ETB**. The digital **ETB** also provides a Video Focus idea in every speaking lesson.

There is a *Watch* callout question which encourages students to notice something about the model presentation/conversation in the video (e.g. body language). This feature is often picked up in the *Reflect* callout. Notes for the *Watch* callout are provided in the **ETB**.

Activity B Functional Language

Functional language is highlighted for students to notice. Students can try to do the activity in the book from memory first and then check their answers when you replay the video. Giving students a critical thinking task, such as analyzing and categorizing the key phrases, will help them to prepare for structuring their presentation or conversation later in the lesson.

International English

This feature exposes students to differences in vocabulary, language, and spelling between American (US) English and British (UK) English. Establish with the students that the flag with the stars and stripes is for the USA and the one with the crosses is for the UK, and that English is spoken in both countries. Remind them that while this is true, some words are different and some words are pronounced the same, but spelled differently. Equally, some words are spelled the same and pronounced differently! Tell students that they will see American English words used in this course, but that British English is also correct. It is important that while they are aware of the differences, you and they choose one variety to use, especially in exams.

Pronunciation

Pronunciation activities in the **Language Book** are about communicating clearly and intelligibly. Students will practice saying sounds and words accurately, by copying you, their teacher, and by listening to and repeating the audio. The sounds featured here have been chosen because they are difficult for many non-native speakers and may require additional practice. Students are then encouraged to identify other words with the same sounds and practice saying them.

Activity C Planning

The planning stage of the lesson allows students to brainstorm lots of ideas before having to speak. Activity C helps them prepare their ideas before organizing them in D. You could use a cooperative learning routine to encourage students to generate ideas (see **TB p. 20**).

Activity D Preparation

Students use their ideas from C to prepare a presentation/ conversation, guided by the template provided in the book. Students will prepare presentations individually and conversations in pairs. Often students are asked to choose one or two ideas to take forward from C. Encouraging students to make choices is an important part of this course, because it promotes engagement and critical thinking.

At this level, students are encouraged to write notes to prepare for a presentation, rather than writing the presentation out in full.

Activity E Practice & Production

This is the productive activity when all students get the chance to speak. For the Presentation lessons, choose a few students each lesson to perform to the class—keep a record so each student gets a chance to perform over the course of the year. If students don't perform to the whole class, have them perform to each other in small groups. Encourage students to show appreciation for each other's efforts, e.g. by clapping or saying *Good job!*

For the conversation lessons, it is enough that they have the conversation with a friend; they don't need to perform it.

The activity ends with a *Reflect* callout feature for students to think about how they did and circle. Encourage them to be honest here and tell them that it is easy to forget to do things when we are nervous, but that speaking gets easier with practice! Notes for the *Reflect* callout are provided in the digital **ETB**.

Talk About It

Lesson Objectives

- to prepare and practice a conversation giving opinions about art
- to recognize and reproduce words with silent *gh*

Materials
Video; Audio Track 14

Warm Up

Have students look back at the pictures in their **Language Book** and choose one that they like. Have them share it with a partner and say why they like it.

A TB p. 238 **Watch and listen. Which picture did Stephen paint?**

- Tell students they are going to watch a video of two friends talking about paintings in a home. Ask *Do you think they will have the same opinions?*
- Introduce the comprehension question *Which picture did Stephen paint?* Play the video and check the answer. Ask additional questions; for example, *Whose home are they in?* (Stephen's) Play the video again and have students notice Stephen's body language when he agrees or disagrees.

Answer
the fourth painting (the landscape)

B **Watch again. Check (✔) the sentences or questions you hear.**

- Have students read the question and sentences.
- Play the video again and have students check the sentences they hear. Read the phrases aloud and have students raise their hands for the ones they checked.
- Read the responses again and ask students to think about the opinion they give: positive, negative, or neutral. Tell them to notice your tone of voice and body language as you say them. Have them say *positive* and raise their hands, *negative* and lower their arms, or *neutral* and put their hands out in front of them. (Positive: 5, 8; Neutral: 7; Negative: 2, 3, 4, 6)

Answers
1; 2; 3; 4; 5; 7

International English

Point to the flags and elicit which phrase is American English and which phrase is British English. Point out that *quite* in American English usually means *a lot*. In British English, depending on intonation, it can mean *a lot* or *kind of*. Ask *Which phrase do we use?*

Pronunciation Silent *gh* 1

TRACK 14 TB p. 214 **Listen and say.**

- Hold up your right hand and ask *Left hand or right hand?* Elicit *right*. Write it on the board and say *right*. Have students repeat the word. Ask if they can hear the *g* and *h* in the middle of the word (no—they are silent letters in this word).
- Play the audio and have students repeat the words. Repeat if necessary.
- Say *These words are used in the video. What other words do you know with these sounds?* Have students discuss in pairs to try to remember any other words they know that also have a silent *gh*. Write these on the board and drill all the words at the end.

Suggested Answers
eight, night, neighbor, through, high

C **Plan. Choose two pictures in this book. Then complete.**

- Tell students they are going to plan their own conversation about pictures.
- Draw or project the table onto the board. Show students a picture you chose from the **Language Book** and ask them to help you by suggesting reasons why you might like it. Complete the table with these opinions.
- Now have students choose two pictures they either like or dislike from the **Language Book** and have them work individually to complete the table with information about the two pictures they have chosen.

D **Prepare notes for your conversation. Use your ideas from C and phrases from B.**

- Play the video again as a model.
- Then do an example conversation with the class, using your plan. Build up the conversation by making notes of students' suggestions on the board. Ask questions to help, e.g. *Do you like the picture? Why? Do you agree or disagree?*
- Have students work in pairs to prepare their conversation. They can choose two or three pictures from their plans to talk about.

E **Practice with a friend.**

- Have students practice their conversation with their partner as many times as they need to. Remind them to take turns, listen when their partner is speaking, and nod their head to agree or shake their head to disagree. Encourage them to show their partner the pictures in their books as they talk about them. Monitor and provide praise and help as needed.

Cool Down

Ask pairs if they agreed on a picture that they both liked. Make a list of these pictures on the board and have a vote for the class's favorite picture.

Practice **Student's App:** Speaking Skills Practice; Speaking Video

Lesson 6 Walkthrough: Write About It

The second productive skills lesson focuses on the mechanics of writing, e.g. punctuation, word-building, and sentence-building. There is always a model text, as well as a brainstorm/planning stage, for the final production task. The structure of the lesson is similar to Lesson 5.

Activity A Contextualized Writing Mechanics

Activity A presents the lesson's writing focus through a model text. It is important to ask students comprehension questions to ensure they have understood the text, since they will be expected to produce their own writing based on this model by the end of the lesson. Some additional comprehension questions are provided in the digital **ETB**. The teaching notes take an inductive approach, by encouraging students to look at the model and notice the mechanic.

Activity B Controlled Practice

Activity B builds on A by having students practice using the target writing mechanic. Encourage them to use the model in A as a guide.

Activity C Planning

Activity C teaches students to brainstorm and plan before writing by providing a graphic organizer to help students collate their ideas. Stronger students can be given the Challenge printout from the Resource Bank which has another column/section to complete.

Activity D Production: Writing Task

Activity D is the productive writing task. Encourage students to do a draft version, then either peer or self-correct, before writing their final version, since research shows that feedback is more useful between drafts and it gets students into the habit of self-correcting. As well as the Challenge printout mentioned for C, there are two other writing printouts, which can be downloaded and printed from the Resource Bank: the standard template can be used by most students for their final written piece. Less-confident students can have the Support printout which gives them more scaffolding to complete the same task as the rest of the class. Stronger students should be encouraged to expand on the model given in A by recycling language from previous lessons and giving more examples where relevant.

As with the Speaking lesson, there is a *Reflect* callout, which relates to the mechanic explored in A and B. Focus on this callout before students write their final draft and give students time to self-correct their work where necessary. Notes are provided in the digital **ETB**.

Cool Down

Cool Down activities give closure to the lesson. They are designed to get students thinking about what they learned and might include a game to review new language and concepts, or provide an opportunity to share classwork completed during the lesson.

Write About It

Lesson Objectives

- to learn how to identify and use different parts of speech
- to plan and write two cinquain poems

Materials

(Optional) a simple poem to recite to the class (WU); colored pens/pencils; (optional) Challenge, Standard, and Support writing printouts from the Resource Bank, one per student (Activities C and D)

Warm Up

Ask students if they know any poems by heart either in their own language or in English. Invite volunteers to recite a poem they know (in any language). Alternatively, recite a simple poem and ask students what they liked or disliked about it.

A Read the poems. Circle the nouns, adjectives, and verbs.

- Have students look quickly at the poems and say how we can see they are poems even before we read (short lines, no punctuation at the ends of the lines, each new line starts with a capital letter). You can point out that not all poems are like this, but many are. Ask students *Which poem is about the countryside? Which poem is about the city?*
- Check students know what a noun is: something that is an object, a person, a thing, or a place—something we can use as a subject. Have students find and circle all the nouns with a blue pen/pencil. Check answers, then repeat this for the adjectives and verbs. Check the meaning of each first: adjectives describe nouns, and verbs describe actions or events. Have students circle each group using a different color: adjectives in red and verbs in green (or other colors they may have). Ask students what words are not circled in each poem (*in the* and *with*). Point out how easy it is to make a poem just by joining nouns, adjectives, and verbs together.
- Finally, have students read the poems again and decide which one they prefer. Take a vote with a show of hands for the class favorite.

Answers

	Flowers	Rain
Nouns:	colors, field, poppies	people, umbrellas
Adjectives:	big, red	quiet, soft, wet
Verbs:	blowing, smiling, dancing,	falling, dripping, splashing, walking

Practice **Student's App:** Writing Practice

B Follow the instructions. Complete the poem.

- Read each line of the instructions and ask students to give the corresponding lines from the poems in A.
- Highlight the title "The Beach" and have students close their eyes and imagine being on a beach. Say *What words does it make you think of?*
- Elicit possible adjectives to complete line 2 of the poem in B. Then have students complete their poems individually. Remind them to refer to the instructions. Encourage them to be creative and write something different from their friends!
- Have students compare their finished versions with a friend. Check if they followed the instructions correctly. Ask if any students would like to read their poem to the class.

C Plan. Think about writing poems. Choose two titles and complete.

- Tell students they now have a chance to write two of their own cinquain poems. Point out that two possible titles have been provided, "School" and "Art" but that they can also think of their own title for the third column. Brainstorm some ideas and write their suggestions on the board.
- Tell students to plan one poem on either school or art and one poem on a topic of their choice. Have them follow the instructions in B to complete the table for their two poems. Encourage them to think about the topics they're writing about and to be as creative as possible. Challenge printouts can be handed out at this point.

D Write your two poems.

- Have students use their plan in C to write a rough draft of each poem in their notebook.
- Have students self-correct or exchange their work with a friend and peer-correct. You can put a checklist of points for students to look out for on the board (e.g. spelling; commas; capital letters; correct use of nouns, adjectives, and verbs).
- Have students correct any mistakes and write their final poems neatly on paper or on the Support and Standard printouts from the Resource Bank. Allow them time to illustrate their poems.

Cool Down

Have students read their poems to the class, without saying the title. Then ask the other students to guess what the title is.

Lesson 7 Walkthrough: Think It Over

The final lesson in the **Language Book** encourages students to reflect on what they have learned and what they want to explore further. Students are not expected to articulate all their ideas in English. It is important that the students reflect for themselves rather than being told what they studied, as this gives them another opportunity to develop as independent thinkers while also beginning to take responsibility for their learning and learning styles. This lays the groundwork for Assessment for Learning and Learning to Learn approaches. At this level, their responses will help you to adapt future lessons to suit your learners' needs and to make targeted suggestions for further practice.

What did I do?

This question focuses students on the activities they completed during the unit, both in and outside of the **Language Book**. Help them to recognize that they are able to do a lot of different things, and bring in props to trigger memories.

Encourage students to make a personal and creative response to the question by choosing activities independently to draw or write about. This allows you to see what students found interesting and challenging, and what they feel they've achieved. Ask students to think about why they enjoyed certain activities and didn't enjoy others. Ask them how they felt when they were doing something they found difficult and how they felt when they had finished the task.

What did I learn?

The purpose of this question is to find out what students think they have learned, rather than what *you* think they have learned. Explain that ideas can be content-related, as well as to do with language. In early units, brainstorm ideas on the board for students to choose from or to help them think of others. In later units, have students discuss their ideas in pairs, but be careful not to pair quieter students with dominant ones, as it is important for each student to have the opportunity to make a personal response. The digital **ETB** provides differentiation activities to support this question.

How did I learn? / What was my favorite part?

These two questions alternate across the units. Their purpose is to help students to begin to identify personalized learning strategies.

For *How did I learn?* encourage students to think about what helped them to remember something, e.g. repeating something a lot of times in a drill or through a cooperative learning routine, using the **Student's App** on **Navio** at home, or creating a mental picture of the vocabulary.

What was my favorite part? gets students to personalize their learning. Encourage them to notice that our favorite part is often the way we learn best. Have students think about how they can make the learning more enjoyable for themselves. This helps them to start taking responsibility for their personal learning journey.

How well did I do?

This question asks students to evaluate their own progress. However, answers will only be valuable if students feel they can be honest. You may find it helpful to explain what it means to analyze ourselves and to provide some concrete examples to help them understand, e.g. *If you can remember 20 words, color in the paint pot with five brushes. If you can remember one or two, color in the paint pot with one brush.* Let them know that it's OK to color in the first paint pot; it just means they need to do more practice. You can suggest targeted practice to suit different students' needs, such as the grammar printouts from the Resource Bank or the **Student's App** on **Navio**.

What can I do next?

Encourage students to think of all the different ways they can continue their English learning journey outside of the classroom, including use of new media, e.g. apps, video games, vlogs. Brainstorm ideas as a class. In Units 1 and 2, you can use the suggested words as prompts. Encourage students to be creative with their ideas and to make suggestions based on the things they identified as enjoyable. Follow up in the next lesson by asking questions, e.g. *What did your mom say when you sang the song? Tell me about the English movie you watched.*

Looking Forward

This features a teaser question about the next unit, which also shows how people are linked in different ways through different activities and roles in their lives. Brainstorm possible answers and review these predictions in the first lesson of the next unit to see who was correct.

Further Review & Recycling

Regular recycling of new language helps increase exposure and build confidence and understanding.

Put It Together communicative games come after every two units, providing an opportunity to review and recycle the language learned in the previous lessons. These fun activities are designed to encourage students to use the language in context and to want to play again and again.

Plays review and recycle language from Units 1–5 and Units 6–10 in amusing contexts, which could be used as mid-year or end-of-year performance pieces.

Think It Over

Lesson Objectives

- to review what has been learned in the unit
- to reflect on the unit and their own progress
- to think about learning strategies and how to continue learning at home

Warm Up

Spell out words from either pp. 10–11 or p. 14. Spell them quite quickly. As soon as students recognize what the word is, they raise their hands. When the majority of students have their hands raised, ask what the word is and then ask if it is a *type* of art or a word used to *describe* art. Suggested words: *sculpture* (type), *detailed* (describe), *bright* (describe), *portrait* (type), *collage* (type), *sketch* (type)

Read the questions and draw or write your answers.

- Give students time to think about and discuss activities in the unit before they complete each question. Explain that they can choose to either write a few words or sentences or to draw a picture. Allowing students to make a personal response will help them retain knowledge and engage with the learning points.

What did I do?

- Give students a few minutes to look back through the unit at the different activities they did. Ask questions about the unit or write questions on the board for students to discuss in pairs or small groups; for example, *What did you sing about? What stories did you read? Where did you hear about paper art?*
- Encourage students to identify something in the unit that they found challenging or something that was particularly memorable for them. Students can draw or write about their chosen activity.

What did I learn?

- Have students talk to a partner about what they remember from the unit—stories, words, phrases, people, types of art.
- Ask questions about the unit to help students think about what they learned; for example, *What did you learn about having a conversation in English? Can you make new questions or answers? What did you learn about art in different countries? What did you learn about writing in English? What else did you learn?* Elicit ideas from the class and discuss them together.
- Encourage students to draw a picture or write sentences about their learning outcomes.
- Have students talk to a friend about what they think they have learned.

How did I learn?

- Ask students how they learned the artwork words in Lesson 1. Elicit ideas (by seeing the words next to the pictures, by doing the visualization activity, by hearing the words in the story, by doing a writing or speaking activity).
- Then ask students about Lesson 3. Encourage students to think about the pronunciation and spelling of the words they learned in this lesson. Ask *What helps you remember how to say/spell these words?*
- Have students draw or write about the activities that helped them learn. Then have them compare their answers in pairs and think about what was similar and what was different in how they learned. *Ask do we all learn in the same way?*

How well did I do?

- Ask students to color in the number of paint pots that represents how well they think they learned the content (i.e. the more pots they color, the more they feel they have learned). Ask *What do you understand? What do you need to practice more?* Encourage students to look back through the unit to see how much they remember, what they did well, and what they found difficult.

What can I do next?

- Brainstorm ideas with the class about what they can do to continue to learn (e.g. watch the videos again, sing the song again, talk about pictures they like or don't like, write another poem). Encourage them to suggest their own ideas for different activities they can do.
- Draw students' attention to the options in the box. Encourage students to think about what they can do at home to improve their English using the verbs in the box as prompts, for instance, read the stories or poems again, practice using the new words to describe things at home or pictures on websites, listen to English on TV, and act out the dialogues with friends.
- Ask students to choose one or more activities from the list (read, practice, listen, act out) that they will do to practice their English.
- Once students have completed the page in their books, have them discuss with a friend what they drew or wrote. Did they choose the same activities or different ones?
- Ask students if there is one activity from the unit that they would like to repeat now.

Looking Forward

- Draw students' attention to the character at the bottom of the page. Ask *Who's this?* and elicit what they remember about her. (Poppy discussed pictures with Larry in Explore Language 2.) Ask *Which after-school club do you think she goes to?* Encourage students to make predictions about Poppy's after-school club and what Unit 2 will be about. Tell students they will find out in the first lesson of the next unit.

Practice **Resource Bank:** Unit Test
Student's App: Vocabulary and Grammar Review

Lesson 1 Walkthrough: Get Ready to Read

There are two sections to this lesson: Section 1 is always a Visible Thinking Routine (VTR) (see **TB p. 20**). Section 2 contains pre-reading activities and previews a reading skill which will be explored in more detail in later lessons. The teaching notes on this page are flexible, so you can tailor lessons to suit your learners. You can either choose to do the VTR and pre-reading activities in one lesson, or alternately spend longer developing the VTR discussion and start the next lesson with the pre-reading activities, then go straight into the reading. There is no Cool Down activity in the main teaching notes, but an extension activity provided in the **ETB** may be used as a Cool Down.

Warm Up

Warm Up activities are designed to generate interest in the topic and activate schema to help students make connections between their own experiences and the readings. Activities are purposely not vocabulary-focused to give the **Literacy Book** a distinct first language (L1) feel.

The **ETB** provides a quick Two-Minute Review activity for each Lesson 1, which provides a link between the previous unit and the existing unit. You can choose to do both the Two-Minute Review and the Warm Up or just one or the other, to suit the needs of your class.

Activities A, B, C Visible Thinking Routine: See, Think, Wonder / Think, Pair, Share / Step Inside / Question Starts

Activities A, B, and C relate to a Visible Thinking Routine (VTR). Each routine uses a striking image connected to the unit's topic to foster thoughtful and constructive classroom discussions.

For See, Think, Wonder, allow students to think silently for one minute at each step of the routine. Then take ideas from the class. After the first flurry of ideas, encourage students to keep looking and to see more things. Explore the difference between students seeing on their own and seeing things together (group discovery). You can allow some discussion in L1 here, but try to re-formulate the students' ideas into simple English. Avoid leading students to an answer by keeping supporting questions open, e.g. *What (else) do you see / think / wonder about the picture? What colors / shapes do you see? Why do you think that?*

For Think, Pair, Share, Step Inside, and Question Starts give students a minute to look at the picture and encourage them to think about what they can see. Have them share their ideas and write useful words on the board. This provides students with a bank of vocabulary to draw on during the discussion part of the routine. Make sure students have enough time to think about their own ideas before they discuss in pairs or groups, as this will lead to a richer discussion.

Model class discussions for each of the VTRs are provided in the teaching notes. When students are sharing their ideas, encourage other students to say if they agree or not, using language like: *Us too. / We agree. / We have a different idea. / Really? / Good question!* They should also feel able to guide the discussion by asking questions, such as *Why do you say that?* Make sure you write down students' questions and ideas on construction paper or post-it notes, so you can revisit them later on in the unit.

Transition

The **Transition** is a discussion question or questions designed to move you smoothly between the two sections of this lesson (VTR and pre-reading activities). This helps students make connections between the ideas they explored in the VTR and the reading. Alternately, you can use this question as a Warm Up, if you decide to start the pre-reading activities in the next lesson.

Activity D Activate Schema

Activity D poses a discussion question for students to apply the work they did in the VTR even more closely to the unit's topic. Have students discuss the question in pairs before sharing their ideas as a class. You can write up their ideas and suggestions in graphic organizers on the board, to develop critical thinking skills.

Activity E Skill Preview

Activity E previews the unit's reading skill. This will be addressed fully in the second Get Ready to Read lesson. You are not expected to actively teach the skill in Lesson 1. The goal is to introduce the concept gently and attune students to look for and/or use it as they read.

Get Ready to Read

Lesson Objectives

- to activate prior knowledge about art
- to encourage students to observe and interpret through a See, Think, Wonder Visible Thinking Routine (VTR)
- to preview the reading skill of identifying facts and opinions

Materials
(Optional) VTR printout from the Resource Bank (Activities A, B, C)

Warm Up

Ask students to raise their hands if they enjoy art. Elicit different types of art (e.g. painting or drawing pictures, taking pictures, making models or sculptures) and which ones they have tried. Ask *Do you prefer looking at pictures or paintings? Do you know the names of any famous artists?*

See, Think, Wonder

A Look at the picture. What do you see?

Students are going to do a See, Think, Wonder VTR to explore the image of a painting.

- Ask students *What do you see?* Give them a minute to look at the picture. Then elicit one or two examples using the phrase *I see …* before asking students to share in small groups or pairs. Then share ideas as a class. Make sure students limit their answers to what is visible, not how they interpret it.

Here's an example of this part of the routine.
Teacher: What do you see?
Student A: I see a boy and a light.
Teacher: Tell us more about the light. What can you see?
Student A: It's really big. The boy is touching the glass.
Student B: There are butterflies.
Teacher: Great. What else do you see?
Student B: He's in a forest. It's dark!

B What do you think?

- Say *I think the boy is very small. What do you think about the picture?* Elicit a response from a student. Then ask *What makes you say that?* and encourage the student to give a reason.
- Give students one to three minutes to think about the picture silently. Then have students work in small groups to share their ideas before sharing as a class. Encourage them to give reasons for their answers and provide language help when needed.

Here's an example of this part of the routine.
Teacher: What do you think?
Student A: I think this is a dream.
Teacher: What makes you say that?
Student A: (It looks like) the light is flying!
Teacher: What else do you think?
Student B: I think the light is hot.
Student C: I don't think so. His hand isn't burned.

C What do you wonder?

- Say *I wonder why the boy is so small.* Then ask students *What do you wonder? What questions do you have?* Give them one minute to think silently.
- Have students discuss their ideas in groups or as a class. Allow students to be creative and accept all their ideas.

Here's an example of this part of the routine.
Teacher: What do you wonder?
Student A: (I wonder) who the boy is.
Teacher: Good question. What do you think?
Student A: Maybe he's from the future!
Student B: He might be an alien!
Teacher: OK, what else do you wonder?
Student C: Does a giant own the light?

Transition

Ask students if they have ever painted a picture like this. Ask *Do you like it? Do you prefer simple paintings or ones with a lot of things happening?* Have them discuss in small groups.

D Think and discuss. When do you draw pictures and when do you take photos? Why?

- Have students think about the last time they drew a picture or took a photo. Ask them to think about where they were, and why they drew the picture / took the photo. Have students discuss in pairs.

E Read. Then underline the facts and circle the opinions.

This activity previews the reading skill of understanding facts and opinions.

- Tell students the picture shows Emil, who appears in the next story. Refer students to the text. Have them work in pairs to underline the facts and circle the opinions.
- To check answers, project the text onto the board. Invite students to underline a fact or circle an opinion.

Answers
Facts: I've run out of paint!; It's cheap and she has so many colors.
Opinion: Mrs. Blanche has the best paint.

Now read **True Colors**

Lesson 2 Walkthrough: Reading 1, Fiction

The reading lessons aim to support the development of literacy and to foster a love of reading, to encourage students to become lifelong readers.

There is one fictional and one nonfictional text in each unit. Fictional texts are laid out to emulate storybooks inspired by ESL/L1 materials and expose students to language in context, which may be slightly above level. This is because research shows that with the right support, reading slightly above level can significantly improve overall reading skills.

Nonfictional texts give students a chance to learn new concepts and vocabulary, as well as broaden their view of the world. They also often appeal to reluctant readers. Nonfictional texts are laid out to look like nonfiction books, websites, and articles to give a realistic and aspirational feel to the book.

Warm Up

This **Warm Up** allows you to review the ideas generated at the end of the previous lesson in preparation for the reading. Alternately, if you are carrying the lesson straight on from the previous page, use this activity to transition between the pre-reading and reading part of the lesson.

Reading Approach

First Reading: Engage with the Text

The purpose of the first reading stage is to engage students and help them become familiar with the text. This sets the scene for the comprehension and analysis work that will come next. Before they read, encourage students to identify things in the pictures that they find interesting, surprising, or unusual. Engagement is more important than vocabulary at this stage, so it's fine for students to point if they are unable to name what they see.

For this first exposure to the text read it out loud, play the video, or have students listen to the audio and follow along in their books. To help students feel comfortable and enjoy watching/listening to the story, have everyone seated in a circle at the front of the class. This is a great opportunity for students to see and hear how to read fluently and with expression, so if you are reading, use character voices and facial expressions where appropriate. Pause only to ask prediction questions, which can help to motivate students and encourage them to want to find out what happens next. Do not spend time analyzing the language at this point; full comprehension is not necessary for students to enjoy a text.

Words in Context, see **TB p. 56.**

Second Reading: Analyze the Text & Features

Ensure students get to explore the text in a variety of ways to keep them motivated and active participants in the learning process. If you read the text out loud in the first reading stage, have students read chorally in the second stage, or have them read silently with or without the audio.

The purpose of the second reading stage is to analyze the text and features using basic comprehension questions provided in the teaching notes and the callout questions from the colored boxes in the **Literacy Book**.

The teaching notes tell you the purpose of the questions, e.g. gist, detail, making connections, personalization, fact, language focus and give ideas about how to exploit them.

One reading in each unit includes a Text Focus point written in blue, often with arrows pointing to the area of the text being highlighted. The teaching notes provide support to help you address these Text Focus points as part of the second reading stage. There is usually an additional extension activity in the digital **ETB** to give students additional practice.

Third Reading: Interact with the Text

The third reading stage gives students the chance to interact with the text on a more personal level. Activities include discussion and role-play to encourage further exploration of character or plot, or text analysis, e.g, summarizing, writing captions, and diagram construction to compare and contrast information.

The video or Story Player is available on the **Student's App** on **Navio** for students to watch again at home.

International English

This feature exposes students to differences in vocabulary, language, and spelling between American (US) English and British (UK) English. Establish with the students that the flag with the stars and stripes is for the USA and the one with the crosses is for the UK, and that English is spoken in both countries. Remind them that while this is true, some words are different, and some words are pronounced the same, but spelled differently. Tell students that they will see American English words used in this course, but that British English is also correct. It is important that while they are aware of the differences, you and they choose one variety to use, especially in exams.

To make the most of this feature, set up a class ebook where students can add the international English words and phrases as they appear in the book. This could be a wiki or shared document that students can access and edit at home. They could also find an image to illustrate the word. At various points during the year, have a quiz to see how many British and American English words students remember.

Fiction: *True Colors*—Fantasy

Lesson Objectives

- to read a fantasy story about a boy who helps people
- to make a personal connection to the reading

Materials
Audio Tracks 5 and 6

Warm Up

Ask students to name as many things as they can that they use in an art lesson; set a target of ten items. Then ask students to scan the pictures and see if they can find the items they named.

TRACK 5 TB p. 227 Reading Approach

First Reading: Engage with the Text

- Have students look quickly at the title of the story and the pictures and say what they think it is about. Ask why they think the story is called *True Colors* (see Language Note in the **ETB**).
- Play the audio while students read. Ask students *Who do you think is the most important person in the story? Why?*
- When you come to the end of p. 11, stop and answer the prediction question in the green box: *What is Emil going to paint next?* Elicit suggestions. Ask students *What would you like to paint with True Colors?* Then continue the story and see if students' ideas were correct.
- Ask students *Do you think Emil uses the True Colors paint well? Would you do the same thing?*
- Read the whole text before looking at the Words in Context.

TRACK 6 TB p. 228 Words in Context

- Play the audio and have students repeat the words.
- Have students race to find the words in the reading.
- Tell students they can sometimes **think about whether a word is a noun, adjective or verb to figure out the meaning** (see TB p. 22). Have them discuss their ideas with a partner, using L1 if necessary.
- Then bring the class together and use these discussion points to confirm the meanings.

owner (p. 10) Ask students to look at the picture of the shop. Ask them *Whose is the shop?* (Mrs. Blanche's) *Does Mrs. Blanche have a boss?* (No, she is the owner so she works for herself.)

run out of (p. 10) Ask *What happened to Emil's paints?* (He used all of them, so he needs more.) Ask students what things they run out of in their daily life (e.g. battery on their phone).

choice (p. 10) Ask students if the word is a noun/thing or a verb/action (a noun). Ask *What verb is it related to?* (choose) Ask students to finish the definition: *Your choice is the thing that you …* (choose).

croissant (p. 11) Have students find and point to the croissant in the picture. Ask if they have ever tried a croissant and if they know which country croissants come from (France).

exclaims (p. 12) Ask *Is it a noun or a verb?* (a verb) *What does the verb do here?* (It tells us how Emil speaks.) *How does Emil feel when he exclaims "This is amazing!"?* (excited)

Second Reading: Analyze the Text and Features

- Have students read the story silently. To keep them focused, ask them to look for a phrase that they think says something about Emil's character. Elicit suggestions.
- Ask some questions to check comprehension; for example, *What does the True Colors paint do?* (It makes the paintings into real objects.) *What does Emil like doing with his new paint?* (helping people)
- Discuss the questions in the green boxes.
  - **Language Focus** (p. 13): *What does* He saves the day *mean?* Ask students if they can give an explanation of the phrase. If they are having difficulty, ask *Were things good or bad before he used his True Colors? How about after?*
  - **Personalization** (p. 15): *When you finish a piece of art, are you always happy with it?* Ask students the question and have them raise their arms to indicate *yes* and lower their arms to indicate *no*. Have students discuss in pairs why they are sometimes not happy with their piece of art and what they do.
- Discuss the text focus: *Why do you think the author chose to make this **fantasy** story happen in a real-life setting instead of a fictional one?* Give students some thinking time, then have them discuss their ideas in pairs.

International English

Point to the flags and elicit that *apartment* is American English and *flat* is British English. Ask *Which word do we use?* Point out that *apartment* is also sometimes used in British English.

Third Reading: Interact with the Text

- Play the audio again and have students repeat the direct speech in the story with appropriate intonation.
- Then have students take turns to read sections of the text in pairs.

Cool Down

Ask students what part of the story they liked best and why.

Lesson 3 Walkthrough: Explore the Reading

This lesson allows students to explore the previous text further with comprehension, analysis and discussion activities.

Activity A Reading Comprehension

Start this lesson with oral comprehension questions to remind students about the text. Have a Group Time discussion about the story (see **TB p. 21**). The teaching notes suggest *Wh-* questions you can ask to help students to remember the gist and details of the reading (*who, where, what, when, why*). Play the video to review the story if you don't want to read the text as a class again.

The lesson then moves on to a heads-down activity which allows you to check students' understanding of the reading. If there are areas that you find students don't understand, you can return to the text and address these before moving on to the analysis part of the lesson.

Activity B Analysis

Activity B is an age-appropriate analysis task, which asks students to think critically about what they have read and to consider the causes, problems, solutions, or consequences. They will need to look back at the reading to answer questions. Help students find a strategy for doing this by encouraging them to look at the pictures and scan the text for key words, rather than re-reading the whole text again.

Activity C/D Post-reading Discussion, Writing & SEL

One activity in each fiction Explore the Reading lesson has a SEL competency focus. Productive think and write or discuss questions are designed to help students make connections between the text and their own knowledge and understanding of the world through a SEL competency. There are often opportunities here for critical literacy, as students can be encouraged to consider the point of view of different characters.

Explore the Reading

Lesson Objectives

- to understand and analyze *True Colors* through reading comprehension activities
- to explore the SEL competency of developing relationship skills by providing help to those who need it
- to make a personal connection to the reading

Warm Up

Read the first part of some phrases from the story (pp. 10–15) and have students find and call out the second half of the sentence or phrase; for example, *Have you run out of ...* (paint again?) *You should be careful ...* (with it.) *He decides to start ...* (a new painting.) *Will it come ...* (to life, too?) *I told you to take ...* (the key).

A Read and write *True* or *False*.

- Help students remember the story by asking some questions using the five *Ws* (*where, who, why, what, when*) and *how*: *Where does Emil find the True Colors paint?* (in the art supply store) *Who is the owner of the store?* (Mrs. Blanche) *Why is True Colors special?* (It makes paintings become real.) *How does Emil use the special paint?* (He helps people.) *What makes Emil happy at the end of the story?* (His neighbors like his paintings.)
- Refer students to the first sentence and example answer. Ask them to find something in the text that shows that the answer is false. (Mrs. Blanche uses his name, and Emil says, "You know me too well!")
- Have students complete the activity, compare their answers with a friend, and say why they chose *True* or *False*.
- Nominate individual students to read a sentence and say *True* or *False*. Ask if everyone agrees.

Answers
1 *False* 2 False 3 True 4 False 5 True 6 True

B Read and match the sentences to the characters.

- Refer students to the characters and quickly review who each one is. Tell them that the sentences are all things the characters might say and that they should match the sentences to the characters based on what they know from the story.
- Have students complete the activity. Then project it onto the board and have students come and draw lines to match, or ask students to raise their hands to give a number and letter.

Answers
1 *b* 2 d 3 e 4 a 5 f 6 c

Practice Student's App: Reading Practice

C Think, draw, and write. How would you use True Colors to help other people? Why?

This activity explores the SEL competency of developing relationship skills by providing help to those who need it.

- Give your own example by drawing a quick picture on the board and asking students to guess how to complete the sentence; for example, draw a table with a big bowl of pasta and a salad and your friend looking pleased. Elicit the sentence *I would paint a nice dinner for my friend, because she's always tired at the end of the day* (or similar).
- Give students some thinking time to decide what they would paint to help other people. Have them draw it in the box, then complete the sentence.
- Have students compare their ideas in pairs or small groups. Ask if any students would like to share their idea with the class.
- Draw on the SEL competency of providing help to those who need it. Ask students *Who does Emil help in the story? Is this usually a good way to make friends? Can you think of a time you helped someone? What happened? How did you feel? How else can you help other people? Why is it good to help other people?* Do a Think, Pair, Share routine to discuss the questions (see TB p. 20).

Cool Down

Ask students to leave their books open showing their drawing from C and invite students to walk around the class and look at other students' ideas. Ask them to look for an original or interesting idea, a good picture, or the best way to help someone. After a few minutes, ask students if they found any of these things and which one they liked best.

Lesson 4 Walkthrough: Get Ready to Read

This lesson provides pre-reading activities, including a reading skill focus, to prepare students for the second text.

Activity A Reading Skill Focus

The reading skill that was previewed in Lesson 1 is explored and practiced here. The activity takes an inductive approach to learning, with students being encouraged to practice the reading skill and notice how it can help them understand the reading before the skill is named in the skills box.

Activity B Reading Skill Practice

Students practice the reading skill from Activity A before they apply it to the forthcoming reading. When they have finished, discuss what students think and encourage them to say why they think it.

Activity C Pre-reading Discussion

The discussion question relating to the reading on the next pages personalizes the learning and encourages students become active participants. They either connect the reading to their own lives or think and express opinions. You can vary the activity by using a Think, Pair, Share VTR or a Cooperative Learning Routine such as a Rally Robin (see **TB p. 20**).

Cool Down

As in the **Language Book**, Cool Down activities give closure to the lesson. They are designed to get students thinking about what they learned and might include a game to review reading skills or an activity to encourage students to make a personal response to what they have read.

Get Ready to Read

Lesson Objectives

- to review the reading skill of identifying facts and opinions
- to activate prior knowledge about how art can help people

Materials

Different genres of music (Activity C)

Warm Up

Pay some compliments to a few students in the class; for example, *I think you're a kind person. Your writing is really neat. Your backpack is a cool color!* Then encourage students to turn to the person or people next to them and pay them a compliment about their clothes, hair, eyes, books, backpack, achievements in class, abilities, or personality (where appropriate).

Ask students *Do you feel good now? It's a great way to start the day and make friends!*

A Read and write *Fact* or *Opinion*.

Students are going to practice the reading skill of identifying facts and opinions.

- Say *You're my English class, and you're a great class!* Ask students which is a fact and which is an opinion. Ask them if they used facts or opinions to say nice things to their friends in the Warm Up.
- Give students some time to read the sentences and decide if they are facts or opinions.
- To check answers, read the sentences and have students raise their arms and say *Fact!* or lower their arms and say *Opinion!*
- Have students read the skills box about facts and opinions. Ask *Why do you think it's important to recognize the difference between a fact and an opinion?* Have students discuss their ideas in small groups. Elicit some ideas. Guide students to begin thinking about all the different information they might read on websites, blogs, and so on. Are these always completely fact-based? Learning to question things when they read them and being able to distinguish between facts and opinions is an important life skill, as it will help students to make good decisions.

Answers

1 Fact 2 Fact 3 Opinion 4 Fact 5 Opinion

B Look at *True Colors* again. Find three facts and three opinions about Emil and his art.

- Give students some time to look back at the story and find either a fact or an opinion about Emil and his art. Ask for one suggestion for a fact and one for an opinion and ask if the others agree.
- Now have students complete the activity and compare their answers with a friend.
- Invite students to read something they put in either the Facts or Opinions section without saying which it is. Have the others call out Fact or Opinion and check that everyone agrees.

Suggested Answers

Facts
1 Emil runs out of paint.
2 Emil paints a still life.
3 Emil helps the old man.

Opinions
1 Emil's work is beautiful.
2 Helping people is fun.
3 The new paint is amazing.

C Think and discuss. How can art help people?

- Ask students to think of a way that art can help the person who makes it and also how it can help the people who experience it. Guide students to think about different kinds of art (music, drawing, painting, sculpting, modeling, writing, photography, etc) and to consider what kinds of art they enjoy doing and how it makes them feel (both while they are doing it and at the end). Encourage them to think about how doing art helps them to express ideas or emotions. Then have students think about how they feel when they listen to a great piece of music, or look at a beautiful painting. Does it inspire them or make them feel happy/excited? Does it challenge them or make them want to find out more about what the artist was thinking about?
- Bring some different genres of music into class and have students listen and draw, write, or color how it makes them feel. Have students talk about what they wrote or drew with a friend. Encourage students to see how art can develop ideas and imaginative thinking.
- Finally, ask students if they think art helps the people who make it or the people who experience it more. Give students some time to think and then discuss their ideas in small groups.

Cool Down

Read some sentences about your school and have students stand up if it is a fact or sit down if they think it is an opinion; for example, *This school is a great place to learn.* (Opinion) *There are [number] classrooms in this school.* (Fact) *I love coming to school.* (Opinion) *This school is bigger than my last school.* (Fact) *The teachers are really nice here.* (Opinion)

Now read **My Guide to Photography**

Lesson 5 Walkthrough: Reading 2, Nonfiction

The structure of the reading lessons, whether fiction or nonfiction, allows students to be exposed to the text multiple times. This helps them to connect oral and written forms, which is important for the development of reading skills. There is a focus on reading for analysis and pleasure, rather than simple mechanics. Students will gain independence with each reading as you progress through the course.

One reading lesson in each unit is supported by a video. Digital storytelling is helpful because it transcends language and culture by engaging students in a way that is both visual and auditory, as well as textual. Learners can make connections to previous experiences more easily, think critically about new information, and use their own knowledge to fill in any gaps in understanding.

Videos can be used as part of the overall reading strategy: as a way of engaging students with the text; as part of the process of analysis; and as a tool to help them interact with the text on a more personal level. The digital **ETB** provides extension activities for each video lesson. If you aren't able to play the video in class, have students watch it at home prior to the lesson. See The Flipped Classroom Approach, **TB p. 15**.

Warm Up

See **TB p. 48**.

Reading Approach

The three-step reading approach is the same for fictional and nonfictional texts (see **TB p. 50**). The teaching notes give many different ideas to use within these steps throughout the course.

The digital **ETB** provides extension activities for checking comprehension further, using the video, and highlighting and exploiting each reading genre.

Words in Context

Each reading lesson has a **Words in Context** box which pulls out certain key words from the text for students to explore in greater detail. It is recommended you look at these Words in Context after the students have read the text at least once through. This is so that the first reading can be about enjoyment and engagement, rather than vocabulary learning. Don't pre-teach these words; it is more valuable to offer students strategies to help them decode the meaning for themselves. Different strategies are suggested in the notes, with more on **TB p. 22**.

Introduce a different strategy in each lesson and encourage pairs to use a combination of strategies to help them decode the words. It is fine for students to use L1 for this, to enable them to express their thoughts and ideas clearly. Ask students which strategies they used to help them understand the new words.

Then ask questions (provided in the notes) to check understanding and clarify meaning. Effectively you are providing students with tools which will help them to figure out the meaning of other unfamiliar words they encounter in the future.

It should be noted that these words have been highlighted to help students' comprehension of the texts; they are not part of the course's key language and will not appear in any assessment material.

Nonfiction: *My Guide to Photography*—Instructional Text

Lesson Objectives

- to read an instructional text about photography
- to learn about photography through CLIL (arts and humanities): exploring how to compose and take a good photo
- to make a personal connection to the reading

Materials

Audio Tracks 7 and 8; Video; a selection of interesting photos (e.g. landscapes, portraits, wildlife, buildings, sports, etc).

Warm Up

Display a selection of interesting photos. Give students time to circulate and look at them and then have them discuss in pairs how each of the photos makes them feel.

TRACK 7 TB p. 228 Reading Approach

First Reading: Engage with the Text

- Have students look at the photos in the reading and say if they have taken similar ones. Are their photos as good as the ones on the pages?
- Play the video to help students understand the reading. Alternately, play the audio and have students listen and read.
- After each tip, stop the video and ask students to say if they think the tip is easy or difficult to do.
- Then look at the Words in Context.

TRACK 8 TB p. 228 Words in Context

- Play the audio and have students repeat the words.
- Have students race to find the words in the text.
- Tell students they can sometimes **use the sentence or paragraph before to guess the meaning of the new words** (see TB p. 22). Have them discuss their ideas with a partner, using L1 if necessary.
- Then bring the class together and use these discussion points to confirm the meanings.

frame (p. 18) Ask students to find another way of saying "the frame" in the same paragraph (*the shape of the photograph*).

elements (p. 18) Ask if they can think of another word to use in place of *elements* here (*things* or *parts*).

zoom in (p. 19) Ask *If you zoom in on something in your photo, do you make it look bigger or smaller?* (bigger) *What word gives us a clue?* (close)

horizontal/vertical (p. 19) Have students look at the pictures. Ask them which one is longer from side to side (horizontal) and which is longer from top to bottom (vertical). Ask *Which is better for taking a picture of a giraffe?* (vertical)

Second Reading: Analyze the Text and Features

- Play the audio and have students follow along in their books. Ask some questions to check comprehension; for example, *Does Huan Chen like to have many things or few things in her photos?* (few)
- Then discuss the questions in the green boxes.
  - **Personalization** (p. 18): *What kind of photos do you usually take?* Ask students to raise their hands if they often take photos of people, places, nature, sports, or something else and why.
  - **Personalization** (p. 19): *Do you prefer the horizontal or the vertical photo?* Ask students the question and have them raise their hands for vertical and stretch their hands out to the sides for horizontal. Take a vote and then elicit reasons.
  - **CLIL Focus** (p. 20): *Do you have a photo that follows the Rule of Thirds?* Ask for a volunteer to explain the rule of thirds. For homework, have students look for or take a photo that they can display in the next lesson to show this rule.
  - **Personalization** (p. 22): *Do you find tips useful, or do you prefer to do things your own way?* Ask students the question and have them discuss it in pairs. Then tell them to raise their arms to indicate that they find tips useful and lower their arms to indicate they prefer to do things their own way. Encourage them to give examples to back up their opinions.

Third Reading: Interact with the Text

- Play the audio again and have students pretend they are holding a camera and following each of Huan's tips in real time.

Cool Down

Ask students to look around the classroom and decide what they would like to take a photo of. Ask them to decide which tips can help them make their photo as good as possible. Have students discuss in pairs.

Next Lesson: Ask students to bring in their favorite photo and a photo that shows the rule of thirds for the next lesson.

Practice **Student's App:** Nonfiction Video

Lesson 6 Walkthrough: Explore the Reading

This lesson follows the same structure as the first *Explore the Reading* lesson with comprehension, analysis, and discussion activities to explore the second reading text. It also provides further practice of the reading skill.

Activity A Reading Comprehension

Before doing **Activity A**, have a team quiz, or group/pair discussion with books closed to check students' comprehension of the text. This can be a nice routine to have at the beginning of each *Explore the Reading* lesson.

Activity B Text Analysis & Practice

This text analysis activity usually involves practicing the unit reading skill. Have students answer the questions individually first. Then they can look back on the reading in pairs to check their answers.

Activity C/D Discussion, Writing & CLIL Focus

Productive think and write or discuss questions enable students to learn about a subject area through the reading and to see language used in a real-world context.

One activity in each nonfiction Explore the Reading lesson has a CLIL focus. There are often extension ideas in the **ETB** to explore this further.

Spelling Patterns

A spelling pattern box is always attached to one of the *Explore the Reading* lessons in each unit. This highlights a high-frequency letter combination with examples taken from the previous reading. The spelling activity is supported by audio, but the focus of the activity should be on reading (there is targeted pronunciation work in the **Language Book**). Students listen to a set of words with a letter pattern, notice where those letters appear, and complete the words to reinforce understanding. What matters most at this stage is that students are actively thinking about how written words are constructed.

The second part of the audio spells out each word, allowing students to check and correct their spelling. Students should be encouraged to read the words aloud to establish a connection between the sound of the word and the way it is written.

Finally, students find other words within the reading with the same spelling patterns. Making connections with other words, reinforces pattern recognition and helps students learn to decode more effectively when reading. See Spelling Patterns, **TB p. 13**.

Explore the Reading

Lesson Objectives

- to understand and analyze *My Guide to Photography* through reading comprehension activities
- to practice the reading skill of identifying facts and opinions
- to learn about photography through CLIL (arts and humanities): exploring what makes a good photo
- to make a personal connection to the reading
- to identify and reproduce words with *–ent*

Materials

Video; Audio Tracks 7 and 9; a selection of three or four different photos to show students (e.g. a mountain landscape, a close-up of an insect, a portrait of someone's face, or a blurry picture of a fast-moving car) (Activity C)

TRACK 7 TB p. 228 Warm Up

Ask students if they can remember the tips from the previous lesson about taking good photos (don't worry if they don't remember the exact wording). Write them on the board and ask if they can remember the order they came in in the text. Then play the video or audio to see if they remembered the tips and their order correctly. If students brought in photos displaying the rule of thirds, display them on the wall and give students a minute to circulate and look at each other's work.

A Read and choose the answer.

- Before students open their books, find out what they remember from the reading. Ask *How many tips did Huan give?* (five) *What does she call the shape of the photo?* (the frame) *What different formats can you use for your photos?* (vertical or horizontal) *Why should we follow the rule of thirds?* (to make photos more interesting) *Where can you put the focus of the photo?* (in the foreground or the background)
- Refer students to the example question and answer, and ask them to find something in the text to justify the answer. (p. 18, I like to fill the frame with only one thing.)
- Have students complete the activity and try to find something in the text to justify each answer. Check answers as a class.

Answers

1 a 2 c 3 b 4 a 5 b

B Read and write *Fact* or *Opinion*.

- Remind students of the difference between facts and opinions with the sentences *You're my English class* (fact) and *You're a fantastic class!* (opinion).
- Give students time to complete the activity. To check answers, read the sentences and have students raise their arms for a fact and lower their arms for an opinion.
- Discuss the sentences in more detail to further explore the CLIL focus of the value of photos as art (not just mementos).

Answers

1 Opinion 2 Opinion 3 Fact 4 Fact 5 Opinion

C Think and write. Describe your favorite photo. Why do you like it?

Students are going to connect the reading to their own experiences. This draws on the art objective of understanding what makes a good photo.

- Choose one of the photos you brought in and elicit how to complete the description from the class. Write this model answer on the board.
- Have students look at their favorite photo and write their own description using the template provided. Point out that they need to try and explain why they like it. If students haven't brought in a favorite photo, they can do this from memory, or choose one of the photos you brought in to describe.
- Ask if any students would like to share their descriptions with the class. You could display all the favorite photos on a wall and have students listen and decide which of the photos their classmate is talking about.

TRACK 9 TB p. 228 Spelling Pattern *–ent*

Listen and write. Then check your answers.

- With books closed, write *–ent* on the board.
- Play the first part of the audio and have students repeat each word. Then have them open their books. Play the first part of the audio again and complete as many words as they can.
- Then play the second part of the audio for students to check their spelling and complete any missing words. Ask *Which word sounds different?* (invent: in this word the second syllable is stressed) Have students underline *ent* and notice that it appears at the end of each word. Ask students to read the words aloud.
- Have students scan the text on pp. 18–21 to find more words with a final *ent*. Invite them to read the words aloud then write all the *–ent* words in a word cloud.

Answers

1 present 2 intelligent 3 parent 4 ingredient
5 invent
In the reading: element; experiment

Cool Down

Do a collaborative *Spelling Bee* with the words from the spelling pattern activity. See TB p. 27.

Practice Resource Bank: Spelling Printout
Student's App: Reading Practice; Spelling Pattern Practice

Lesson 7 Walkthrough: Think Together

Think Together brings the unit full circle to consider the key concept question. This acts as the thread for all the lessons related to the readings. The teaching notes support you to address this question.

Warm Up

Students are encouraged to revisit the Lesson 1 VTR image to see if their perceptions have changed or shifted now that they know more about the topic. Review their initial ideas and see if students can offer more information or link the image more explicitly to the unit's topic.

In the digital **ETB** there is a Two-Minute Review idea. This is a quick, fun activity which reviews both of the readings in the unit to help students make connections between the two. You can choose to do this instead of, or as well as, the Warm Up.

Activity A Text Comparison

Activity A is a text-to-text comparison task which lays the foundations for more communicative comparison analysis in higher levels. Learning how to compare and contrast is an important skill which has been shown to: improve students' ability to memorize content; develop higher-order thinking skills; strengthen comprehension skills; and improve writing skills. Graphic organizers are used throughout the course to help students organize content and ideas and to guide them towards becoming more effective learners.

If you have not done the Two-Minute Review, it may be beneficial to have students brainstorm what they remember about both texts before you start.

Activities B/C Speaking Routine

Activities B and **C** have a text-to-world base. Students are first given time to think and make connections to prior knowledge. They then explore ideas through a Think, Pair, Share VTR or a cooperative learning routine, such as Roundtable, Three-step Interview, Numbered Heads Together, or Round Robin (see **TB p. 20**). Cooperative learning routines create opportunities for purposeful communication and collaboration which encourages students to become actively engaged in their learning.

My Reading Journal

Students give a personalized response to the readings and reflect on the unit as a whole. The goal is to foster self-reflection as a learning tool, to help students to see the importance of the learning process, to encourage them to think critically about texts and to express preferences, and motivate and empower them to want to learn more.

Think Together

Lesson Objectives

- to make connections between the readings
- to explore the key concept: Why do people make art?
- to reflect on the unit and provide personal thoughts and opinions

Materials

Large pieces of paper, one per group (Activity B)

Warm Up

Have students look back at the VTR image on pp. 8–9 and ask *Do you now have any new ideas about the image? Do you now have an answer for any of the things you wondered about it?*

Ask *Why do you think the artist made this picture?* Have students work in pairs and then share their ideas with the rest of the class.

A Think and write. Compare and contrast *True Colors* and *My Guide to Photography*. What did you learn?

- Draw or project the Venn diagram onto the board. Ask students to look back at the two readings and try to find one similarity. Elicit a suggestion and write it in the center.
- Have students continue to compare and contrast the two readings in pairs, and then draw and complete the Venn diagram in their notebooks. Encourage them to try to find at least three similarities and differences. To check answers, invite students to come and write one thing in the Venn diagram.
- Finally, ask students to write about one or more things they learned from each reading.

Suggested Answers

True Colors: 1 Is about how helping people is good 2 Emil is a painter and uses a paintbrush and paints. 3 Emil paints a bee; *My Guide to Photography*: 1 Is about how to take a good photo 2 Huan Chen is a photographer and uses a camera 3 Huan Chen takes a photo of a butterfly; Both readings: 1 Are about having fun with art 2 Emil and Huan Chen want to stop their pictures being boring 3 Emil promises to paint a portrait and Huan Chen takes a portrait picture of her brother; What did you learn?: Students' own answers.

B Think and discuss. Choose one subject you would like to paint or take photos of. Explain why. Do a Roundtable.

- Have students read the instructions. Give one example answer: *I'd like to take one photo of my own face every day. Then I can see how I change in a year!* Point out that not all the ideas have to be brilliant—sometimes simple suggestions help other people think of new creative ideas.
- Set the class up for the Roundtable cooperative learning routine (see TB p. 20).
- Give groups some thinking time. Then designate one person in each group to start and remind them to write what their idea is and why. Point out that they can keep going around the table until they have no more ideas.
- Have groups read and discuss their ideas. Ask each group what they thought their best ideas were.

C Draw the thing you chose in B.

- Ask students to draw one thing they would like to paint or take a photo of in the space provided.
- Ask students *Are you happy with your picture? Is it like you imagined?*
- Ask students how they felt while drawing their picture. Remind students that the purpose of this activity is to reflect on why they make art and how it makes them feel.
- Introduce the key concept question *Why do people make art?* Give students time to think about everything they learned from the readings and their own feelings when making art. Encourage them to write their ideas in a spidergram around the key concept question. Then invite students to share their ideas with the class. Praise students for good thinking and for providing good ideas.

My Reading Journal

How does reading about art make you feel? What do you want to do next?

These questions personalize what students have learned in the unit and encourage them to want to learn more.

Give an example, then give students some thinking time and have them complete their answers. Invite students to share their answers with the class.

Ask *Do you all want to make some art, or do some people want to look at some art?* Point out that enjoying art is also a very valuable way to spend our time!

Example Answer

Reading about art makes me want to do something new! I want to take photos of ten different things on my way home today and then think about how to improve them!

Cool Down

Have students leave their books open with their drawings from C. Encourage them to walk around the classroom, looking at the different drawings. At the end, ask which drawings were interesting or unusual.

Practice **Resource Bank:** Unit Test
Student's App: Key Concept Practice

UNIT 2

How Long Is It?

Unit Overview

Themes

Experiments

Time

Synopsis

In this unit students will learn about different experiments and ways of measuring time. They will think about the importance of time and how being able to measure time can help people. They will learn about timelines and words to describe time. They will plan and prepare a presentation giving advice about using time and write instructions for an experiment using target language from the unit.

Language Book

Vocabulary
experiment, float, height, length, measure, pour, scale, thermometer, weight, width
p. 64

Explore Language
Future Predictions: *Going to* and *Will*
p. 65

Global Citizenship
Why do we measure time?
calendar, century, decade, hour, millennium, minute, month, second, year
p. 66

Explore Language
Future Plans: Present Progressive
p. 67

Take the Stage
Presentation: giving advice
p. 68

Write About It
The process of an experiment
Word building: nouns to adjectives
p. 69

Think It Over
Review and Reflection
p. 70

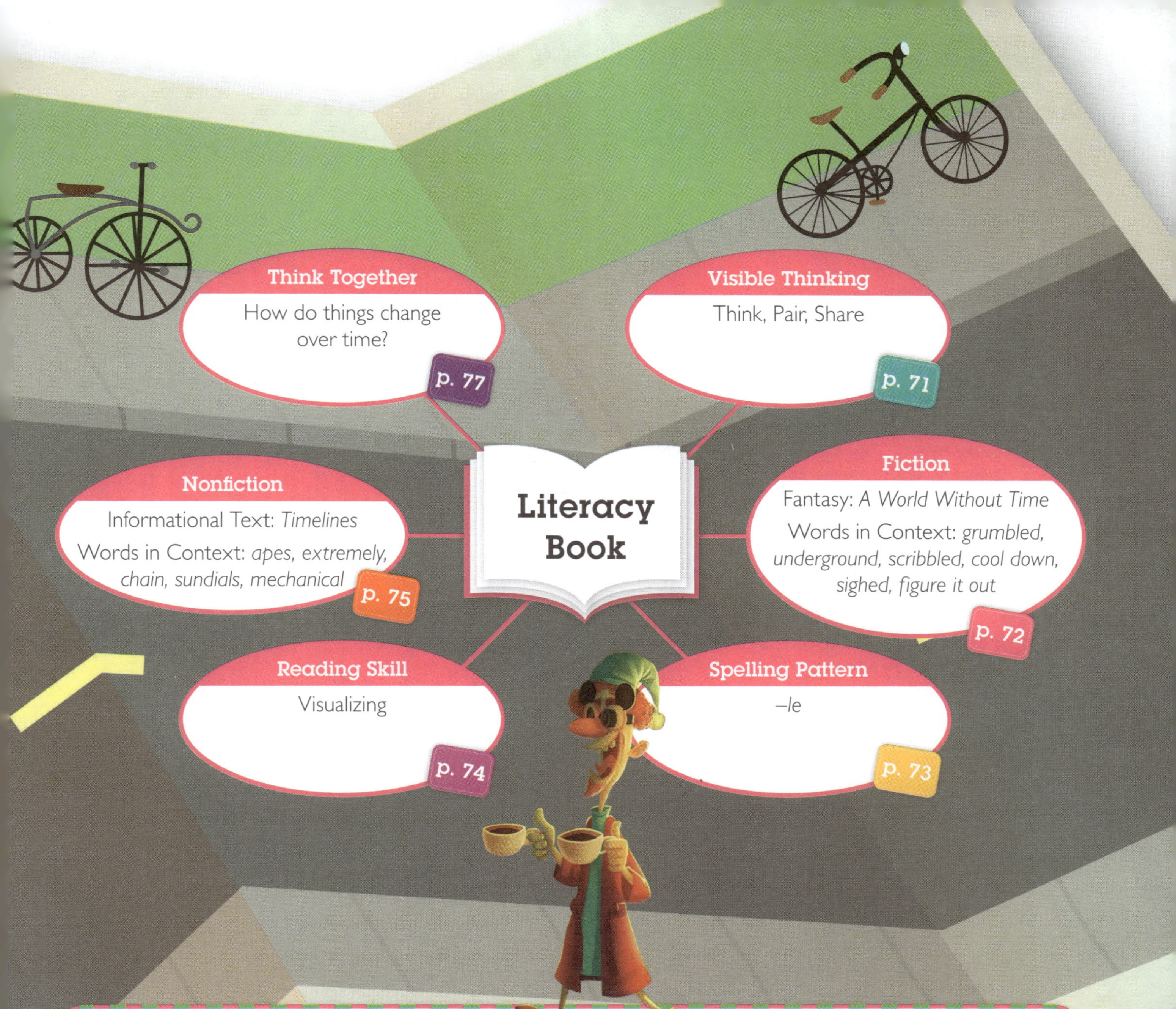

Language and Literacy Connections

The connecting theme in Unit 2 is measuring time and how things change over time.

	Language	Literacy
Vocabulary	**Set 1:** experiments **Set 2:** time	**Fiction:** length, measure **Nonfiction:** length, measure, centur(ies), decade, second, year(s)
Grammar	**Future Predictions: *Going to* and *Will*** We're going to do a science experiment. The stick will go down at one end. **Future Plans: Present Progressive** What are you doing on Saturday? I'm playing soccer in the morning.	**Fiction** You'll figure it out. **Nonfiction** Timelines help us predict how things are going to change. What will come next?
Skills	**Pronunciation:** word stress 1	**Reading:** visualizing **Spelling Pattern:** *–le*
International English	scale/scales; schedule/diary	

Vocabulary

Lesson Objectives

- to learn vocabulary to describe experiments: *experiment, float, height, length, measure, pour, scale, thermometer, weight, width*
- to sing a song about doing experiments

Materials
Audio Tracks 15 to 18; Video

Warm Up

Ask students what they recently learned in science class. Ask *What did you do? How did you learn? Did you use objects, or did you read from books?* Then have students discuss with a partner.

A TRACK 15 TB p. 214 **Listen and find. Which ball bounces the highest?**

- Have students look at pp. 22–23 and say what they can see and where it is happening. Have them find and point to Poppy from the previous unit (she's sitting down, next to the boy with the thermometer). Ask *Does this look like a typical science lesson? Does it look like fun?*
- Play the audio and have students point to the words and pictures as they listen.
- Ask the comprehension question *Which ball bounced the highest?* and elicit the answer. Play the audio again for students to check.
- Remind students of the challenge at the end of Unit 1: *Which after-school club do I go to?* Elicit that Poppy goes to a science club after school.

Answer
the golf ball

B TRACK 16 TB p. 214 **Listen, say, and number the pictures in A.**

- Play the audio and have students point to the pictures and say the words.
- Tell students to listen again and write numbers next to the words in the picture. Do the example together (scale).
- Check answers by calling out a word and having students say the number. Then have everyone repeat the word.

Answers
1 *scale* 2 length 3 width 4 height 5 weight
6 experiment 7 thermometer 8 measure
9 pour 10 float

International English

Highlight the differences between the two words and elicit *scale* is American English and *scales* is British English. Drill the pronunciation of both and ask *Which one do we use?*

C TRACK 17 TB p. 214 **Close your eyes. Listen, visualize, and say.**

- Prepare students for the visualization (see TB p. 21).
- Play the audio, allowing students to visualize the ideas as they listen. Make sure students know not to speak until they hear the word *say*.
- Have students mime a few of their visualizations in pairs. (e.g. holding a hand up for *height*, pouring for *pour*, etc.).

D **Look and write.**

- This activity develops critical thinking as students categorize the vocabulary under different headings. Check students know the meaning of *equipment* (objects you need to do something) and *measurements* (to say how big, long, or heavy something is). Elicit one word for each of the columns and then have students finish the activity individually. Have them compare their answers with a friend.
- Draw or project the activity onto the board and invite students to complete one item each in the appropriate column.

Answers
Equipment for experiments: scale, thermometer
Actions: float, pour, measure
Measurements: *height*, weight, width, length

E TRACK 18 TB p. 215 **Listen and complete. Then watch and sing.**

- Have students turn their books over so they can't see the song lyrics. Tell them the title of the song is *Measure It!* Ask students *What units of measurement do you know?* and elicit suggestions.
- Play the song once, allowing students to listen and enjoy it.
- Have students turn their books back over. Explain that some words in the song are scrambled and they have to unscramble them. Ask *Can you guess what they are?* Encourage them to look at the vocabulary words in the picture dictionary to help them. Play the song again, this time pausing for students to write their answers.
- Check answers as a class.
- Play the song video and encourage students to sing along.

Answers
1 *length* 2 height 3 weight 4 Measure 5 Measure
6 experiment 7 thermometer 8 width

Cool Down

Play *Running Spelling* (see TB p. 26) with the new vocabulary from this lesson.

Practice **Student's App:** Vocabulary Practice; Song Video

Explore Language

Lesson Objectives

- to learn how to talk about the future using *going to* and *will*
- to practice vocabulary for talking about an experiment

Materials

Audio Tracks 19 and 20

Warm Up

Ask students to predict six things they think they will do in this lesson. Write them in note form in a corner of the board and refer to them at the end of the lesson.

A TRACK 19 TB p. 215 **Listen and read. What are the students measuring?**

- Have students look at the pictures on p. 24 and say what they can see and what they think the people are doing. Play the audio and have students follow in their books.
- Ask the comprehension question *What are the students measuring?* and elicit the answer.
- Ask students *What words about experiments from the previous lesson can you find in the story?* (experiment, weight, measure, scale)

Answer

the weight of air

B **Look at A. Complete.**

- Write or project the table onto the board.
- Refer students to the first sentence in the table. Have students find it in the story and complete it in the table. Have students complete the next blank, then ask *Are these sentences about the present or future? How do we know?* (future: *going to* and *will*)
- Have students work in pairs to complete the rest of the table.
- Nominate students to read the completed sentences aloud, and complete the table on the board.
- Ask students *When we use "going to," what always comes first?* (the verb be) *What comes after?* (a verb) Ask *What comes after "will"?* (also a verb) Point out that verbs after *going to* and *will* are in the base form. Elicit the negative forms of *are going to* and *will* (*aren't going to* and *won't*). Then highlight the two questions and encourage students to notice the word order (question word + be + subject + *going to* + verb; question word + *will* + verb).
- Have students look at the Grammar tip *Remember*. Point out that we don't use *to* after *will*.

Answers

're; going to; will; won't; am; going to; will

C **Think and discuss. Then choose.**

- Have students work in pairs to read and discuss the sentences. Tell them they can look at the table in B and at the story to help them circle the correct options. Then check answers.

Answers

1 going to 2 will

D TRACK 20 TB p. 215 **Listen and say.**

- Tell students they will hear some sentences using *going to* and *will*. Play the audio and have students listen and repeat. For ideas on how to vary the drills, see TB p. 23.

E **Read and choose.**

- Refer students to the example question and answer and elicit why the answer is *'s going to*. (We have information to help us make a prediction.)
- Have students work individually to circle the correct options.
- Check answers and write them on the board.

Answers

1 *'s going to* 2 we'll 3 won't 4 It's going to

F **Look and write your predictions. Then compare.**

- Have students look at the pictures and say what they can see happening.
- Then refer them to the example sentence. Ask why that prediction is correct (because we can see it about to happen).
- Have students complete the predictions for the other pictures and then compare their ideas in pairs. Encourage pairs to take turns making additional predictions about the pictures; for example, *I think that boy will win; I think the coin will stop; I think he will go to the park; I think he'll go home.* Remind students that they can use phrases like *I agree / I disagree* after their partner makes a prediction.
- Check answers as a class.

Suggested Answers

1 *'re going to have a race* 2 won't stop the coin
3 's going to fall 4 will/won't swim

Cool Down

Refer students to the list of their predictions for this lesson (see the Warm Up). First have them phrase the predictions using *going to* or *will* and then have them say if their predictions were correct or not.

Practice **Resource Bank:** Grammar Printout
Student's App: Grammar Practice

Global Citizenship

Lesson Objectives

- to learn vocabulary for talking about time: *calendar, century, decade, hour, millennium, minute, month, second, year*
- to explore why we measure time and how we experience time
- to practice listening for gist and details

Materials
Audio Tracks 21 to 23; Audio Track B; a world map (D)

Opening Question

Ask students what time it is and how they know. Ask *How do you tell the time?* (clock, smartphone) *When do you usually check the time? Why?*

Then ask the question *Why do we measure time?* Give students time to think before eliciting ideas.

A TRACK 21 TB p. 215 **Listen to Anton talk to his dad about time. When did people first use clocks?**

- Ask students what they can see on the page. Say *Find a month.* (September) *Find a year.* (1629)
- Play the audio and have students point to the words or pictures as they listen.
- Ask the comprehension question *When did people first use clocks?* Elicit the answer, then play the audio again for students to check. See the digital **ETB** for further comprehension questions.

Answer
nearly a millennium ago

B TRACK 22 TB p. 215 **Listen, say, and number the pictures in A.**

- Play the audio and have students point to the pictures and say the words.
- Tell students to listen again and number the pictures in the order they hear them. Do the example together (calendar).
- Write or project the answers onto the board.

Answers
1 *calendar* 2 millennium 3 century 4 decade
5 year 6 month 7 hour 8 minute 9 second

TRACK B TB p. 215 **Visualization**

The TTL has a visualization audio track for this vocabulary set. (See TB p. 21.)

C Complete the timeline. Write the measurements of time in order.

- Draw or project the timeline across the board. Choose two of the words and ask students where to place them.
- Give students time to match the words from A with the numbers on the timeline and then compare with a friend. Invite individual students to come to the board and write a word on the timeline.

Answers
second, minute, hour, *day*, *week*, month, year, decade, *century*, millennium

D TRACK 23 TB p. 215 **Now listen to Salma and Markus. Which clock is older?**

- Have students look at the two pictures and notice where the speakers are from. Have them find the countries on a map. Elicit what they know about Egypt or Germany already.
- Then ask students what they can see in the two pictures and how old they think the objects are.
- Listening for gist: play the audio and have students listen for the answer to the gist question *Which clock is older?* Elicit the answer.

Answer
The sundial is older.

E Listen again and complete.

- Listening for details: have students read and complete as many of the sentences as they can. Play the audio and stop after *... used the sun to tell the time.* Point out the example answer.
- Play the rest of the audio and have students check their answers or complete the sentences. Check answers.

Answers
1 *sun* 2 sunny 3 shadow 4 300 5 bird 6 dance

Discussion Questions

- Draw students' attention to the discussion questions: *When does time feel slow for you? Why? How does measuring time help people?* Have students discuss the questions in pairs (see **ETB**).
- Return to the opening question to ask again: *Why do we measure time?* and discuss any further ideas students may have.
- Guide them to the conclusion that measuring time helps us interact with and be respectful of others' plans, and that time often moves slowly when you're not having fun.

Cool Down

Do a time quiz. Read out some unusual definitions of different periods of time for students to guess the time period, e.g. *What is 5,214 weeks long?* (a century) *Thirty-six of these make three years—what are they?* (months) *Some people can run 100 meters in less than 10 what?* (seconds)

Practice **Student's App:** Vocabulary Practice; Listening Practice

Explore Language

Lesson Objectives

- to learn how to use the present progressive for future plans
- to practice using vocabulary to describe time

Materials
Audio Tracks 24 and 25

Warm Up

Ask *What activities do you do after school? What time do you do activities? What time do you do your homework? What time do you have dinner? What time do you go to bed?* Have students discuss their schedules in pairs.

A TRACK 24 TB p. 215 **Listen and read. When are the children going to start their project?**

- Ask students *What can you see in the picture?* and *What do you think the teacher is giving the children?*
- Play the audio and have students follow the dialogue in their books.
- Ask the comprehension question *When are the children going to start their project?* Elicit the answer.

Answer
now

B Look at A. Complete.

- Write or project the table onto the board.
- Refer students to the incomplete question in the table and have them find it in A. Elicit the answer and write it on the board. Ask *What kind of word is "are"?* (a verb)
- Have students work in pairs to complete the rest of the sentences.
- To check answers, elicit the completed sentences and fill in the table on the board. Have students notice that all the sentences include *be* + *going to* + verb and point out that this is the present progressive. Ask students *What do we usually use the present progressive for?* (to talk about things happening now) *Are the sentences in A about things happening now?* (no, the future) *How do we know they're about the future?* (There are phrases that refer to times in the future, for example, on Saturday.)

Answers
are; 'm; playing; are taking

C Think and discuss. Then choose.

- Check that students understand the meaning of *arrangements* (when you plan or agree to do something, often with someone else).
- Have students work in pairs to read and discuss the sentence. Tell them they can look at the table and the dialogue in A to help them circle the correct option. Then check the answer as a class.

Practice **Resource Bank:** Grammar Printout
Student's App: Grammar Practice

- Refer students to the Grammar tip *Watch Out*. Ask them why we don't use *will* in the sentences in A (because we are talking about future arrangements, or plans we have made; *will* is used for making a prediction).

Answer
future arrangements

D TRACK 25 TB p. 215 **Listen and say.**

- Play the audio and have students listen and repeat. For ideas on how to vary the drill, see TB p. 23.

E Read Sara's schedule and complete.

- Draw or project the schedule onto the board. Refer students to the first sentence and elicit how they can find out the answer.
- Have students complete the sentences individually and then compare their answers with a friend.
- Ask individual students to read their completed sentences aloud and ask if everyone agrees. Write the verbs on the board or project the activity and complete it so everyone can check their answers. Have students check that they all have the verb *be* in their answers.

Answers
1 *is practicing* 2 are coming 3 aren't meeting; is going
4 isn't flying 5 is arriving

International English

Have students look at both words and elicit *schedule* is American English and *diary* is British English. Pay careful attention to the pronunciation of *schedule* **/'skedju:l/**. Ask *Which word do we use?*

F Write your schedule for Saturday. Then compare. Who is busier?

- Draw a schedule on the board, just for one day—Saturday. Fill in a few activities of your own; for example, 10:00 clean the house, 1:00 lunch with Maria, 3:00 correct homework. Elicit sentences from the class (using you) for your schedule; for example, *You're cleaning the house on Saturday morning.*
- Have students write their own Saturday schedule in their notebooks. If they have no arrangements made, they can invent some! Note: if appropriate for your class, you can choose a different day for them to write about.
- Divide the class into pairs. Have two students read aloud the example question and answer. Then have students ask and answer questions about each other's schedules in their pairs.
- Ask each pair whose schedule is busier.

Cool Down

Have pairs write an imaginary weekend schedule for a TV character or famous person, then share one thing their character/person is going to do with the class.

Take the Stage

Lesson Objectives

- to prepare and give a presentation giving opinions and advice about using time
- to recognize and reproduce words with different stress patterns

Materials

Video; Audio Track 26

Warm Up

Have students make a *Word Tree* in pairs (see TB p. 27). Tell them to write the word *Time* at the base and then build their tree. Invite some pairs to share their word trees with the class.

A TB p. 238 **Watch and listen. What did Lewis do while he was practicing his talk?**

- Tell students they are going to watch a video of a boy talking about using time well. Have students make some predictions using *will* about what he might say and then watch the video to see if they were correct.
- Introduce the comprehension question *What did Lewis do while he was practicing his talk?* Play the video again and then ask students for the answer. Ask additional questions; for example, *What's Lewis's best advice?* (make a list of things to do) Play part of the video again and have students notice where Lewis is looking while he's giving his presentation.

Answer

He cleaned his room.

B Watch again. Check (✔) the sentences you hear.

- Have students read the sentences.
- Play the video again and have students complete the activity. Read the sentences and have students raise their hands for the ones they checked. Have students read the phrases again and ask them to categorize them into three groups: introducing what you want to say (1, 2), giving advice (3, 5, 7), and ending (8).

Answers

1; 2; 3; 5; 7; 8

Pronunciation Word Stress 1

TRACK 26 TB p. 215 **Listen and say.**

- Read the first phrase from B with the wrong stress on *something and important*: someTHING, imporTANT. Ask students if it sounded right. Read the phrase again correctly and point out that the part of a word we say more strongly can help others understand us.
- Play the audio and have students listen and count the syllables. They should notice that in these words the stress is on the first syllable for two syllable words and on the middle syllable for three syllable words. Play the audio again and have students repeat the words.
- Tell students these words are all in the video. Have them look for other words from the unit that have the same stress patterns in pairs, then elicit ideas and write them on the board in two sections. If they have any difficulty, ask them to place these words in the correct group: *measure, sunshine, prediction, teacher, progressive, circus, opinion.* Drill all the words at the end.

C Plan. Think about advice for using time in the best way. Then complete.

- Tell students they are going to plan their own presentation about how to use time well.
- Draw or project the *At Home* part of the plan in C onto the board. Give students time to think and then elicit more ideas for planning time at home. Write them on the board.
- Now have students work individually to complete the plan in their book for each of the three categories. Point out that, like Lewis, they should choose four or five important points to present.

D Prepare your presentation. Use your ideas from C and phrases from B.

- Play the video again as a model and remind students to watch with their own presentation in mind.
- Ask students which phrases from B they can use in the Introduction (1 and 2). Do the same for the Middle (Advice) section and the Ending.
- Have students transfer their ideas from C into the template in D in note form.

E Practice with a friend. Then share with your class.

- Now have students practice their presentation with a friend. Remind students that it is important to look directly at the audience and speak clearly.
- Invite volunteers to come to the front of the classroom to give their presentation. Have the audience give a round of applause after each presentation.

Cool Down

Play *Change It Round* (see TB p. 25) with the following section of Lewis's presentation on the board:

I think it's very important to plan your time. Here are some tips. I find that the best thing to do is to make a list every day. Always do the things you have to do first, and then the things you want to do! So, my advice is do your homework first.

Practice **Student's App:** Speaking Skills Practice; Speaking Video

Write About It

Lesson Objectives

- to learn how to use word building to make adjectives from nouns
- to plan and write an experiment

Materials

(Optional) Challenge, Standard, and Support writing printouts, one per student (C and D)

Warm Up

Have students remember the experiment with the two balloons on p. 24. Have them describe the equipment and experiment, with each student saying a few words before you choose someone else to continue.

A Read the instructions. Circle the three adjectives describing the ice cubes.

- Have students read the text quickly and say what kind of text it is. (instructions for an experiment) Ask some questions to check comprehension; for example, *What equipment do you need for this experiment?* (four glasses, four ice cubes, a teaspoon, salt, sugar, sand, stopwatch)
- Check that students remember what an adjective is. Ask students to find three adjectives to describe the ice cubes (all in step 1). Have students join you in using their hands to reinforce the meaning of *wide* (hands spread side to side), *long* (hands spread, one near your body and the other out in front), and *high* (hands spread up and down).

Answers

wide; long; high

B Look at A. Complete.

- Elicit or remind students what a noun is. Draw or project the table onto the board. Have students find the adjective in A that corresponds to the noun width. Elicit the answer and write it in place.
- Then have students complete the rest of the table and compare with a friend. *Height* is not mentioned in A, but students should remember it from the Vocabulary lesson.
- Ask students to come to the board and each write an answer in the table. Check that everyone agrees and that the spelling is correct. Have students read the words aloud and check pronunciation.

Answers

wide; height; long

C Plan. Look at the experiment and think about these questions.

- Ask students to look at the illustrations for the experiment. Ask them to say what is similar to the experiment in A and what is different. (Similar: ice cubes, measurements, glasses, sunny place, melting; different: breaking one ice cube, only two ice cubes.)
- Tell students that they are going to write instructions for this new experiment using the instructions in A as a model. Ask the class the first question and elicit the answer (there are six steps in the experiment). You can hand out the Challenge printouts at this point.
- Have students answer the other questions individually and then compare their answers with a friend.

Answers

1 six 2 two glasses, two ice cubes, a hammer, a stopwatch 3 3 cm. wide, long, and high 4 which ice cube melts first 5 The broken ice melted first. Breaking the ice cube into a few large pieces makes it melt faster.

D Write the instructions and results for the experiment.

- Encourage students to look at step 1 in A and elicit the beginning of the instructions for the experiment in C. (*To do this experiment, you need …*)
- Have students continue to write the instructions individually in their notebooks. Remind them to use their plan and to look at A as a model.
- Have students self-correct or exchange their work with a friend and peer-correct. You can put a checklist of points for students to look out for on the board (e.g. spelling, commas, capital letters, correct use of nouns and adjectives).
- Have students correct any mistakes and write their final instructions neatly on paper. Alternatively, hand out the Support and Standard printouts from the Resource Bank. Allow them time to illustrate their experiment.
- Have each student compare their instructions with another student and see how similar or different they are. They may find useful phrases they can incorporate into their own instructions.

Suggested Answers

1 To do this experiment, you need two glasses, two ice cubes that are 3 cm. wide, 3 cm. long, and 3 cm. high, a hammer, and a stopwatch. 2 Put one ice cube in glass A and break the other ice cube into pieces with a hammer. 3 Put the pieces of ice in glass B. 4 Put the glasses in a sunny place. 5 Set a stopwatch and wait 30 minutes. 6 Check the ice cubes. Which ice cube melted first? Results: The ice cube in glass B melted first. Breaking it into a few large pieces makes it melt faster.

Cool Down

Play *Simon Says* with the instructions from A (see TB p. 27).

Practice **Student's App:** Writing Practice

Think It Over

Lesson Objectives

- to review what has been learned in the unit
- to reflect on the unit and their own progress
- to think about learning strategies and how to continue learning at home

Warm Up

Play the *Yes/No Game* (see TB p. 27) with words from pp. 22–23 or p. 26 and some that do not appear in the unit. Ask them to identify when words were in the unit. Suggested words: *thermometer* (Y), *knife* (N), *calendar* (Y), *second* (Y), *shadow* (N), *width* (Y), *speed* (N), *measure* (Y), *decade* (Y), *pour* (Y), *fly* (N), *century* (Y), *scale* (Y), *plate* (N), *month* (Y), *sculpture* (N).

Read the questions and draw or write your answers.

- Give students time to think about and discuss activities in the unit before they complete each question. Explain that they can choose to either write a few words or sentences or to draw a picture. Allowing students to make a personal response will help them retain knowledge and engage with the learning points.

What did I do?

- Give students a few minutes to look back through the unit at the different activities they did. Ask questions about the unit or write questions on the board for students to discuss in pairs or small groups; for example, *What did you sing about? What stories did you read? Where did you hear about different types of clocks?*
- Encourage students to identify something in the unit that they found challenging or something that was particularly memorable for them, but tell them not to choose their favorite activity yet. Students can draw or write about their chosen activity.

What did I learn?

- Have students talk to a partner about what they remember from the unit—stories, words, phrases, people, experiments.
- Ask questions about the unit to help students think about what they learned; for example, *Can you find new words that you didn't know before? Can you make new questions or answers? What did you learn about experiments? What else did you learn?* Elicit ideas from the class and discuss them together.
- Tell students to draw a picture or write sentences about their learning outcomes.

What was my favorite part?

- Have students look back through the unit and decide what they enjoyed the most. Tell them it can be an activity they found fun, a text they enjoyed reading, a favorite character, or a favorite action. They should try to choose just one and draw a picture or write about it. Explain that when we like something, it is often easier to learn.

How well did I do?

- Ask students to color in the number of thermometers that represents how well they think they learned the content (i.e. the more thermometers they color, the more they feel they have learned). Ask *What do you understand? What do you need to practice more?* Encourage students to look back through the unit to see how much they remember what they did well and what they found difficult.

What can I do next?

- Brainstorm ideas with the class about what they can do to continue to learn (e.g. watch the videos again, think about the time again and make a sundial, practice word stress, make predictions about friends). Encourage them to suggest their own ideas of things they can do.
- Draw students' attention to the options in the box. Encourage students to think about what they can do at home to improve their English using the verbs in the box as prompts. Suggestions might include: watch English-language programs on TV; share what they learned in class with other friends or family (explaining things to others is a great way to consolidate your learning); sing the song from this unit again with friends (or learn and sing a new song from the radio); find out more about some of the experiments in this unit.
- Ask students to choose one or more activities from the list (watch, share, sing, find out) that they will do to practice their English.
- Once students have completed the page in their books, have them discuss with a friend what they drew or wrote. Did they choose the same activities or different ones?
- Ask students if there is one activity from the unit that they would like to repeat now.

Looking Forward

- Draw students' attention to the character at the bottom of the page. Ask *Who's this?* and elicit what they remember about him. (Mr. Sim appears in the Vocabulary and Explore Language 2 lessons; he is the science teacher.) Ask *What's under Mr. Sim's table in his classroom?* Ask students to make predictions about what's under the table and what Unit 3 is about. Tell them they will find out in the first lesson of the next unit.

Put It Together

To further review and recycle the language in Units 1 and 2, play the game, *Give a Reason!*, on pp. 34–35. See TB p. 206 for teaching notes.

Practice **Resource Bank:** Unit Test
Student's App: Vocabulary and Grammar Review

Get Ready to Read

Lesson Objectives

- to activate prior knowledge about time
- to encourage students to observe and interpret through a Think, Pair, Share VTR
- to preview the reading skill of visualizing changes

Materials
(Optional) VTR printout from the Resource Bank (A, B, C); (optional) strips of paper and glue or staples for students to make their own Möbius strip

Warm Up

Write the word *time* in the middle of the board and draw a circle round it. Ask students to think of all the words that can go before the word *time* to make mini-phrases. Give the examples *good time* and *lunchtime* and write the words *good* and *lunch* around the central word on the board. Give students time to think, then invite them to the board to write more answers. Possible answers include: home time, bedtime, free time, spend time, breakfast time, dinnertime

Think, Pair, Share

A Look at the picture. How does the artist represent time? Think about it.

Students are going to do a Think, Pair, Share VTR to explore the image of the Möbius strip on pp. 24–25.

- Start by asking students what they can see in the picture. Encourage them to use adjectives, such as colors and shapes. If students don't know a word, ask them to describe it so that you can provide it in English.
- Then write the question *How does the artist represent time?* on the board. Check that students understand this means how the artist shows time in this picture. Give students one or two minutes to think silently, so that they form their own ideas. Tell them to cross their arms when they have thought of some ideas.

B Discuss with your partner.

- Ask a volunteer to read the first speech bubble. Ask students *Do you agree with this person?*
- Divide the class into pairs and have students share their ideas. Encourage them to discuss any questions they might have and to think of possible answers together.
- Circulate and encourage students to expand on their ideas by asking *What makes you say that?* Remind students to use phrases like *Me, too* and *Really? I don't think so*, and *Yes, I agree* to help the conversation feel more natural. Provide vocabulary where necessary.

C Share your ideas with the class.

- Ask pairs to share their ideas about the picture with the class. Encourage students to use *we*, as they are talking about their partner's opinion, too.

Here's an example of this part of the routine.

Teacher: (Student A), what do you and your friend think?
Student A: We think the broken body parts represents time.
Teacher: That's interesting! Can you tell us more?
Student B: Things break and change after years.
Teacher: Great. Any other ideas?
Student C: We think the strip shows time.
Teacher: In what way?
Student C: There's no end and no beginning.
Student D: It shows time goes round in a circle like a clock.

Transition

Draw the infinity symbol ∞ on the board and ask if students have seen it before and if they know what it means. Elicit or give the word *infinity*. Point out that it looks like the Möbius strip and ask if they can guess the meaning. (Like the Möbius strip, it doesn't finish and just goes around and around.)

D Make lists. What words do we use to talk about time? What do we use to measure time?

- Draw or project the table onto the board. Elicit one or two examples for each column and write them in the table. You can include the word *infinity* in the *Measure Time* column. Give students time to discuss ideas in pairs and then invite students to come to the board and write more words in each column.

Suggested Answers
Talk About Time: *early*; day; long; morning; afternoon; night
Measure Time: *hour*; second; minute; watch; clock; sun; phone

E Think and discuss. Look at the first two pages of *A World Without Time*. What is the problem? Imagine one way to fix the problem.

This is a preview of the reading skill of visualizing changes.

- Have students look at the picture on pp. 26–27 (you could project them onto the board) and discuss what they think the problem is. (People don't know what time it is, as there's no sun.) If necessary, ask some prompt questions: *Do you think it is night or day? How do you know?* Tell students it always looks like this in the town because it is underground.
- Give students time to imagine a solution. Have them discuss in pairs and then as a class.

Now read A World Without Time

Fiction: *A World Without Time*—Fantasy

Lesson Objectives

- to read a fantasy story about an underground world
- to make a personal connection to the reading

Materials
Audio Tracks 10 and 11; Video

Warm Up

Divide the class into groups of three. Ask the groups to think of as many words as possible to describe the picture on pp. 26–27. They should classify all of their words under the headings *Objects*, *People*, and *Adjectives*. Elicit examples for each category; for example, Objects: *houses*, *bridge*, *road*, *lamp*; People: *old man*, *construction workers*/*man driving a steamroller*, *people waiting at a bus stop*; Adjectives: *dark*, *angry*, *tall*. Then ask *Do you think this would be a good place to live?*

TRACK 10 TB p. 228 Reading Approach

First Reading: Engage with the Text

- Have students look at the pictures and title and ask students the prediction questions *What's Ooleck's problem? What do you think he's going to do?* Elicit answers.
- Play the video or audio and pause after each character's name is mentioned. Have students pronounce the names then find and point to them in their books.
- Play the video/audio to the end and ask if anyone's predictions were correct.
- Then look at the Words in Context.

TRACK 11 TB p. 229 Words in Context

- Play the audio and have students repeat the words.
- Have a word race to find the words in the story.
- Remind students they can sometimes **think about whether the new word is a noun, verb, or adjective to figure out meaning** (see TB p. 22). Have them discuss their ideas with a partner, using L1 if necessary.

grumbled (p. 26) Ask students *What's happening? How do you think Ooleck feels? What does his voice sound like?* Have them grumble the line *Working time already?*

underground (p. 27) Ask *Where do they live? Can they see the sun? What animals do you know that live underground?*

scribbled (p. 29) Ask *Is it a noun, an adjective, or a verb?* (a verb) Ask *What do you think Ooleck is doing?* (writing/drawing) *Do you think his writing is slow and careful or quick and not very tidy?* (quick) Have students either mime scribbling their name or ask them to scribble it in their notebook and say if it looks neat.

cool down (p. 30) Ask *When tea cools down, does it get hotter or colder?*

sighed (p. 31) Ask *Is* tired *a noun, verb, or adjective?* (verb) *What does it tell us about the way Ooleck is feeling when he says, "I still can't solve it"?* (he is tired, disappointed, sad) Have students sigh while saying the phrase.

figure it out (p. 31) Ask *Do you think Zeena means he will give up or he will find a solution? How do we know?* (She says the answer is under his nose.)

Second Reading: Analyze the Text and Features

- Now allow students to read the story silently. Remind them not to worry if there are parts of the text they don't understand. To keep them focused, ask them to count how many ideas Ooleck suggests. Elicit answers.
- Ask some comprehension questions to check understanding: *Why were some people working and some people still sleeping?* (They had no way to know the time.) *How will a way to tell the time help them?* (People won't be late or early—they'll do things at the right time.)
- Discuss the questions in the blue boxes.
  - **Making Connections** (p. 27): *Why is it important to measure time?* Elicit students' opinions and ask what problems it causes the people living in Undergroundia when they can't measure time. What problems would they have if they couldn't tell what time it was?
  - **Language Focus** (p. 30): *Why does Zeena repeat the word* silly *several times?* Give students some thinking time and then ask for their suggestions. (She's probably getting impatient.)
  - **Language Focus** (p. 31): *What does* right under your nose *mean? Do you know a similar expression in any other language?* Ask students if they can explain the expression. (It's something you should be able to see easily but for some reason you can't see it!) Ask students if they know a similar expression in their own language.

Third Reading: Interact with the Text

- Play the video again and have students repeat all of Ooleck's direct speech when he grumbles (p. 26, p. 29), thinks (p. 30), and sighs (p. 31).
- Divide the class into pairs, designate a role for each student (Zeena or Ooleck), and have them act out the story. Remind them they only need to say the direct speech.

Cool Down

Have students imagine all the things they couldn't do if they lived in Undergroundia and didn't have sunshine, and then share their ideas with the class. Make a list on the board and decide which are essential for quality of life.

Practice **Student's App:** Fiction Video

Explore the Reading

Lesson Objectives

- to understand and analyze *A World Without Time* through reading comprehension activities
- to explore the SEL competency of self-management through setting plans and working toward goals
- to identify and practice words ending in *le*

Materials

(Optional) Video (A); Audio Tracks 10 and 12; handwritten cards with quotations from the story (WU)

Warm Up

Play *Who Said It?* (see TB p. 27) using these sentences: *I need to invent a way of measuring time.* (Ooleck) *Good idea.* (Zeena) *Don't be so silly.* (Zeena) *It's taken seven candles so far.* (Ooleck) *The answer is probably right under your nose.* (Zeena)

A Read and answer.

- Before students open their books, find out what they remember from the story. Ask *Where do the people in the story live?* (underground in Undergroundia) *What is their problem?* (They have no way to tell the time.) *Who is Ooleck?* (an inventor) *How do you think Ooleck will find the solution?* (He will realize he can use candles to measure time.) Play the video or audio again to check answers.
- Refer students to the first question and elicit the answer. Ask them to find something in the text that shows this answer. (*In the giant cave outside …* (p. 26), *Undergroundians spent their whole lives underground* (p. 27).
- Have students complete the activity. Check answers as a class and have students say where they found each answer.

Answers

1 Ooleck and Zeena live in a cave underground / in Undergroundia. 2 Ooleck wakes up because he hears the noise of the workers. 3 The tooth scraper and the two-wheeled cycle. 4 Ooleck shares three ideas: beard time, tea time, and cycle time. 5 Ooleck burns seven candles.

B Think and write. What is Ooleck like?

- Refer students to the example answer and ask why Ooleck is silly. (Some of his ideas are a bit crazy!)
- Have students think about more adjectives or phrases that can describe Ooleck. Ask students to consider what he decides to do and how he does it.
- Write or project the activity onto the board and have students write new words or phrases around his name. Encourage students to notice that Ooleck is organized (he uses a brainstorming technique) and determined (he doesn't give up even when the problem is hard).

Suggested Answers

silly; smart; creative; motivated/determined; organized

C Think and discuss. What solution does Zeena have for telling time? Why doesn't she tell Ooleck?

- Ask students what they think Zeena's solution for telling time was and why she didn't tell Ooleck. Have students work in pairs and look back at the reading for ideas.
- Elicit suggestions from students. Encourage them to justify their answers with reference to the reading.

Suggested Answer

Zeena's solution is to use melting candles to measure time. She doesn't tell Ooleck because she wants him to figure it out on his own.

D Think and discuss. What does Ooleck need to do to reach his goal of measuring time? What do you do to reach your goals?

This activity addresses the SEL competency of self-management by having students reflect on how they set plans and work toward their own goals.

- Ask guiding questions to draw out Ooleck's working method and why it is a good one; for example, *What's his method for thinking about the problem?* (He sits down and starts making notes of ideas.)
- Ask students to think about what they do when they have a goal they want to achieve. Give them time to think and then have a Group Time discussion (see TB p. 21). Ask *Do you think you can use Ooleck's way of working to help you achieve your goals?*

TRACK 12 TB p. 229 **Spelling Pattern –*le***

Listen and write. Then check your answers.

- With books closed, point to something purple in the classroom. Ask them what color it is and write the word on the board. Say the word, underline the letters *le*, and have students repeat it.
- Play the first part of the audio and have students repeat each word. Then have them open their books. Play the first part of the audio again and have them complete as many words as they can.
- Play the second part of the audio and have students check their spelling and complete any missing words. Have students underline *le* and notice that it appears at the end of each word.
- Have students find more words with the –*le* ending in the reading. Invite students to read the words aloud, then have them write all the –*le* words from the lesson in a word cloud.

Answers

1 handle 2 whale 3 trouble 4 purple 5 castle
In the reading: whole, candle, cycle

Cool Down

Play *How Many Words?* with sentences from the reading. (See TB p. 26.)

Practice Resource Bank: Spelling Printout
Student's App: Reading Practice; Spelling Pattern Practice

Get Ready to Read

Lesson Objectives

- to practice the reading skill of visualizing changes
- to activate prior knowledge about how people and things change
- to encourage students to consider how visualizing can help us predict the future

Warm Up

Ask students to look around the classroom and say how it has changed since the beginning of the school year (maybe there are new pictures, new pencils, or different displays).

Ask students *What other changes do you think can happen in this room? What can make it better?*

A Think, draw, and share. Ooleck visualizes a man standing in the town square growing a beard. Draw the man's face as it changes over time.

Students are going to practice the reading skill of visualizing changes.

- Ask students to remember Ooleck's silly ideas for measuring time—measuring a man's beard growing, timing someone cycling around Undergroundia, and timing a cup of tea cooling. Tell them they will think about the beard idea now.
- Project the three pictures of the man onto the board. Ask students to think about how the man's face and beard change over time. Give students time to complete the three pictures. While they are doing this, draw your own changes onto the projected pictures on the board.
- When students have finished, have them compare their pictures with a friend. Then show them your pictures and see how different they are.
- Refer students to the skills box about *visualizing*. Point out that this is something very useful for us to do while reading as it helps us imagine the story, how things might look, what the characters are like, and the setting. This all helps us make predictions about the story and understand it. It also helps us to feel involved in a story, making reading a more interesting, exciting, and personal experience.

B Think, draw, and write. Choose something that changes over time. Visualize the changes.

- Elicit some suggestions for things that change over time—if necessary, you could prompt students to think about children growing, plants producing flowers, the weather changing with the seasons, food cooking, and so on. Write their ideas on the board.
- Ask students to choose one of these and try to visualize what changes will take place. They should draw the changes in the spaces provided and write a suitable time reference at the top of each picture.
- Then divide the class into pairs and have them tell each other about the changes they visualized. Ask *Do you think your partner's visualizations were realistic?*
- Ask if any students would like to share their ideas with the rest of the class.

C Think and discuss. Look at the timeline on the next page. What changes does it help you visualize?

- Have students look at the timeline at the beginning of the text. First, ask students *What can you see?* (animals, plants, dinosaurs, monkeys, humans, etc.) Check students understand that the events on the left of the timeline were longer ago than the events on the right.
- Now have students discuss with a partner what changes the timeline shows and if there is anything that they don't understand on the timeline or that is new information for them. One thing that may surprise students is that dinosaurs and people are so far apart. Many people believe that they lived at the same time, but the dinosaurs died about 65 million years before humans appeared.
- Ask students to share any doubts or questions they have. Tell them that the reading may help answer their questions.

Suggested Answers

I see a lizard/dinosaur/ape/person. The timeline tells me about how animals have changed over many years.

Cool Down

Have students visualize, then act out the following: a dinosaur dancing; a lizard playing soccer; a frog swimming; a fish singing; a bird eating breakfast; a monkey climbing a tree.

Now read Timelines

Nonfiction: *Timelines—* Informational Text

Lesson Objectives

- to learn about chronology through timelines
- to read an informational text about timelines
- to practice the reading skill of visualizing change
- to make a personal connection to the reading

Materials

Audio Tracks 13 and 14

Warm Up

Draw a timeline on the board with key years from your life, e.g. the year you started school, the year you finished your studies, the year you started teaching, and so on. Have students guess what happened in each year. Write in the facts when they guess correctly.

TRACK 13 TB p. 229 Reading Approach

First Reading: Engage with the Text

- Have students close their books. Write the following on the board: first life on earth, people, dinosaurs, primates, amphibians, reptiles. Explain any words that students don't understand. Ask *Which came first? Which came next?* and have students guess the order.
- Then play the audio while students follow along in their books. Stop after *Human beings appear* and check the timeline against the earlier predictions.
- Play the audio to the end, then look at the Words in Context.

TRACK 14 TB p. 229 Words in Context

- Play the audio and have students repeat the words.
- Have a race to find the words in the text.
- Play the audio again and tell students to **use pictures in the reading to help establish the meaning of the new words**. Have them discuss their ideas with a partner, using L1 if necessary.
- Then bring the class together and use these discussion points to confirm the meanings.

apes (p. 35) Have students look at the pictures. Ask *How are monkeys, apes, and humans different?* (Apes are bigger than monkeys and have no tails. Both have hair on their bodies, which is different from humans.)

extremely (p. 36) Ask *Do you think the bikes were very bumpy or not at all? What word gives us a clue?* (the name Boneshaker) *Do you think* extremely *is stronger than* very *or not as strong?*

chain (p. 36) Elicit that a chain is part of the bike and have them find it in the picture.

sundials (p. 37) Ask *What is this object used for?* (telling the time) *Does it go inside or outside?* (outside) *What gives us a clue about how it works?* (the word *sun* at the beginning).

mechanical (p. 37) Elicit that *mechanical* is an adjective, which describes the clock. Ask *What other objects are mechanical?* (wind-up toys, robots, etc) *How are these mechanical objects similar?* (They are all machines, they all have moving parts.)

International English

Have students notice the different spelling of the words. Point out that they are pronounced the same.

Second Reading: Analyze the Text and Features

- Now give students time to read the text silently and find which timelines show the longest and shortest periods of time (longest: history of life on Earth, pp. 34–35; shortest: history of bikes, pp. 36–37). To check understanding, ask *When did life start on Earth?* (3.8 billion years ago)
- Have students answer the questions in the blue boxes.
  - **Making Connections** (p. 34): *What different ways can we show time passing?* Invite suggestions from students—they will now have ideas from the previous reading and from this one.
  - **Fact** (p. 36): *John Dunlop invented rubber wheels filled with air in 1888. Biking became more comfortable.* Ask students why it was more comfortable (the air acted like a cushion). Do they think this was the most important change to happen to bikes? Why or why not?
  - **Personalization** (p. 37): *Which timeline do you think is most interesting? Why?* Have students discuss their ideas with a partner. Then have students vote for the most interesting timeline.
- Discuss the text focus: *A timeline shows us events in the order they happened. What is the benefit of seeing the* ***chronology*** *of events?* Give students some thinking time, then have them discuss the question in pairs.

Third Reading: Interact with the Text

- Ask students to visualize traveling back in time to use either the draisine bike or the sundial. Encourage them to think about what would be good and bad about each experience. Have them share their ideas in pairs, then compare and contrast the draisine bike with the smart bike or the sundial with the smart watch. Which pair found the most similarities/differences?

Cool Down

Work as a class to build a timeline on the board. Ask students to think of all the ways that people wrote before the modern pen, from making marks on stones with other stones to using chalk, pencils, and feathers and ink, and what might happen in the future.

Explore the Reading

Lesson Objectives

- to understand and analyze *Timelines* through reading comprehension activities
- to practice the reading skill of visualizing change and predicting the future
- to learn about measuring time through CLIL (math): exploring how timelines can help us predict change
- to make a personal connection to the reading

Materials

Some images of futuristic developments to project or show students (WU)

Warm Up

Project onto the board or show students pictures from the internet of some futuristic predictions (e.g. a flying car, a robot teacher, teleportation, or time travel with people watching dinosaurs). For each one, ask students *Do you think it will be possible in the future?* and *When in the future do you think it might happen?*

A **Read and complete.**

- Before students open their books, find out what they remember from the reading. Ask *How many different timelines did the reading show?* (three) *What were they about?* (life on Earth, bikes, measuring time) *When did the first bike appear?* (1816) *Why did bikes become more comfortable?* (James Dunlop invented rubber wheels filled with air.) *In which century did smartwatches appear?* (the 21st century)
- Refer students to the completed example sentence and ask them to find where this information is in the reading (p. 34, at the beginning of the first timeline).
- Have students complete the activity, referring to the text to justify their answers. Then have students compare their answers with a partner.
- To check answers, project the activity onto the board and invite students to come and complete one space each or ask students to read a sentence aloud. Ask if everyone agrees.

Answers

1 *3.8 billion years ago* 2 370 million years ago
3 200,000 years ago 4 running along the ground
5 decade 6 Atomic

B **Think and discuss. Think about the future. Predict what will happen.**

- Remind students of the pictures you showed them in the Warm Up and point out that people are inventing or imagining new things every day! Ask the class for possible ways to finish the prediction about bikes; for example, In the future, bikes will … (not have wheels—they will float above the ground).
- Ask students *What do you think will happen in the future?* Give them some time to look at the three timelines and imagine what might happen next for each. Then have them compare their ideas with a friend. Ask if any pairs would like to share any ideas that were particularly interesting, probable, or funny! Try to elicit at least one or two ideas for the future, for every timeline.

C **Think and write. Look at the timeline below. Add your predictions from B.**

This activity draws on the math focus of looking at how timelines help us predict change. It also encourages students to connect the reading to their own predictions.

- Draw or project the timeline in C onto the board. Ask students for one of their predictions about the future from B and where to place it on the timeline.
- Have students do the activity in their books and then compare their timelines in groups. Ask *Are your timelines the same?*

D **Think and write. Look at the timeline above. When were you born? When were your parents and grandparents born? If you don't know, make a guess!**

- Mark one line on the timeline on the board for when your parents were born. Show it to students and have them guess what happened then. Confirm the answer and next to the line write the sentence *My parents were born.*
- Have students mark lines on the timeline in C to show when they, their parents, and their grandparents were born. Then have them show and tell in pairs.
- Ask if any students would like to share their dates with the class. Find out how many students had the same events in these years. Ask *How is life different now from when your grandparents were born?* Give students a minute to think, then elicit one idea from each student.

Cool Down

Make a short quiz based on the information about timelines. Divide the class into two teams, or groups of four, and have them raise their hands to give an answer and win a point for each question. Alternately, this can be played with the whole class to see how much students remember.

Possible questions: *True or false: Life appeared on Earth 4.8 million years ago.* (False; 3.8 billion years ago) *What type of animals are snakes and lizards?* (reptiles) *When did human beings develop?* (200,000 years ago) *What was the name of the bike invented in 1867?* (Boneshaker) *What did people start to make in the 1920s?* (children's bikes) *Who were the first people to use sundials?* (the Egyptians) *Which nationality invented mechanical clocks?* (Italians) *True or false: Smartwatches became popular in the 1990s.* (False; the 2010s)

Practice **Student's App:** Reading Practice

Think Together

Lesson Objectives

- to make connections between the readings
- to explore the key concept: How do things change over time?
- to reflect on the unit and provide personal thoughts and opinions

Warm Up

Have students look back at the VTR image on pp. 24–25 and ask *Do you now have any new ideas about the image? Are there things you can see in the image that you now think are more important?*

Have students compare their ideas in pairs and then ask for suggestions.

A Look at the pictures. How do things change? Draw.

- Project the two pictures onto the board and ask students *What can you see?*
- Have students look back at the story on pp. 26–31 and remember how the story ended. Ask them *Do you think Ooleck was close to finding a solution?* Have students draw a picture illustrating what they think happened next.
- Have them draw a picture of the latest development in the bike timeline in the other box and then compare their drawings with a friend.
- Ask students if their pictures were very similar or very different. If different, ask them to explain how.

B Think and write. Make a timeline of your life.

- Draw a timeline on the board and insert some key dates from your life or the life of someone famous. (born, started school, started university, became a teacher, moved to a different place, etc.)
- Have students make their own timeline, showing key events in their life. They should label it with short phrases and illustrate it with small pictures if they have time. Give them a minute to reflect on their finished timeline to consider how their own lives have changed over time. Have them look at their finished timelines and consider how their own lives have changed over time.

C Think about the timeline of your life. What events did you put on it? Do a Three-Step Interview.

- Ask two students to read the example sentences in the speech bubbles. Have students suggest how they could complete the second bubble. Then elicit some follow-up questions they could ask, e.g. *When did it happen? What happened after that? What happened next? How did you feel?*
- Set the class up for the Three-Step Interview cooperative learning routine (see TB p. 20). Remind students they need to listen carefully when they interview their partner, as they will tell the other students in their group what they have learned.
- After students have shared what they learned in their groups ask *Did you learn anything interesting about your partner?* and invite students to share any interesting information with the class.
- Introduce the key concept question: *How do things change over time?* Ask students to remember all the changes they learned about in the readings or about each other's lives. Encourage them to expand their thinking to changes they know about elsewhere in their lives, e.g. places that have changed. Have them also consider how ideas change over time as people learn from what has gone before. How have their ideas changed over the course of the unit? Have students discuss their ideas in small groups. Circulate and give students praise for good thinking.

My Reading Journal

What do you want to learn more about? Choose something from one of the readings.

This question focuses on personalization and encourages students to start taking responsibility for their own learning. Give students some thinking time to consider their answers. You can give an example answer of your own first.

Have students write their own sentences and then discuss their answers in pairs or small groups.

Example Answer
I want to learn more about smartwatches, because I think they will be more important in the future.

Cool Down

Play a version of *Find Someone Who* (see TB p. 25). Ask students to think about one thing they enjoyed doing in this unit. Have them circulate and talk to as many people as possible about their chosen activity. When they find someone who liked the same activity, they should stop and have a conversation about why they liked it. Did they like things for the same reasons or different reasons?

Practice Resource Bank: Unit Test
Student's App: Key Concept Practice

UNIT 3

Be My Friend

Unit Overview

Themes

Friendship

Trust

Synopsis

In this unit students will learn about emotions, friendship, and what it means to be a good friend. They will find out about some very special friendships and look at why people experience certain emotions. They will plan and give a presentation about a good friend and write an email to a friend about their feelings using target language from the unit.

Language Book

Vocabulary
calm, confident, embarrassed, grateful, lonely, nervous, proud, relaxed, stressed, upset
p. 80

Explore Language
First Conditional Statements
p. 81

Global Citizenship
What does it mean to be a friend?
break a promise, forgive, get along well with, have a falling out with, keep in touch with, laugh at, tell a secret, make a promise, make friends with
p. 82

Explore Language
First Conditional Questions
p. 83

Take the Stage
Presentation: talking about your friend
p. 84

Write About It
An Email to a Friend
Word building: *and, so, because,* or *but*
p. 85

Think It Over
Review and Reflection
p. 86

Literacy Book

Think Together
What makes a good friend?
p. 93

Visible Thinking
Step Inside
p. 87

Fiction
Story: *Trust Me*

Words in Context: *toddlers, capital, entertaining, trust, genius*
p. 91

Nonfiction
Informational Text: *A Friendly Message*

Words in Context: *communicate, translate, typed, award, personal, friendship*
p. 88

Reading Skill
Describing and understanding characters
p. 90

Spelling Pattern
–ed
p. 89

Language and Literacy Connections

The connecting theme in Unit 3 is friendship and how to be a good friend.

	Language	Literacy
Vocabulary	**Sets 1:** emotions **Set 2:** friendships	**Nonfiction:** grateful, lonely, proud, upset, make friends with **Fiction:** embarrassed
Grammar	**First Conditional Statements** If I get lost, I'll stay calm. **First Conditional Questions** If someone tells you a secret, what will you do?	**Nonfiction** You'll find a way to communicate if you want to! **Fiction** If you study a bit more next time, you'll do a lot better. If we run, will we get away?
Skills	**Pronunciation:** silent *l*	**Reading:** describing and understanding characters **Spelling Pattern:** *–ed*
International English	get along with / get on well with; have a falling out with / fall out with	

Vocabulary

Lesson Objectives

- to learn vocabulary to describe emotions: *calm, confident, embarrassed, grateful, lonely, nervous, proud, relaxed, stressed, upset*
- to sing a song that explores different emotions

Materials
Audio Tracks 27 to 30; Video

Warm Up

Ask students to think about their day yesterday and how they felt throughout the day. Have them draw a quick timeline in their notebooks and then explain to a friend what they did and how they felt at different moments in the day. Ask students for all the adjectives they used to describe their emotions and write them on the board.

A TRACK 27 TB p. 216 **Listen and find. Did Dani have a good day?**

- Have students look at pp. 36–37 and say what they can see. Ask them to compare and contrast what they see in the picture with their own school. Draw attention to the man in the picture and ask *Who's this?* Establish that it is Mr. Sim from Unit 2.
- Play the audio and have students point to the words or pictures as they listen.
- Remind students of the challenge at the end of Unit 2: *What's under my table in my classroom?* If necessary, play the audio again to check the answer. (Dani's lunchbox is under Mr. Sim's table.)
- Ask the gist question *Did Dani have a good day?* and elicit the answer. Ask *Why or why not?*

Answer
He had a good day in the end.

B TRACK 28 TB p. 216 **Listen, say, and number the pictures in A.**

- Play the audio. Have students point to the pictures and say the words.
- Tell students to listen again and write numbers next to the words in the picture. Do the example together. (proud) If students need more time to write their answers, pause the audio.
- Check answers by calling out a number and having students call out the word. Ask a few individual students to repeat each word to check pronunciation.

Answers
1 *proud* 2 nervous 3 lonely 4 upset 5 calm
6 relaxed 7 embarrassed 8 stressed 9 confident
10 grateful

C TRACK 29 TB p. 216 **Close your eyes. Listen, visualize, and say.**

- Prepare students for the visualization (see TB p. 21).
- Play the audio, allowing students to visualize the ideas as they listen.
- Have students work in pairs. Students should take turns miming one of the emotions from the visualization and have their partner guess what it is.

D **Look and write.**

- Tell students they are going to categorize the vocabulary into two sets. Ask students why the words *relaxed* and *upset* are in different groups. Elicit that *relaxed* is a positive feeling and *upset* is negative. Now give students time to decide about the other adjectives and write them in the correct column in their books.
- Draw or project the table onto the board and invite students to come to the board and complete one item each in the appropriate column.

Answers
Smiley face: *relaxed*; confident; calm; proud; grateful
Sad face: *upset*; nervous; stressed; embarrassed; lonely

E TRACK 30 TB p. 216 **Listen and complete. Then watch and sing.**

- Point to the song title *You'll Be Fine*. Ask *What do you think the song will be about?* and elicit suggestions.
- Then play the song once, allowing students to listen and enjoy it.
- Have students complete as many of the missing words as they can, using the initial letters as clues. Point out that all the words they need are on pp. 36–37, so they can check their spelling.
- Play the song again, this time pausing for students to write any missing answers. Then check answers as a class.
- Play the song video and encourage students to sing along and act out all of the emotions in the song.

Answers
1 *nervous* 2 relaxed 3 grateful 4 embarrassed
5 proud 6 upset

Cool Down

Play *Running Spelling* (see TB p. 26) with the new vocabulary from this lesson.

Practice **Student's App:** Vocabulary Practice; Song Video

Explore Language

Lesson Objectives

- to learn how to use first conditional statements
- to practice vocabulary for talking about emotions

Materials
Audio Tracks 31 and 32

Warm Up

Brainstorm places in the world where students would like to go (countries or cities) and write their ideas on the board. Ask *How do you think you would feel at the beginning of a trip like this?*

A TRACK 31 TB p. 216 **Listen and read. How does Lizzie feel about her trip?**

- Have students look at the pictures on p. 38 and ask *What can you see? What do you think the people in the pictures are talking about?* Draw their attention to the girl on the right in the first picture and establish that it's Hana from the previous lesson.
- Play the audio and have students follow in their books.
- Ask the gist question *How does Lizzie feel about her trip?* and elicit the answer. Ask *What words about emotions from the previous lesson did you see and hear in this story?* Play the audio again for students to check. (nervous, excited, upset, calm, lonely)

Answer
She's excited.

B Look at A. Complete.

- Write or project the table onto the board.
- Refer students to the first sentence in the table. Have students find it in the dialogue and complete it in the table. Elicit the answer and write it on the board.
- Have students work in pairs to fill in the blanks and complete the table.
- Nominate students to read the completed sentences aloud. Ask if everyone agrees and complete the table on the board.
- Ask students *What do we need to make a first conditional sentence?* (if + simple present verb in one part, will + verb in the other part) Ask students *Can you change the order and put* if *in the middle?* (yes) Point out that there is a comma in the first sentence, but that if we change the word order and put *if* in the middle of the sentence, we don't use a comma. Ask students how they could change the order of the first sentence in the table.
- Have students look at the Grammar tip *Watch Out*. Ask students *What form of the verb do we use after "if"?* (simple present) *And in the other part of the conditional sentence?* (will + base verb). Point out that we never use *will* in the same part of the sentence as *if*.

Practice Resource Bank: Grammar Printout
Student's App: Grammar Practice

Answers
get; 'll; help; if; ask

C Think and discuss. Then choose.

- Have students look at the sentence in C. Give them some thinking time and then have them work with a partner to choose an answer and discuss.
- Read the sentence and answer options and have students raise their hands for the option they chose. Confirm the answer. Point out that the *will* part of the sentence talks about the possible outcome of something that is happening in the present.

Answer
1 a possible action in the future

D TRACK 32 TB p. 216 **Listen and say.**

- Play the audio and have students listen and repeat. For ideas on how to vary the drill, see TB p. 23.

E Read and complete.

- Refer students to the completed example sentence and elicit why we use *do* in the first part of the sentence and *feel* in the second part (feeling proud is the predicted result of doing well.).
- Have students complete the other sentences and compare answers with a friend.
- Project or write the answers on the board for students to check.

Answers
1 *do; 'll feel* 2 don't work; won't get 3 borrow; 'll be
4 're; 'll be

F Write and complete. Then compare. Who has more sentences?

- Tell students that in this activity, they need to think of different ways to finish each sentence. Elicit some more examples for ending the first sentence, e.g. … I'll finish my homework.
- Give students some time to think of two or three endings for each sentence (they can write more if they want). Point out that the second sentence uses can't—this is a little different but still follows the rule of if + simple present. Then have students compare with a partner and combine their ideas. Remind students to check they are using the simple present and *will* in the right places.
- Invite pairs to share different ways to finish each sentence. Ask each pair how many sentences they made in total. Who wrote the most sentences?

Cool Down

Have students build conditional sentences around the class, contributing one word each. You can start each sentence by giving the first word (e.g. *If* …) and also add in new words if you think the sentence needs redirecting.

Global Citizenship

Lesson Objectives

- to learn vocabulary for talking about friendships: *break a promise, forgive, get along well with, have a falling out with, keep in touch with, laugh at, make a promise, make friends with, tell a secret*
- to explore what it means to be a friend
- to practice listening for gist and details

Materials

Audio Tracks 33 to 35; Audio Track C; a world map (D)

Opening Question

Ask the opening question: *What does it mean to be a friend?* Have students discuss in pairs and then elicit opinions. Ask students *What can happen if people aren't good friends?*

A TRACK 33 TB p. 216 **Listen to Paula talk to her mom about friendship. Who's Kari?**

- Tell students they are going to listen to a conversation between a daughter and her mom about friendship. Ask students *What do you think is happening in each picture? Do you think they are friends?*
- Play the audio and have students point to the words or pictures as they listen.
- Ask the comprehension question *Who's Kari?* Elicit answers, then play the audio again for students to check.

Answer

Paula's mom's friend

International English

Elicit which expressions are American English and which are British English. Point out that the American English phrases are used in the dialogue but that both are correct.

B TRACK 34 TB p. 216 **Listen, say, and number the pictures in A.**

- Play the audio and have students point to the pictures and say the words.
- Tell students to listen again and number the pictures in the order they hear them.
- Check answers by asking volunteers to call out the numbers and asking others to respond.

Answers

1 *forgive* 2 make a promise 3 laugh at 4 make friends with 5 break a promise 6 get along well with 7 have a falling out with 8 keep in touch with 9 tell a secret

TRACK C TB p. 216 **Visualization**

The TTL has a visualization audio track for this vocabulary set. (See TB p. 21.)

C Read and complete.

- Have students quickly read the text without thinking about how to complete the blanks yet. Ask students *Do you think Beth is a good friend? Why or why not?* (not always—she's often late!)
- Refer students to the example answer and point out it comes from the phrase on p. 40, *get along well with*. Have students complete the activity and compare answers.
- Check answers as a class.

Answers

1 *get* 2 tell 3 laugh 4 made 5 broke 6 forgave

D TRACK 35 TB p. 216 **Now listen to Carla and Sem. Where did they meet their friends?**

- To generate interest, have students look at the two pictures and notice where each child is from. Ask students *Where are these countries?* Use a map to find them.
- Have students look at the pictures and ask them *How do you think the people in these pictures are feeling? What do you think they're going to talk about?*
- Listening for gist: Ask the gist question *Where did they meet their friends?* and elicit suggestions. Play the audio, then check the answer.

Answer

at school

E Listen again and answer the questions.

- Listening for details: have students look at the example answer and ask them to answer as many questions as they can.
- Play the audio again and have students answer the remaining questions.

Answers

1 *She was five.* 2 She lives in another city. 3 They send photos and videos. 4 He was six. 5 No, he was nervous. 6 His friends helped him.

Discussion Questions

- Draw students' attention to the discussion questions: *What different kinds of friendships do you have? Why are friends important?* Have students discuss the questions in small groups (see **ETB**).
- Return to the opening question to ask again: *What does it mean to be a friend?* Ask students if listening to Paula, her mom, Carla, Sem, and their own friends has given them any new ideas to answer that question.

Cool Down

Play *Board Race* with the word *friends* (see TB p. 25).

Practice **Student's App:** Vocabulary Practice; Listening Practice

Explore Language

Lesson Objectives

- to learn how to make questions using the first conditional
- to practice using vocabulary to describe friendship

Materials
Audio Tracks 36 and 37

Warm Up

Brainstorm activities that students are expecting to do later today. Write key words on the board, then ask what can go wrong with each one (e.g. *do homework—forget your books!*). For each problem, see if students can suggest a creative solution.

A TRACK 36 TB p. 217 **Listen and read. Does Amit tell Lizzie's secret?**

- Ask students *What can you see in the picture? What do you think the boys are doing?*
- Play the audio and have students follow the dialogue in their books.
- Ask gist question *Does Amit tell Lizzie's secret?* Elicit the answer and then play the audio again for students to check.

Answer
No, he doesn't.

B **Look at A. Complete.**

- Write or project the table onto the board.
- Refer students to the first incomplete question in the table and have them find it in the dialogue and write it in the table. Elicit the answer and write it on the board.
- Have students work in pairs to complete the second question.
- Invite students to come to the board to write one word each in the blanks. Have students identify the question word *how*. Ask *What kind of word follows a question word?* (a verb) Write *Lizzie will feel angry if you break a promise* onto the board and have students compare this to the first question in the table. Point out that *will* and the subject change places in the question form.

Answers
will; if; break; If; will; feel

C **Think and discuss. Then choose.**

- Give students time to read the sentence, think about their answer, and then discuss with a friend.
- Read the sentence and answer options and have students raise their hands to show the option they chose.
- Refer students to the Grammar tip *Remember*. Look at the first question in the table again and ask students to identify which part contains a problem and which part is asking about the result of that problem. (Asking about the result comes first; the problem is second.) Remind students that when a question or sentence starts with the result, we don't need to use a comma. Ask *If the sentence starts with* If*, do we need a comma in the middle?* (yes)

Answer
first conditional

D TRACK 37 TB p. 217 **Listen and say.**

- Play the audio and have students listen and repeat. For ideas on how to vary the drill, see TB p. 23.

E **You're moving to a new school. Choose a or b. Write.**

- Tell students to imagine they are moving to a new school. How do they feel?
- Draw students' attention to the two boxes and tell them to imagine they are writing questions from the point of view of a friend who is not moving. Point out these questions are all about possible future problems. Refer students to the example answers and ask *Which word follows the question words?* (will)
- Then have students choose one box, a or b, and use the prompts to write full questions.

Answers
a
1 *How will you contact me if you lose my email address?*
2 How will you feel if you don't make friends?
3 What will happen if you don't like your new school?
b
1 *What will you say if people laugh at your English?*
2 Who will you talk to if you get lonely?
3 What will you say if you don't like your new home?

F **Look at E. Ask and answer. Who has the most positive ideas?**

- Have students work in pairs or small groups to ask and answer their questions. Make sure there is at least one person who wrote questions for a and one who wrote questions for b in each pair or group.
- Ask students if they heard any good ideas and invite them to share them.

Cool Down

Play the *Chain Game* with first conditional questions and answers (see TB p. 25). Play in teams. Ask a question, e.g. *What will you do if it's raining after school?* and have students take turns to answer it by starting *If it's raining …* Students have to remember their teammates' answers as well as say their own. Which team can keep the chain going the longest? Ask a student to suggest a new question and play again.

Practice **Resource Bank:** Grammar Printout
Student's App: Grammar Practice

Take the Stage

Lesson Objectives

- to prepare and give a presentation about similarities and differences between friends
- to recognize and reproduce words with a silent *l*

Materials
Video; Audio Track 38

Warm Up

Divide the class into pairs. Give them two minutes to find three ways that they are the same and three ways that they are different. Encourage them to ask each other yes/no questions to make the task simpler; for example, *Do you like …? Do you have …? Do you play …?*

A TB p. 238 **Watch and listen. What's the difference between the two friends?**

- Tell students they are going to watch a video of a girl named Rania talking about her best friend. Ask *Do you think they will be very similar or very different?* Play the video.
- Introduce the gist question *What is the difference between the two friends?* Elicit the answer, then play the video again to check. Ask questions to check comprehension; for example, *How tall is Suyin?* (the same height as her friend) Play the video again and ask students to notice Rania's body language when she talks about her friend.

Answer
She doesn't like playing sports, but her friend does.

B Watch again. Check (✔) the sentences you hear.

- Have students read the sentences.
- Play the video again and have students complete the activity. Read the sentences and have students raise their hands for the ones they checked. Play the video again and have them correct the unchecked phrases.
- Ask students to categorize all the phrases into three groups: things they do together (3), phrases to talk about similarities (1, 2, 4, 5, 6), and phrases to talk about differences (7, 8, 9).

Answers
1; 2; 4; 5; 7; 8; 9

Pronunciation Silent *l*

TRACK 38 TB p. 217 **Listen and say.**

- Walk from one side of the classroom to the other and ask students *What am I doing?* Elicit and write *walking* on the board. Say the word and ask students *Can you hear a "l" sound in the word?* (no) Point out that *l* is a silent letter in this word.
- Read the words aloud. Then play the audio and have students repeat the words. Repeat if students need more practice. Ask students if they hear the letter *l* in the other words.
- Say *These words are used in the video. What other words do you know that are pronounced in the same way?* Have students work in pairs. If they have any difficulty, remind them of these words: *calm, would, should, salmon.* Write all the words on the board and drill them for pronunciation.

C Plan. Think about a friend. Then complete.

- Tell students they are going to plan their own presentation about one of their friends, like the one in the video. Draw or project the plan in C onto the board and elicit what kind of information needs to go into each box.
- Then have students complete the plan in their notebook with information about their best friend.

D Prepare your presentation. Use your ideas from C and phrases from B.

- Play the video again as a model and remind students to watch with their own presentation in mind.
- Refer students to the template in D and elicit that the middle section is where they will talk about their friend's character and appearance, the things they do together, and how they are similar and different. Have students transfer their ideas from C into the template, using the phrases from B where appropriate.

E Practice with a friend. Then share with your class.

- Now have students practice their presentation with a friend. Remind students that, like Rania in the video, they should smile while they are speaking and sound interested in talking about their friend.
- Invite volunteers to come to the front of the classroom to give their presentation. Have the audience give a round of applause after each presentation.

Cool Down

Play *Change It Round* with the following sections of the presentation (see TB p. 25):

Suyin is kind and helpful. She always talks to you if you feel lonely or upset. If you tell her a secret, she won't tell anyone else. We have the same interests and hobbies: modern dance, cooking, and watching movies.

There is only one difference between us. Suyin loves playing sports, but I don't!

Have students work in groups to rewrite the underlined sections.

Practice Student's App: Speaking Skills Practice; Speaking Video

Write About It

Lesson Objectives

- to learn how to use the conjunctions *and*, *because*, *so*, *but*, *or*
- to plan and write an email to a friend about feelings

Materials

(Optional) Challenge, Standard, and Support writing printouts, one per student (C and D)

Warm Up

Ask students to remember something funny that happened in the last few days that they talked about or will talk and laugh about with their best friend. Have them share their memories with a partner and then ask if any students would like to share their ideas with the class.

A Read the email. Circle *and*, *because*, *but*, *or*, *so*.

- Have students quickly read the email and say if Robbie had a good or bad day overall. (bad) Ask some further comprehension questions; for example, *Did Robbie's day start well or badly?* (It started OK.)
- Have students find and circle all the examples of *and*, *because*, *but*, *or*, and *so*. Ask students which word introduces why something happened (because), which one combines similar ideas in the same sentence (and), which one combines contrasting ideas in the same sentence (but), which one gives two alternates (or), and which one introduces a result (so). Have them find a sentence from the email to illustrate each definition.

Answers

Hi Arif,

What a day! It started OK. I felt proud in science *because* I got a good grade on my project. We listened to a really interesting poem in English, but then everything changed in history. I was tired, so I fell asleep. Suddenly, I woke up. Everyone laughed at me, and my teacher was annoyed. Now I have to do extra homework or stay after school for an hour! Then in math, I was stressed because we had a test, and at lunchtime I was upset because my friend kicked my ball into the river.

Oh well, perhaps tomorrow will be better. We have art first, and we're going to paint a mural at the playground. I'm really excited about that.

Bye, Robbie

B Read and choose.

- Read the example sentence aloud and ask students why *but* is the correct answer (they are two opposite ideas—the second part is not a result of the first).
- Now have students complete the activity and compare answers with a friend.
- Write or project the answers onto the board for students to check.

Practice Student's App: Writing Practice

Answers

1 *but* 2 so 3 and 4 because 5 or

C Plan. Think about your day at school yesterday. Then complete.

- Draw or project the table onto the board. Refer students to the example and elicit some alternate ways they could complete the third column using different conjunctions, e.g. *and happy; but then I felt sick; so I played well.*
- Then look at the next row and elicit an example from students for each column.
- Have students complete their table with subjects, feelings, and the continuations. Encourage them to use different conjunctions in each row. You can hand out the Challenge printout at this point.

D Write an email to a friend about your feelings yesterday.

- Tell students they are going to write an email to a friend. Elicit how they can start their email—say *Hi*, then give an idea about the day; for example, *What a day!* or *I had a fantastic day!* or *My day was very normal …*
- Then have students continue the email in their notebooks following the model in A and using their ideas from C. Point out they can change the order of the information; for example, *I was upset in history, because the teacher was annoyed*, or *The history teacher was annoyed with me, so I was upset.*
- Have students self-correct or exchange their work with a friend and peer-correct. You can put a checklist of points for students to look out for on the board (e.g. spelling, commas, capital letters, conjunctions).
- Have students correct any mistakes and write their final instructions neatly on paper or hand out the Support and Standard printouts from the Resource Bank.
- Have students share their finished email with a friend and see if they have any similarities. Ask *Who had the better day?*
- Ask students if they used the conjunctions correctly. If they are not sure, they can check with a friend or ask for your help. Allow them time to make any further changes to their work.

Cool Down

Play *Never-Ending Sentence* by using the conjunctions from this lesson (see TB p. 26).

Think It Over

Lesson Objectives

- to review what has been learned in the unit
- to reflect on the unit and their own progress
- to think about learning strategies and how to continue learning

Warm Up

Do a quick quiz on the content of the unit. Divide the class into two teams and give points to the first team of students to raise their hands (not call out!) and then give the right answer. Suggested questions: *What's the name of the song in this unit?* (*You'll Be Fine*) *Where is Lizzie going?* (New York) *Where did Sem live before the USA?* (Namibia) *What's the name of Dani's friend?* (Amit) *What does Suyin love doing?* (playing sports) *Which teacher was annoyed with Robbie?* (his history teacher)

Read the questions and draw or write your answers.

- Give students time to think about and discuss activities in the unit before they complete each question. Explain that they can choose to either write a few words or sentences or to draw a picture. Allowing students to make a personal response will help them retain knowledge and engage with the learning points.

What did I do?

- Give students a few minutes to look back through the unit at the different activities they did. Ask questions about the unit or write questions on the board for students to discuss in pairs or small groups; for example, *What did you sing about? What stories did you talk about? What did you write about?*
- Encourage students to identify something in the unit that they found challenging or something that was particularly memorable for them. Students can draw or write about their chosen activity.

What did I learn?

- Have students talk to a partner about what they remember from the unit—stories, words, phrases, people, emotions.
- Ask questions about the unit to help students think about what they learned; for example, *What did you learn about being a good friend? What did you learn about different conjunctions? What else did you learn?* Have students discuss their ideas in pairs.
- Encourage students to draw a picture or write sentences about their learning outcomes.

How did I learn?

- Ask students how they learned the emotion words in Lesson 1. Elicit ideas (by seeing and miming the words, by doing the visualization activity, by hearing the words in the story, by doing a writing or speaking activity).
- Then encourage students to think about how they learned throughout the unit; for example, how did they develop their listening skills?
- Encourage students to draw a picture or write about some of the activities that helped them learn. Then have them compare their answers in pairs and think about what was similar and what was different about how they learned. *Ask do we all learn in the same way?*

How well did I do?

Ask students to color in the face that best expresses how well they think they learned the unit content (i.e. the happier the face they color, the more they feel they have learned). Ask *What do you understand? What do you need to practice more?* Encourage students to look back through the unit to see how much they remember, what they did well, and what they found difficult.

What can I do next?

- Ask students to think about what they can do at home to improve their English. Have them suggest some verbs that they can use (e.g. watch, read, think, practice, sing) and write the verbs in their books. Students can look back at the previous units to get more ideas. Encourage students to suggest their own ideas for different activities they can do.
- Have students choose several activities that they would like to do and write them in their notebooks. They can then share their ideas with a partner.

Looking Forward

Draw students' attention to the character at the bottom of the page. Ask *Who's this?* and elicit what they can remember about him. (Amit discussed secrets with Dani in Explore Language 2) Ask students *Can you guess where his uncle works?* Elicit predictions about Amit's uncle and Unit 4, and tell students they will find out in the first lesson of next unit.

Practice **Resource Bank:** Unit Test
Student's App: Vocabulary and Grammar Review

Literacy

Get Ready to Read

Lesson Objectives

- to activate prior knowledge about friendship
- to encourage students to observe and interpret through a Step Inside VTR
- to preview the reading skill of describing and understanding characters

Materials
(Optional) VTR printout from the Resource Bank (A, B, C)

Warm Up

Ask all students to remember a time when a friend helped them and how. Have students discuss with a partner.

Step Inside

A Look at the picture. Choose a person, animal, or thing. What can they see?

- Students are going to do a Step Inside VTR to explore the image on pp. 40–41. This routine encourages them to step inside a person or object that they can see and imagine their point of view. (See TB p. 20.)
- Ask students *What can you see in the picture?* Elicit suggestions (donkeys, grass, trees, umbrella, kids, girls, bowl of food, adult, hat, coat, gloves).
- Ask students to imagine that they are one of the people, animals, or things in the photo. Tell students *You are putting yourself in their shoes,* and explain this concept.
- Ask students *What can you see (from that person, animal, or thing's viewpoint)?* Encourage them to think about the surroundings. Ask them, for example, *What is she you doing? What is she wearing? How is she feeling? Hot or cold? Excited or bored?* Have students discuss their ideas in pairs and then as a class.

Here's an example of this part of the routine.
Student A: This donkey is hungry! It sees some little humans and one big one.
Teacher: Great. What else can the donkey see?
Student A: It sees some food. The food smells good!
Teacher: OK, Student B, what can your person, animal, or thing see?

B What do you think they believe?

- Tell students again that they need to imagine what's happening in the head of the person, animal, or thing they chose. Check students understand that *believe* means to have an opinion about something. Say *I think the woman believes those donkeys are friendly. What does your person, animal, or thing believe?*
- Give students time to think about the person, animal, or thing they have chosen and their thoughts and opinions. Have students discuss their ideas in pairs and then as a class.

Here's an example of this part of the routine.
Teacher: Who did you decide to be in in the picture?
Student A: The girl with the bowl.
Teacher: OK, so what does she believe?
Student A: She believes that the other children are her friends.
Student B: She believes the donkeys are friendly.
Student C: She believes they like food!

C What do you think they care about?

- Say *I care about the environment, so I always recycle.* Then ask students *If you care about something, is that thing important to you or not?* (yes)
- Ask students to think about what is important to the people, animals, or things in the picture. Give students time to think then discuss in pairs. Elicit ideas.

Here's an example of this part of the routine.
Student A: The donkey cares about food! It doesn't want to be hungry.
Teacher: Does it care about the people?
Student A: Yes, it likes people.
Teacher: Why do you think that?
Student A: Its head is forward.
Student B: But its ears are back. I don't think it likes the people.

Transition

Ask students *Who is making friends in the picture? Do you think people and animals can be friends?* Take a vote and then discuss as a class.

D Think, discuss, and write. What are some ways to make a new friend? Make a list.

- Ask students to remember how they made or met one of their friends. Ask for a couple of suggestions about how to make a new friend.
- Give students time to think of more ideas and then discuss ideas in pairs. Have them choose and write their four best ideas.

E Think and discuss. How do you think a new student in a class feels?

This is a preview of the reading skill of describing and understanding characters.

- Ask students *Have you ever had the experience of being a new student in a class? Is it a fun or a scary experience?* Ask students to imagine how a new person in their class would feel and how they could help them. Have students discuss their ideas in pairs and then as a class.

Now read **A Friendly Message**

Nonfiction: *A Friendly Message*—Informational Text

Lesson Objectives

- to read an informational text about two children making friends
- to learn about sociology and technology through CLIL (science): making connections between social relationships and communication
- to make a personal connection to the reading

Materials

Audio Tracks 15 and 16

Warm Up

Use the first blue box questions on p. 42 for a Warm Up discussion: *Do you ever write notes? Who do you write them to?* Have students discuss their ideas with a partner. Then ask the class *What situations do people write notes in?* (To remind someone to do something, to let someone know about something that happened when they weren't there, to give useful information, etc.)

TRACK 15 TB p. 229 Reading Approach

First Reading: Engage with the Text

- Have students look at the title and pictures on pp. 42–43. Ask *Who can you see? Do you think they are friends?* Draw students' attention to the picture of the note. Ask them *What language is the note written in?* See if they can guess what the problem in the story is.
- Play the audio while students follow along in their books. Ask *What words can you think of to describe Amanda?*
- Then look at the Words in Context.

TRACK 16 TB p. 230 Words in Context

- Play the audio and have students repeat the words.
- Have students race to find the words in the text.
- Tell students they can sometimes **use knowledge of the structure of words to help establish the meaning of new words** (see TB p. 22). Have them discuss their ideas with a partner, using L1 if necessary.
- Then bring the class together and use these discussion points to confirm the meanings.

communicate (p. 42) Ask *What type of word is it?* (a verb) Ask *What is the problem? What other way to communicate could Amanda use?*

translate (p. 43) Ask *What language did Amanda write in? What language did the smartphone give her? Can you translate any languages?*

typed (p. 43) Elicit that *typed* is a verb. Have students mime typing on a smartphone and ask where else they might type (e.g. a computer keyboard).

award (p. 43) Elicit what type of word it is (a noun). Elicit that an award is a positive thing and that the phrase *for being kind* tells us this. Ask *What do you think the school gave her?*

personal (p. 44) Ask *What type of word is it?* (an adjective) *Do you know a similar word?* (person). Elicit that a personal message is written for one person to read.

friendship (p. 45) Ask *What type of word is it?* (a noun) *Do you know a similar word?* (friend) Elicit that *friendship* is the a situation between friends.

Second Reading: Analyze the Text and Features

- Have students read the story without the audio and find how many people were happy as a result of Amanda's note (Amanda, Rafael, their parents, the school directors).
- Discuss the other question in the blue box as a class.
  - **Making Connections** (p. 45): *Do you have any friends who speak different languages at school and at home?* Ask students why this happens and whether it is a disadvantage or not. Elicit some ideas, but don't correct them. Give them time, either in class or at home, to do some online research about children who speak different languages. Find out if students' ideas have changed. (It is often an advantage—children usually learn the second language quickly, and learn other languages more easily later on.)

Third Reading: Interact with the Text

- Have students read the text again, underline the key events, and circle any words that show how the characters are feeling at each point in the story.
- Divide the class into groups of three or four to compare ideas. Then have them mime each section of the story, focusing on the key events and using the words they circled; e.g. part 1: Rafael looking upset, the teacher talking to him, and Amanda about to give him a note.

Cool Down

Read some phrases that don't actually appear in the story but which students can imagine one character saying. Have students say who they think said each one.

Suggested phrases: *This is for you.* (Amanda to Rafael) *Your daughter is very kind!* (Rafael's parents) *We are proud of you and want to give you this award.* (the school director) *Amanda is my best friend.* (Rafael) *Rafael, do you understand the activity?* (the teacher) *Mom, I don't want to go to school!* (Rafael—before he had a new friend!)

Explore the Reading

Lesson Objectives

- to understand and analyze *A Friendly Message* through reading comprehension activities
- to learn about sociology and technology through CLIL (science): making connections between social relationships and communication
- to identify and practice words ending in *–ed*

Materials
Audio Track 17

Warm Up

Give students a minute to look at Amanda's message to Rafael from p. 42 (in English). Then with books closed, have them work in pairs to write as much of the note as they can remember. Tell them to focus on the main ideas, rather than word for word accuracy. Then have them compare their version with Amanda's. How much did they remember?

"H_ll_, R_f_ _l. W_ _ld y_ _ l_k_ t_ s_t w_th m_ t_d_y? L_ _k f_r m_ _nd _ w_ll sh_w y_ _ wh_r_ _ s_t. W_ c_n c_l_r _r s_mply t_ll sc_ry st_r_ _s. Th_nk y_ _ f_r y_ _r t_m_."

A Read and match.

- Refer students to the example sentence. Elicit that *so* gives a result and *because* tells us the reason.
- Have students complete the activity and then compare their answers with a friend. Nominate pairs of students to read aloud a first and second part. Write the answers on the board.

Answers
1 b 2 f 3 a 4 d 5 c 6 e

B Read and write *True* or *False*.

- Refer students to the first sentence and ask *Is it is true or false?* (False. She invited him to sit with her.)
- Have students complete the activity. Ask students to read sentences and have the others raise their hands if the answer is true and lower them if it is false.

Answers
1 False 2 False 3 True 4 False 5 True 6 True

C Think and discuss. How could you use an app to help you with something you do every day?

This activity explores the CLIL focus of making connections between social relationships and communication.

- Ask students which app Amanda used and how it helped her. (She used Google Translate to write her message.) Divide the class into pairs and ask them to think of other apps that could help them in their everyday life. If necessary, brainstorm a list of apps first and build a list on the board.
- Discuss some of the students' ideas as a class. Have students decide which app seems the most useful.

D Think and discuss. Then complete the graphic organizer. What other ways can Amanda and Rafael communicate with each other?

Students are going to connect the reading to the wider world. This draws on the CLIL focus of making connections between social relationships and communication.

- Ask students to imagine you don't speak any English or any of their language. Wave hello to them and smile. Then point to the board, mime writing, and look around you and show that you can't see a board pen. Some students will point to it. Say *We just had good communication without speaking each other's language. How did we do it?* (mime, actions, pointing)
- Ask students to think about other ways Amanda and Rafael could communicate together. Have them compare ideas with a friend and then complete the graphic organizer with their best ideas.

Suggested Answers
They could mime, use hand gestures, point to things, or play games on a computer.

TRACK 17 TB p. 230 Spelling Pattern –ed

Listen and write. Then check your answers.

- With books closed, write *–ed* on the board. Play the first part of the audio and have students repeat each word. Then have them open their books. Play the first part of the audio again and have them complete as many words as they can.
- Play the second part of the audio and have students check their spelling and complete any missing words. Have students underline *ed* at the end of each word and read the words aloud.
- Ask students *What verb form are all of these words in?* Elicit that these are all simple past verbs ending in *ed*. (Note that *annoyed* can be an adjective, but it is a simple past verb here.)
- Then ask students to find more words in the text that end in *ed*. Invite them to read the words aloud. Have students write all the *ed* words from the lesson in a word cloud.

Answers
1 waited 2 annoyed 3 decided 4 recognized
5 slipped 6 hugged
In the reading: moved; decided; used; called; typed; clicked; copied; explained; received; talked

Cool Down

Have students draw a picture of their favorite part of the story of Amanda and Rafael. Then have them share with students around them. This could make part of a wall display.

Practice **Resource Bank:** Spelling Printout
Student's App: Reading Practice; Spelling Pattern Practice

Get Ready to Read

Lesson Objectives

- to encourage students to consider how we can understand characters from what they do or say
- to review and practice the reading skill of describing and understanding characters
- to preview the SEL competency of social awareness through evaluating others' emotional reactions

Materials

Large sheets of paper, one per group (C)

Warm Up

Play *Shark* (see TB p. 26) with some of the adjectives from A or B. Suggested words to use: *friendly, proud, nervous, lonely, confident.*

A Read and complete. What is Amanda like?

Students are going to review and practice the skill of describing and understanding characters.

- Remind students of the words they used in the Warm Up game. Ask them which of these adjectives they think are true about Amanda.
- Decide on the answer for the first sentence with the whole class, and then have students complete the activity individually.
- To check answers, ask students to read complete sentences aloud and check if everyone agrees.
- Introduce the SEL competency of evaluating others' emotional reactions. Ask students *What did Amanda want Rafael to feel when he saw the note? Why? What did Amanda imagine Rafael was feeling before?*
- Have students read the skills box about understanding characters. Tell students that the choices, thoughts, words, and actions that characters make are all things that help to develop the themes and plot in a story. Sometimes characters symbolize certain qualities, such as courage, which gives us clues to help us understand the overall message or theme in the text. You could also point out that in some stories characters are more important than the plot. Can they think of any examples of stories like this? Understanding characters in a story, or real people in an article, also helps us understand the people we know.

Answers

1 kind 2 clever 3 friendly 4 proud

B Think, write, and discuss. How would you describe Rafael before and now? Why?

- Read the adjectives and have students raise their hands and say *Positive!* or lower their hands and say *Negative!*
- Ask students to remember the story and say if Rafael's emotions were more positive before or after Amanda's note.
- Then have students complete the sentences by choosing some of the adjectives in the box. Have them compare sentences with a friend. Invite pairs to share whether their answers were the same or different.

Suggested Answers

Before, Rafael was upset, lonely, stressed, and nervous.
Now, he's grateful, happy, and (more) confident.

C Think and discuss. Look at the two characters from *Trust Me*. What do you think they are like?

- Have students look at the pictures two girls who are the main characters in the story. Ask students to think of adjectives to describe them from looking at the pictures.
- Have them share their ideas in small groups. Have one group member act as scribe to capture their group's ideas on a large sheet of paper. Display the sheets of paper on the wall. Tell students they'll check their ideas later after they have read the story.

Cool Down

Students are going to use adjectives describe characters in different stories in the **Literacy Book**. Have students discuss their ideas in pairs.

Suggested characters: Ooleck and Zeena from *A World Without Time* (p. 26); Emil and Mrs. Blanche from *True Colors* (p. 10).

Now read **Trust Me**

Fiction: *Trust Me*—Story

Lesson Objectives

- to read a story about two friends who are very different
- to practice the reading skill of describing and understanding characters
- to make a personal connection to the reading

Materials

Audio Tracks 18 and 19; Video; sheets of paper with character adjectives from the previous lesson (Text Focus)

Warm Up

Ask students the first blue callout question from p. 48: *Who's your oldest friend?* Have students tell a partner about their oldest friend and what makes them special friends. Ask students if they are still good friends with that person and if anyone has their oldest friend in this class.

TRACK 18 TB p. 230 Reading Approach

First Reading: Engage with the Text

- Play the video or audio while students follow along and read.
- When students reach the point of the blue callout box on p. 52, stop and have them answer the question: *Do you know what to do in this situation?* Have students discuss their ideas with a partner. Then elicit suggestions. Continue the video to see if they had the same ideas as Luana.
- Then look at the Words in Context.

TRACK 19 TB p. 230 Words in Context

- Play the audio and have students repeat the words.
- Have students race to find the words in the story.
- Tell students we can sometimes **use the words around the new words to guess their meaning** (see TB p. 22). Have them discuss their ideas with a partner.
- Then bring the class together and use these discussion points to confirm the meanings.

toddlers (p. 48) Have students look at the picture of the two children. Ask students what age they think the toddlers are. (One to three years old—a toddler is a child who is learning to walk.) Ask *Have you had the same friend since you were a toddler?* and elicit answers.

capital (p. 49) Ask *What's the capital of China?* and then have students read ahead to find the answer. Elicit the names of other capital cities around the world.

entertaining (p. 50) Have students find the word and look at the previous sentence. Elicit that *not boring* gives us a clue. Ask *If her stories are not boring, what do you think they are like?* (probably funny and exciting)

trust (p. 52) Ask *Does Maria trust Luana? How do we know?* (The picture shows that she follows her advice.) *If you trust someone, will you tell him or her a secret?* (yes)

genius (p. 53) Elicit that *genius* is an adjective. Ask *Do you think a genius is a positive or negative description of someone?* (Positive, because Maria is hugging Luana.) Encourage students to use what just happened in the story to suggest some synonyms, e.g. *smart, intelligent.*

Second Reading: Analyze the Text and Features

- Now give students time to read the story at their own pace without video or audio. To focus them, ask them to look for one way that Maria helps Luana and one way that Luana helps Maria.
- Ask students if they think the pictures also tell us something about the characters of Maria and Luana.
- Ask some comprehension questions to check understanding: *Are Maria and Luana very similar to each other?* (No, they're very different.) *Did the event with the book change their friendship?* (No, they were still friends.)
- Have students answer the questions in the blue boxes.
  - **Making Connections** (p. 50): *Why is Luana upset?* Ask students to look at the advice Maria gives her and imagine what happened on the test.
  - **Critical Thinking** (p. 51): *Did Luana really see a wolf?* Ask students what they think and why. (No—she didn't know the color of the wolf, and it doesn't sound like a very real story!) Point out Luana is enjoying using her imagination.
  - **Personalization** (p. 53): *Can you think of a difficult time when you helped your best friend?* Ask if any students would like to share a story with the class.
- Discuss the text focus: ***Comparing** characters helps us understand them better. What do these details tell you about Maria and Luana?* Tell students to think of all the differences and similarities between the way the two girls act. Then have them discuss what they learn about the characters from these actions, e.g. Luana is distracted and prefers reading stories to studying; Maria is a strong character who thinks she knows the best way of doing things. Tell students to review the adjectives suggested for each character in the previous lesson. What do they agree/disagree with? Invite them to make changes or add new adjectives to the sheets of paper.

Third Reading: Interact with the Text

- Put students into groups and give each group a problem, e.g. *Luana and Maria are lost in the forest. What do they do?* Have students discuss how Maria would solve the problem and then how Luana would solve it. Have each group join up with another group and compare ideas.

Cool Down

Play *What's the Scene?* (see TB p. 27).

Practice **Student's App:** Fiction Video

Explore the Reading

Lesson Objectives

- to understand and analyze *Trust Me* through reading comprehension activities
- to practice the reading skill of describing characters and understanding how they act
- to explore the SEL competency of social awareness through evaluating others' emotional reactions
- to make a personal connection to the reading

Materials
Video or Audio Track 18

TRACK 18 TB p. 230 **Warm Up**
Play *Who Said It?* by reading phrases from the story (see TB p. 27). Suggested phrases: *What's the capital of China?* (M) *Umm … Sorry, what?* (L) *If you study a bit more next time, you'll do a lot better.* (M) *I once saw a wolf in the forest.* (L) *Wow! Were you scared?* (M) *I made friends with the wolf.* (L) *So, what do we do?* (M) *Best friends always help each other.* (L) Play the video or audio again to check answers.

A Read and complete with *Maria* or *Luana*.

- Before students open their books, have a quick quiz to find out what they remember from the reading. Put students into two teams and have them take turns to answer a question. If they get it wrong, it passes to the other team to answer. Ask *What did the two girls share?* (toys and secrets) *Who was better in school?* (Maria) *Why was Luana upset?* (She didn't do very well on the test.) *Where did they decide to go the next day?* (swimming / the Blue Waterfalls) *How did they escape the bear?* (They lay down and they didn't move.)
- Draw students' attention to the first sentence in A. Decide on how to complete it with the whole class. Ask students if they can find something in the reading to justify the answer. (p. 49: *At school, Maria gets along well with everyone.*)
- Have students complete the activity, referring to the reading to justify their answers. Have students compare their ideas in pairs.
- To check answers, ask students to read the completed sentences aloud.

Answers
1 Maria 2 Maria 3 Luana 4 Maria 5 Luana 6 Luana

B Read and answer.

- Decide on the answer to the first question together as a class. Elicit that the reading does not give us the answer directly, but we can infer it from what we have learned about Maria's character.
- Have students complete the activity and then compare their answers with a friend.
- Ask pairs of students to read their questions and answers aloud. Ask if everyone agrees.

Suggested Answers
1 She wants everyone to do well on the test.
2 She got caught lying. 3 She didn't do well on the test.
4 She wants to cheer up Luana. 5 Luana knew how to stay safe.

C Think and write. Are you more like Maria or Luana? Why?

- If necessary, quickly elicit adjectives to describe the characters of Maria and Luana. Then ask students to decide who they are more like and to write a sentence explaining why.
- Have students share their sentences with a friend. Encourage students to say whether they agree or disagree with what their friend has written.
- Invite volunteers to read their sentence to the class. Then have a show of hands to see how many students think they're more like Maria and how many think they're like Luana.

D Think and discuss. How can you tell when your friends are upset? What do you do to help them?

- Use this activity to explore the SEL competency of evaluating others' emotional reactions. First, ask students *Who gets upset in the story?* (Luana) *How do we know she is upset?* (She looks sad.) *What does Maria do to try to make her feel better?* (She suggests a fun activity.)
- Ask students *What do people look like when they are upset?* and then *How do people act when they are upset?* Elicit ideas for both and write them on the board.
- Have a Group Time discussion (see TB p. 21) about how students can tell if their friends are upset and what they can do to help them. Ensure that they do not discuss other friends in the class. If necessary, write some prompts on the board; for example, *My friend … acts … when he/she is upset. I … to make him/her feel better when he/she is upset.*

Cool Down
Have students discuss, agree on, and write a Friendship Rules poster for the class. Ideas could include: *We listen to each other; We say kind things; We help each other; We take turns; We share; We take care of each other.* Provide language help where necessary, but don't contribute ideas. It's important that the students lead the discussion.

Practice Student's App: Reading Practice

Think Together

Lesson Objectives

- to make connections between the readings
- to explore the key concept: What makes a good friend?
- to reflect on the unit and provide personal thoughts and opinions

Warm Up

Have students look back at the VTR image on pp. 40–41 and ask *Do you now have any new ideas about the people in the image and what they believe or care about? Why? How do you think this image connects to the two stories you read?*

Have students compare their ideas in pairs and then ask for their suggestions.

A Think and discuss. Which of these ideas is in both readings in this unit? Find a sentence in each reading to support your answer.

- Have students complete the activity individually and then work with a friend to discuss ideas and identify sentences in the readings that support their answers.
- Check answers and ask students to give supporting sentences.

Suggested Answers
2; A Friendly Message: p. 44 She explained that Rafael used to feel really nervous about going to school, so she was grateful to Amanda for helping him feel less nervous.
Trust Me: p. 53 Best friends always help each other.

B Think and discuss. How do you help your friends? How do your friends help you? Do a Numbered Heads Together routine.

- Elicit one example of when students in the class help their friends. Then set up the class for a Numbered Heads Together cooperative learning routine (see TB p. 20).
- Have students work in groups to discuss together all the ways they help their friends and how their friends help them.
- When each group has finished their discussion, use the routine to nominate students to from each group to share their group's ideas. Ask the others to listen and say if they also discussed that idea.
- Ask if any students learned a new way to help their friends that they'd like to do in the future.

C Think, read and write. Think of a time when a friend helped you. Write a thank-you message to him or her.

- As an example, work with the whole class to write a thank-you message from Rafael to Amanda (in English). This will allow you to show the message can be expanded; for example, *Thank you for sitting with me and being my friend. Now I don't feel lonely. You are very kind, and you will always be my friend!*
- Have students write a message to a friend who helped them in their notebooks. Point out the *–ing* form of the verb after *Thank you for ...* If students finish quickly, encourage them to expand the message by saying how the thing that their friend did made a difference to them.
- Ask if any students would like to share their message with the class.
- Introduce the key concept question. *What makes a good friend?* Ask students to remember all the ways to be a good friend they've read about in this unit, their classmates' ideas, and their own experience of having a good friend.
- Have students discuss their ideas in pairs. Give each pair some colored paper and have them choose one idea to write down. Make a colorful wall display from the students' ideas, with the question *What makes a good friend?* in the middle.

Practice Resource Bank: Unit Test
Student's App: Key Concept Practice

My Reading Journal

Which reading did you like more? Circle the title and write why.

This question encourages students to give a personal response to the reading. Give students some thinking time to consider their answer and have them circle and complete their answers. Then have students discuss their answers in pairs or small groups.

Answer
Students' own answers.

Find four words in the readings that have to do with real friendship.

Elicit one example from the class and then have students continue the activity individually. Have them compare with a friend.

Example Answer
kind; trust; sharing; help

Cool Down

Have students make an acrostic (a series of words starting with each letter of the initial word) in small groups with the word *friend*. They should try to use words connected to the meaning of *friend*. If students find it difficult to find words starting with the letters, then point out they can use a word with the letter anywhere in it. These acrostics can form part of your wall display. Example acrostic:

Fun person
Remembers your birthday
Invites you to their party
Entertaining
Never mean
Does kind things for you

UNIT 4

What's Up There?

Unit Overview

Themes

Space

Astronomy

Synopsis

In this unit students will learn about space and space exploration. They will find out about the first man in space and think about why it is important for us to learn about space. They will plan and prepare a conversation about preparing a presentation and will write a magazine interview practicing question words and using target language from the unit.

Language Book

Vocabulary
astronaut, astronomer, comet, galaxy, observatory, planet, shooting star, solar system, spaceship, telescope
p. 96

Explore Language
Modal Verbs: *Have to* and *Must*
p. 97

Global Citizenship
Why is it important to learn about space?
crater, Earth, ice cap, iron, Mars, rock, sand dune, satellite, soil
p. 98

Explore Language
Modal Verbs: *Might* and *Should*
p. 99

Talk About It
Conversation: making offers, showing enthusiasm, saying what you know
p. 100

Write About It
A Magazine Interview
Sentence building: reviewing question words
p. 101

Think It Over
Review and Reflection
p. 102

Literacy Book

Think Together
How do we explore space?
p. 109

Visible Thinking
See, Think, Wonder
p. 103

Nonfiction
Biography: *First Man in Space*
Words in Context: *capsule, attitude, failed, pressed, parachuted, hero*
p. 107

Fiction
Story: *Hope You Like Fish*
Words in Context: *launch, Mission Control, blast, gravity, in sight*
p. 104

Reading Skill
Scanning for specific information
p. 106

Spelling Pattern
Long *i*
p. 105

Language and Literacy Connections

The connecting theme in Unit 4 is space and exploration.

	Language	Literacy
Vocabulary	**Set 1:** space **Set 2:** Mars	**Fiction:** astronaut(s), planet, spaceship, Earth, Mars **Nonfiction:** astronaut, planet, Earth
Grammar	**Modal Verbs: *Have* to and *Must*** An astronaut has to speak Russian. You don't have to be good at sports. I must go to the gym. You mustn't give up. **Modal Verbs: *might* and *should*** It might be too heavy. It might not be wide enough. We should clean up the glass. We shouldn't leave it here.	**Fiction** You must sit down! You chimps shouldn't think about food all the time! **Nonfiction** They had to learn to survive on their own.
Skills	**Pronunciation:** word stress 2	**Reading:** scanning for specific information **Spelling Pattern:** long *i*
International English	never give up / you must never give up	high school / secondary school

Vocabulary

Lesson Objectives

- to learn space vocabulary: *astronaut, astronomer, comet, galaxy, observatory, planet, shooting star, solar system, spaceship, telescope*
- to sing a song about astronomy

Materials
Audio Tracks 39 to 42; Video

Warm Up

Write the word *space* in the middle of the board and ask students what words they think of when they think about space. Write them on the board around the central word and then ask students if they can see any of the words on pp. 48–49.

A TRACK 39 TB p. 217 **Listen and find. What does Amit want to be?**

- Have students look at pp. 48–49 and ask *What can you see?* and *Where is it happening? What are the children doing in the picture?* (looking at the stars) Ask students if they can see Amit from Unit 3.
- Play the audio and have students point to the words and pictures as they listen.
- Ask the comprehension question *What does Amit want to be?* and elicit answers. Play the audio again to check.
- Remind students of the challenge at the end of Unit 3: *Where does my uncle work?* Ask *Can you answer Amit's question now?* and elicit the answer (he works in an observatory). If necessary, play the audio again to check.

Answer
an astronaut

B TRACK 40 TB p. 217 **Listen, say, and number the pictures in A.**

- Play the audio. Have students point to the pictures and say the words.
- Tell students to listen again and write numbers next to the words in the picture. Do the example together (astronaut).
- Check answers and ask a few students to repeat each word to check pronunciation.

Answers
1 *astronaut* 2 telescope 3 observatory 4 comet
5 shooting star 6 planet 7 spaceship 8 astronomer
9 galaxy 10 solar system

C TRACK 41 TB p. 217 **Close your eyes. Listen, visualize, and say.**

- Prepare students for the visualization (see TB p. 21).
- Play the audio, allowing students to visualize the vocabulary as they listen.
- Then have students work in pairs to mime one of the words they visualized for their partner, who has to guess the word.

D **Look and write.**

- Project or draw the Venn diagram in D on the board. Explain to students that they are going to categorize the words into things that are in space and things that aren't in space. Point out the word *astronaut*, which fits in both categories.
- Give students some thinking time; then have them complete the activity in pairs. To check answers, invite students to the board to complete the diagram.

Answers
In Space: *comet*; galaxy; shooting star; planet; solar system
Not in Space: *observatory*; astronomer
Both: *astronaut*; spaceship; telescope

E TRACK 42 TB p. 217 **Listen and complete. Then watch and sing.**

- Have students look at the title of the song, *The Astronomer's Song*, and ask them *What do you think the song will be about? Who do you think is singing the song?*
- Then play the song once, allowing students to listen and enjoy it.
- Explain to students that some words are missing and they have to complete them. Ask *Can you guess what words they are?* Encourage them to look at the first letter and complete as many words as they can. Point out that all the words they need are on pp. 48–49, so they can check their spelling.
- Play the song again, this time pausing for students to complete any missing answers. Then check answers as a class.
- Play the song video and have students watch and sing along. Play the song video again and have students add actions for what the astronomer does or says in the song.

Answers
1 *planets* 2 observatory 3 telescope
4 shooting star 5 spaceship 6 astronaut

Cool Down

Play *Draw It!* (see TB p. 25) with the vocabulary from this lesson.

Practice **Student's App:** Vocabulary Practice; Song Video

Explore Language

Lesson Objectives

- to learn how to use modals of obligation: *have to* and *must*
- to practice using space vocabulary

Materials
Audio Tracks 43 and 44

Warm Up

Tell students to imagine they are astronauts and have them walk around the classroom as though they have landed on the moon.

A TRACK 43 TB p. 217 **Listen and read. Why does Alfie want to go to the gym?**

- Have students look at the picture on p. 50 and ask *What can you see? What do you think the people are talking about? Can you see Alfie from the previous lesson?* (He's in the middle here.)
- Play the audio and have students follow the dialogue in their books.
- Ask the gist question *Why does Alfie want to go to the gym?* and elicit the answer. Then ask students why they think Alfie wants to get fit. (He wants to be an astronaut.) Ask *What space words did you see and hear in this story?* (astronaut, Space Station)

Answer
He wants to get fit.

International English

Ask *Do the two sentences mean the same thing?* (yes) Have students say the two phrases with real enthusiasm. Elicit which phrase is American English and which phrase is British English. Ask *Which do we use?*

B Look at A. Complete.

- Write or project the table onto the board.
- Refer students to the first sentence in the table. Have them find it in the dialogue and complete it in the table. Elicit the answer and write it on the board.
- Have students work in pairs to fill in the blanks and complete the table.
- Nominate students to read the completed sentences aloud, ask if everyone agrees and complete the table on the board. Elicit what comes after *have to* and *must* (an infinitive / base form verb) Highlight the *have to* statement and question, and elicit that we add *Do* to make the question but that the word order stays the same. Highlight the *must* statement and question and elicit how the word order is different (subject + *must* + infinitive changes to *must* + subject + infinitive for the question).

Practice **Resource Bank:** Grammar Printout
Student's App: Grammar Practice

- Draw students' attention to the Grammar tip *Look*. Ask *Why do you think some students make the mistake of putting "to" after "must"?* (because of *have to*) Remind them that *must* is like *can, will,* or *should*: there is no need to include *to*!

Answers
has to; have to; go; mustn't; have to

C Think and discuss. Then choose.

- Have students look at the sentences and answer options. Give them some thinking time and encourage them to look at the table and the dialogue to help. Then have them discuss their answers with a partner.
- Read the questions and have the class call out the correct word. Check everyone agrees and confirm the answers.
- Ask students if *You mustn't give up* and *You don't have to give up* have the same meaning. (No, the first sentence is telling us not to do something, and the second is saying it isn't necessary.)

Answers
1 need 2 don't need

D TRACK 44 TB p. 217 **Listen and say.**

- Play the audio and have students listen and repeat. For ideas on how to vary the drill, see TB p. 23.

E Read an astronaut's email to his children and choose.

- Have students read the email quickly and say where the astronaut is writing from (space).
- Refer students to the example answer and elicit why it is *must*. (This is something that is necessary.) Now have students complete the activity individually and then compare answers with a friend.
- To check answers, invite students to read complete sentences aloud.

Answers
1 *must* 2 have to 3 don't have to 4 must

F Ask and answer with *have to, don't have to, must,* or *mustn't.*

- Tell students to imagine they are astronauts answering questions about their job. Look at the questions and elicit one possible answer for each one from the class; for example, *You must play basketball every day. You have to do a lot of homework!*
- Then have students continue to give more suggestions in pairs.
- Ask if the pairs found any answers they'd like to share with the class.

Cool Down

Play *Simon Says* with modals (see TB p. 27). Use actions connected with the theme of space (e.g. *look through a telescope, go in a spaceship, watch a shooting star, count the planets*).

Global Citizenship

Lesson Objectives

- to learn vocabulary for talking about Mars: *crater, Earth, ice cap, iron, Mars, rock, sand dune, satellite, soil*
- to explore why it is important to learn about space
- to practice listening for gist and details

Materials
Audio Tracks 45 to 47; Audio Track D; a world map (D)

Opening Question

Ask students the opening question: Why is it important to learn about space? Give students time to think and then elicit some opinions.

A TRACK 45 TB p. 217 **Listen to an astronaut talk about Mars. What do people call this planet?**

- Have students look at p. 52 and say what they can see. Tell students they are going to listen to an astronaut talk about Mars.
- Play the audio and have students point to the words and pictures as they listen.
- Ask the comprehension question *What do people call this planet?* and elicit the answer. Play the audio again for students to check.

Answer
the Red Planet

B TRACK 46 TB p. 218 **Listen, say, and number the pictures in A.**

- Play the audio and have students point to the pictures and say the words.
- Play the audio again and have students write numbers next to the words in the pictures. Do the example together (Mars).
- Check answers by having one student call out a number and nominating another student to respond.

Answers
1 *Mars* 2 Earth 3 ice cap 4 crater 5 iron
6 rock 7 sand dune 8 satellite 9 soil

TRACK D TB p. 218 **Visualization**

The TTL has a visualization audio track for this vocabulary set (see TB p. 21).

C Read and write.

- Have students read the words in the box aloud. Ask if they remember which ones the astronaut used when he talked about Mars. (all except rock and crater)
- Refer students to the example question and answer. Ask them to imagine the comet hitting the ground.
- Have students complete the activity individually and then compare answers with a friend.
- Check answers as a class.

Answers
1 *crater* 2 ice cap 3 sand dune 4 rock 5 Mars
6 satellite

D TRACK 47 TB p. 218 **Now listen to Max and Lily. Do they talk about plants, experiments, or machines?**

- Have students look at the two pictures and notice where each child is from. You could point out the UK and the USA on a world map.
- Ask students what they can see. Ask if they have ever done activities like these and if they enjoyed them.
- Listening for gist: ask the gist question *Do they talk about plants, experiments, or machines?* and elicit suggestions. Play the audio for students to check their ideas.

Answers
Max talks about an experiment with plants. Lily talks about an experiment with a machine.

E Listen again. Write *True* or *False*.

- Listening for details: have students read the sentences before they listen again and think about whether they're true or false. Then play the audio and have students write their answers.
- Check answers. If the answer is false, ask a student to say why.

Answers
1 *True* 2 False 3 False 4 False 5 True 6 False

Discussion Questions

- Draw students' attention to the discussion questions: *Which planet do you want to learn about? Why? How do you think learning about space can help us?* Have students discuss the questions in pairs (see **ETB**).
- For the second question, encourage students to think in terms of the problems we have on Earth (climate change, growing population). Ask the class for their ideas and write them on the board.
- Return to the opening question to ask again: *Why is it important to learn about space?* and ask students if listening to the astronaut, Max, and Lily has given them any new ideas.

Cool Down

Play *Board Race* with the word *space* (see TB p. 25).

Practice **Student's App:** Vocabulary Practice; Listening Practice

Explore Language

Lesson Objectives

- to learn how to use modals: *might* and *should*
- to practice using space vocabulary

Materials
Audio Tracks 48 and 49

Warm Up

Ask students *Do you like making models? What different things have you made models of? What materials did you use?* Make a list of the different models and materials on the board.

A TRACK 48 TB p. 218 **Listen and read. What do the children want to use the mirror for?**

- Ask students *What can you see in the first picture? What do you think the children are making?* (a model spaceship) Ask if they recognize Alfie and Freya from previous lessons.
- Play the audio and have students follow the story in their books.
- Ask the comprehension question *What do the children want to use the mirror for?* and elicit the answer.

Answer
a window for their spaceship

B Look at A. Complete.

- Write or project the table onto the board.
- Refer students to the first incomplete sentence in the table and have them find it in the story in A. Have them complete the sentence in the table. Elicit the answer and write it on the board.
- Have students work in pairs to fill in the blanks and complete the table.
- Invite students to come to the board to write one word each in the table. Ask *What kind of word comes after "might," "might not," "should," and "shouldn't"?* (an infinitive / verb in the base form)
- Refer students to the Grammar tip *Watch Out*. Remind them that the *l* in *should* is silent—we don't pronounce it. Model the pronunciation and have students repeat the word. Then have them read the sentences from the table in A, and check pronunciation of *should*. Ask students *Can you remember any other words with the silent "l"?* (could, would, half, walk, talk)

Answers
might; should; might not; shouldn't; leave

C Think and discuss. Then choose.

- Give students time to read the sentences, think about their answers, and then compare them with a friend. Tell them to look at the table in B and the story in A to help.
- Read the questions and options and have students raise their hands to show the option they chose. Confirm the answers.
- Ask students to think of some more sentences using *might / might not* or *should/shouldn't*. Give them some prompts to get them started; for example, *homework: I might not finish my homework. You should do your homework!* Write their ideas on the board.

Answers
1 should and shouldn't 2 might and might not

D TRACK 49 TB p. 218 **Listen and say.**

- Tell students they will listen to and repeat some sentences using *might* and *should*. Play the audio. Remind students that like the *l* in should, the *gh* in *might* is also not pronounced.
- For ideas on how to vary the drill, see TB p. 23.

E Complete the story with *should, shouldn't, might,* or *might not*.

- Ask students *What is happening in the pictures? Do you think it's a funny story or a scary story?*
- Tell students that they need to complete the sentences using *should, shouldn't, might,* or *might not*. Refer students to the first sentence and example answer. Ask why *might* is correct here. (because they aren't sure if it's a tunnel) Have students complete the activity individually, then check answers.

Answers
1 *might* 2 should 3 shouldn't 4 might not

F Look at the story in E. Ask and answer.

- Tell students they are going to imagine what happens next in the story in E. Ask why the character says *It might not be safe.*
- Tell students that they need to imagine the answers to the two questions. Read the first question, *What might be in the tunnel?* Have students read the suggested answer aloud and then repeat with the second question, *What should they do?*
- Give students time to imagine more answers to these questions and then have them share their ideas by asking and answering in pairs.
- Ask if any pairs would like to share their ideas with the class.

Cool Down

Play *Disappearing Sentences* (see TB p. 25) with the sentences from D.

Practice **Resource Bank:** Grammar Printout
Student's App: Grammar Practice

Talk About It

Lesson Objectives

- to prepare and practice a conversation making offers
- to recognize and reproduce words with the stress on the first syllable.

Materials
Video; Audio Track 50

Warm Up

Tell students that in this lesson they will learn to talk about making presentations. Ask students for suggestions of topics that they could do a presentation about and write them all on the board.

A TB p. 238 **Watch and listen. Are Anya and Natalia excited about the presentation?**

- Tell students they are going to watch a video of two friends talking about preparing a science presentation. Ask *Do you think they will have the same ideas?* Elicit ideas and then play the video for students to check.
- Introduce the gist question *Are Anya and Natalia excited about the presentation?* Elicit answers, then ask some more comprehension questions; for example, *What planet do they choose for the presentation?* (Jupiter) Play the video again and have students notice the girls' body language during the conversation.

Answer
Yes, they are.

B Watch again. Check (✔) the sentences or questions you hear.

- Have students read the sentences and questions.
- Play the video again and have students complete the activity. Read the sentences and questions and have students raise their hands for the ones they checked. Play the video again and have students correct the other sentences.
- Read all the sentences and questions and ask students to say if they give suggestions or information (raise hands) or if they show interest or agreement (clap hands). (Give suggestions or information: 1, 3, 5, 7, 9; Show interest or agreement: 2, 4, 6, 8.)

Answers
1; 2; 3; 4; 6; 7; 8

Pronunciation Word Stress 2

TRACK 50 TB p. 218 **Listen and say.**

- Write *interesting* on the board and have the class repeat it. Then say it slowly and have students tell you which syllable is stressed (the first one).
- Read the words aloud, then play the audio and have students repeat the words. Ask them where the word stress lies in each word and confirm it is on the first syllable. Repeat the words slowly so that they can hear if necessary.
- Say *These words are used in the video. What other words do you know from this unit where the word stress is on the first syllable?* Have students work in pairs to find more words with a similar stress pattern. Write all the words on the board and drill them at the end.

Suggested Answers
astronaut; galaxy; telescope; satellite

C Plan. Choose a topic to talk about. Then complete.

- Tell students they are going to plan their own presentation about a topic of their choice.
- Draw or project the graphic organizer onto the board. Tell students the topic that you have chosen (e.g. the moon) and write it in the topic circle. Elicit and fill in some basic information for the other boxes; for example; *I know … where it is* / *I want to know … exactly how far away it is.*
- Divide the class into pairs and have them choose a topic to do a presentation about. Encourage them to choose a topic they find interesting.
- Have them do a Rally Robin cooperative learning routine to generate ideas about the three categories in the graphic organizer (see TB p. 20).
- Then have students complete the graphic organizer with information about their topic.

D Prepare notes for your conversation. Use your ideas from C and phrases from B.

- Play the video again as a model and remind students to watch with their own conversation in mind.
- Prepare notes for an example conversation with your class using your plan from C and building it up with students' suggestions.
- Have students work in pairs to prepare their conversation based on the topic they have chosen and their ideas. Make sure they use their plan from C and phrases from B.

E Practice with your friend.

- Have students practice their conversation in pairs. Encourage them to gradually rely less on their notes, so their conversation becomes more fluid. Remind them to show their enthusiasm for their topic, like the girls in the video. Monitor and provide praise and help as needed.

Cool Down

Play *What's the Next Word?* (see TB p. 27) with the video.

Practice **Student's App:** Speaking Skills Practice; Speaking Video

Write About It

Lesson Objectives

- to review and practice using question words
- to plan and write a magazine interview

Materials

(Optional) Challenge, Standard, and Support writing printouts from the Resource Bank, one per student (C and D)

Warm Up

Ask students *Which famous person would you like to have a conversation with? What question would you like to ask?* Have them share their ideas in pairs. Then invite students to share their ideas with the class.

A Read the magazine interview. Circle the question words.

- Have students look quickly at the interview. Ask students who is in the interview and where they are (a journalist who is on Earth and Lian Starr, an astronaut on the International Space Station). Check that students understand what *Q* and *A* stand for before each part of the interview (*Q* for *question* and *A* for *answer*). Ask some questions to check comprehension; for example, *What did Lian Starr do before she was an astronaut?* (She was a pilot.)
- Ask students to find the first question word in the interview (*How*) and point out that words like this introduce the questions. Have them find and circle all the question words. Ask how many they have found.
- Invite students to raise their hands and read a question each.

Answers

How; Who; Why; Where; What; When

B Look at A. Match.

- Tell students they are going to match the question word to the type of answer it is asking for. Refer students to the example and ask them to find the *How* question in A. (*How did you become an astronaut?*) Explain that a *How* question is asking for details. Have students find the details in the answer. (First she was a pilot, then she trained to be an astronaut.)
- Have students match the other question words to the type of answer it is asking for. They should compare with the answers in A to check they chose the correct definition.
- Check answers, and after each, ask *What information did we find out from this question?*

Answers

1 f 2 a 3 d 4 c 5 b 6 e

C Plan. Choose someone to interview. Think about your questions.

- Tell students they are going to interview someone. You can decide whether this is a famous person (another student will have to pretend to be a famous person) or a parent or other family member (students will carry out their interviews at home for homework).
- Give students time to choose the person they would like to interview.
- Have students refer back to the interview in A to remember all the different ways they can start their questions and to think about the questions they could ask.
- Have students complete the questions for their interview. Tell them to write at least one question for each question word. Monitor and provide language help when needed. You can hand out the Challenge printout at this point.

D Interview someone. Then write your magazine interview.

- Give students time to interview the person they have chosen, using their questions from C. Tell them to make a note of the answers in their notebooks. Explain that answers can be written in note form at this point.
- Once students have carried out the interview, have them write up a rough draft in their notebook, following the layout in A. Tell them that now they need to write full sentences for the answers.
- Have students self-correct or exchange their work with a friend and peer-correct. You can put a checklist of points for students to look out for on the board (e.g. spelling, capital letters, periods, question marks, correct use of question words).
- Have students correct any mistakes and write their final instructions neatly on paper or hand out the Support and Standard printouts from the Resource Bank. Give them time to draw a picture of the person they are interviewing to give their magazine article a more authentic look!

Cool Down

Have students write a short poem called "My Important Things" with just a question word and a very short answer for each line. You can give your own example:

When? Now!

Who? Friends!

What? Adventure!

Where? The ocean!

Why? Fun!

How? Fast ☺

Have students share their poems with friends in the class. These poems could be displayed around the classroom, as they can act as helpful prompts for students when forming questions.

Practice **Student's App:** Writing Practice

Think It Over

Lesson Objectives

- to review what has been learned in the unit
- to reflect on the unit and their own progress
- to think about learning strategies and how to continue learning at home

Warm Up

Project the TTL flashcards (image only) for any of the vocabulary from pp. 48–49 or p. 52 and have students raise their hands as soon as they know what the word is. This could be played as a team game for points.

Read the questions and draw or write your answers.

- Give students time to think about and discuss activities in the unit before they complete each question. Explain that they can choose to either write a few words or sentences or to draw a picture. Allowing students to make a personal response will help them retain knowledge and engage with the learning points.

What did I do?

- Give students a few minutes to look back through the unit at the different activities they did. Ask questions about the unit or write questions on the board for students to discuss in pairs or small groups; for example, *What grammar did you learn about? What games did you play? Where did you hear about experiments?*
- Encourage students to identify something in the unit that they found challenging or something that was particularly memorable for them, but tell them not to choose their favorite activity yet. Students can draw or write about their chosen activity.

What did I learn?

- Have students talk to a partner about what they remember from the unit—stories, words, phrases, people, aspects of space.
- Ask questions about the unit to help students think about what they learned; for example, *Can you find new words that you didn't know before? What did you learn about space or other planets? What did you learn about planning a presentation? What did you learn about writing an interview? What else did you learn?* Have students discuss their ideas in pairs.
- Encourage students to draw a picture or write sentences about their learning outcomes.

What was my favorite part?

- Have students look back through the unit and decide what they enjoyed the most. Tell them it can be an activity they found fun, a text they enjoyed reading, a favorite character, or a favorite action. They should try to choose just one and draw a picture or write about it. Explain that when we like something, it is often easier to learn.

How well did I do?

- Ask students to color in the number of shooting stars that best expresses how well they think they learned the content (i.e. the more stars they color, the more they think they have learned). Ask *What do you understand? What do you need to practice more?* Encourage students to look back through the unit to see how much they remember, what they did well, and what they found difficult.

What can I do next?

- Encourage students to think about what they can do at home to improve their English. Have them suggest some verbs that they can use (e.g. read, practice, listen, interview) and write the verbs in their books. Students can look back at the previous units to get more ideas. Encourage students to suggest their own ideas for different activities they can do.
- Have students choose several activities that they would like to do and write them in their notebooks. They can then share their ideas with a partner.

Looking Forward

Draw students' attention to the character at the bottom of the page. Ask *Who's this?* and elicit what they remember about her. (Freya was in the observatory in the Vocabulary lesson and also helped make the model spaceship in Explore Language 2.) Ask *What do you think she's reading about at the moment?* Elicit predictions about what she's reading and what Unit 4 is about. Tell students they will find out if they were correct in the first lesson of the next unit.

Put It Together

To further review and recycle the language in Units 3 and 4, play the game, *Race Around the Galaxy*, on pp. 60–61. See TB p. 207 for teaching notes.

Practice **Resource Bank:** Unit Test
Student's App: Vocabulary and Grammar Review

Literacy

Get Ready to Read

Lesson Objectives

- to activate prior knowledge about space exploration
- to encourage students to observe and interpret through a See, Think, Wonder VTR
- to preview the reading skill of scanning for specific information

Materials

(Optional) VTR printout from the Resource Bank (A, B, C)

Warm Up

Refer students to the title of the unit, *What's Up There?* Ask students *What do you think is up there?* (the sky/space) Brainstorm as many answers as possible (from clouds and birds to planets, stars, etc.). Write the answers on the board.

See, Think, Wonder

A Look at the picture. What do you see?

- Students are going to do a See, Think, Wonder VTR to explore the image of the Carina Nebula. Helps students with vocabulary where necessary. Give students a minute to look at the picture. Then have students discuss what they see in small groups or pairs and then as a class. Encourage them to be creative and use their imaginations when describing what they see.

Here's an example of this part of the routine.
Teacher: What do you see?
Student A: I see a man riding a horse through space.
Student B: I see pink stars.

B What do you think?

- Ask *What do you think about the picture?* Students should be encouraged to go beyond what they can see and start expressing their thoughts and ideas about the image. Give students one to three minutes to think about the picture silently. Then have students work in small groups to share their ideas before sharing as a class.

Here's an example of this part of the routine.
Teacher: What do you think?
Student A: (I think) this picture was taken in space.
Teacher: What makes you say that?
Student A: It looks like space, and you can see stars.
Student B: I think an astronaut took it in space.
Student C: I don't agree, it looks like it's really far away. I think someone took it here.

C What do you wonder?

- Ask students *What do you wonder?* Tell students that they should think about what they don't know about the picture but would like to know. Give students time to think and then discuss in pairs. Ask pairs to share their ideas with the class.

Here's an example of this part of the routine.
Teacher: What do you wonder about the picture?
Student A: I wonder how many stars are in the picture and how far away they are.
Teacher: That's interesting.
Student B: I wonder what is in the center of the picture—it looks like a monster!
Student C: Is the picture a galaxy?

Transition

Ask students *Would you like to go into space to visit a place like this? Why or why not?* Have students discuss ideas in pairs and then as a class.

D Think and discuss. How do we explore space? What space missions do you know?

- Ask students what they know about exploring space. Write some prompts on the board—*How do astronauts get into space? What special equipment do they need? Do we always need astronauts to explore space?*
- Divide the class into pairs and have students discuss the questions. Then invite pairs to share their answers with the class. You could point out that as well as astronauts and satellites, some animals have also been sent into space.
- Ask students if they know of any space missions. Elicit or point out that as well as the famous missions with astronauts, there are other missions with no astronauts but with machines called probes that visit planets and send back information.

Suggested Answers

To explore space, we use rockets/satellites/astronauts.
I know about the International Space Station and Apollo 13.

E Scan the first page of *Hope You Like Fish*. What is the name of the spaceship?

This is a preview of the reading skill of scanning for specific information.

- Have students look at the beginning of the story on the next page and find the name of the mission—encourage them to scan the text quickly for the name by making it into a race.
- Ask students *What do you think the mission is about? Where do you think they are going?* Elicit suggestions.

Answer

Mars 11

Now read **Hope You Like Fish**

Fiction: *Hope You Like Fish—Story*

Lesson Objectives

- to read a story about space exploration
- to make a personal connection to the reading

Materials

Audio Tracks 20 and 21; handwritten cards with quotations from the story (CD)

Warm Up

Ask students to imagine they're going on a space mission. Say *You can take three personal objects with you into space. What will you take?* Have students think then discuss in pairs.

TRACK 20 TB p. 230 Reading Approach

First Reading: Engage with the Text

- Look at the title and pictures on pp. 58–59 together and ask students *Which animals are on the space mission?* (rabbits and chimps) Clarify that *chimp* is a short word for *chimpanzee*, which is a type of ape native to Africa.
- Ask *Do you know of any animals that have been into space?* Tell them that the first dog to go into space was named Laika in 1957.
- Give students time to read the story silently without the audio. Ask students *Do you think the story is funny?*

TRACK 21 TB p. 231 Words in Context

- Play the audio and have students repeat the words.
- Have students race to find the words in the story.
- Remind students they can often **use the words around the new words to guess their meaning** (see TB p. 22). Have them discuss their ideas with a partner, using L1 if necessary.
- Then bring the class together and use these discussion points to confirm the meanings.

launch (p. 59) Elicit that here the word is used as a verb. Ask *What is the spaceship about to do?* (leave, go into space) Ask students to find another instance of *launch* in the story (*launch pad* on p. 58). Elicit that *the* tells us *launch pad* is a noun. We can figure out it's the platform a spaceship leaves from.

Mission Control (p. 58, p. 61, p. 63) Read the sentence from p. 58: *Mission control checks everything.* Have students find a picture of mission control (p. 59). Ask *Who works there?* (the animals directing the space mission) *Why does mission control check everything?* (to see if everything is correct and working)

blast (p. 59) Elicit that *Blast off* happens after the countdown, so we know it is the point when the rocket takes off. Look at the sentence *Fire blasts from the rocket* and have students point to where they see this in the picture. Ask *What do you think it sounds like?* (loud)

gravity (p. 61) Ask students if they have a word similar to *gravity* in their own language. Elicit that the word *float* in the sentence tells us that the astronauts don't fall when there is zero gravity, so we can figure out that *gravity* is what makes things fall to the Earth.

in sight (p. 63) Refer students to the sentence *There is nothing else in sight.* Elicit that the verb *see* is in the same word family as *sight*. Ask *What can they see?* (the ocean) *Anything else?* (no) *So if there is nothing in sight, can you see anything?* (no)

Second Reading: Analyze the Text and Features

- Play the audio and have students read along as they listen.
- Ask some comprehension questions to check understanding: *Are the rabbits happy to be going into space with the chimps?* (no) *Why do the chimps argue?* (because they both want the food)
- Discuss the questions in the red boxes.
  - **Fact** (p. 58): *Marfusha, Enos, and Ham were names of real animals who went to space during the 1950s and 1960s.* Ask *Why do you think a rabbit went into space?* (The scientists first sent insects and then mammals to see what effect space had on them.)
  - **Language Focus** (p. 61): *What does* in charge *mean?* Elicit that it means *to lead*. Ask who is in charge on the rocket? (the rabbits)
  - **Fact** (p. 62): *Not all early space missions were successful.* Ask *What do you think happened to the missions that were not successful?* (Some didn't even take off, some crashed, and some had problems in space and couldn't return.)
  - **Critical Thinking** (p. 63): *Why do you think people sent animals into space in the 1960s?* Have students discuss their ideas in small groups. Point out that people didn't know if it was dangerous to go into space, so sending animals helped them see if it was safe for humans.

Third Reading: Interact with the Text

- Play the audio again and have students mime the actions in the story.
- Then divide the class into groups of five and designate a role for each student: Marfusha, Katyusha, Ham, Enos, and one student to be a narrator and mission control. Have each group role-play two pages of the story. Invite three groups with different scenes to perform to the class, so the audience sees the whole story. For more ideas on using role-play, see TB p. 23.

Cool Down

Play *Who Said It?* with phrases from the story (see TB p. 27). Suggested phrases: *Worst day ever.* (Katyusha) *I guess maybe we got distracted.* (Enos) *We're exploring new worlds for science.* (Katyusha) *I've changed my mind!* (Ham) *This isn't the time for a space snack.* (Marfusha)

Explore the Reading

Lesson Objectives

- to understand and analyze *Hope You Like Fish* through reading comprehension activities
- to explore the SEL competency of self-management through attention control and maintaining optimal work performance
- to identify and practice words with a long *i* sound

Materials
Audio Track 22

Warm Up

Read the first part of some phrases from the reading and have students race to find and call out the second half; for example, *I can't believe they're sending us into space with ...* (these guys again). *You landed us in totally ...* (the wrong place). *You're going to cause ...* (an accident). *We said we were ...* (sorry).

A Read and answer.

- Before students open their books, have a team quiz to find out what they remember from the story. Ask *Who is in the rocket?* (two chimps, two rabbits, and two mice) *Why aren't the rabbits happy?* (because the chimps made mistakes last time) *Where are the ducks?* (at mission control on Earth) *Which animals make the rocket crash?* (the chimps) *What are the chimps trying to do at the end of the story?* (catch fish to eat)
- Refer students to the first question in A. Elicit the answer and ask them to find something in the reading to justify it (the first words of the reading—*The launch pad. Just before dawn*). If necessary, clarify the meaning of *dawn*.
- Have students complete the activity, compare answers with a friend, and find something in the reading to justify their answers.
- Nominate pairs of students to read aloud a question and answer.

Answers
1 The launch is just before dawn. 2 They landed in the wrong place. 3 The purpose of the mission is to land on Mars and collect rocks. 4 They float because they are in zero gravity. 5 Marfusha and Katyusha / the rabbits are in charge. 6 The mission lands in the ocean.

B Think and write. What do you think is important to the rabbits? What is important to the chimps? What makes you think that?

- Give students some thinking time to consider what they think is important to the rabbits and to the chimps.
- Then set up a Numbered Heads Together routine (see TB p. 20) to discuss the questions and gather ideas about the story. Nominate students in each group to give their ideas and encourage them to explain what makes them think that by referring to the text.

Practice Resource Bank: Spelling Printout
Student's App: Reading Practice; Spelling Pattern Practice

Suggested Answers
I think the mission is important to the rabbits because they are focused and serious. I think having fun is important to the chimps because they are not serious and get distracted by food.

C Think and discuss. Food distracted Ham and Enos from their mission to Mars. What do you do when something distracts you?

- Ask students to remember what distracts the chimps from their mission to Mars. (food) Ask *What happens when the chimps start to lose their attention to the mission?* (Things go wrong and an accident happens.) *How could the chimps focus better on the mission?* (not bring distractions like snacks)
- Explore the SEL competency of self-management through attention control and maintaining optimal work performance. Ask students *Do you sometimes get distracted? What types of things distract you?* Start off by giving them an example: *I get distracted by my smartphone.* Have students do a Think, Pair, Share routine to discuss the questions. Elicit ideas and write them on the board.
- Ask students to discuss in small groups *How can you stop getting distracted?* Have them make a list of potential solutions. Ask each group for their best ideas. Remind students that in order to do something well, you need to be able to pay attention, stay focused, and ignore distractions. Ask *Who is more serious about the mission—the rabbits or the chimps?*

TRACK 22 TB p. 231 Spelling Pattern long *i*

Listen and write. Then check your answers.

- With books closed, write *hi* on the board and elicit how to pronounce it. Underline the long *i*.
- Play the audio and have students repeat each word. Then have them open their books. Play the first part of the audio again and have them complete as many of the words as they can.
- Play the second part of the audio and have students check their spelling and complete any missing words. Have them underline the *i* in each word and read the words aloud.
- Have students look back at the reading and find more words with the same sound and write them down. Invite students to read them aloud, then have them write all the long *i* words from the lesson in a spidergram or other graphic organizer.

Answers
1 library 2 lion 3 quiet 4 grind 5 migrate
In the reading: I; time; upside; 5 (five); fire; science; mind(s); like; flies; tiny; sight; while; finds

Cool Down

Have a *Spelling Bee* (see TB p. 27) using all of the words from the spelling pattern activity on p. 64.

Get Ready to Read

Lesson Objectives

- to review and practice the skill of scanning for information
- to activate prior knowledge about early space exploration and key figures in space exploration

Warm Up

Do a quick quiz for students on space and space exploration. Divide the class into two teams and have each team nominate a spokesperson. Team members should confer with their spokesperson before he/she raises a hand to provide the team's answer. Give a point for each correct answer. Possible questions: *How many people have walked on the moon—three, eight, or twelve?* (twelve) *What was the name of the first mission to land on the moon—Apollo or Sputnik?* (Apollo) *What's the closest planet to Earth—Mars or Venus?* (Venus) *What's the biggest planet in our solar system—Neptune or Jupiter?* (Jupiter) *How many moons does Mars have—one, two, five, or ten?* (two)

A Scan the timeline. Answer the questions.

This lesson reviews and practices the reading skill of scanning for specific information.

- Refer students to the timeline about space exploration. Ask students the first question and have them raise their hands when they have found the answer in the timeline.
- When all students have their hands raised, check the answer. Ask them how they found the answer—did they read everything, or did they look for information about a woman? Point out the quickest way to find information is often to find the key word and then check the information around it—find *woman*, then check that surrounding text talks about the first woman in space.
- Have students read the skills box about scanning and explain this is what they just did—or at least students who found the answer quickly did this! Ask students if they can think of any instances in their lives outside the classroom when scanning would be useful. They might mention looking for key information on a website or looking up information in the index of a book. Ask *Do we scan when we read a story?* (perhaps beforehand to find out if it's something we want to read, but to enjoy a story we need to read in more detail).

Answers

1 Valentina Tereshkova 2 Neil Armstrong became the first person to step foot on the moon. 3 340 days

B Scan the first page of *First Man in Space*. Then answer the questions.

- Ask students if they know the name Yuri Gagarin. Have them look quickly at pictures on the next page and say what they think his job was. (astronaut)
- Remind students they need to find the answer to the two questions quickly, so they will need to scan the text for the information. Ask them what word or words in each question to look for (*born* and a year in question 1 and *parents/work* in question 2).
- Have students scan the first page of the reading and raise their hands when they know the answers. Ask if it was quicker scanning for the information than reading everything line by line from the beginning.

Answers

1 1934 2 on a farm

C Think and discuss. What kind of person explores space? What skills do you think astronauts need?

- Elicit one or two suggestions from the whole class and then have students continue thinking individually about the questions. Write prompts on the board to help guide them: *What do you need to be able to do in space? Can you do these things? How can you learn how to do them?*
- When they have had time to think, divide the class into pairs and have them share their ideas with a partner.
- Then ask the pairs to share their best ideas with the rest of the class. Continue until all the ideas have been shared.
- Ask students *Do you think you have any of the skills or qualities you need to be an astronaut?* Have a show of hands and invite a few students who raised their hands to say why they think they would make a good astronaut.

Cool Down

Tell students that they will be reading more about Yuri Gagarin in the next lesson. Ask students to predict and write down one thing they think they'll learn about him.

Now read **First Man in Space**

Nonfiction: *First Man in Space—Biography*

Lesson Objectives

- to read a biography about a famous astronaut
- to learn about Yuri Gagarin and astronauts in general
- to make a personal connection to the reading

Materials

Audio Tracks 23 and 24; Video

Warm Up

Do a Total Physical Response (TPR) activity with students. Have students mime as you say: *Five—put on your helmet. Four—hold the controls* (like a steering wheel!). *Three—say "Ready to launch!" Two—push the red button! One—get ready ... zero—lift off!* (a lot of shaking and sound effects!)

TRACK 23 TB p. 231 Reading Approach

First Reading: Engage with the Text

- Have students read the prediction they made at the end of the last lesson to a partner.
- Play the video. Alternately, play the audio and have them follow in their books.
- Pause the video/audio in different places and ask students to say what they think will come next; for example, at the end of p. 66, ask *Will Gagarin's secret mission be successful?* At the end of p. 68, *What will he do now that he's in space?*
- At the end of the video ask students how many of their predictions were correct. Then look at the Words in Context.

TRACK 24 TB p. 231 Words in Context

- Play the audio and have students repeat the words.
- Play the video again and tell students to **use pictures/actions/events in the video to help establish the meaning of the new words** (see TB p. 22). Have them discuss their ideas with a partner, using L1 if necessary.
- Then bring the class together and use these discussion points to confirm the meanings.

capsule (p. 66) Ask students to read the sentence it is in and elicit that *tiny* gives us a clue about what a capsule is like. Tell students to try to imagine the situation. Ask *What does his capsule look like?* (a chair, a lot of controls, and very little space to move!)

attitude (p. 67) Ask students *Did Yuri have a positive or negative attitude?* (positive) *How do we know?* (he smiled a lot)

failed (p. 67) Ask *Did the launches go into space?* (no, it was too dangerous) Ask students if they can think of something people can fail. Remind them also of Luana from Unit 3 who failed her test because she didn't study.

Practice **Student's App:** Nonfiction Video

pressed (p. 68) Ask *What did the people press?* (an ignition button). Have students mime pressing a button.

parachuted (p. 69) Have students read the clue in the next sentence: *landed in a field.* Ask *How did he land in the field?* and invite a student to draw Yuri with a parachute on the board.

hero (p. 69) Ask *How do you think people felt about Gagarin?* (They loved him: they gave him awards and named streets after him.)

Second Reading: Analyze the Text and Features

- Play the audio and read along while they listen. Pause the audio in places and ask questions to check understanding, e.g. *What was Yuri Gagarin the first man to do?* (go into space)
- Discuss the questions in the red boxes.
  - **Making Connections** (p. 66): *In Russia, an astronaut is called a* cosmonaut. *In China, an astronaut is known as a* taikonaut. Ask students what they think the different parts of the words mean—what about *astro–/cosmo–/ taiko–*? (They mean stars, space, and the universe.) Ask them what they know about *–naut.* (It comes from a Greek word meaning "sailor".)
  - **Making Connections** (p. 67): *In those days, no one knew what effect being in space would have on a human.* Ask *Can you remember how people knew that it was possible to survive a trip into space and back?* (They had sent animals first.)
  - **Fact** (p. 68): *Gagarin traveled to 203 miles above Earth. His flight went around Earth once and lasted a total of 108 minutes.* Ask *What do you think Gagarin did in that time?*
  - **Personalization** (p. 69): *What other famous astronauts do you know?* Ask *Do you know the name of the first person to walk on the moon?* (Neil Armstrong)
- Discuss the text focus *How do you know this is a* ***biography****?* Give students some thinking time, then have them discuss the question in pairs. Elicit some features of a biography.

International English

Tell students that high school is for children aged 13–18 in the USA. In the UK, children usually start secondary school aged 11.

Third Reading: Interact with the Text

- Have students read the text silently, write down three things they learned, and rank these in order of interest. Have students share their opinions in pairs.

Cool Down

Finish with another TPR activity—this time of Gagarin arriving back home: *Five—you're getting close to earth ... Four—you landed (with a bump!). Three—turn off the engine. Two—open the door. One—take off your helmet. Zero—wave to the people!*

Explore the Reading

Lesson Objectives

- to understand and analyze *First Man in Space* through reading comprehension activities
- to practice the reading skill of scanning for specific information
- to learn about space exploration through CLIL (science): understanding the qualities needed to be an astronaut
- to make a personal connection to the reading

Materials
Video or Audio Track 23

TRACK 23 TB p. 231 Warm Up

Play the video or audio from the previous lesson again and have students raise their hands when they hear the thing they found most interesting in the previous lesson. At the end ask *Did everyone find the same things interesting? Has anyone changed their minds?*

A Read and write *True* or *False*.

- Before students open their books, have a quick team quiz to find out what they remember from the reading. Ask *What was Yuri Gagarin the first man to do?* (go into space) *Where was he from?* (Russia) *Why was he chosen for the mission?* (He had good skills and attitude.) *How much time did Gagarin spend in space?* (less than two hours / 108 minutes) *What did they name after him?* (streets and a town)
- Refer students to the first sentence in A and ask them to quickly find the answer and to say why. (False—20 air force pilots were chosen) Ask them to remember the best way to find information like this in a text—find the key words (in this case, *air force pilots*) and then check that the information is about the same thing you're looking for. This is called scanning.
- Have students complete the activity using these scanning techniques to find something in the reading to justify their answer. Check answers as a class.

Answers
1 False 2 True 3 False 4 True 5 True 6 True

B Think, discuss, and write. Imagine you meet Yuri Gagarin. What do you ask him?

- Elicit first from the class some topics that students could ask questions about: his feelings, when he was a child, his training, the capsule, and so on. Make a list of these on the board to enable students to be more wide-ranging in their questions.
- Elicit one example question and then do a Round Robin (see TB p. 20) to gather more questions. One student from each group should be responsible for writing down the questions. Ask the groups to share their questions with the rest of the class.
- Then have students work individually to choose the three questions they would most like to ask Yuri Gagarin. Tell them they can choose questions generated by their own group or a different group, if they prefer.

C Think and write. Which characteristics do you think make a good astronaut? Use the words to write sentences.

Students are going to connect the reading to their own ideas about what makes a good astronaut. This draws on the CLIL science focus of learning about space exploration.

- Refer students to the adjectives in the box. Ask them to decide which characteristics a good astronaut needs. Point out they can use more adjectives than those in the box. Remind them of the skills they discussed in C of the *Get Ready to Read* lesson. Do they have a different opinion after reading the text?
- When they have chosen their adjectives, have students write a short paragraph about what makes a good astronaut. Have them write first in their notebooks and then on paper when they are happy with their sentences. Give them time to illustrate their sentences. These could then be displayed as part of a Space themed wall display.

Suggested Answer
A good astronaut is smart, healthy, and brave. It is also good to be friendly so that you get along with the other astronauts.

D Think and discuss. Would you make a good astronaut? Why or why not?

- Elicit some of the characteristics that students wrote about in C.
- Give students some thinking time to decide if they would be a good astronaut and why and then share their ideas with a friend or in small groups. Ask if any students would like to share their conclusions with the class.

Cool Down

Ask each student to choose a profession and think why they would be good at it. Then have them circulate around the class asking other students about their chosen profession. Listen in and write some of the professions you hear on the board. Have students return to their seats, and ask the class if they can remember a student who talked about each of the professions on the board and why they thought they would be good at it. Tell students they can't answer about themselves! Write their suggestions on the board next to each profession and ask the students named to confirm if the information is correct or not. Remind students that it is important to pay attention when other people are speaking.

Practice Student's App: Reading Practice

Think Together

Lesson Objectives

- to make connections between the readings
- to explore the key concept: How do we explore space?
- to reflect on the unit and provide personal thoughts and opinions

Materials

Large sheets of paper, two per group (B and C)

Warm Up

Have students look back at the VTR image on pp. 56–57 and ask *Do you now have any new ideas about the image?* Have students discuss in pairs and then ask for suggestions. Write the transition question you asked in the first *Get Ready to Read* lesson on the board: *Would you like to visit a place like this?* Ask if students have changed their minds now they have read more about traveling in space.

A Compare and contrast the space missions in *Hope You Like Fish* and *First Man in Space*.

- Draw or project the Venn diagram onto the board. Ask students to suggest one thing that they can put in the right-side area that is only true about the Yuri Gagarin reading; for example, *The mission was a success.* Then elicit from students a fact for the middle (the middle part is for things that are true for both readings); for example, *Both have rockets.*
- Have students copy the diagram into their notebooks and look back at the readings on pp. 58–63 and pp. 66–69 to find more things they can include in each area of the diagram. Have students share their ideas in groups.
- Introduce the key concept question *How do we explore space?* Ask what ways to explore space they've learned about in this unit (sending animals into space and sending a human into space). Encourage them to think of other ways we can explore space.

Suggested Answers

Both: 1 have rockets 2 are about space
3 are based on true stories
Hope You Like Fish: 1 is about animals 2 is a story
3 has drawings 4 mission isn't successful
First Man in Space: 1 is about human astronauts
2 is a biography 3 has real photographs
4 mission is successful

B Think and discuss. What do you imagine the astronauts on a space mission hear? What do they see? What do you think it feels like in space? Do a Roundtable.

- Students are going to use their imagination to think about what it is like in space. Have students read the questions and elicit an example answer for each one. Then give them a minute to think of their own ideas.
- Set up the class for a Roundtable cooperative learning routine (see TB p. 20). Designate one person to start in each group and have students take turns to write answers to any of the questions.
- Give groups time to review and discuss all the answers at the end. Encourage them to say if they agree or disagree and to add any more ideas they think of during the discussion.

C Complete the Y chart with your ideas from B.

- Have students change groups. Give each group a large sheet of paper and have them copy the Y chart onto it. Have them pass the paper around their group so that each student can add one idea in each section, remembering the suggestions generated from the Roundtable routine they did in B. Give them time to review all the ideas on the chart at the end.
- Project the Y chart onto the board and have students volunteer ideas.

My Reading Journal

Look back at the unit. What questions do you have?

This question encourages students to think about what else they want to learn.

Give students time to think and write at least two questions, then discuss in pairs or small groups.

Ask students to raise their hands to give a question they'd like to know the answer to. Ask if anyone in the class knows or can suggest ideas for the answer.

Example Answers

When will the first people walk on Mars? What do astronauts eat?

What's your opinion of this unit?

This question encourages students to give a personal response to the unit. Give students time to look back at the unit and then complete their answers. Have them share their ideas with a friend.

Ask if any students would like to share their answers with the class.

Answer

Students' own answers.

Cool Down

Have students draw their favorite part from either reading and write a short description of what happened (e.g. a drawing of a rocket leaving Earth's atmosphere; *Yuri Gagarin became the first man to enter space at 6.18 a.m. on April 12, 1961*). Have them show and describe their drawing to students near them. These can then make a wall display.

Practice **Resource Bank:** Unit Test
Student's App: Key Concept Practice

UNIT 5

So That's How They Did It

Unit Overview

Themes

Trade in the past

Travel in the past

Synopsis

In this unit students will learn about Vikings and how people in the past used to trade and travel. They will learn about the Silk Road and think about why people used to trade and how travel has changed over the years. They will plan and prepare a conversation to practice trading and negotiating and write a character profile of a Viking to learn how to give examples.

Language Book

Vocabulary

crops, fight, helmet, hunt, shield, stew, sword, village, warrior, weave

p. 112

Explore Language

Used to: Statements

p. 113

Global Citizenship

Why did people trade and explore in the past?

coins, fur, honey, jewelry, leather, necklace, pottery, silk, spices, wheat, wood

p. 114

Explore Language

Used to: Questions

p. 115

Talk About It

Conversation: negotiating

p. 116

Write About It

A Character Profile

Sentence Building: giving examples

p. 117

Think It Over

Review and Reflection

p. 118

Literacy Book

Think Together
How has travel changed from ancient times?
p. 125

Visible Thinking
Think, Pair, Share
p. 119

Fiction
Folk Tale: *Sinbad's First Voyage*
Words in Context: *wealthy, penniless, boarded, sank, strength, stranger, troubles*
p. 123

Nonfiction
Informational Text: *The Silk Road*
Words in Context: *goods, faraway, network, routes, merchants, preserved, thieves*
p. 120

Reading Skill
Identifying points of view
p. 122

Spelling Pattern
Soft *c*
p. 124

Language and Literacy Connections

The connecting theme in Unit 5 is how people traveled and traded in the past.

	Language	Literacy
Vocabulary	**Set 1:** Vikings **Set 2:** trade and travel	**Nonfiction:** fur(s), pottery, silk, spice(s) **Fiction:** coins, jewelry, pottery, silk, spice(s), wheat
Grammar	***Used to*: Statements** The children used to work, too! Viking children didn't use to go to school. ***Used to*: Questions** What did they use to eat? Did they use to sleep on the ships? Yes, they did.	**Fiction** My father used to be a wealthy merchant. It used to cost 20 gold coins to get a place on a ship. **Nonfiction** Merchants used to travel on the Silk Road to trade goods. How did people use to do it?
Skills	**Pronunciation:** /s/ or /z/	**Reading:** identifying points of view **Spelling Pattern:** soft *c*
International English	figure out / work out	

Vocabulary

Lesson Objectives

- to learn vocabulary to talk about Vikings: *crops, fight, helmet, hunt, shield, stew, sword, village, warrior, weave*
- to sing a song about being a Viking

Materials
Audio Tracks 51 to 54; Video

Warm Up

Ask students to think about someone from 1,500 years ago, going on an adventure. Ask questions and build up a picture on the board (it doesn't have to be very artistic). Ask *How is the person traveling? What is the person wearing? What is the person carrying? Does the person have anything on his/her head? What's the person eating?* Now have students look at pp. 62–63 and say if they can see any of their ideas on the page.

A TRACK 51 TB p. 218 **Listen and find. When did the Vikings arrive in England?**

- Have students look at the picture on pp. 62–63. Ask *What can you see? When do you think this is happening?* Ask students if they recognize the girl in the image (Freya from Unit 4). Tell them the boy with the dark hair is named Oliver. Say *Can you see what Freya is giving Oliver?* (a sword)
- Play the audio and have students point to the words and pictures as they listen.
- Ask the comprehension question *When did the Vikings arrive in England?* and elicit the answer. Play the audio again to check.
- Remind students of Freya's challenge at the end of Unit 4: *What am I reading about at the moment?* If necessary, play the audio again to check the answer. (She's reading a book about Vikings.)

Answer
in around 700 CE

B TRACK 52 TB p. 218 **Listen, say, and number the pictures in A.**

- Play the audio. Have students point to the pictures and say the words.
- Tell students to listen again and write numbers next to the words in the picture in the order they hear them.
- Check answers and ask a few students to repeat each word to check pronunciation.

Answers
1 *crops* 2 stew 3 hunt 4 village 5 weave
6 warrior 7 fight 8 helmet 9 sword 10 shield

C TRACK 53 TB p. 218 **Close your eyes. Listen, visualize, and say.**

- Prepare students for the visualization (see TB p. 21).
- Play the audio, allowing students to visualize the vocabulary as they listen.
- Then have students draw what they imagined for their partner, who has to guess the word.

D Look and write.

- This activity develops critical thinking, as students have to decide how to categorize the different vocabulary items from the picture dictionary scene. Project or draw the graphic organizer on the board and tell students that they have to work in pairs to agree on the words associated with each category. As an example, elicit one word that can be associated with *warriors*.
- Give students some time to complete the activity. Then invite students to come to the board to fill in the shapes. Ask if everyone agrees.

Answers
Food: stew; crops
Warriors: fight; sword; shield; helmet
Clothes: weave
Homes: village
Animals: hunt

E TRACK 54 TB p. 218 **Listen and choose. Then watch and sing.**

- Have students look at the title of the song, *The Viking Life*. Ask *What do Vikings do? Where do they live? What do they eat?* Elicit suggestions and write them on the board.
- Then play the song once, allowing students to listen and enjoy it.
- Explain that students have to choose between two words to complete the lyrics. Ask *Can you guess what the correct words are?* Have students read the song and circle any answers they know.
- Play the audio again and have students check and circle the correct words. Then check answers as a class.
- Play the song video and have students watch and sing along. Then play the song video again and have students sing and mime actions for the verbs (weave, hunt, and fight).
- Ask students *Do you think the Viking life sounds exciting or like a lot of work?*

Answers
1 *Weave* 2 crops 3 Hunt 4 animals 5 sword
6 shield 7 warrior 8 Fight

Cool Down

Play *Draw It!* (see TB p. 25) with the vocabulary from this lesson.

Practice **Student's App:** Vocabulary Practice; Song Video

Explore Language

Lesson Objectives

- to learn and practice how to make *used to* statements
- to practice using vocabulary about Vikings

Materials
Audio Tracks 55 and 56

Warm Up

Ask students *What are your favorite free-time activities?* and write their suggestions on the board. What is the most popular free-time activity?

A TRACK 55 TB p. 219 **Listen and read. What did Viking children do in their free time?**

- Have students look at the pictures on p. 64. Ask *What can you see? What do you think the people are talking about?* Ask students if they recognize the girl on the left—it's Freya from the previous lesson and from Unit 4.
- Tell students they are going to listen to a conversation about Viking children.
- Play the audio and have students listen and follow the story in their books.
- Ask the comprehension question *What did Viking children do in their free time?* and elicit answers. Did any students suggest these as favorite activities in the Warm Up?

Answers
swim, go ice-skating, and play ball games

B **Look at A. Complete.**

- Write or project the table onto the board.
- Have students discuss and complete the grammar table in pairs using the story.
- When they have completed the table, invite students to come up to the board and fill in one word each. Ask if everyone agrees. Discuss the word order and verb forms together, but let your class guide the discussion. If you feel that students need more guidance, the **ETB** provides a differentiation activity to help you support students as they explore the grammar table.
- Have students look at the Grammar tip *Watch Out*. Ask *What verb form is* used? (past) *Why do we use* use *and not* used *after* didn't? Elicit the answer or remind students that the simple past is shown through *didn't* and that we use the base form of the verb after *didn't*.

Answers
used; work; didn't use; go

C **Think and discuss. Then choose.**

- Have students look at the sentence and answer options. Give them time to think and encourage them to look at the table in B and the story in A to help. Then have them discuss their answer with a partner.
- Read the statement and have the class raise their hands for the correct answer. Confirm the answer.

Answer
1 often

D TRACK 56 TB p. 219 **Listen and say.**

- Play the audio and have students listen and repeat. (See TB p. 23 for ideas on how to vary the drill.)

E **Read about life in the past and complete.**

- Have students read the conversation quickly and say if Grandpa's life as a child was similar or different from their own.
- Refer students to the example answer and elicit why it is *used to* (a positive, repeated action in the past). Have students complete the activity and then compare answers.
- To check answers, ask students to read complete sentences aloud.

Answers
1 *used to* 2 use to 3 used to 4 use to 5 use to
6 used to

F **Look and write five sentences. Then compare.**

- Have students look at the picture and elicit some sentences about what they can see happening. Ask students *Do you think this picture is in the past or present?* Point out that it is about the past, but some things are wrong.
- Ask one student to read the example sentences aloud; elicit one more thing that is wrong in the picture. Give students time to find and write five sentences about the picture using either *used to* or *didn't use to*.
- Then have students take turns to say sentences in pairs. Ask *Did you have the same sentences or different sentences?*
- Invite pairs to share their sentences. Which pair has the most different sentences?

Suggested Answers
People didn't use to drive cars. They used to ride horses. They didn't use to have airplanes. They didn't use to eat ice cream. They didn't use to wear jeans. They used to wash clothes in the river. They didn't use to watch television. They didn't use to have headphones.

Cool Down

Play *Running Sentences* (see TB p. 26) with key sentences from the lesson; for example, *We didn't use to have computers. / In their free time they used to go ice-skating. / Viking children didn't use to go to school. / Vikings used to weave their own clothes from wool.*

Practice **Resource Bank:** Grammar Printout
Student's App: Grammar Practice

Global Citizenship

Lesson Objectives

- to learn vocabulary about trade and travel: *coins, fur, honey, jewelry, leather, necklace, pottery, silk, spices, wheat, wood*
- to explore why people traded and explored in the past
- to practice listening for gist and details

Materials

Audio Tracks 57 to 59; Audio Track E; a world map (D)

Opening Question

Ask students the opening question: *Why did people trade and explore in the past?* Check students understand that *trade* means to buy and sell. Give students time to think and then elicit opinions. Don't correct students at this point; they will find out more about the topic during the lesson.

A TRACK 57 TB p. 219 **Listen to Becky talk to her mom. Name three things the Vikings traded for spices, silk, and pottery.**

- Have students look at p. 66 and say what they can see. Tell students they will hear a girl talking about what she learned in school about the Vikings.
- Play the audio and have students point to the words and pictures as they listen.
- Play the audio again and ask the comprehension question *Name three things the Vikings traded for spices, silk, and, pottery.* Elicit answers.

Answers

three of the following: wood; wool; fur; leather; fish; honey

B TRACK 58 TB p. 219 **Listen, say, and number the pictures in A.**

- Play the audio and have students point to the pictures and say the words.
- Play the audio again and have students number the words in the order they hear them.
- Check answers by inviting students to call out the numbers and asking others to respond.

Answers

1 *fur* 2 silk 3 spices 4 wheat 5 pottery 6 wood 7 leather 8 necklace 9 jewelry 10 coins 11 honey

TRACK E TB p. 219 **Visualization**

The TTL has a visualization audio track for this vocabulary set. (See TB p. 21.)

C Read and complete.

- Ask a volunteer to read the complete example sentence. Ask students what word tells us the answer is *spices* (cooking).
- Have students complete the activity and then compare answers with a partner. To check answers, ask pairs to read a question and answer aloud.

Answers

1 *spices* 2 necklace 3 honey 4 jewelry 5 leather 6 wheat

D TRACK 59 TB p. 219 **Now listen to Ari and Jing. How did the two groups of people travel?**

- To generate interest, have students look at the two pictures and notice where each child is from. Ask students *Where are these countries?* Use a map to find them.
- Have students look at the pictures and ask them *What can you see?* Ask if they have seen or been in boats like these before and where.
- Listening for gist: play the audio and have students listen for the answer to the gist question *How did the two groups of people travel?* Have students compare ideas and then elicit answers.

Answers

The Maoris traveled in canoes, and the Chinese explorers traveled in huge ships called junks.

E Listen again and choose.

- Listening for details: have students look at the sentences and choose the correct answer for as many as they can.
- Play the audio and have students check their answers and answer any they missed. Check answers as a class.

Answers

1 *building* 2 sun 3 birds and whales 4 1st 5 pottery 6 700

International English

Elicit that *figure out* is American English and *work out* is British English. Ask *Which do we use?*

Discussion Questions

- Draw students' attention to the discussion questions: *Would you like to be a trader or an explorer? Why? What's more important, trading or exploring?* Have students discuss the questions in small groups (see **ETB**).
- Return to the opening question to ask again: *Why did people trade and explore in the past?* Divide the class into pairs and have them think of as many reasons as possible. Then discuss as a class.

Cool Down

Make a simple quiz using the lesson vocabulary, e.g. *Name two things made with wheat.* (bread, biscuits, etc.) As soon as students know the answer, have them raise their hands. This can be played as a team game with points for correct answers.

Practice Student's App: Vocabulary Practice; Listening Practice

Explore Language

Lesson Objectives

- to learn and practice how to make questions with *used to*
- to practice vocabulary related to trade

Materials
Audio Tracks 60 and 61

Warm Up

Ask students to name their favorite foods. Make a list on the board. Have students imagine they are going on a long journey and they can take only one food with them to eat every day. Ask them to choose something from the board and tell a partner. Ask some students for their choices and find out if the others agree.

A TRACK 60 TB p. 219 **Listen and read. Why is Freya glad that she wasn't a Viking?**

- Ask students *What can you see in the picture? What do you think the woman is talking about?* Ask if they can find Freya from earlier lessons (she's the girl in the purple shirt).
- Play the audio and have students listen and follow the dialogue in their books.
- Ask the gist question *Why is Freya glad that she wasn't a Viking?* and elicit the answer. Ask *Have you ever tried dried fish? Would you like to?*

Answer
because the Vikings used to eat dried fish every day

B Look at A. Complete.

- Write or project the table onto the board.
- Have students discuss and complete the grammar table in pairs using the dialogue.
- When they have completed the table, invite students to come up to the board and fill in one word each. Ask if everyone agrees. Discuss the word order and verb forms together, but let your class guide the discussion. If you feel that students need more guidance, the **ETB** provides a differentiation activity to help you support students as they explore the grammar table.
- Refer students to the Grammar tip *Watch Out*. Tell students that *used to* in the past has the same meaning as *usually* in the present (both mean something that happened regularly). Have students work in pairs to write two versions of the same sentence, one using *usually* in the present and one using *used to* in the past; for example, *I usually eat lunch at 12:00. I used to eat lunch at 12:00.*

Answers
use; to; use; to; did

C Think and discuss. Then choose.

- Give students some time to read the sentence and think about their answer. Then have them compare their ideas with a friend.
- Read the sentence and answer options and have students raise their hands to show the option they chose. Check everyone agrees.
- Remind students that *use + to* is an unusual verb, as it can only be used in the past, not the present.

Answer
1 the past

D TRACK 61 TB p. 219 **Listen and say.**

- Play the audio and have students listen and repeat. For ideas on how to vary the drill, see TB p. 23.

E Choose and write questions. Guess your partner's answers.

- Ask students if they can remember what their lives were like when they were five years old. Ask if they can remember something that was different.
- Elicit a question from the list of verb phrases and write it on the board. When you write *use to* in the question, check with students: *With "d" or no "d"?*
- Ask students to guess what your answer is to this question—*Yes, I did* or *No, I didn't.* Write the two possible answers on the board and circle the one with the majority vote. Then confirm the answer.
- Divide students into pairs and have them write more *Did you …?* questions for their partner using the verbs in the box. Tell them to guess their partner's answers and write them in the second column of the table.

Suggested Answers
Did you use to love riding a bike? Did you use to speak English? Did you use to live in a different place? Did you use to go swimming? Did you use to walk to school? Did you use to like vegetables? Did you use to be scared of animals?
Yes, I did. / No, I didn't.

F Look at E. Ask and answer. Were you right?

- Tell students they will ask their partner the questions they wrote in E. Have a pair of students read the example in the speech bubbles first.
- Then have students ask and answer. Tell them to listen to their partner's answers and put a checkmark next to the answers they predicted correctly.
- Ask if any students predicted all of their partner's answers correctly.

Cool Down

Play *Pass the Whisper!* (see TB p. 26) with the questions in D.

Practice **Resource Bank:** Grammar Printout
Student's App: Grammar Practice

Talk About It

Lesson Objectives

- to prepare and practice negotiating in a conversation
- to recognize and reproduce words with /s/ or /z/

Materials
Video; Audio Track 62

Warm Up

Ask students *Do you collect anything? What do you like to collect?* Make a list on the board. Who has the most unusual collection?

A TB p. 238 **Watch and listen. Is there a trade?**

- Tell students they are going to watch a video showing a conversation between friends talking about their collections. Ask students *Have you seen soccer cards before?*
- Introduce the gist question *Is there a trade?* and have students predict the answer. Point out that here *a trade* means to swap items rather than to buy or sell. Say *You give me your pencil and I give you my pen. That's a trade.*
- Play the video and have students raise their hands when they hear the answer. Encourage students to say what gave them the answer. Then ask some more comprehension questions; for example, *What soccer cards are they collecting?* (World Cup) Play the video again and have students notice the boys' body language and tone of voice as they negotiate.

Answer
Yes

B **Watch again. Check (✔) the sentences or questions you hear.**

- Have students read the sentences and questions.
- Play the video and have students complete the activity. Read the sentences and questions and have students raise their hands for the ones they checked.
- Read the checked phrases 3, 4, 5, 6, and 8 again and ask students to say if they give suggestions (clap hands) or if they mean *yes* (raise hands) or *no* (lower hands). (Suggestions: 3, 5; Yes: 8; No: 4, 6)

Answers
1; 3; 4; 5; 6; 8

Pronunciation /s/ or /z/

TRACK 62 TB p. 219 **Listen and say.**

- Demonstrate the two sounds for students to copy. Make the voiceless /s/ sound first (a hissing sound). Then make the voiced /z/ sound (a buzzing sound). If students put their hands on their throat, they should feel their vocal cords vibrate when they make the /z/ sound.
- Read the words aloud, then play the audio and have students repeat the words.
- Say *These words are used in the video. What other words do you know with this sound?* Elicit ideas and write them on the board in two columns (e.g. *silk, clothes*). Drill the pronunciation of each word.

Suggested Answers
/s/ sword, stew, skating, spices
/z/ animals, warriors, coins

C **Plan. Think about items to trade. Then answer.**

- Tell students they are going to plan their own conversation about trading items with a friend.
- Ask students what items they can see in the pictures across pp. 70–71. Ask *Do you have any of these things?* Tell students to imagine they have three of the items and they want to trade them. Write your own example on the board: *I have an eraser I want to trade, because my friend gave me a new one yesterday.* Have students think of three things they have that they want to trade and why.
- Now ask students what items they want to get. Give an example: *I want to trade the soccer cards for the comics because I want to read them!* Have students decide on three things they want and why. Then give them time to complete the table.

D **Prepare notes for your conversation. Use your ideas from C and phrases from B.**

- Play the video again as a model and remind students to watch with their own conversation in mind.
- Prepare notes for an example conversation with the class, using your plan from C. Build up the conversation on the board, using the students' suggestions.
- Have students work in pairs and compare the items they have and the items they want. Have them plan a conversation in their notebooks where they trade something and disagree about another trade. They can use the phrases from B by substituting the objects for the ones they want to trade; for example, *If I give you <u>a pen</u>, will you give me <u>a pencil</u>?*

E **Practice with a friend.**

- Have students practice their conversation as many times as they need to. Encourage them to gradually look at their notes less often so their conversation becomes more fluid. Remind them that if they disagree with their partner, they should do so politely! Monitor and provide praise and help where needed.

Cool Down

Play *What Was the Last Word?* (see TB p. 27) with the video.

Practice **Student's App:** Speaking Skills Practice; Speaking Video

Write About It

Lesson Objectives

- to identify examples
- to practice using example phrases to give examples
- to plan and write a character profile

Materials

(Optional) Challenge, Standard, and Support writing printouts from the Resource Bank, one per student (C and D)

Warm Up

Ask students what they like to do with their best friend and have them discuss the question in small groups. Then invite groups to share ideas and capture these in a spidergram on the board.

A Read the character profile. Circle the words used to give the examples.

- Have students look quickly at the character profile and see if any of the activities in the text match the activities on the board. Ask students *Which people are talked about in the text? Who is the main character?* (Eric is the main character; the other characters are his sisters, brothers, parents, grandparents, and best friend Rolf.) Ask some additional comprehension questions; for example, *What did Eric look like?* (fair hair, blue eyes) *How old was he?* (ten years old)
- Ask students to scan the first paragraph for a list of activities. Explain that these are examples of the kinds of activities Eric and Rolf did together. Ask *What phrase introduces the examples?* (for example)
- Have students read the rest of the text and circle more phrases that introduce examples. When they finish, ask how many different phrases they have (there are three). Ask students to say the phrases they found and read a section of the text that uses the phrase. Draw students' attention to the way commas are used to list the examples

Answers

for example, for instance, such as

B Match. Then complete with *for example*, *such as*, or *for instance*.

- Point out that 1–5 are beginnings of sentences and a–e are the endings that complete them. Look at number 1 as a class: invite a volunteer to read the full sentence, then ask students if they can also use *for example* or *for instance* in this sentence (yes). Point out that the only difference is the comma after *for example* and *for instance* but that all the phrases can be used in the same way. Tell students that *for instance* is used more in writing than speaking. Ask students what word in 1 gives them a clue to figure out the correct ending (countries). Remind them to look for clues when completing the other sentences.
- Have students complete the other sentences in their notebooks and compare with a friend. Ask if they chose the same ways to complete them each time.
- To check answers, invite students to read complete sentences aloud and ask if everyone agrees on the ending. Ask if any students used a different phrase to introduce the examples and remind them to check whether they used commas correctly.

Answers

1 e 2 b 3 a 4 c 5 d

C Plan. Invent a Viking character and complete.

- Tell students they a going to plan a Viking character profile. Have students look at p. 72 in their books (or project it) and decide who they want to describe. Point out they will need to use their imagination to complete most of the information.
- Do a visualization routine to generate ideas. Encourage students to imagine they are the character they have chosen. Ask *What's your name? How old are you? What do you look like? Where do you live? Who do you live with? Do you have brothers and sisters? What activities do you do? What are you doing now? What things do you like? What do you dislike doing?*
- Have students complete their plans, using the ideas generated by the visualization as a prompt. You can hand out the Challenge printouts at this point.

D Write your character profile.

- Have students write a draft of their character profile in their notebooks, based on their plan in C. Remind them to use A as a model and to give examples using the example phrases.
- Have students self-correct or exchange their work with a friend and peer-correct. You can put a checklist of things for students to look out for on the board (e.g. spelling, commas, capital letters, periods, use of examples and example phrases).
- Have students correct any mistakes and write their final instructions neatly on paper. Alternatively, hand out the Support and Standard printouts from the Resource Bank.
- Have students read their descriptions in small groups. Ask *Are your characters similar or very different?* Have each group nominate one description for the whole class to hear.

Cool Down

Play *Simon Says* (see TB p. 27) with actions from this lesson, e.g. *play warrior games, hunt for animals, carry wood, go fishing, tell stories, play board games.*

Practice **Student's App:** Writing Practice

Think It Over

Lesson Objectives

- to review what has been learned in the unit
- to reflect on the unit and their own progress
- to think about learning strategies and how to continue learning at home

Warm Up

Give short definitions of some of the vocabulary from pp. 62–63 or p. 66. Have students raise their hands when they know the word. This can be played as a team game for points. Suggested definitions: *What's the name of a Viking soldier?* (a warrior) *People made clothes from this—it's from China.* (silk) *This is money made from metal.* (coins) *Vikings wore this on their heads.* (helmet) *This is the food the Vikings ate.* (stew) *People used these to make their food taste good.* (spices) *Bees make this.* (honey) *This is food that you grow in the ground.* (crops) *Vikings used this to fight other people.* (sword)

Read the questions and write or draw your answers.

- Give students time to think about and discuss activities in the unit before they complete each question. Explain that they can choose to either write a few words or sentences or to draw a picture. Allowing students to make a personal response will help them retain knowledge and engage with the learning points.

What did I do?

- Give students a few minutes to look back through the unit at the different activities they did. Ask questions about the unit or write questions on the board for students to discuss in pairs or small groups; for example, *Who did you write about? What did you talk about? What story did you read? Where did you hear about different boats?*
- Encourage students to identify something in the unit that they found challenging or something that was particularly memorable for them. Students can draw or write about their chosen activity.

What did I learn?

- Have students talk to a partner about what they remember from the unit—stories, words, phrases, people, facts about Vikings.
- Ask questions about the unit to help students to think about what they learned; for example, *What new words do you know? What new questions can you say? What did you learn about the Vikings or other explorers? What did you learn about New Zealand and China? What else did you learn?*
- Encourage students to draw a picture or write sentences about their learning outcomes.
- Once students have written their statements, have them talk to a friend about what they think they learned.

How did I learn?

- Ask students how they learned the Viking words in Lesson 1. Elicit ideas (e.g. by seeing and miming the words, by doing the visualization activity, by hearing the words in the story, by doing a writing or speaking activity).
- Encourage students to think about how they learned throughout the unit; for example, how did they develop their speaking skills?
- Have students draw a picture or write about some of the activities that helped them learn. Then have them compare their answers in pairs and think about what was similar and what was different about how they learned. Ask *do we all learn in the same way?*

How well did I do?

- Ask students to color in the number of boats that best expresses how well they think they learned the content (i.e. the more they color, the more they feel they have learned). Ask *What do you understand? What do you need to practice more?* Encourage students to look back through the unit to see how much they remember, what they did well, and what they found difficult.

What can I do next?

- Encourage students to think about what they can do at home to improve their English. Have them suggest some verbs that they can use (e.g. read, practice, watch, find out, sing) and write the verbs in their books. Students can look back at the previous units to get more ideas. Encourage students to suggest their own ideas for different activities they can do.
- Have students choose several activities that they would like to do and write them in their notebooks. They can then share their ideas with a partner.

Looking Forward

Draw students' attention to the character at the bottom of the page. Ask *Who's this?* and elicit what they remember about her. (Jennifer was the librarian talking about Vikings in Explore Language 2.) Ask students where they think she travels to next. Elicit predictions about her trip and Unit 6. Point out that they will find out if they were correct in the first lesson of the next unit.

Play 1

To further review and recycle the language in Units 1–5, have students practice and perform the play, *Time Traveler,* on pp. 140–141. See TB p. 211 for teaching notes.

Practice **Resource Bank:** Unit Test; Mid-year Test
Student's App: Vocabulary and Grammar Review

Get Ready to Read

Lesson Objectives

- to activate prior knowledge about the past
- to encourage students to observe and interpret through a Think, Pair, Share VTR

Materials

(Optional) VTR printout from the Resource Bank (A, B, C)

Warm Up

Ask students *Who lived in our country 2,000 years ago? Where did they live? What kinds of towns and houses did they live in?* Ask students *Have you heard of any other ancient civilizations?* Brainstorm a list on the board.

Think, Pair, Share

A Look at the picture. A long time ago people made this. Why did they make it and who were they? Think about it.

Students are going to do a Think, Pair, Share VTR to explore the image of an ancient settlement, The Guyaju ruins in Yanqing county, Beijing.

- Ask students what they can see in the picture and elicit some ideas. Provide vocabulary where necessary.
- Then ask students *Who do you think made this? Why do you think they made it?* Give students one or two minutes to think independently and form their own ideas. Tell them to cross their arms when they've thought of some ideas.

B Discuss with your partner.

- Invite two volunteers to read the speech bubbles. Ask students *Do you agree with this?*
- Have students work in pairs to share ideas about who built the place in the picture and why. Encourage them to discuss any questions they might have and to think of possible answers together. Encourage students to expand on their ideas by asking each other *What makes you say that?* and other questions. Provide vocabulary where necessary.

C Share your ideas with the class.

- Ask pairs to share their ideas about the picture with the class. Encourage students to use *we*, as they are talking about their partner's opinion, too.

Here's an example of this part of the routine.

Teacher: (Student A), what do you and your friend think?

Student A: We think this place is in the desert somewhere, maybe in the Middle East. We think it might have been built by a tribe there.

Teacher: Interesting! Why do you think they might have built it?

Student B: We think they wanted to live here.

Teacher: What would it be like to live here?

Student B: Uncomfortable. The caves are small.

Student C: But there are many caves. We think everyone had their own cave.

Teacher: OK, does anyone have any different opinions about this picture?

Transition

Ask students *Where do you think the people who lived here before went? Why do you think they left, and how did they travel?*

D Think and discuss. How did people travel in the past?

- Have students discuss means of transportation in the past in small groups.
- To expand the discussion, write some prompts on the board to encourage students to start thinking of different ways people traveled, e.g. *How far? Why? What? Where? When?* Students should begin to recognize that how people traveled varied depending on the distance they were traveling, the purpose of their journey, the load they were carrying, and the country/area and time they lived in. They might also mention that even in the same place/time, richer people would often have traveled differently from poorer people.
- Invite each group to share some of their ideas.

E Think and discuss. Look at the reading on the next page. Is it a story or an article? Do you see any characters?

- Have students look at the reading on p. 74 or project it onto the board. Ask students *What images can you see?* Elicit suggestions. (a map, picture of ceramics, picture of men and camels, portrait of man)
- Ask *Do you think this is a story or an article? How do we know?* Have students discuss their ideas in pairs.
- Invite pairs to share their ideas with the class and find out if everyone agrees. You could point out that stories often have pictures of key characters.

Suggested Answers

It looks like an article because there are headings, maps, and pictures of objects. I don't see any characters.

Now read The Silk Road

Nonfiction: *The Silk Road—* Informational Text

Lesson Objectives

- to read an informational text about a historic trade route
- to make a personal connection to the reading

Materials

Audio Tracks 25 and 26; Video

Warm Up

In pairs, ask students to think of all the animals they can that people use for work or travel. Have them make a list and then compare with another pair. Tell them to add any animals they didn't think of to their original list.

TRACK 25 TB p. 231 Reading Approach

First Reading: Engage with the Text

- Refer students to the title of the reading. Check students know what silk is and how it is made. (It is made from very fine threads produced by silk worms—similar to spider web—which is then made into a cloth.)
- Have students read the text silently. To focus them ask: *What does the blue line on the map show?* (the Silk Road) *What do you think the red dots show?* (important towns on the Silk Road)

TRACK 26 TB p. 231 Words in Context

- Play the audio and have students repeat the words.
- Have students race to find the words in the reading.
- Tell students they can sometimes **use the separate parts of a word to help establish the meaning of the new words** (see TB p. 22). Have them discuss their ideas with a partner, using L1 if necessary.
- Then bring the class together and use these discussion points to confirm the meanings.

goods (p. 74) Ask what word in the first paragraph helps us to understand *goods*. (trade) Ask *What do people do with goods?* (sell them) *Why do goods go on planes and ships?* (they are sold in different countries)

faraway (p. 74) Point out that there are two parts to this word. Elicit the meaning of the two parts: *far* and *away*. Ask *Does that help you understand the meaning of the word?*

network (p. 74) Elicit what the two parts of the word are (*net* and *work*). Have students point to the picture showing a network of routes. Ask them how this is similar to a net. Draw a picture of a net on the board. (Both have a lot of different lines crossing each other, the lines are all connected.)

routes (p. 74) Have students identify a similar word (path) and elicit that routes are the paths we travel from one place to another place. Ask *Where does a sea route go?* (across the sea)

merchants (p. 74) Elicit that the pronoun *their* tells us merchants were people and the verb and noun *trade goods* helps us to understand who the merchants were and what they did.

preserved (p. 74) Elicit which words help us to understand *preserved* (food and longer). Ask *What did the spices help people do with food?* (stop it from going bad because people didn't have refrigerators)

thieves (p. 74) Ask *Do you think the thieves are good or bad people? What do you think they do?* Elicit that the words *it was safer to travel in a big group* give us a clue about what the thieves did.

Second Reading: Analyze the Text and Features

- Play the video to reinforce understanding.
- Ask some comprehension questions to check understanding: *Where was the start of the Silk Road?* (Eastern Europe) *Where was the end?* (China)
- Have students do a Think, Pair, Share routine (see TB p. 20) to discuss the facts in the blue boxes.
  - **Fact** (p. 74): *In ancient China, soldiers and workers used to get paid in silk.* Ask students why they think this happened.
  - **Fact** (p. 75): *People traveling on the Silk Road also spread diseases.* Ask students how they think this happened.
- Discuss the text focus: *Which details are **evidence** of the author's main idea?* Give students some time to look back through the text and identify what the main idea of the article is and what information shows this, then have them discuss the question in pairs.

Third Reading: Interact with the Text

- Tell students to imagine a reader wants to know whether they should read the article or not. Have them work in pairs to summarize the article. To do this, have students first decide on and circle key words or phrases in the text. Have them use these to identify the main ideas. Finally, have them read the text again and decide which details are important to understand the main ideas and which information is unnecessary. Have them write a short paragraph to summarize the text, then invite pairs to share these summaries with the class.

Cool Down

Read the first part of some key phrases from the reading. Have students race to find the second half and raise their hands to provide the answer. Suggested phrases: *It wasn't that easy to trade with …* (people in faraway places). / *These routes connected …* (to create a path from Eastern Europe to China) / *Silk was light and it used to be …* (as valuable as gold).

Practice **Student's App:** Nonfiction Video

Explore the Reading

Lesson Objectives

- to understand and analyze *The Silk Road* through reading comprehension activities
- to review and practice the reading skill of identifying the main idea
- to learn about important places through CLIL (history): understanding the significance of the Silk Road
- to make a personal connection to the reading

Warm Up

Ask students if they can think of what countries would be on the Silk Road and then ask them which one they would most like to visit and why. Have students discuss in pairs and then elicit ideas.

A Make a list. What did people trade on the Silk Road?

- Before students open their books, have a team quiz to find out what they remember from the reading. Ask *Where did the Silk Road start and end?* (Eastern Europe to China) *Who traveled on the Silk Road?* (merchants and traders) *Why did they use the Silk Road?* (to sell and buy things) *What other things moved along the Silk Road?* (ideas, culture, inventions, diseases) *When did people stop using the Silk Road?* (around the 1400s)
- Refer students to the list in A. Ask them if they can remember any of the items that were traded in the reading, and write one or two on the board as an example. Then have students look back at the reading again and make a list of all the things they can find.
- Have students compare their answers with a friend and see if they can expand their lists.
- Invite students to read an item each. Tell students to listen and add anything missing from their lists.

Answers
tea; furs; pottery; spices; silk; ideas; culture; inventions; paper; printing press

B Read and write *True* or *False*.

- Refer students to the first sentence and have them say whether it is true or false and why. (False—traders used to trade silk, not wear it.)
- Have students complete the activity and be prepared to say why they chose *false* for some answers.
- Ask students to read aloud a sentence each and say *True* or *False*. Ask if everyone agrees. If false, ask a student to explain why.

Answers
1 False 2 True 3 True 4 False 5 True 6 True

C Think and check (✔). What's the main idea of the reading?

Students are going to identify the main point that the reading makes about the Silk Road. This draws on the CLIL history focus of understanding the significance of the Silk Road trade route.

- First, set students up for a Rally Robin (see TB p. 20) to brainstorm all the reasons they think the Silk Road was important. Then have them read the three statements about the reading.
- Give students some thinking time to decide which of the three statements is the main idea of the reading and then have them compare their ideas with a friend.
- Read the statements and have students raise their hands for the one they chose as most important.

Answer
1 The most important thing people traded on the Silk Road was knowledge.

D Think and discuss. Would you like to travel on the Silk Road? What would you trade from your country?

- Ask students if they know what products from their country were traded in the past. If they don't know, give them some time to research online or ask them about products that could be traded today. Ask *Do you think any of these products would be good for trading on the Silk Road? Why do you think that?*
- Have students discuss with a friend what would be good or bad about traveling and working on the Silk Road and what they would like to trade. Then have a Group Time discussion to share ideas (see TB p. 21). Take a class vote for who would or wouldn't like to travel on the Silk Road.
- Point out that the Silk Road is still interesting for tourists to visit. Ask students *What do you think tourists might be interested in seeing, visiting, and learning about on the Silk Road?* Have students discuss their ideas in pairs and then share with the rest of the class. (Tourists can see a lot of different cultures from the Eastern Mediterranean culture of Greece and Turkey through the plains of Uzbekistan and Mongolia and into China, past mountains, caves, and historical buildings, and can travel on a high-speed railway.)

Cool Down

Play the *Chain Game* (see TB p. 25) using items that could be traded on the Silk Road. Start the chain with the sentence *I'm a merchant on the Silk Road, and I sell tea.*

Practice **Student's App:** Reading Practice

Get Ready to Read

Lesson Objectives

- to review and practice the reading skill of identifying points of view
- to learn about first- and third-person narration to tell a story

Warm Up

Ask students how many characters they can remember from the stories they have read so far in this book. (Unit 1: Emil, Mrs. Blanche, Mr. and Mrs. Durand [Emil's neighbors]; Unit 2: Ooleck, Zeena; Unit 3: Luana, Maria; Unit 4: Marfusha and Katyusha [rabbits], Enos and Ham [chimps]) Write them on the board. For each one they recall, ask what they remember best about the character.

A Read. Then look at the reading *Trust Me* in Unit 3 again. Who is telling the story in each sentence? Write *narrator*, *Maria*, or *Luana*.

- Before students look back at the story *Trust Me* (pp. 48–53) in their books, ask if they can remember the characters and the main events of the story. Ask students *Can you remember which animal the two friends found in the forest?* (a bear)
- Elicit who the narrator of story is—the person who is not in the story but who tells us about what happens.
- Have students read the three sets of sentences in A and decide who is telling the story. Have them look back at the story on pp. 48–53 to check. Point out they should have one answer for each person.
- Check answers and ask students how they know who is telling the story.
- Refer students to the skills box about different points of view. Ask students *Do you like it better when a character tells the story or the narrator tells the story? Why? How is it different?* Have students discuss their ideas in pairs. Students might mention that it's more personal when a character tells the story and that it makes it easier to understand what the character is thinking or feeling and why they act in a certain way. This can help us to have a better understanding of the events in the story. Encourage them to also think about why having a character telling a story might be a disadvantage, e.g. we don't get to see what other characters are thinking. You could also point out or elicit that characters might sometimes tell a story in a certain way to make themselves look better; another character might tell the story in a different way!

Answers
1 Maria 2 narrator 3 Luana

B Read, think, and discuss. Look at the pictures and read the beginning of the story. Complete the story. First, tell it from the narrator's point of view. Then, retell it from the character's point of view.

- Refer students to the pictures or project them onto the board. Ask students *What can you see happening in the pictures? What do you think the story is about?* Elicit a few ideas.
- Have students read the beginning of the story under the pictures and ask *Does it give the narrator's point of view or the character's point of view?* (the narrator's point of view). Have students work in pairs or small groups to use the pictures to write the continuation of the story from the narrator's point of view.
- Ask if any pairs or groups would like to read aloud their completed version of the story from the narrator's point of view.
- Now have pairs and groups work together to change the story to the character's point of view. This can be done orally, but point out that they can add in extra information about what the character is thinking; for example, *I'm traveling on a train, and it's really exciting!*
- Ask groups/pairs to retell their stories to a different group/pair. Ask them how their stories were similar/different.

C Think and discuss. Read the first sentence of *Sinbad's First Voyage* on the next page. Who's telling the story?

- Have students turn to p. 78 and read the first sentence. Have them discuss in pairs who is telling the story. Elicit the answer and ask one student to say why they think that. Ask if everyone agrees.

Answer
Sinbad / the main character

Cool Down

Tell students they are are going to think about what characters might be thinking in different stories in the **Literacy Book**. Show different scenes from the stories and ask *What is* (name) *thinking?* Give students a couple of minutes to discuss their ideas for each scene in pairs.

Suggested scenes: p. 10 Mrs. Blanche when Emil buys the bottle of True Colors; p. 11 Emil when his picture becomes real; p. 29 Ooleck when he can't come up with an answer to his problem; p. 63 one of the rabbits when the spaceship lands in the ocean; p. 63 one of the chimps when the spaceship lands in the ocean.

Now read **Sinbad's First Voyage**

Fiction: *Sinbad's First Voyage—* Folk Tale

Lesson Objectives

- to read a folk tale about a traveler and his adventures
- to make a personal connection to the reading
- to think about point of view when telling a story

Materials
Audio Tracks 27 and 28

Warm Up

Ask students *Can you think of a good adventure story?* (book or movie) *What do all good adventure stories need?* Have students discuss ideas in pairs.

TRACK 27 TB p. 231 **Reading Approach**

First Reading: Engage with the Text

- Refer students to the title and ask them *Have you ever heard of Sinbad or any of the stories about him?* Have students look at the pictures in the story and guess what type of story it is.
- Ask students to close their books. Play the audio and have students follow in their books. Pause in different places and ask students *What do you think will happen next?* Then continue the audio to confirm.

TRACK 28 TB p. 232 **Words in Context**

- Play the audio and have students repeat the words.
- Have students race to find the words in the story.
- Remind students they can sometimes **use the separate parts of words and their knowledge of similar words to help establish the meaning of new words** (see TB p. 22). Have them discuss their ideas with a partner, using L1 if necessary.
- Then bring the class together and use these discussion points to confirm the meanings.

wealthy (p. 78) Have students read the paragraph about Sinbad's father. Ask *If he was a merchant and traded jewelry and silk, what can we imagine about him?* (He was rich.)

penniless (p. 78) Ask students *Did Sinbad spend all the money?* (yes) *What is another word for* penniless? (poor) Elicit that the word itself also gives us a clue: we can divide it into two: *penny* (a small coin) and *less* (without).

boarded (p. 80) Elicit that *The Rose* is the name of a ship. The context suggests this is the start of a journey, so we can guess that *boarded* means *to get on* the ship. Have students mime boarding a boat.

sank (p. 82) Ask *What happens when you fall into the sea and go* deeper and deeper? Have students mime sinking.

strength (p. 82) Point out they know another similar sounding noun—*length*. Ask what adjective *length* comes from (long) and if they can guess the adjective *strength* comes from (strong).

stranger (p. 83) Point out what Sinbad said just before. (He was on a *strange beach*.) Ask *Has he seen this beach before?* (no) *So what is a stranger?* (a person we haven't met before)

troubles (p. 84) Ask *What do you think he meant when he said* I thought my troubles were over, but…? (More trouble is coming now.) *What does "trouble" mean in this sentence?* (danger, a bad situation: the next picture gives us a clue)

Second Reading: Analyze the Text and Features

- Have students read the folk tale silently. Focus them by asking them to answer the following questions: *What was the only thing Sinbad had left from his father?* (his dagger) *How did he get money to go on the ship?* (He worked hard.)
- Use Think, Pair, Share to discuss the questions in the blue boxes.
  - **Personalization** (p. 78): *What do you think of Sinbad's friends?* Remind students they talked about what it means to be a friend in Unit 3. Ask students *Do you think his friends are good friends?* (No, they leave when he has no more money.)
  - **Language Focus** (p. 80): *What does* The world was my oyster *mean? Is there a similar phrase in your language?* Ask *Was Sinbad doing new things in new places and enjoying it? Do you think he had a lot of new opportunities?* (The phrase means you have opportunities to do anything you want.)
  - **Language Focus** (p. 84): *What does* Take that! *mean?* Ask *What is Sinbad doing when he says "Take that!"?* (throwing the dagger at the sea monster) Ask *When do people say* Take that? (when they're fighting—it is a phrase used in adventure stories, not real life!)
  - **Personalization** (p. 85): *Stories of Sinbad the Sailor are from* The Thousand and One Nights. *Would you like to read about Sinbad's other journeys?* Have students give reasons for their answer, then take a quick vote.

Third Reading: Interact with the Text

- Have students work in pairs to imagine what happened on Sinbad's next voyage. Give them time to draw his adventures, then have them tell the story to another pair, either from Sinbad's point of view or a narrator's.

Cool Down

Play a game of *Simon Says* (see TB p. 27) with some of the actions from the story (e.g. *work hard, trade with people, the ground is shaking, sink deeper and deeper, throw your dagger, greet the prince*).

Explore the Reading

Lesson Objectives

- to understand and analyze *Sinbad's First Voyage* through reading comprehension activities
- to explore the SEL competency of self-management by overcoming obstacles and creating strategies for more long-term goals
- to make a personal connection to the reading
- to recognize and reproduce words with the soft *c* sound

Materials
Audio Track 29

Warm Up

Play *Who Said It?* by calling out the phrases (see TB p. 27). Suggested phrases: *See you around, Sinbad!* (Sinbad's friends) *It's a whale!* (the sailors) *Take that!* (Sinbad) *I'm sure the king would like to thank you.* (the prince) *That was my first voyage. I went on many more.* (Sinbad)

A Complete the story map.

- Before students open their books, find out what they remember about the story. Write the following questions on the board and have students answer them in groups. *Why was Sinbad poor?* (because he spent all his father's money) *Where did he get the money to travel?* (He worked hard.) *What did the sailors think the whale was?* (an island) *Where did Sinbad work for almost a year?* (the king's palace)
- Look at the story map in A together. Elicit from the class what should go in the first box (all the main characters). Have students scan the story and tell you who to write in the box.
- Have students continue completing the story map individually and then compare with a friend to see if they agree about the beginning, middle, and end. Elicit some ideas.

Answers
Characters: *Sinbad*; Sinbad's father; Sinbad's friends; Maruf; sailors; men on island; Prince Zayn; the King
Setting: Sinbad's father's house; Sinbad's own house; the port; *The Rose* (ship); desert island; the king's palace
Beginning: Sinbad wastes money; becomes a sailor/merchant
Middle: lands on a whale; almost drowns; saves the king's horse
End: works for the king; goes home

B Read and answer.

- Refer students to the first question. Have students find the answer. Then ask if they can find something in the story that justifies the answer. (p. 79—*A man I knew, Maruf, told me there was work in the port.*)
- Have students continue the activity individually. Then have them compare answers in pairs.
- Check the answers and ask students to tell you something from the story that justifies each answer. Ask *Do you think Sinbad was good at overcoming challenges?* and elicit reasons.

Answers
1 He worked at the port. 2 He wanted to become rich and see the world. 3 He saved it and then paid to go on a ship. 4 He held on to a piece of wood. 5 He used the dagger to save the King's horse.

C Think and discuss. How do you overcome difficulties and challenges?

- Introduce the SEL competency of overcoming obstacles and creating strategies for long-term goals. Start by giving students an example of overcoming a difficulty in your life, e.g. *When my old car stopped working, I had to find a new one. I checked how much money I had and how much I could spend. Then I looked online for the best places to buy cars. I spoke to the people, got a lot of information, and made my new choice. Now I'm very happy with my new car!*
- Give students some time to think of difficulties or challenges they have had, in school or in sports or even video games! Have them think about how they faced the challenges and then discuss with a friend. Ask *Are you like Sinbad?*

TRACK 29 TB p. 232 **Spelling Pattern soft c**

Listen and write. Then check your answers.

- With books closed, write *face* on the board. Say the word, have students repeat, and ask students how the *c* is pronounced: /s/.
- Play the first part of the audio and have students repeat each word. Then have them open their books. Play the first part of the audio again and have them complete as many of the words as they can.
- Play the second part of the audio for students to check their spelling and complete any words they missed. Have them underline each soft *c* and read the words aloud. Ask students if they notice any patterns when they look at the words (the soft *c* comes before either *e* or *i* in each word).
- Have students look back at the reading to find more words with the soft *c* and write them down. Invite them to read them aloud. Then have students draw a big C and write all the soft *c* words from this lesson inside.

Answers
1 face 2 pencil 3 medicine 4 science 5 prince
In the reading: spices; place; surface; piece; Prince; palace

Cool Down

Have students work in pairs to make three sentences, each using at least two of the soft *c* words from the spelling pattern activity; for example, *The prince needs some medicine!* Have pairs choose their favorite sentence and share it with class.

Practice **Resource Bank:** Spelling Printout
Student's App: Reading Practice; Spelling Pattern Practice

Think Together

Lesson Objectives

- to make connections between the readings
- to explore the key concept: How has travel changed from ancient times?
- to reflect on the unit and provide personal thoughts and opinions

Warm Up

Have students look back at the VTR image on pp. 72–73 and ask *Do you now have any new ideas about the image, who might have lived here, and why?* Does it remind you of anywhere you've visited? Have students work in pairs and then share their ideas with the rest of the class.

A Think and write. Look at *The Silk Road* and *Sinbad's First Voyage* again. What did people gain from traveling in the past and what do they still gain from traveling today?

- Make sure students understand *gain* in this context. (*What good things, or benefits, did people get?*) Elicit one idea for each side of the list.
- Have students look back at the readings on pp. 74–75 and pp. 78–85 and find more things that people gained in the past. Then ask them to consider things that people gain today from traveling today.
- Have students compare their lists in pairs. Tell them they can add any new ideas their partner had. Then go around the class and have each pair make a suggestion. Count how many of their ideas appear on both sides of the list. Students should find that many of the benefits in the past still apply today!

Suggested Answers

Past: *explore new places*; met new people; traded goods; became rich; found new ideas; learned languages; learned about new cultures. Today: is quicker, is safer, can be for fun; can meet new people; can trade goods; can find new ideas; can learn new language; can learn about new cultures

B Complete the table. Think about a trip you took. What did you do? What new things did you see and learn?

- Draw or project the table onto the board. Tell students to imagine they are Sinbad. Elicit ideas for each section of the table from Sinbad's point of view.
- Then have students work individually to complete the table with information about the last trip they made.

C Look at the table in B. Do a Round Robin.

- Set the class up for the Round Robin cooperative learning routine (see TB p. 20).
- Designate one person to start in each group and have students each talk about their trip in turn. Encourage other group members to ask additional questions about the trip, e.g. *What did you eat? How did you get there? What did you buy? Do you want to visit again?* Then have each group nominate a spokesperson to tell the class about the group's trips. Other group members can help by prompting where necessary.
- Introduce the key concept question: *How has travel changed from ancient times?* In their groups, ask students to give examples of travel in ancient times that they learned about in this unit—traveling in caravans, the danger of thieves, and so on. Have them write their ideas in a spidergram. Then encourage students to add anything else they know about travel in ancient times, from books or movies.
- Have them draw a second spidergram showing different ways of traveling today. Ask each group to compare and contrast the ideas in the spidergrams and reflect on how travel and the experience of travel has changed over time.
- Ask for suggestions from the class and include as many groups and students as possible. Provide new vocabulary when necessary.

My Reading Journal

What else would you like to learn about the Silk Road?

This question encourages students to want to play an active role in their learning journey.

Give students time to think and then have them complete the sentence in the Reading Journal.

Have students share their ideas in small groups.

Example Answer

I want to find out how people learned to make silk.

Imagine you are talking to Sinbad at the beginning of the story. What advice would you give him?

This question encourages students to reflect critically on the story and Sinbad's behavior.

Give students some time to look back at the story of Sinbad's voyage and think about what advice they could give him. Elicit one or two examples and then have students write their own sentences. Remind them that the structure is *should* + verb.

Have students share their ideas with a friend.

Example Answers

1 You should be more careful with your money!
2 You should choose better friends. 3 You should be careful where you sleep!

Cool Down

Play *Disappearing Words* (see TB p. 25) with key words students associate with this unit. Have them suggest the words (maximum 12–15 words).

Practice Resource Bank: Unit Test; Mid-year Test
Student's App: Key Concept Practice

UNIT 6

Ready for Anything

Unit Overview

Themes

The outdoors

Survival

Synopsis

In this unit students will learn how to survive outdoors, find out about what to do in an emergency, and think about how teamwork is important for outdoor survival. They will plan and prepare a conversation about buying a present for a friend and write a postcard about a summer camp using target language from the unit.

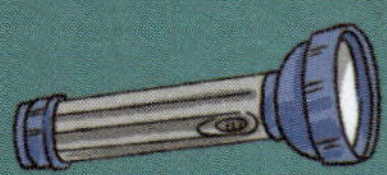

Language Book

Vocabulary
build, crawl, dive, hammock, put up, rope, shelter, survive, swing, tent
p. 128

Explore Language
Present Perfect: Questions
p. 129

Global Citizenship
How is teamwork important for surviving the outdoors?
binoculars, bug spray, compass, first aid kit, fishing rod, flashlight, matches, mosquito net, sleeping bag, sunscreen
p. 130

Explore Language
Present Perfect: Statements
p. 131

Talk About It
Conversation: giving reasons, disagreeing politely, deciding together
p. 132

Write About It
A Postcard
Sentence Building: adding information
p. 133

Think It Over
Review and Reflection
p. 134

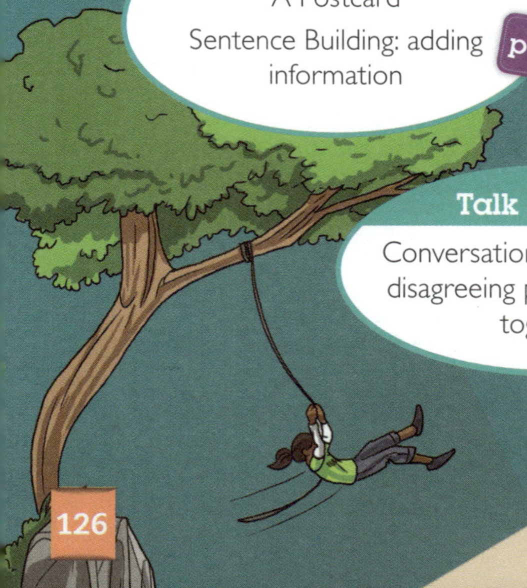

Literacy Book

Think Together
What can you do to survive in an emergency?
p. 141

Visible Thinking
Question Starts
p. 135

Fiction
Story: *Panic or Calm?*
Words in Context: *locked, power outage, handle this, spare, gasped, blushed, stuck*
p. 139

Nonfiction
Instructional Text: *SOS*
Words in Context: *wilderness, pretend, attention, attach, reflection, target, dots and dashes*
p. 136

Reading Skill
Understanding a sequence of events
p. 138

Spelling Pattern
st–
p. 137

Language and Literacy Connections

The connecting theme in Unit 6 is survival and being prepared.

	Language	Literacy
Vocabulary	**Set 1:** actions and survival **Set 2:** camping equipment	**Nonfiction:** build, put up, survive, tent, flashlight **Fiction:** flashlight
Grammar	**Present Perfect: Questions** Have you ever slept under the stars? Yes, I have. No, I haven't. **Present Perfect: Statements** I've traveled to a lot of dangerous places.	**Fiction** Have you ever wanted to panic? I don't think Alex has remembered my STOP lesson.
Skills	**Pronunciation:** *ph* as **/f/**	**Reading:** understanding a sequence of events **Spelling Pattern:** *st–*
International English	flashlight/torch; bug spray / insect repellent; sunscreen / sun cream; program/programme	trail/footpath; flashlight/torch; power outage / power cut

Vocabulary

Lesson Objectives

- to learn vocabulary to talk about actions and survival: *build, crawl, dive, hammock, put up, rope, shelter, survive, swing, tent*
- to sing a song about surviving on a desert island

Materials
Audio Tracks 63 to 66; Video

Warm Up

Write *on a tropical island, on a mountain, in a forest, or in the city* on the board. Ask students *Where do you think is the best place to live?* Take a vote. Ask students to give reasons for their answers.

A TRACK 63 TB p. 219 **Listen and find. What was David looking for in the tree?**

- Have students look at the picture on pp. 74–75 and ask them *What can you see? Where are the children? What are they doing?* Draw students' attention to the woman wearing the green top and purple skirt and ask if they remember her. (It's Jennifer, the librarian, from Unit 5.)
- Play the audio and have students point to the words and pictures as they listen.
- Ask the comprehension question *What was David looking for in the trees?* and elicit the answer. Play the audio again to check.
- Remind students of the challenge at the end of Unit 5: *Where do I travel to next?* If necessary, play the audio again to check the answer. (Jennifer travels to a desert island.)

Answer
fruit/mangoes

B TRACK 64 TB p. 220 **Listen, say, and number the pictures in A.**

- Play the audio and have students point to the pictures and say the words.
- Tell students to listen again and number the pictures in the order they hear them. Have students complete the activity individually. Play the audio again if necessary.
- Check answers and ask a few students to repeat each word to check pronunciation.

Answers
1 *crawl* 2 swing 3 dive 4 put up 5 tent 6 build
7 survive 8 hammock 9 rope 10 shelter

C TRACK 65 TB p. 220 **Close your eyes. Listen, visualize, and say.**

- Prepare students for the visualization (see TB p. 21).
- Play the audio, allowing students to visualize as they listen.
- Have students work in pairs. Each student should take turns miming one thing they visualized for their partner to guess.

D Look and write.

- Tell students they are going to match the new words to common phrases.
- Refer students to the example phrase: *crawl along the ground.* Have students mime the action.
- Give students some thinking time, then have them complete the activity in pairs. Project or write the activity on the board, then invite students to come to the front of the class to complete the phrases.

Answers
1 *crawl* 2 dive 3 rope / hammock 4 put up
5 shelter 6 survive

E TRACK 66 TB p. 220 **Listen and complete. Then watch and sing.**

- Have students look at the title of the song, *Desert Island Fun*, and ask them *How do you think you can have fun on a desert island?* Elicit suggestions and write them on the board.
- Play the song once, allowing students to listen and enjoy it.
- Explain that some parts of the words are missing and students have to complete them. Ask *Can you remember what words they are?* Have students read the song and complete any answers they know. Remind students that all of the words that they need are on pp. 74–75, so they can check their spelling.
- Play the song again and have students write any missing answers. Then play the song again and have students check their answers.
- Play the song video and have students watch and sing along. Then check answers as a class.

Answers
1 *survive* 2 hammock 3 tent 4 build 5 dive
6 rope 7 shelter

Cool Down

Play *Physical Spelling* (see TB p. 26) with the new vocabulary from this lesson.

Practice **Student's App:** Vocabulary Practice; Song Video

Explore Language

Lesson Objectives

- to learn how to make present perfect questions
- to practice using vocabulary about survival

Materials
Audio Tracks 67 and 68

Warm Up

Ask students *Do you think you could survive on a desert island? What things would you need to survive?* Have students discuss the questions in pairs.

A TRACK 67 TB p. 220 **Listen and read. What do the children want to cook for dinner?**

- Project the dialogue or have students look in their books. Have them look at the picture and say what they can see. Ask students if they recognize the people (they are David, Alex, and Naima from the previous lesson).
- Play the audio and have students follow the dialogue in their books.
- Ask the comprehension question *What do the children want to cook for dinner?* Elicit the answer, then ask *How do you think they'll cook it?* (over the fire)

Answer
They want to cook fish.

B **Look at A. Complete.**

- Write or project the table onto the board.
- Have students discuss and complete the grammar table in pairs using the dialogue.
- Check answers on the board. Discuss the word order and verb forms together, but let your class guide the discussion. If you feel that students need more guidance, the **ETB** provides a differentiation activity to help you support students as they explore the grammar table.
- Ask students *What do you need to make the present perfect?* (*have*/*has* and a past verb; point out that this is called a *past participle*) Make sure students notice the word *ever* in the question.
- Ask *Do you think these questions are about the past, present, or future?* Give students time to discuss their answer in pairs. Elicit some answers and ask *Why do you think that?* Establish that the questions are about the past and that the past participle is what gives us the clue.
- Have students look at the Grammar tip *Remember.* Elicit that the past participles in the grammar table are irregular because they don't have an *–ed* ending. Have students recall the infinitive and simple past forms of the verbs in the table. Tell students that here the past participle is the same as the simple past, but sometimes they are different. Give an example (e.g. *swam*/*swum*).

Answers
Have; slept; have; Has; put; hasn't; Have; caught; haven't

C **Think and discuss. Then choose.**

- Check students understand what *specific time* means. (that we know exactly when something happened) Give them a little thinking time to choose an answer option and encourage them to look at the table in B and the dialogue in A to help. Then have them discuss their answer with a partner.
- Elicit and confirm the answer. Point out that the word *ever* in a question tells us it is about non-specific time.

Answer
1 non-specific

D TRACK 68 TB p. 220 **Listen and say.**

- Play the audio and have students repeat. For ideas on how to vary the drill, see TB p. 23.

E **Read the participle. Complete.**

- Refer students to the example *swim – swum.* Ask *Is it a regular or irregular verb?* (irregular) *How do you know?* (no *–ed*) Ask if the participle is the same as the simple past. (no: *swam – swum*)
- Have students complete the table with the base form of each verb. Project it onto the board and invite students to come to the board and complete a verb each. Ask if everyone agrees.
- For each verb, ask students if the participle is the same or different from the simple past form.

Answers
1 *swim* 2 see 3 build 4 drink 5 sleep 6 catch
7 put up 8 ride

F **Choose and write questions. Then ask and answer.**

- Tell students they are going to write questions to ask a friend. Elicit the past participles for all the verbs in the box and write them on the board. Then elicit two questions with the first two verb phrases to reinforce the structure of the question.
- Have students write their own questions using the verbs in the box. Remind them to make the first verb agree with the subject.
- Elicit how to make yes/no answers and then have students ask and answer with a friend. Encourage them to answer using complete sentences. They can then change partners and ask again.

Cool Down

Play *Pass the Whisper!* (see TB p. 26) with key questions from the lesson; for example, *Have you ever slept under the stars?*

Practice **Resource Bank:** Grammar Printout
Student's App: Grammar Practice

Global Citizenship

Lesson Objectives

- to learn vocabulary for camping equipment: *binoculars, bug spray, compass, first aid kit, fishing rod, flashlight, matches, mosquito net, sleeping bag, sunscreen*
- to explore how teamwork is important for surviving in the outdoors
- to practice listening for gist and details

Materials

Audio Tracks 69 to 71; Audio Track F; a world map (D)

Opening Question

Ask students the opening question: *How is teamwork important for surviving the outdoors?* Give students time to think and elicit some opinions.

A TRACK 69 TB p. 220 **Listen to Ryan and his friend Josh talk about camping equipment. What are they going to bring home?**

- Have students look at p. 78. Ask *What can you see?* Tell students they will hear two friends talking about things they need for camping.
- Play the audio and have students point to the pictures and words as they listen. Ask them the comprehension question *What are they going to bring home?* and elicit the answer. Play the audio again to check.

Answer

their dirty clothes

International English

Elicit which words are American English and which words are British English. Ask students if they remember hearing any of them before. Ask *Which ones do we use?*

B TRACK 70 TB p. 220 **Listen, say, and number the pictures in A.**

- Play the audio and have students point to the pictures and say the words.
- Play the audio again and have students listen again and write numbers next to the words in the order that they hear them.
- Check answers by having one student call out a number and nominating another student to respond.

Answers

1 *flashlight* 2 binoculars 3 first aid kit 4 sunscreen 5 mosquito net 6 bug spray 7 matches 8 fishing rod 9 sleeping bag 10 compass

TRACK F TB p. 220 **Visualization**

The TTL has a visualization audio track for this vocabulary set. (See TB p. 21.)

C Read and write.

- Tell students they are going to write the correct words/phrases next to the definitions. Look at the example together. Ask *What are the key words that tell us the answer?* (sleep, under, insects away)
- Have students complete the activity individually and then compare their answers with a friend. Ask pairs of students to read aloud a definition and an answer.

Answers

1 *mosquito net* 2 compass 3 first aid kit 4 binoculars 5 flashlight 6 sleeping bag 7 sunscreen

D TRACK 71 TB p. 220 **Now listen to Ryan and Hailey. Which object did they both learn to live without on their trips?**

- To generate interest, have students look at the two pictures and notice where each child is from. Ask students *Where are these countries? What do you know about them?* Use a map to find them.
- Have students look at the pictures and ask them *What can you see?* Ask if they have done activities like this before.
- Listening for gist: play the audio and have students listen for the answer to the gist question *Which object did they both learn to live without on their trips?* Have students compare their ideas and then elicit the answer.

Answer

cell phones

E Listen again. Write *True* or *False*.

- Listening for details: have students look at the sentences. Ask if they can remember if the sentences are true or false.
- Play the audio again and have students complete the activity individually. Check answers.

Answers

1 *True* 2 True 3 True 4 False 5 False 6 False

Discussion Questions

- Draw students' attention to the discussion questions: *Are you a good team member? How? What happens when people don't work as a team?* Have students discuss the questions in pairs (see **ETB**).
- Return to the opening question to ask again: *How is teamwork important for surviving in the outdoors?* Divide the class into small groups and have them think of as many ideas as possible. Encourage them to think about Ryan and Hailey's trips. Invite groups to put their ideas in a graphic organizer and share them with the class.

Cool Down

Play *Mime It!* (see TB p. 26) with the vocabulary from this lesson.

Practice **Student's App:** Vocabulary Practice; Listening Practice

Explore Language

Lesson Objectives

- to learn how to make present perfect statements
- to practice using vocabulary about survival

Materials

Audio Tracks 72 and 73

Warm Up

Play *Board Race* (see TB p. 25) with the word *pets* and have students write as many names of animals that people keep as pets as possible.

A TRACK 72 TB p. 220 **Listen and read. Is David's pet dangerous?**

- Ask students *What can you see in the picture? What do you think the people are talking about?*
- Play the audio and have students follow the story in their books.
- Ask the gist question *Is David's pet dangerous?* Elicit answers, then ask *Would you like to hold David's pet?*

Answer

No, it isn't.

B **Look at A. Complete.**

- Write or project the table onto the board.
- Have students discuss and complete the grammar table in pairs using the story.
- Check answers on the board. Discuss the word order abbreviations (I've, It's), and negative verb forms together, but let your class guide the discussion. If you feel that students need more guidance, the **ETB** provides a differentiation activity to help you support students as they explore the grammar table.
- Ask *How do we make present perfect sentences?* (Have/Has + subject + past participle)
- Refer students to the Grammar tip *Watch Out*. Highlight *It's* in the grammar table and point out that *It's* has two possible meanings and elicit what these are (*It is* and *It has*). Tell students that they should be able to understand the meaning from the context and words that follow. Remind students that the short version *It's* sounds much more natural in spoken English.

Answers

've; traveled; haven't; hasn't; bitten

C **Think and discuss. Then choose.**

- Give students some time to read the sentence and think about their answer. Then have them compare ideas with a friend.
- Read question and answer options and have students raise their hands to show the option they chose. Confirm the answer.

Answer

1 non-specific

D TRACK 73 TB p. 221 **Listen and say.**

- Play the audio and have students repeat. For ideas on how to vary the drill, see TB p. 23.

E **Complete with the present perfect.**

- Tell students they will use the present perfect to complete the sentences. Look at the example sentence together. Elicit why *'ve made* is the answer. (present perfect uses *have/has* + participle) Ask what the long form is (*have made*) and point out this is correct, too.
- Have students complete the activity.
- Check answers and write them on the board.

Answers

1 *'ve made* 2 has ridden 3 haven't visited 4 hasn't swum 5 've built 6 haven't slept

F **Guess about your partner. Choose and write. How many did you get right?**

- Tell students they are going to guess things their partner has done.
- Divide the class into pairs. Have a pair read out the example dialogue, then ask students to use two or three of the verbs in the box to make guesses about you; for example, *You've swum in the ocean. You've eaten Japanese food.* Answer *Yes, I have!* or *No, that's wrong. I haven't done that.*
- Tell students to choose some of the verbs in the box and write three or four guesses about their partner, starting *(Maria) has …*
- When they've finished, have students read their sentences to their partner, who should say whether the guess is right or not. Ensure students use the second-person singular when speaking (e.g. *You've …*). Encourage students to respond using complete sentences. Write these prompts on the board for students to use: *You're right, I have done that. / You're wrong, I haven't done that.* Find out if anyone's guesses were all right.

Cool Down

Play *Running Sentences* (see TB p. 26) with sentences from A and D.

Practice **Resource Bank:** Grammar Printout
Student's App: Grammar Practice

Talk About It

Lesson Objectives

- to prepare and hold a conversation, giving reasons, disagreeing politely, and deciding together
- to recognize and reproduce words with *ph*

Materials
Video; Audio Track 74

Warm Up

Ask students to remember the last present they gave to someone and why they gave it (e.g. was it a birthday present?). Have them discuss in pairs.

A TB p. 238 **Watch and listen. Which four objects do the friends talk about?**

- Tell students they are going to watch a video of four friends trying to choose a present for their friend. Say *What do you think they buy?* and elicit suggestions.
- Introduce the gist question *Which four objects do the friends talk about?* Play the video and have students raise their hands when they hear the answers.
- Ask students *Which do you think is the best present? Which present do they buy in the end?* (the photo album) *Did anyone predict correctly?* Play the video again and encourage students to notice how the friends show they're listening to each other's ideas.

Answers
diary; a (really long cotton) scarf; a (small) flashlight; a photo album

B Watch again. Check (✔) the sentences and questions you hear.

- Have students read the sentences and questions.
- Play the video again and have students complete the activity. Then check answers. Play the video again and ask students to correct the incorrect phrases.
- Read all the phrases and ask students to say if it is a question (raise hands) or a statement (lower hands). Then ask students which phrases are agreeing with a suggestion (4, 8) and which phrases are disagreeing with a suggestion (6, 7). Point out that not all phrases fall into these categories.

Answers
l; 2; 3; 4; 6; 7; 9

Pronunciation *ph* as /f/

TRACK 74 TB p. 221 **Listen and say.**

- Ask students the name of the person who will receive the present (*Sophie*). Elicit how to spell the name, and write it on the board. Underline the *ph* and ask students how it's pronounced—say the /f/ sound and then have them make the /f/ sound.
- Read the words aloud, then play the audio and have students repeat the words.
- Say *These words are used in the video. What other words do you know with "ph"?* Have students work in pairs to try to remember any other words they know that also have *ph* (e.g. *cell phone*). Elicit and write the words on the board. Drill them at the end.

Suggested Answers
alphabet, dolphin, nephew, telephone, telegraph

C Plan. Think about a present for a friend. Then complete.

- Tell students they are going to plan their own conversation about buying a present for a friend.
- Project the table onto the board and work through an example with students. You could talk about a friend of yours who likes cycling and possible ideas; for example, *Idea: helmet; Reason: to be safe.* Ask students for more suggestions and reasons.
- Divide the class into pairs and have them do a Rally Robin cooperative learning routine to generate some gift ideas and reasons for a friend who has a particular interest (e.g. movies, dance, soccer). They can choose a real friend or imagine a friend. Then have them choose some of their ideas to complete the table.

D Prepare notes for your conversation. Use your ideas from C and phrases from B.

- Play the video again as a model and remind students to watch with their own conversation in mind.
- Prepare notes for an example conversation with the class, using your plan from C. Build up the conversation on the board with students' suggestions.
- Have each pair use their ideas from C to plan a conversation where they compare ideas and choose a present. Remind them to adapt phrases from B; for example, *Hmm, I was thinking of a helmet.*

E Practice with a friend.

- Have students practice their conversations as many times as they want. Encourage them to gradually use their notes less often and to try out different phrases, so the conversation becomes more fluid. remind them to ask for, and listen to, each other's opinions. Monitor and provide praise and help where needed.

Cool Down

Play *What's the Next Word?* (see TB p. 27) with the script from the video.

Practice **Student's App:** Speaking Skills Practice; Speaking Video

Write About It

Lesson Objectives

- to identify and practice using *too*, *as well*, and *also* to add additional information
- to plan and write a postcard

Materials

(Optional) Challenge, Standard, and Support writing printouts from the Resource Bank, one per student (C and D)

Warm Up

Ask students *What are all the different ways we can stay in touch with our friends or family when we're on vacation?* Make a list on the board and take a class vote to see which communication method students use most.

A Read the postcard. Circle *too*, *as well*, and *also*.

- Have students look quickly at the text and see if it matches any of their ideas from the Warm Up. Ask students *Who wrote the postcard? Where is she at the moment? Is she having a good time?* (Lara; summer camp; yes, she is) Draw students' attention to the address on the right. Ask *Whose address is this?* (Lara's mom and dad's house)
- Ask students to scan the text and circle all the examples of *too*, *as well*, and *also*. Say *Do we use these words to repeat information or give more information?* (give more)
- Call on students to read the text a line at a time and for the others to raise their hands when a circled word is said. Ask students which words come at the end of the sentence (*as well*, *too*) and which at the beginning (*also*). Ask them to find the example of *also* in the middle of a sentence and identify which word comes next. (the main verb) Ask *Which word has a comma before it?* (*too*) *Which word has a comma after it?* (*also*) *Does also always have a comma after it?* (no—only when it's at the start of a sentence, not in the middle)

Answers

Also, my cell phone doesn't work here on the mountain
The teachers are very friendly, and the kids are as well
The weather's been good, too
I've done so many different activities, including watersports—swimming, sailing, and water skiing as well
and we've also made a sail from an old sheet.

B Read and complete.

- Tell students they are going to use the words in the box to complete the sentences. Ask a student to read the example sentence (number 1). Ask why *Also* is correct here (it's at the beginning of the sentence).
- Have students complete the other sentences. When they have finished, have students compare answers with a friend. Ask if they chose the same ways to complete them each time.
- Invite students to read aloud completed sentences and ask if everyone agrees. If some students have used *too* and *as well* in different places, remind them to check the commas: *too* has a comma before it, *as well* doesn't.

Answers

1 *Also* 2 too 3 also 4 as well

C Plan. Imagine you are at the summer camp for a week. Think about these questions.

- Write or project the questions onto the board and elicit an example answer for each one, e.g. *1 theater and music, 2 some new friends and a great music teacher, 3 sunny and very hot—best to stay inside! 4 We did a concert, and I forgot the words to the song!*
- Put students into groups and have them do a Round Robin cooperative learning routine (see TB p. 20) to generate more ideas for each question.
- Then have students choose some of these ideas to include in their own plan. Have them write their plan individually. Hand out the Challenge printouts at this point.

D Write a postcard about your week at the summer camp.

- Elicit from students how the information from your plan can be made into a postcard. Use phrases from the postcard in A to expand the ideas into a complete postcard.
- Have students complete their postcard in their notebook. Remind them to use *too*, *as well*, and *also*.
- Have students self-correct or exchange their work with a friend and peer-correct. You can put a checklist of points for students to look out for on the board, e.g. spelling; capital letters; commas; correct use of *too*, *as well*, and *also*.
- Have students correct any mistakes and write their final instructions neatly on paper. Alternatively, hand out the Support and Standard printouts from the Resource Bank. Remind them that, as it's a postcard, they need to include an address! Give students time to circulate and read each other's postcards. Ask students to suggest whose Summer Camp sounds the most fun.

Cool Down

Play *Simon Says* (see TB p. 27) with some summer camp activities. You can extend the game by saying *Simon Says play tennis and play the guitar as well!* and have students try to mime two things at the same time!

Practice **Student's App:** Writing Practice

Think It Over

Lesson Objectives

- to review what has been learned in the unit
- to reflect on the unit and their own progress
- to think about learning strategies and how to continue learning at home

Warm Up

Play *Unscramble* (see TB p. 27) with any of the words from TB pp. 74–75 or p. 78.

Read the questions and draw or write your answers.

- Give students time to think about and discuss activities in the unit before they complete each question. Explain that they can choose to either write a few words or sentences or to draw a picture. Allowing students to make a personal response will help them retain knowledge and engage with the learning points.

What did I do?

- Give students a few minutes to look back through the unit at the different activities they did. Ask questions about the unit or write questions on the board for students to discuss in pairs or small groups; for example, *What did you sing about? What story did you read? What survival trips did you hear about?*
- Encourage students to identify something in the unit that they found challenging or something that was particularly memorable for them, but tell them not to choose their favorite activity yet. Students can draw or write about their chosen activity.

What did I learn?

- Have students talk to a partner about what they remember from the unit—stories, words, phrases, people, facts about survival.
- Ask questions about the unit to help students think about what they learned; for example, *What survival words do you know? What phrases can you use to make suggestions and agree or disagree? What did you learn about survival? What else did you learn?*
- Encourage students to draw a picture or write sentences about their learning outcomes.
- Once students have written their statements, have them talk to a friend about what they think they have learned.

What was my favorite part?

- Have students look back through the unit and decide what they enjoyed the most. Tell them it can be an activity they found fun, a text they enjoyed reading, a favorite character, or a favorite word. They should try to choose just one and draw a picture or write about it.
- Explain that when we like something, it is often easier to learn.

How well did I do?

- Ask students to color in the number of tents that best expresses how well they think they learned the unit content. Ask *What do you understand? What do you need to practice more?* Encourage students to look back through the unit to see how much they remember, what they did well, and what they found difficult.

What can I do next?

- Brainstorm ideas with the class about what they can do to continue to learn (e.g. learn more about surviving outdoors; write another postcard).
- Encourage students to think about what they can do at home to improve their English. Have them suggest some verbs that they can use (e.g. *read*, *practice*, *watch*, *sing*) and write the verbs in their books. Students can look back at the previous units to get more ideas. Encourage students to suggest their own ideas for different activities they can do.
- Have students choose several activities that they would like to do and write them in their notebooks. They can then share their ideas with a partner.

Looking Forward

Draw students' attention to the character at the bottom of the page. Ask *Who's this?* and elicit what they remember about him (David was with the kids camping in Explore Language 1 on p. 76 and also talking about his pet snake in Explore Language 2 on p. 80). Ask students if they can guess what his son's name is. Elicit some suggestions for names and some predictions about the topic of Unit 7, then tell students they will find out if they were correct in the first lesson of the next unit.

Put It Together

To further review and recycle the language in Units 5 and 6, play the game, *The Great Outdoors*, on pp. 86–87. See TB p. 208 for teaching notes.

Practice **Resource Bank:** Unit Test
Student's App: Vocabulary and Grammar Review

Get Ready to Read

Lesson Objectives

- to activate prior knowledge about survival skills
- to encourage students to observe and interpret through a Question Starts VTR
- to preview the reading skill of understanding the sequence of events

Materials

(Optional) VTR printout from the Resource Bank (A, B, C)

Warm Up

Ask students *Where do you think would be the most difficult place on Earth to live? Why?* Have students discuss in pairs, then elicit different environments and reasons why it would be difficult to live there (e.g. desert, mountains, the Arctic).

Question Starts

A Think about the picture. Then brainstorm questions. Write a list.

Students are going to do a Question Starts VTR to explore the image of the two girls on a snowy mountain.

- Have students look at the picture for a minute and then say what they can see. If students don't know a word in English, ask them to describe what they see so you can provide the word.
- Draw students' attention to the question words. Ask *What questions do you have about the picture?* Give students a few minutes to write questions in their notebooks, based on the prompts.
- Elicit ideas and write all suggestions on the board, helping students correct their questions when needed.

B Look at your list from A. Which questions seem the most interesting? Discuss them with the class.

- Ask students to look at their list of questions individually and identify the questions they would most like to know the answers to.
- Tell students that they are going to practice negotiation skills by working as a group to decide which three questions they want to ask. Have them work in groups of three to review the questions and discuss possible answers. This will help them decide which questions they think are the most interesting. Discuss the questions as a class and decide on the most interesting questions. Encourage students to listen to each other's questions and suggest answers where appropriate.

Here's an example of this part of the routine.

Teacher: Which questions seem the most interesting? What do you really want to know?

Student A: Why do the two girls in the picture look nervous?

Student B: I don't think that girl's nervous. I think she's cold! Why isn't she wearing a jacket or a hat?

Teacher: Interesting questions. What other questions do you have?

Student C: Why is she carrying so many pots?

Student D: Where are they?

Student C: I think it's Mount Everest. Are they climbing Mount Everest?

C What new ideas or questions do you have now? Talk about your ideas with your partner.

- Encourage students to use the picture to think about more global questions or ideas. Encourage students to think beyond this picture, but tell them they can use their previous questions as a starting point. Refer students to the example questions and give them a couple of minutes to think of their own questions. Then have students share their questions in pairs and discuss any possible answers. Encourage them to be as creative as possible.

Transition

Ask students *Have you ever been in a situation like the one in the picture? Do you think you could live in a place like this? What would you need to do to survive?*

D Think, discuss, and write. What does *survival* mean? What things do humans need to survive? Make a list.

- Ask students if they can explain the word *survival*. If not, ask *If you survive, do you live?* (yes) *Is it usually a difficult or easy situation?* (difficult)
- Elicit a couple of ideas of things that humans need to survive (e.g. water, air). Have students work in pairs or small groups to make a list of all the things they think we need to survive.
- Invite students to share their lists with the class.

Suggested Answers

Survival means staying alive. Humans need food, water, air, and shelter to survive.

E Think and discuss. Look at *SOS* on the next page. How many different survival ideas are there? How do you think they are connected?

This is a preview of the reading skill of understanding a sequence of events.

- Have students look at the pictures on pp. 90–95 (or project them onto the board) and find and count the survival ideas. Elicit ideas from the class. Encourage students to say how they think the ideas are connected.

Suggested Answers

I see four ideas. They are connected because they are all about calling for help.

Now read SOS

Nonfiction: *SOS*—Instructional Text

Lesson Objectives

- to read an instructional text about survival skills
- to make a personal connection to the reading

Materials

Audio Tracks 30 and 31; Video; (optional) flashlight; ball (CD)

Warm Up

Write the following on the board: *(a) the beach, (b) the mountains, (c) a lake or river, (d) a forest, (e) a farm.* Ask students *Where do you prefer to visit? Why?* Have students discuss in pairs, then take a class vote.

TRACK 30 TB p. 232 **Reading Approach**

First Reading: Engage with the Text

- Refer students to the title. Ask if they know what *SOS* means. Ask *When do people send an SOS message?* Elicit or tell students it's a way of saying *Help!*
- Play the audio and have students follow in their books.

TRACK 31 TB p. 232 **Words in Context**

- Play the audio and have students repeat the words.
- Have students race to find the words in the reading.
- Remind students they can sometimes **read the next words or sentence to get clues to explain the meaning of a new word** (see TB p. 22). Have them discuss their ideas with a partner, using L1 if necessary.
- Then bring the class together and use these discussion points to confirm the meanings.

wilderness (p. 90) Have students look at the picture. Ask *What can she see all around her?* (trees, plants, wild country) *What gives us a clue?* (the word *wild* in *wilderness*)

pretend (p. 90) Ask students to read the whole paragraph. Ask *Are they lost?* (no) *What are they going to do?* (act out being lost and calling for help)

attention (p. 91) Have students read the whole sentence. Ask students how teachers usually get attention in their classes.

attach (p. 91) Have students look at the picture. Ask *How can you attach a whistle to a backpack?*

reflection (p. 92) Ask students *When you look in a mirror, what do you see? What happens if you shine a light on a mirror?*

target (p. 92) Ask *What's the important verb in the sentence?* (aim) *What else can we aim at a target?* (e.g. an arrow)

dots and dashes (p. 93) Have students point to the dashes. Elicit that the words *a little longer* tell them which the dashes are. Let a student demonstrate dots and dashes with a flashlight.

Second Reading: Analyze the Text and Features

- Play the video and have students raise their hands for something they think is a good idea.
- Ask some questions to check understanding, e.g. *What ways does Mia have of sending an SOS message?* (build an SOS with rocks and branches on the ground, make letters in the snow and fill with something dark, write letters in sand, use a flashlight)

International English

Elicit that *trail* and *flashlight* are American English and *footpath* and *torch* are British English. Ask students if they remember hearing any of these before. Ask *Which ones are used in the reading?*

- Discuss the questions in the orange boxes.
  - **Text Focus** (p. 90): *How does the author use the characters and setting to make the information interesting?* Ask students for their ideas. (The author uses a fictional story to give the facts about survival. This way, the characters and setting make us more involved or connected, and we remember the important information better.)
  - **Making Connections** (p. 92): *What can you use to make a reflection if you don't have a mirror?* Ask students for their ideas (e.g. glasses, a CD, the screen of your smartphone).
  - **Fact** (p. 93): *Morse code was invented in 1838 by Samuel Morse as a way of sending messages over wires.* Ask students how they think people communicated before this. (by letter, which was very slow; with wires, the message could travel at the speed of light)
  - **Creative Thinking** (p. 95): *What other ways can you think of to call for help?* Have students discuss in pairs, then ask them for their ideas (e.g. shouting, banging the SOS signal on a tree or rock, making a fire).

Third Reading: Interact with the Text

- Have students work in pairs to discuss the pros and cons of each of the four ways of calling for help. They should decide which would be most effective and why. Put each pair with a pair who chose a different idea and have them present their arguments to each other. Ask if any students changed their minds after hearing their classmates' arguments.

Cool Down

Play *Pass the Ball* (see TB p. 26) and have each student say one thing they learned from the reading.

Practice **Student's App:** Nonfiction Video

Explore the Reading

Lesson Objectives

- to understand and analyze *SOS* through reading comprehension activities
- to learn about emergency management through CLIL (science): understanding different survival skills
- to recognize and reproduce words starting with *st–*

Materials
Audio Track 32

Warm Up

Have students take turns miming one of the four methods of calling for help (whistle, mirror, SOS, and flag) for each other to guess.

A Read and check (✔). Which of these details can you find in the reading?

- Before students open their books, have a team quiz to find out what they remember from the reading. Ask *How many different methods for calling for help were there in the text?* (four) *Who can remember the Morse code for SOS?* (dot, dot, dot, dash, dash, dash, dot, dot, dot) *How can you make an SOS signal?* (rocks and branches, something dark on the snow, letters in the sand, Morse code, flashlight, flag) *What can you use to make a flag?* (the rain cover from a tent, jacket, or other clothing) *Where are Mrs. Collins and her students?* (in the wilderness)
- Refer students to the example sentence in A and ask if they can find something in the reading that justifies the answer. (p. 93, *The international signal for help is the letters SOS.*)
- Have students complete the activity individually and compare their answers with a friend.
- To check answers, read the statements, and have students raise their hands for yes and lower them for no. For the yes statements, ask one student to find something in the reading to justify it.

Answers
1; 3; 4; 6

B Think and discuss. Why do you think it is important to know more than one way of signaling for help?

- Have students think about the question, then compare ideas in small groups, using the prompt in the example speech bubble.
- Elicit ideas.

C Think, draw, and write. Think of a survival story you know or make one up. Draw the story. Then write about it.

Students are going to connect the reading to their own experience. This draws on the CLIL science objective of understanding different survival skills as part of learning about emergency management.

- Tell students a survival story you know about or something that happened to someone you know. For example, *A girl was skiing when there was an avalanche, and a lot of snow fell on her. No one could see her, so she pushed her ski pole up through the snow, and it worked like a flag!* Make a quick drawing of this on the board and elicit a short caption to write: *She was under the snow, but they found her because she used her ski pole like a flag!*
- Have students think, draw, and write a caption about a survival story they know or one they make up.
- Have students work in groups to show each other their pictures and explain what happened.

TRACK 32 TB p. 232 Spelling Pattern *st–*

Listen and write. Then check your answers.

- With books closed, write the word *storm* on the board and have students repeat it. Underline the letters *st* and say *st– st– storm*. Have students repeat the sound and then the word.
- Play the first part of the audio and have students repeat each word. Then have them open their books. Play the first part of the audio again and have them complete as many of the words as they can.
- Then play the second part of the audio again for students to check their spelling and complete any missing words. Have them read the words aloud.
- Have students look back at the reading to find more words beginning with *st–* and write them down. Invite students to read the words aloud. Then have them draw the outline of a storm cloud and write all the *st-* words from this lesson inside. Encourage them to add any other *st*-words they can think of and display the storm clouds on the wall.

Answers
1 storm 2 strong 3 striped 4 straight 5 stairs
In the reading: stopped; starting; strap; start; stamp; stuff; stomachs

Cool Down

Have students all leave their books open to show their drawing of the survival situation from C. Encourage students to circulate around the room, looking at their friends' work. Ask them to look for as many different methods as they can to signal for help, a different method from the ones in the reading, a particularly good drawing, or a good description. Ask them to provide feedback on what they found.

Practice **Resource Bank:** Spelling Printout
Student's App: Reading Practice; Spelling Pattern Practice

Get Ready to Read

Lesson Objectives

- to review and practice the reading skill of understanding the sequence of events
- to activate knowledge about how to deal with an emergency
- to explore the SEL competency of self-management by exhibiting positive motivation, hope, and optimism

Warm Up

When you are beginning this lesson, make sure you say the following phrases (or similar). Then write them on the board in random order and ask students to remember what order you said them in: *Good morning/afternoon, everyone! Who can tell me what day it is today? Do you all have your books today? Are we all ready to begin the lesson?*

A Read the sentences. Then look at the reading *First Man in Space* in Unit 4 again. Sequence these events in the order they happened.

This lesson practices the reading skill of understanding a sequence of events.

- Ask students what they can remember about Yuri Gagarin (they read about him in Unit 4). Have students raise their hands to say what they remember. Then have them read *First Man in Space* again (pp. 66–69).
- Have students read the statements in A and elicit which event came first. Have them continue the activity in pairs.
- Check the answers as a class.
- Refer students to the skills box about understanding the sequence of events. Ask if the sentences in A are a sequence—*Is there more than one? Do we know the order? Are they connected?* Elicit answers, then ask students how they think knowing the sequence of events helps them understand the text. They might suggest that it helps them to remember what happened and that it helps them understand why things happened (e.g. why Gagarin became famous). If students seem unsure, you could ask them to retell a famous folk tale in your country by recalling the beginning, middle, and end of the story. By sequencing in this way, students will have told the key elements of the story in a logical way, and even if not all the details are there someone unfamiliar with the story would be able to understand what happened.

Answers

1 Yuri Gagarin was born in 1934 in a small farming village in Russia. 2 In 1960, 20 air force pilots were chosen for a secret mission. 3 On the day of the launch, Gagarin was calm as he waited for blast-off. 4 When *Vostok 1* returned to Earth, Gagarin parachuted down. 5 Soon, Gagarin was one of the most famous people in the world.

B Look at the pictures. Sequence the events. Tell the story.

- Ask students to look at the pictures and say what they can see happening in each one.
- Have students study the pictures and say which happened first. Then have them decide the order of the others individually.
- Say *Number 1* and have students say the letter of the picture that comes first. Check everyone agrees.

Answers

a 4 b 3 c 1 d 2

C Think and discuss. No one is at home and you are locked outside. What do you do?

- Have students discuss the questions through a Numbered Heads Together cooperative learning routine (see TB p. 20). When they have shared all the ideas they can in their groups, call out numbers and have all the students with that number share their group's suggestions. Ask if there are any more ideas to add.
- Then ask students *Have you been in this situation?* and have them share experiences in pairs or small groups.

Cool Down

Have students work in pairs to compare their morning routines. Write on the board *Wake up. / Put on your shoes. / Have breakfast. / Wash your face. / Go to school. / Clean your teeth. / Get dressed.* Have students tell each other the order they do these things and see if they have the same sequence or a different one from their partner.

Now read **Panic or Calm?**

Fiction: *Panic or Calm?—Story*

Lesson Objectives

- to read a story about remaining calm when frightened
- to make a personal connection to the reading

Materials

Audio Tracks 33 and 34

Warm Up

Have students brainstorm a list of all the things they can't do at home if there is no electricity. Write their ideas in a list on the board and ask *Has this ever happened in your house?* Ask which is the most difficult to do..

TRACK 33 TB p. 232 Reading Approach

First Reading: Engage with the Text

- Before listening, refer students to the title and have students discuss the first orange callout question:
  What is the difference between panicking and staying calm? Ask *Which word means you feel like everything is going wrong and you can't stop it?* (panicking). Point out that staying calm is the opposite of panicking. Have students show you a panicking face and a calm face.
- Play the audio while students follow along in their books.
- At the end of the first page, pause the audio and ask *Do you think Alex will panic or stay calm?* Then continue the audio. After the next page, pause again and elicit that the story shows Alex both panicking and staying calm, to compare them.

TRACK 34 TB p. 233 Words in Context

- Play the audio and have students repeat the words.
- Have students race to find the words in the story.
- Remind students we can sometimes **use the sentence before and the next words or sentence to get clues to explain the meaning of a new word** (see TB p. 22). Explain that **understanding how characters are feeling can also give us clues**. Have them discuss their ideas with a partner, using L1 if necessary.
- Then bring the class together and use these discussion points to confirm the meanings.

locked (p. 98) Ask *What happened when Alex pushed the door?* (It didn't open.) Elicit that *she couldn't get in* helps us to understand the word *locked*. Ask *Why couldn't she get in?* (she doesn't have a key)

power outage (p. 98) Ask students *What happened to the lights?* (They went out.) *Why?* (no electricity) Elicit that different clues help us understand the meaning here. (*out* in the first part of the second word, *Every light in the city died*, in the previous sentence)

handle this (p. 99) Ask *Does Alex think she can solve her problem?* (yes) Have students read on to find a phrase that means the same thing *I can do this.*

spare (p. 100) Ask *Why do you think the key is in the plant?* (for someone who forgets their key!) Ask *Is this a good idea?*

gasped (p. 101) Ask students how they think Mom is feeling (surprised, worried). Elicit that is it not easy to speak when you're surprised. Have students act being surprised and saying *sorry I'm late* at the same time. Point out that this is gasping!

blushed (p. 101) Ask *How do you think Alex is feeling?* (embarrassed because she panicked) *What usually happens to your face when you are embarrassed?*

stuck (p. 101) Ask if students can think of a similar word (stick). Point out that *stuck* is the past participle of stick. Ask how knowing this helps us to understand the phrase *stuck in traffic* (if we stick something with glue it doesn't move, so we can guess that bus wasn't moving because there were a lot of cars.

Second Reading: Analyze the Text and Features

- Give students some time to read the story silently. To focus them while they read, ask *Why didn't Alex go into her house?* (There was no one at home.)
- Use Think, Pair, Share to discuss the questions in the orange boxes.
  - **Making Connections** (p. 99): *Why is it a good idea for Alex to sit down and think?* Students might conclude that if we are sitting and still, we think better than if we are moving and panicking!
  - **Personalization** (p. 101): *What does it feel like to be lost and alone?* Ask students *Have you ever been in this situation? How did it feel?*
- Discuss the text focus: *Look at how these pages are organized. What do you see? How do you think this organization helps show us the **sequence of events** in this story?* Give students some thinking time, then have them discuss the questions in pairs. Elicit suggestions and write them on the board (e.g. the stories are color-coded, with headings at the top of each section, so you can easily follow one story and then the other).

Third Reading: Interact with the Text

- Play the audio again and have half the class mime being Alex in the *Panic* story and the other half mime being Alex in the *Calm* story.

Cool Down

Ask students how they think the story would be different if there wasn't a power outage. Have students discuss their ideas in pairs and then share with the class.

Explore the Reading

Lesson Objectives

- to understand and analyze *Panic or Calm?* through reading comprehension activities
- to understand the sequence of events
- to explore the SEL competency of self-management by exhibiting positive motivation, hope, and optimism
- to make a personal connection to the reading

Warm Up

Read some phrases from the story *Panic or Calm?* and ask students to say if they refer to panicked Alex (raise arms in panic) or calm Alex (assume thinking position!). Suggested phrases: *Alex's head started spinning.* (P) *She sat down in the backyard.* (C) *I can handle this.* (C) *Alex ran into the street.* (P) *Alex searched the faces in the crowd for Mom.* (P) *She looked around the backyard.* (C) *She began to cry.* (P) *Alex made a plan.* (C) *I've been fine.* (C)

A Think and write. Choose the *Panic* story or the *Calm* story. Then write a timeline and sequence the main events.

- Before students open their books, find out what they remember about the story. Have them discuss the following questions in pairs. *Why was Alex scared?* (because she was alone and it was dark) *Where was her mom?* (on the bus coming home) *What did panicked Alex do next? And calm Alex?* (ran toward the shops; sat down to think) *Who found panicked Alex?* (Mrs. Bryson) *How did Mom feel when she found Alex at home?* (happy that everything was OK)
- Draw or project the diagram onto the board. Elicit what the next action was for the panic story and then for the calm story. Write them both on the board (panic on one side and calm on the other).
- Have students choose one version of the story and complete the timeline in their books. Remind them to look back at the story to find the sequence of events and to focus on the main events, not the details.
- Have students compare their versions with a friend to see if they agree about the sequence.
- Have a student who wrote a *panic* timeline read their sentences while the class listens and acts them out. Does everyone agree the order is correct? Repeat with a student who wrote a *calm* timeline.

Suggested Answers

Panic: *The front door was locked.* The lights went out. Alex ran downtown. Alex was lost and began to cry. Mrs. Bryson started to walk home with her and then they met Mom.
Calm: The front door was locked. The lights went out. Alex remembered why Mom was late. Alex found the spare key. Alex waited at home until Mom came home.

B Think and write. What are the steps for STOP? How did Alex use them in the *Calm* story?

This activity explores the SEL competency of self-management by exhibiting positive motivation, hope, and optimism.

- Write or project the table onto the board. Ask students *What does the "S" stand for?* Elicit *Sit down.* Have students look back at the reading and find how Alex used this advice in the story.
- Have students continue the activity individually. Then have them compare in pairs.

Answers

S Sit down; Alex sat in the backyard and took a deep breath.
T Think; Alex remembered Mom saying something about the car being fixed.
O Observe; Alex saw the potted plant with the spare key for the house.
P Plan; Alex decided to stay home.

C Think and discuss. Imagine the story from Mom's perspective. How do you think she felt? Why?

- Have students work in pairs to imagine the story from Alex's Mom's point of view. Have them consider how she must have felt, both before and after she saw Alex.
- Then ask pairs to share their ideas with the class.

Suggested Answer

I think Mom was worried about Alex and wanted to get home quickly. She says, "I was worried about you in power outage!"

D Think and discuss. Why do you think keeping calm and positive is important?

- This activity further explores the SEL competency of self-management by exhibiting positive motivation, hope, and optimism Ask students *How did keeping calm and positive help Alex?* (She found a good solution because she was calm and took time to think.)
- Have students work in pairs to discuss why they think keeping calm and positive is important in other situations and then have a Group Time discussion to share ideas (see TB p. 21).

Cool Down

Play *Simon Says* (see TB p. 27) with some of the main actions from the story; for example, *run toward the stores / sit down and think / start to cry / look around the backyard / make a plan / say "I can handle this" / find the spare key / search the crowd for Mom's face.*

Practice **Student's App:** Reading Practice

Think Together

Lesson Objectives

- to make connections between the readings
- to explore the key concept: What can you do to survive in an emergency?
- to reflect on the unit and provide personal thoughts and opinions

Warm Up

Have students look back at the VTR image on pp. 88–89 and ask *Do you now have any new ideas about the image? Do you have any advice for the people in this situation? Do you think you could now do better in this situation?*

Have students compare their ideas in pairs and then ask for their suggestions.

A Read and match the advice to the character.

- Ask students if they remember the characters in the pictures and if they remember what the two readings were about. (The first was about surviving in the wilderness and sending SOS messages, and the other was about staying calm.)
- Elicit which character corresponds to the first advice: *Sit down, think, observe, and then plan.* (the first picture on the top left—Alex's teacher from *Panic or Calm?*) and ask students to explain why (she taught her students the STOP advice to stay calm).
- Have students work individually to look back at the readings and match the advice to the character, and then let them compare with a friend. Check answers as a class.

Answers
1 Mrs. Bryson 2 Yuki 3 Mia 4 Micaela 5 Joe

B Think and write. Imagine you are stuck on a deserted island. Choose three items from your classroom to bring with you to help you survive. What are they? Why did you choose them?

- Tell students to imagine they are stuck on a desert island. Elicit an example of something they could bring from their classroom and encourage them to say why they would bring it; for example, *A flashlight so we could see in the dark, and so we could use it to signal SOS!*
- Divide the class into pairs and have them choose three items from their classroom to bring with them. Encourage them to think of and write why they chose them.
- Ask if any pairs would like to share their ideas with the class.

C On the island, what is your plan to survive? What do you do first? What do you do next? Sequence your survival ideas. Do a Think, Pair, Share.

- Tell students they are going to do a Think, Pair, Share routine to discuss and sequence their ideas for surviving on a desert island (see TB p. 20). After students have had time to think, elicit two or three ideas of what students think they need to do (e.g. find water, make a tent or shelter, make an SOS signal). Use these examples to elicit more words for sequencing ideas (e.g. *then, after that, finally*).
- Divide the class into pairs and have them continue to think of things they need to do to survive. Have them sequence their survival ideas using suitable sequencing words.
- Have pairs read their plan for survival to the class, and then take a class vote on which pair has the best plan.
- Introduce the key concept question: *What can you do to survive in an emergency?*
- Give students some time to think. Encourage them to consider what they know from school emergency procedures, books, movies, TV, and news articles, alongside what they learned in this unit. Have them discuss the question in small groups and present their ideas in a spidergram.

Practice Resource Bank: Unit Test
Student's App: Key Concept Practice

My Reading Journal

What was something new you learned this unit?

This question encourages students to reflect on their own learning.

Have students look back at the information in this unit and then write a sentence about something they learned.

Example Answer
I learned that you can use a CD as a mirror to signal to a ship or a plane.

Who might find this unit useful? What information will you share?

This question encourages students to make connections between what they have read and the world around them.

Encourage students to think of someone they know who does the sort of activities that might mean that they need survival skills someday. Then have them complete the sentences in their book.

Example Answer
I think my friend Anna might find this unit interesting, because she often goes walking in the mountains. I will share the ideas about making a flag out of a jacket.

Cool Down

Encourage students to engage in further self-reflection by writing the following questions on the board and having students discuss them in pairs: *Which reading did you like best? Why? Which picture do you think best represents the unit?*

UNIT 7

Every Last Drop

Unit Overview

Themes

Man-made water resources

Conserving water

Synopsis

In this unit students will learn about the water cycle, find out about different kinds of technology that provide clean water and think about how communities can save water. They will plan and prepare a presentation comparing two pictures and write a fact file about Niagara Falls using target language from the unit.

Language Book

Vocabulary
drain, faucet, flow, flush, pipe, pond, reservoir, water plant, well
p. 144

Explore Language
Gerunds as Subjects
p. 145

Global Citizenship
How can communities save water?
banks, bucket, canals, dam, drought, flood, hose, irrigate
p. 146

Explore Language
Prepositions: After Adjectives
p. 147

Take the Stage
Presentation: describing pictures
p. 148

Write About It
A Fact File
Paragraph Building: pronouns
p. 149

Think It Over
Review and Reflection
p. 150

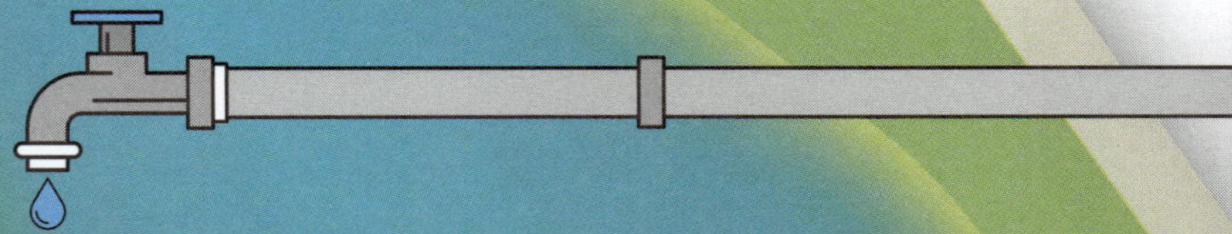

Think Together
How do you use water every day?
p. 157

Visible Thinking
Think, Pair, Share
p. 151

Literacy Book

Fiction
Story: *The New Dam*

Words in Context: *respected, powerful, creek, salmon, direct, hold*
p. 155

Nonfiction
Informational Text: *Clean Water for All*

Words in Context: *humid, advertising, vapor, bacteria, practical, steam, pump*
p. 152

Reading Skill
Understanding inferences
p. 154

Spelling Patterns
–ful and *–fully*
p. 156

Language and Literacy Connections
The connecting theme in Unit 7 is water and how we use it.

	Language	Literacy
Vocabulary	**Set 1:** the water cycle **Set 2:** water	**Nonfiction:** faucet, pond, drought(s) **Fiction:** pond, dam, drought, flood
Grammar	**Gerunds as Subjects** Saving water is important. **Prepositions: After Adjectives** This canal is famous for houseboats. I'm good at it now.	**Nonfiction** Having clean water is extremely important to our health. Drinking water from rivers, lakes, or ponds is safe with Lifestraw. **Fiction** Waiting for the rain isn't helpful.
Skills	**Pronunciation:** /dʒ/ and /g/	**Reading:** understanding inferences **Spelling Patterns:** *–ful* and *–fully*
International English	faucet/tap; hose / hose pipe	liter/litre; vapor/vapour; faucet/tap

Vocabulary

Lesson Objectives

- to learn vocabulary to talk about the water cycle: *drain, faucet, flow, flush, pipe, pond, reservoir, water plant, well*
- to sing a song about the water cycle

Materials
Audio Tracks 75 to 78; Video

Warm Up

Play *Board Race* with the word *water* (see TB p. 25).

A TRACK 75 TB p. 221 **Listen and find. Where does all the water we don't drink go back to?**

- Have students look at the pictures on pp. 88–89 and ask *What can you see?* Tell students they are going to hear a conversation with David from the previous unit. Ask students *What can you remember about David?* (He's an explorer and has a large pet snake.)
- Play the audio and have students point to the words and pictures as they listen.
- Ask the gist question *Where does all the water we don't drink go back to?* and elicit the answer. Play the audio again to check.
- Remind students of the challenge at the end of Unit 6: *What's my son's name?* Ask *Can you answer David's question now?* Play the audio again to check if necessary. (Julio)

Answer
into the rivers

B TRACK 76 TB p. 221 **Listen, say, and number the pictures in A.**

- Play the audio and have students point to the pictures and say the words.
- Play the audio again and have students write numbers next to the words in the order they hear them.
- Check answers and ask a few students to repeat each word to check pronunciation.

Answers
1 *pipe* 2 well 3 pond 4 water plant 5 reservoir
6 drain 7 faucet 8 flush 9 flow

International English

Elicit that *faucet* is American English and *tap* is British English. Point out that both words are correct English and ask *Which do we use?*

C TRACK 77 TB p. 221 **Close your eyes. Listen, visualize, and say.**

- Prepare students for the visualization (see TB p. 21).
- Play the audio, allowing students to visualize the vocabulary as they listen.
- Then have students draw what they imagined for their partner, who then guesses the word.

D Look and write.

- Tell students they are going to categorize the words into two groups: things that collect water and things that move water. Refer students to the examples. Ask *What does a pond collect?* (rain) *How does a faucet move water?* (Turn it on and water comes out—it moves!)
- Give students time to complete the activity in pairs. Project or draw the table on the board and invite students to come up to the board and add a word each. Confirm answers.

Answers
Collects Water: *pond*, well, water plant, reservoir
Moves Water: *faucet*, pipe, drain, flush, flow

E TRACK 78 TB p. 221 **Listen and complete. Then watch and sing.**

- Have students look at the title of the song, *Where Does the Water Go?*, and ask them what answers they think they will find in the song.
- Play the song once, allowing students to listen and enjoy it.
- Explain some of the words in the song are scrambled and students have to unscramble them. Ask *Can you guess what words they are?* Have students read the song and complete any words they know. Remind students that all of the words that they need are on pp. 88–89, so they can check their spelling.
- Play the song again, and have students write any answers they missed. Then check answers as a class.
- Play the song video and have students watch and sing along. Then play the song video again and have students invent some actions to do (e.g. flowing movement for *into the river it flows*).

Answers
1 *flows* 2 pond 3 faucet 4 drain 5 pipes 6 plant

Cool Down

Play *Unscramble* (see TB p. 27) with the vocabulary in this lesson.

Practice **Student's App:** Vocabulary Practice; Song Video

Explore Language

Lesson Objectives

- to learn how to use gerunds as subjects
- to practice vocabulary about saving water

Materials

Audio Tracks 79 and 80

Warm Up

Brainstorm with students all the activities they do during the day that use water, and display them in a graphic organizer on the board.

A TRACK 79 TB p. 221 **Listen and read. What does Julio choose to do in the end?**

- Have students look at the pictures on p. 90 and ask them *What can you see? What is he doing?* Establish that the boy is Julio, David's son, from the previous lesson.
- Play the audio and have students follow the story in their books.
- Ask the gist question *What does Julio choose to do in the end?* Elicit the answer, then ask *Why does he choose this?* (because it doesn't use water) Ask how many of their ideas from the Warm Up were mentioned in the story.

Answer

He chooses to watch TV.

B Look at A. Complete.

- Write or project the table onto the board.
- Have students discuss and complete the grammar table in pairs using the story.
- When they have finished, have students call out the answers and write them on the board. Discuss the word order and verb forms together, but let your class guide the discussion. If you feel that students need more guidance, the **ETB** provides a differentiation activity to help you support students as they explore the grammar table.
- Write *I like cupcakes. Cupcakes are delicious!* on the board and ask students to identify the subject in each sentence (I; Cupcakes). Point out or elicit that usually the subject in a sentence is a pronoun or noun. Ask students how we can make a verb into the subject of the sentence. (use the *–ing* form) Point out that by adding *–ing*, the verb has become an activity and acts as a noun.
- Say *When a verb is the subject, do we follow it with "be" in the singular or plural?* Have students find an example in the table to illustrate their answer (singular; for example, *Washing fruit is necessary*).
- Write *washing* and *watching* on the board and elicit the base form of the verbs (*wash* and *watch*). Point out that we just have to add *–ing* to these words to make the gerund.
- Have students look at the Grammar tip *Remember.* Ask students for the base form of *swimming* and *running* (run, swim). Point out that spellings for the gerund can be irregular. Here, we have doubled the final consonant before adding *–ing.* Ask students if they know why (the base verbs end in consonant, vowel, consonant).

Answers

Saving; is; Washing; Bathing

C Think and discuss. Then choose.

- Have students look at the sentence in C. Give them some thinking time and encourage them to look at the table in B and the story on p. 90 to help. Then have them discuss their answer with a partner.
- Read the question and invite a student to call out the answer they chose. Check everyone agrees and confirm the answer.

Answer

1 in general

D TRACK 80 TB p. 221 **Listen and say.**

- Play the audio and have students repeat. For ideas on how to vary the drill, see TB p. 23.

E Complete the new sentences with gerunds.

- Tell students they are going to complete the sentences with gerunds. Refer students to the example. Ask *What happened to the verb when it became an activity and the subject of the sentence?* (It used the *–ing* form.)
- Have students complete the sentences. Check answers and ask if everyone agrees. Check the spelling of *getting* to make sure students have the double *t* and *swimming* to make sure students have the double *m.*

Answers

1 *Growing* 2 Drinking 3 Watering 4 Getting
5 Swimming

F Choose and write sentences with gerunds. Then compare. How many are the same?

- Elicit which box contains activities and which contains adjectives. Look at the example sentence *Running for an hour is tiring* and ask *Do you agree?* Have students identify the activity and the adjective in the sentence, then ask if students can replace *tiring* with another adjective.
- Have students write their own gerund sentences using the activities and adjectives in the boxes. Then have students take turns saying a sentence in pairs. Tell them to say *Match!* if any of their sentences are the same. Which pair has the most matches?

Cool Down

Play *Mime It!* with the gerunds in F (see TB p. 26).

Practice **Resource Bank:** Grammar Printout
Student's App: Grammar Practice

Global Citizenship

Lesson Objectives

- to learn vocabulary for talking about water: *banks, bucket, canals, dam, drought, flood, hose, irrigate*
- to explore how communities can save water
- to practice listening for gist and details

Materials
Audio Tracks 81 to 83; Audio Track G; a world map (D)

Opening Question

Ask students the opening question: *How can communities save water?* Give students time to think and then elicit opinions.

A TRACK 81 TB p. 221 **Listen to Tarek talk to his uncle about the Aswan High Dam. When did building start on the dam?**

- Have students look at p. 92 and ask *What can you see?* Ask if students know what a dam is. (something we build to block the flow of water and make a reservoir) Ask *Do you know of any dams in your country?* Tell students they will hear a conversation about a dam.
- Play the audio and have students point to the pictures and words as they listen.
- Ask the comprehension question *When did building start on the dam?* and elicit the answer. Play the audio again to check.

Answer
in about 1960

B TRACK 82 TB p. 221 **Listen, say, and number the pictures in A.**

- Play the audio and have students point to the pictures and say the words.
- Play the audio again and have students write numbers next to the words in the order they hear them.
- Check answers by inviting volunteers to call out the numbers and asking others to respond.

Answers
1 *flood* 2 dam 3 banks 4 canals 5 drought
6 irrigate 7 bucket 8 hose

TRACK G TB p. 221 **Visualization**
The TTL has a visualization audio track for this vocabulary set. (See TB p. 21.)

International English

Elicit that *hose* is American English and *hosepipe* is British English and ask *Which do we use?*

C Read and complete.

- Tell students they are going to use the words in the box to complete the text. Ask a volunteer to read the example sentence. Ask why *drought* is correct here. (A drought happens when it doesn't rain.)
- Have students complete the activity individually and then compare their answers with a friend. Have students take turns reading a completed sentence aloud.

Answers
1 *drought* 2 bucket 3 irrigate 4 hose 5 canals
6 banks

D TRACK 83 TB p. 222 **Now listen to Mesi and Tarek. Are the traditional water inventions still in use today?**

- To generate interest, have students look at the two pictures and notice where each child is from. Ask students *Where are these countries?* Use a map to find them.
- Have students look at the pictures and ask them *What can you see?* Ask if they have ever seen something like this in their own country.
- Listening for gist: play the audio and have students listen for the answer to the gist question *Are the water inventions still in use today?* Have students compare ideas and then elicit the answer.

Answer
Yes, they are.

E Listen again. Write *True* or *False*.

- Listening for details: have students look at the sentences and remember what they heard. Ask if they think they know any of the answers.
- Play the audio and have students complete the activity. Check answers.

Answers
1 *True* 2 False 3 True 4 False 5 True 6 False

Discussion Questions

- Draw students' attention to the discussion questions: *How do people in your community save water? Why is it important not to waste water?* Have students discuss the questions in small groups (see **ETB**).
- Guide students to conclude that every small thing we do can make a difference, and that while it may seem that there is water all around us in the oceans, it's very precious.
- Return to the opening question to ask again: *How can communities save water?* Divide the class into pairs and have them find as many ways as possible.

Cool Down

Play *Running Spelling* (see TB p. 26) with the new vocabulary from this lesson.

Practice **Student's App:** Vocabulary Practice; Listening Practice

Explore Language

Lesson Objectives

- to learn how to use adjectives with prepositions
- to practice vocabulary about water

Materials
Audio Tracks 84 and 85

Warm Up

Brainstorm with students all the different types of homes where people live and sleep (e.g. house, apartment, castle, igloo). Ask students *Which would you prefer to live in? Why?* Have students discuss in pairs.

A TRACK 84 TB p. 222 **Listen and read. Does the man like living on a houseboat?**

- Ask students *What can you see in the picture?* Ask them if they mentioned this place to live in the Warm Up.
- Play the audio and have students follow the dialogue in their books.
- Ask the gist question *Does the man like living on a houseboat?* Elicit the answer, then ask *Would you like to live on a houseboat?*

Answer
Yes, he does.

B Look at A. Complete.

- Write or project the table onto the board.
- Have students discuss and complete the grammar table in pairs using the dialogue.
- When they have finished, have students call out the answers and write them on the board. Discuss word class and word order together, but let your class guide the discussion. If you feel that students need more guidance, the **ETB** provides a differentiation activity to help you support students as they explore the grammar table.
- Write *I'm at good painting* on the board and ask students if there is a problem with the sentence. Elicit that the adjective and preposition are in the wrong order: the rule is adjective + preposition.
- Refer students to the Grammar tip *Look.* Point out that both *bored of* and *bored with* are correct.

Answers
for; good; with; tired

C Think and discuss. Then choose.

- Give students time to read the sentence, look at A for examples, think about their answer, then discuss with a friend.
- Read the sentence and answer options and have students raise their hands to show the option they chose.

Answer
1 or

D TRACK 85 TB p. 222 **Listen and say.**

- Play the audio and have students listen and repeat. For ideas on how to vary the drill, see TB p. 23.

E Read and complete.

- Tell students they are going to complete the questions with a preposition. Refer students to the example and point out the preposition *of* that goes with *proud.* Also point out that the preposition at the end of the sentence is common in English (though not in other languages).
- Have students complete the activity individually. Point out they can find an example of all the adjectives with the correct preposition either in the dialogue or in the grammar table.
- Write or project the answers onto the board for everyone to check.

Answers
1 *of* 2 of 3 in 4 at 5 for 6 with/of 7 of
8 about

F Look at E. Ask and answer.

- Tell students they are going to ask and answer the questions in E. Ask two students to read the two example sentences. Ask students to identify which of the questions in E they are answering (questions 2 and 8). Then have students raise their hands if each sentence is also true for them. Have a student ask you one of the example questions and supply a new answer using adjective + preposition + noun; for example, *I'm afraid of big dogs!* Remind students that there are two possible ways of answering—with a noun or with the *–ing* form after the preposition.
- Have students ask and answer the questions from E and say if their partner's answer is true for them, too.

Cool Down

Play *Running Sentences* (see TB p. 26) with sentences from this lesson.

Practice **Resource Bank:** Grammar Printout
Student's App: Grammar Practice

Take the Stage

Lesson Objectives

- to prepare and practice a presentation describing a picture
- to recognize and reproduce words with /ʤ/ and /g/

Materials
Video; Audio Track 86

Warm Up

Brainstorm with the class all the different ways people have fun with water—swimming and watersports, water parks, fishing, water fights, and so on. Draw a spidergram on the board.

A TB p. 239 **Watch and listen. Which picture does Stephen like best?**

- Tell students they are going to watch a video of a boy talking about two pictures with water in them. Have students looks at the pictures and say what they can see.
- Introduce the gist question *Which picture does Stephen like best?* Play the video and have students raise their hands when they know the answer. Ask them why he likes it (it looks like fun). Play the video again and encourage students to notice Stephen's body language as he gives the presentation.

Answer
the second one

B **Watch again. Check (✔) the sentences you hear.**

- Have students read the sentences.
- Play the video and have students complete the activity. Read the phrases and have students raise their hands for the ones they checked.
- Read the checked sentences again and ask students to say if they are part of the description (raise hands), describe similarities (clap hands), or describe differences (fold arms). (Description: 2, 4; Similarities: 1, 5; Differences: 6, 7)
- Ask students to notice which phrases are in the simple present (e.g. number 2) and which are in the present progressive (e.g. number 4).

Answers
1; 2; 4; 5; 6; 7

Pronunciation /g/ and /ʤ/

TRACK 86 TB p. 222 **Listen and say.**

- Demonstrate the two sounds for students to copy. Write *a huge garden* on the board. Ask students to say the phrase. Point out the letter *g* in each word. Say the words separately and have students repeat each one.
- Read the words aloud, then play the audio, and have students repeat the words. Ask students what letter comes after the letter *g* when it is pronounced /ʤ/ (*e*; point out it can also be *i*, as in *changing*).
- Say *These words are used in the video. What other words do you know have the same sound?* Have students say the words again and then work in pairs to try to remember any other words they know that also have the /ʤ/ and /g/ sounds (e.g. /ʤ/ sound: *giant*; /g/ sound: *guide*). Write them on the board in two columns and then drill them for pronunciation.

Suggested Answers
/g/ go, give, grow, irrigate
/ʤ/ generous, suggestion

C **Plan. Choose two pictures from this book. Then complete.**

- Tell students they are going to plan their own presentation that involves describing two pictures.
- To give an example, choose two pictures from p. 92 that students have already seen (e.g. banks and drought) and elicit information about them to complete the table.
- Then have students choose two pictures from their book and use them to complete the table.

D **Prepare your presentation. Use your ideas from C and phrases from B.**

- Play the video again as a model and remind students to watch with their own presentation about their pictures in mind.
- Write some example presentation notes on the board, using your plan from C and adding to it with students' suggestions.
- Have students use the pictures they chose and their plan from C to write notes for their presentation. Remind them to adapt phrases from B to fit their pictures (i.e. keep the part in green and change the rest of the phrase). Encourage them to use both the simple present and present progressive in their notes.

E **Practice with a friend. Then share with your class.**

- Then have students practice their presentation with a friend. Remind students that it is important to look directly at the audience and speak clearly.
- Invite volunteers to come to the front of the classroom to give their presentation. Remind students they need to show the audience the pictures they're talking about. Have the audience give a round of applause after each presentation.

Cool Down

Choose a picture from either a **Language Book** or **Literacy Book** unit that students have already completed. Describe the picture and have students draw what you describe. Then hold up the picture you were describing and have them hold up their own version. Ask students whose drawing is closest to the original.

Practice **Student's App:** Speaking Skills Practice; Speaking Video

Write About It

Lesson Objectives

- to identify and practice using pronouns
- to plan and write a fact file

Materials

(Optional) Challenge, Standard, and Support writing printouts from the Resource Bank, one per student (C and D)

Warm Up

Prepare students to do a visualization (see TB p. 21). Say *Imagine you are on a boat on the biggest river in South America, going through the rain forest. What can you see around you? What plants or animals can you see? What can you hear? There is something big in the water … What is it? Where are you going, and what will you see there?*

Have students open their eyes, ask the questions again, and have students share with a friend what they visualized.

A Read the fact file. Circle the pronouns.

- Have students scan the text quickly and find places, animals, and people. After one minute, ask *What did you find?* and elicit answers. (places: South America, Ecuador, Venezuela, Bolivia, Brazil, Colombia, Peru, mountains, Atlantic Ocean, Belém, rainforest; animals: fish, anaconda/snake; people: Martin Strel, 400–500 different groups of people)
- Write the question *What did you find?* on the board and elicit the answer *I found …* Write this on the board below the question. Circle *I* and *you* and ask students if they know what these words are called. (pronouns) Ask what they do. (refer to people or things before the verb)
- Have students scan the text and circle all the examples of pronouns—point out *I* and *you* are not here, but other pronouns are.
- Read the text a line at a time and have students raise their hands when they hear a pronoun.

Answers

It; It; They; He

B Look at A. Complete.

- Project or draw the table onto the board and highlight the example. Explain that the first *It* refers to the Amazon River. Have students read the first two sentences in A again and ask *Why is it used here?* (*It* refers to something that the text talked about in the previous sentence, so it isn't necessary to repeat the name.)
- Have students complete the rest of the table by finding the nouns in A and then compare answers with a friend.
- Elicit the nouns for each pronoun and complete the table on the board.

Answers

The Amazon River; the anaconda; green anacondas; Martin Strel

C Plan. Read the facts about Niagara Falls. Then match.

- Tell students they are going to match facts to questions. Review what information each question word is asking for. Point out the facts about Niagara Falls in the box and the example given for *What?* Ask them to identify the *Where* information in the box and complete the space in their book. Hand out the Challenge printouts at this point.
- Check answers as a class.

Suggested Answers

1 *one of the largest waterfalls in the world* 2 between Canada and the USA 3 Nik Wallenda walked across the falls on a rope / visitors from all over world 4 Nik Wallenda walked across the falls on a rope / visitors from all over world 5 30 million visitors a year 6 flows at about 56.3 km. per hour

D Write your fact file.

- Tell students they are going to write a fact file about Niagara Falls, like the one in A. Ask students to help you write a paragraph about Niagara Falls using the information from C. Elicit the first paragraph and write it on the board. Then elicit how the next paragraph might continue.
- Have students write a rough draft of the rest of the fact file in their notebook. Remind them to use the text in A as a model.
- Have students self-correct or exchange their work with a friend and peer-correct. You can put a checklist of points for students to look out for on the board (e.g. spelling, capital letters, commas, periods, correct use of pronouns).
- Have students correct any mistakes and write their final instructions neatly on paper. Alternatively, hand out the Support and Standard printouts from the Resource Bank. Give students time to circulate and look at each other's fact files.

Cool Down

Have students pretend they are Nik Wallenda, walking over Niagara Falls on the tightrope. Say *You're in the USA—start walking!* As they are miming walking and balancing, call out questions for them to answer, but tell them to keep miming as they give the answers! For example, *How many people visit Niagara Falls every year?* (30 million) *Where is it?* (between Canada and the US) *How fast does the water flow?* (about 56.3 km. per hour) *What's your name?* (Nik Wallenda!) *Where do the visitors come from?* (all over the world) *You're in Canada! Well done!*

Practice Student's App: Writing Practice

Think It Over

Lesson Objectives

- to review what has been learned in the unit
- to reflect on the unit and their own progress
- to think about learning strategies and how to continue learning

Warm Up

Play *Shark* (see TB p. 26) with key vocabulary from pp. 88–89 and p. 92. Ask students to say a sentence using the word when they guess correctly.

Read the questions and draw or write your answers.

- Give students time to think about and discuss activities in the unit before they complete each question. Explain that they can choose to either write a few words or sentences or to draw a picture. Allowing students to make a personal response will help them retain knowledge and engage with the learning points.

What did I do?

- Give students a few minutes to look back through the unit at the different activities they did. Ask questions about the unit or write questions on the board for students to discuss in pairs or small groups; for example, *What did you sing about? Where did the man on p. 94. live? Where did you hear about inventions to use with water? Which pictures did you talk about in your presentation?*
- Encourage students to identify something in the unit that they found challenging or something that was particularly memorable for them. Students can draw or write about their chosen activity.

What did I learn?

- Have students talk to a partner about what they remember from the unit—stories, words, phrases, people, ways of saving water.
- Ask questions about the unit to help students to think about what they learned; for example, *Do you know any new words that you didn't know before? What did you learn about saving water? What did you learn about writing a fact file? What else did you learn?*
- Encourage students to draw a picture or write sentences about their learning outcomes.
- Once students have written their statements or drawn a picture, have them talk to a friend about what they think they have learned.

How did I learn?

- Ask students how they learned the water cycle words in the Vocabulary Lesson. Elicit ideas (e.g. by seeing and miming the words, by doing the visualization activity, by hearing the words in the story, by playing a game).
- Encourage students to think about how they learned throughout the unit; for example, how did they develop their writing skills?
- Encourage students to draw a picture or write about some of the activities that helped them learn. Then have them compare their answers in pairs and think about what was similar and what was different about how they learned. Ask *do we all learn in the same way?*

How well did I do?

- Ask students to color in the glass of water that best expresses how well they think they learned the unit content (i.e. the more full the glass, the more they feel they have learned). Ask *What do you understand? What do you need to practice more?* Encourage students to look back through the unit to see how much they remember, what they did well, and what they found difficult.

What can I do next?

- Brainstorm ideas with the class about what they can do to continue to learn (e.g. watch the videos again; sing the song again or learn a new one).
- Encourage students to think about what they can do at home to improve their English. Have them suggest some verbs that they can use (e.g. read, practice, watch, find out more) and write the verbs in their books. Students can look back at the previous units to get more ideas. Encourage students to suggest their own ideas for different activities they can do.
- Have students choose several activities that they would like to do and write them in their notebooks. They can then share their ideas with a partner.

Looking Forward

Draw students' attention to the character at the bottom of the page. Ask *Who's this?* and elicit what they remember about her. (Ruby, Julio's mom, was talking to the man on the houseboat in Lesson 4 on p. 94.) Ask *What do you think her job is?* Elicit suggestions and predictions about Unit 8. Explain that students will find out if they were right in the first lesson of the next unit.

Practice **Resource Bank:** Unit Test
Student's App: Vocabulary and Grammar Review

Literacy

Get Ready to Read

Lesson Objectives

- to activate prior knowledge about the importance of water
- to encourage students to observe and interpret through a Think, Pair, Share VTR
- to preview the reading skill of understanding inferences

Materials

(Optional) VTR printout from the Resource Bank (A, B, C)

Warm Up

Ask students to think of every time during the day that they use a faucet (e.g. to brush their teeth, to drink, to wash their hands, to wash the dishes). Make a list on the board. Ask if they think it is the same all over the world or if some people use more or less water. Have students discuss ideas in pairs.

Think, Pair, Share

A Look at the picture. What do you think they're doing? Why? Think about it.

Students are going to do a Think, Pair, Share VTR to explore the image of people taking samples of water.

- Start by asking students what they can see in the picture. Provide vocabulary where necessary.
- Then write the questions *What do you think they're doing? Why do you think they're doing this?* on the board. Give students one or two minutes to think so that they form their own ideas. Tell them to cross their arms when they have thought of some ideas.

B Discuss with your partner.

- Ask two volunteers to read the speech bubbles. Ask students *Do you agree with what the first person said?*
- Divide the class into pairs and have students share their ideas about the picture. Encourage them to discuss any questions they might have and to think of possible answers together.
- Circulate and encourage students to expand on their ideas by asking each other *What makes you say that?* Provide vocabulary where necessary.

C Share your ideas with the class.

- Ask pairs to share their ideas about the picture with the class. Encourage students to use *we*, as they are talking about their partner's opinion, too.

Here's an example of this part of the routine.

Teacher: What do you think about the picture?
Student A: We think they're scientists checking the water.
Teacher: OK, why do you think they're checking the water?
Student A: To see if it's dirty or clean.
Student B: We think it's dirty. They're wearing masks.
Teacher: Does anyone have a different idea?
Student C: They don't know if the water is dirty. They are being careful.
Student D: We think they're police officers looking for clues.
Student C: What makes you say that?
Student D: Sometimes police officers wear those clothes.

Transition

Ask students if they have ever been in a place like the one in the picture. Ask *Would you drink this water? Would you swim in it?*

D Think and discuss. Why is it dangerous to drink dirty water?

- Ask students *What can happen if people drink dirty water?* Have students discuss their ideas in pairs. Then elicit ideas and write them on the board. Ask them if they know why dirty water can make us sick.
- Then ask students the types of places where they shouldn't drink the water. Have students discuss this in pairs and then elicit as many suggestions from different pairs as possible.

Suggested Answers

It can have bacteria/germs. It can make you sick.

E Think and discuss. Look at the pictures. What do you think each invention does?

This is a preview of the reading skill of understanding inferences.

- Refer students to the pictures (or project them onto the board). First ask what they can see in each of the pictures and then ask them to think about what each invention does. Have them compare ideas with a partner and then ask the class for their ideas.
- Ask if everyone agrees and if students can add any more ideas.

Now read **Clean Water for All**

Nonfiction: *Clean Water for All*—Informational Text

Lesson Objectives

- to read an informational text about the importance of clean water
- to learn about the environment through CLIL (science): exploring inventions that provide clean water
- to make a personal connection to the reading

Materials
Audio Tracks 35 and 36

Warm Up

Ask students to imagine they don't have clean water at home. Have students work in groups to brainstorm all the things they wouldn't be able do in that situation and decide which one they would miss the most.

TRACK 35 TB p. 233 Reading Approach

First Reading: Engage with the Text

- Refer students to the title and ask them *What do you think* Clean Water for All *means?* Have them guess what the reading is about.
- Have students read the text individually and check their predictions about the text.

TRACK 36 TB p. 233 Words in Context

- Play the audio and have students repeat the words.
- Have students race to find the words in the reading.
- Review all the strategies students have learned so far for figuring out the meaning of new words (see TB p. 22). Have them discuss these words with a partner.
- Ask which strategies they used. Then bring the class together and use these discussion points to confirm the meanings.

humid (p. 106) Have students underline words that help them figure out the meaning of *humid* in both the sentences with this word (water in the air, hot).

advertising (p. 106) Ask what the purpose of billboards like this usually is. (to sell things) Elicit that the first part of the word, *ad*, gives us the clue. (Students will be familar with writing ads from previous levels.)

vapor (p. 106) Ask *Where does the water come from?* (the air) *Is it liquid in the air?* (no—like part of the air)

bacteria (p. 107) Have students point to the picture. Ask *Are bacteria alive?* (yes) *Are some of them bad? Why?* (yes, they are sometimes dangerous, they can make you sick)

practical (p. 107) Have students find the word and the sentences that come after it. Ask *Do you think something* practical *makes life easier or harder?* (easier: Lifestraw is light to carry).

steam (p. 108) Ask *How can we make steam?* (by heating hot water) Students might also mention steam in a shower.

pump (p. 109) Have students point out the sequence of actions in the picture as you read them: You cycle to a river. You pedal to power a pump. The water flows. Ask *What does the pump do?* (pulls water from the river)

International English

Elicit which words are American English and which words are British English. Highlight the spelling differences between *liter/litre* and *vapor/vapour.*

Second Reading: Analyze the Text and Features

- Play the audio and have students follow along in their books.
- Ask some comprehension questions to check understanding, e.g. *How much water do we need to drink every day?* (six glasses a day)
- Discuss the questions in the orange boxes.
  - **Text Focus** (p. 106): *What is the purpose of the diagrams?* If necessary, ask students if they think they could understand the inventions with no diagrams.
  - **Personalization** (p. 106): *What's the climate like in your area?* Brainstorm the words that can be used to describe a climate—*dry, humid, cold, hot, rainy,* and so on. Ask *Which of these describes your climate?*
  - **Making Connections** (p. 107): *You need a microscope to see bacteria.* Ask students if they think bacteria are generally big or small (tiny). Ask students what other things people use microscopes to see. (Doctors and scientists study things in the body and tiny living things.)
  - **CLIL (science)** (p. 109): *What other inventions to make clean water do you know?* Ask students *Do you have something in your house to filter water? Do you know of any other inventions to make water clean?*

Third Reading: Interact with the Text

- Write the *Wh-* question prompts on the board and have students work in small groups to write five questions about the reading (tell them the answers must be in the text).

Cool Down

Have students swap the questions they wrote in the Third Reading stage with another group. Have groups race to answer the questions correctly.

Explore the Reading

Lesson Objectives

- to understand and analyze *Clean Water for All* through reading comprehension activities
- to learn about the environment through CLIL (science): exploring the effectiveness of inventions that provide clean water

Warm Up

Write the names of the four water-purifying methods on the board. In groups of three, have students take turns to mime using a method for the others to guess, e.g. Water Billboard—look up at the billboard and turn on a faucet to get the water; Lifestraw—bend down and mime drinking through a big straw; Eliodomestico—mime pouring seawater into the boiler pot; Cycloclean—mime pedaling.

A Read and answer. Write *Water Billboard*, *Lifestraw*, *Eliodomestico*, or *Cycloclean*.

- Before students open their books, have a team quiz to find out what they remember from the reading. Ask *How many methods for making clean water were there in the reading?* (four) *Which one doesn't use a machine or moving parts?* (Lifestraw) *Why do hikers like Lifestraw?* (It's practical.) *Where was Cycloclean invented?* (Japan) *What country uses Water Billboards?* (Peru)
- Have students look at the picture of each invention in A and ask volunteers to explain briefly how each works.
- Refer students to the first sentence and ask students which invention it describes. (Cycloclean) Encourage them to tell you what word or phrase from the text tells them this. (work with your legs)
- Have students complete the rest of the activity individually and compare their answers with a friend.
- Check the answers and ask if everyone agrees. If necessary, confirm with the reading.

Answers

1 Cycloclean 2 Lifestraw 3 Water Billboard
4 Cycloclean 5 Eliodomestico 6 Lifestraw

B Think and write. Choose one of the four inventions. What are its advantages and disadvantages?

- Do one of the inventions as an example with the whole group (e.g. Water Billboards). Project or draw the diagram on the board and give students some thinking time. Ask them for their ideas on what the advantages and disadvantages of Water Billboards are. Ask them to think about what it needs to work, space, and how easy it is to move. Write their ideas on the board.
- Now divide the class into pairs and have them choose one of the other three options to analyze. Then have pairs compare with each other. If they chose the same invention, ask how similar their ideas were. If they chose different inventions, ask which one seems to have more advantages.

Suggested Answers

Water Billboard
Advantages: uses water from the air, easy to use
Disadvantages: doesn't produce much water, very big, can't carry it
Lifestraw
Advantages: easy to carry and use, lightweight
Disadvantages: need to replace it after a while
Eliodomestico
Advantages: good for hot and sunny places, easy to use, doesn't need electricity
Disadvantages: can only do a little bit of water at a time, doesn't work in the shade
Cycloclean
Advantages: good for emergencies, doesn't need electricity
Disadvantages: large, needs a lot of human energy

C Think and discuss. Which invention would be best for where you live? Why?

This activity encourages students to connect the ideas they learned about in the reading to real-life situations in their own community. It draws on the CLIL science and environmental studies objective of exploring the effectiveness of different clean water inventions.

- Ask students to discuss in pairs which invention would be most useful for where they live. Encourage them to consider all the issues they discussed in B when making a decision, e.g. climate, environmental factors, practicality. Ask the class for their opinions and reasons and then take a class vote by a show of hands.

Cool Down

Ask students to imagine they don't have clean water at home and they want to make lemonade. In pairs, have students decide which of the inventions they would use and have them draw a sequence of pictures to show how they would make the lemonade, from cutting and juicing to serving.

Practice **Student's App:** Reading Practice

Get Ready to Read

Lesson Objectives

- to practice the reading skill of understanding inferences
- to make predictions about character, setting, and plot

Materials

A backpack with some of the following items or similar: a tennis ball / table tennis paddle or similar; a tourist book about a different country or other interest; pet food or other item connected with a pet; a car key or bike lock; a gallery or theater ticket or brochure or similar (WU)

Warm Up

Tell students you've just found a backpack and you want to know to whom it belongs. Remove the items one by one and place them on your desk. Point out there is no identification. Ask students what we can say about this person from the items that are in the backpack. Have students discuss ideas with a friend and then share with the class; for example, *He/She likes sports. He/She went to X on vacation or maybe is going to go to X? He/She drives a car / rides a bike.*

A Think and check (✔). Look at the scene. What can you infer from the text and picture?

Students are going to practice the reading skill of understanding inferences.

- Project the picture onto the board or have students look at it in their books. Ask *What can you see in the picture? Are there people outside or inside? What's the weather like outside? What is the man outside doing? What do you think is happening? What do you think will happen next?*
- Have students check all the sentences they think they can infer from the text and picture.
- Check answers, by having students ask each other questions in pairs to confirm understanding. Model an example first, so students know the kind of questions to ask. Suggested questions include:
  1 *Did the rain ruin the party?* (no) *Why do you think that?* (the picture shows people smiling)
  2 *Is everyone going to leave?* (no) *Why do you think that?* (the picture shows people holding drinks and talking)
  3 *Do you think they'll have the party inside?* (yes) *Why do you think that?* (the picture shows most people are inside already, they have drinks, they're talking, they look like they're having fun, it's wet outside)
  4 *Do you think they expected the rain?* (no) *Why do you think that?* (The picture shows a barbecue, which we usually have in good weather; the text says "the food is getting wet." It's unlikely someone would have taken it outside if they expected rain.)
- Refer students to the skills box about making inferences. Ask students *Were you given all the information about the picture, or did you make inferences (guesses)?* (inferences) Elicit some answers, then ask students why they think being able to make inferences is an important skill. Have students discuss ideas in pairs. If necessary, point out that writers don't always give us all the information in words. Sometimes thinking about our own experiences in combination with the information we're given, can give us a better understanding of the plot and what characters might be thinking, as well as what motivates them.

Answers

They'll have the party inside instead.
No one expected the rain.

B Think and discuss. Look at the picture from *The New Dam*. What inferences can you make about the characters and the setting?

- First ask students *What can you see in the picture?* Give them a minute to think about the picture individually. Elicit some ideas and help with vocabulary, as necessary.
- Then have students use what they can see to make guesses or inferences about the place and the characters. Ask for suggestions to complete the example sentences and then have students carry on making more inferences in pairs.
- Elicit ideas and encourage students to give reasons for their answers.

Suggested Answers

The younger man looks angry/frustrated.
The village is small / in the countryside.

C Think and discuss. Look at B. Predict what you think will happen in this story.

- Give students some thinking time to look at the picture in B and their inferences again, and to use these to make predictions about the story *The New Dam*. Have them discuss their ideas about the story in pairs or in small groups. Ask students if they had the same ideas. Then ask for volunteers to share their ideas with the class.

Cool Down

Ask students which picture from this lesson they think looks like it shows a more interesting story. Have them discuss their ideas in pairs. Encourage them to give reasons, then have a class vote to see which picture is the most popular.

Now read **The New Dam**

Fiction: *The New Dam—Story*

Lesson Objectives

- to read a story about sharing water
- to make a personal connection to the reading

Materials
Audio Tracks 37 and 38; Video

Warm Up

Have students look at the inference question in the orange box on p. 112: *What do you think is wrong with the river?* Point to the pictures of the river at the top and bottom of the page. Ask students *What do you think the problem is?* Elicit suggestions and let them know they will find out the answer when they read the story.

TRACK 37 TB p. 233 Reading Approach

First Reading: Engage with the Text

- Refer students to the title and elicit or check students understand what a dam is. Then play the audio while they follow along in their books.
- After each page, pause and ask students *What do you think will happen next?* Then continue the audio to confirm.
- Play the audio to the end, then look at the Words in Context.

TRACK 38 TB p. 234 Words in Context

- Play the audio and have students repeat the words.
- Have students race to find the words in the story.
- Remind students they can sometimes **use the separate parts of the words and the type of word to help establish the meaning** (see TB p. 22). Have them discuss their ideas with a partner, using L1 if necessary.
- Then bring the class together and use these discussion points to confirm the meanings.

respected (p. 112) Ask *Did the people like the river? Why?* (Yes, it gave them drinking water and fish.) *Was it always good to them?* (No, sometimes it flooded the fields.) Ask students to imagine how they feel about something that is good but can also be dangerous. Elicit other examples (electricity, the sun, the ocean).

powerful (p. 112) Elicit that it is an adjective (here it describes the river) and that the word *power* gives us a clue to its meaning. Ask students if they can think of a synonym (strong).

creek (p. 112) Remind students that the story said the river was powerful. *Does this look like a powerful river?* (no) Ask students whether *creek* is a word for a big or a small river.

salmon (p. 112) Elicit that a *salmon* is a kind of fish and that we can find this information in the next sentence.

direct (p. 113) Ask *Is* direct *a verb or a noun?* (a verb) Have them read the sentence again and ask if they know a word that could replace direct here (move). Ask *How does the dam work?* (It stops the river from going into the village and directs or moves it towards Kingstown.)

hold (p. 115) Ask students to imagine a wooden dam with a strong river against it—what will happen? Will it hold?

Second Reading: Analyze the Text and Features

- Play the video to consolidate understanding of the story. Ask students to raise their hands when they see a character does something positive and fold their arms when a character makes a bad decision. Ask *Did it take a long time to build the dam?* (yes, months)
- Then discuss the questions in the orange boxes.
  - **Critical Thinking** (p. 113): *Why did people start building dams?* Encourage students to think about the situation in the village. Ask *Was it better or worse after the dam?*
  - **Language Focus** (p. 114): *"The frog doesn't drink up the pond in which it lives." What do you think this means?* Check understanding of *pond* (small lake). Then have students discuss the sentence in pairs. If necessary, guide them by asking if frogs need water to drink (yes) and to live in (yes). Ask *What happens if a frog drinks all the water?* (It can't live.) Ask if Wabaunsee's friend is only talking about frogs when he says this. (No—he's saying that we must all respect nature.)
- Discuss the text focus: *When characters have a* ***problem****, they must find a* ***solution****. How does Wabaunsee find a solution?* Have students discuss their ideas in pairs. Ask if they think Wabaunsee found the solution on his own. (No—he worked with the engineer.)
  - **Personalization** (p. 117): *Find out about the biggest dam in your country. What does it do?* For homework, have students find out about dams in their country on the internet.

Third Reading: Interact with the Text

- Ask students if they think the story would be different if the villagers blocked the river and the town suffered. How? Why? Have them discuss their ideas in small groups and then tell another group their new version of the story.

Cool Down

Ask students if they have changed their minds about any of the inferences they made regarding character and setting in the previous lesson. Have students discuss ideas. Tell them that it is important to continuously update their thinking when they get new information.

Practice Student's App: Fiction Video

Explore the Reading

Lesson Objectives

- to understand and analyze *The New Dam* through reading comprehension activities
- to practice the reading skill of understanding inferences
- to explore the SEL competency of relationship skills by demonstrating leadership skills and, when necessary, being assertive and persuasive
- to make a personal connection to the reading
- to recognize and reproduce words with the spelling *–ful* and *–fully*

Materials

Video; Audio Tracks 37 and 39

TRACK 37 TB p. 233 Warm Up

Have students brainstorm all the words they can remember from the reading. Then play the video or audio and have students check off any words they hear mentioned. Ask students how many words they checked off and what they were.

A Read and match.

- Before students open their books, find out what they remember about the reading. Give them three answers and have them work in pairs to write possible questions for the answers. Answers could include: 1 Kingstown (Where was the dam? Where did Wabaunsee go?) 2 the engineer (Who did Wabaunsee work with to find a solution?) 3 months (How long did it take to build the new dam?)
- Refer students to the problems on the left in A. Explain that for each problem there is a solution on the right. Elicit the solution for the first problem.
- Have students complete the activity individually and then compare answers with a friend.
- To check answers, ask one student to read a problem and another student to read the corresponding solution.

Answers

1 d 2 c 3 b 4 a

B Read and answer. Write *T* for sentences from the text and *I* for inferences.

- Refer students to the example sentence. Ask them to find where in the text this is mentioned. (in the first line on p. 112) Explain that some of the sentences aren't actually mentioned in the text but can be inferred instead.
- Have students continue the activity individually. Then have them compare answers in pairs.
- Check the answers and ask if everyone agrees. Ask students to tell you where in the text they found the sentences marked with a T.

Answers

1 *T* 2 T 3 I 4 T 5 I 6 T

C Think and discuss. How did Wabaunsee react to his village's problem? How would you react in a similar situation?

This activity explores the SEL competency of demonstrating leadership skills and, when necessary, being assertive and persuasive.

- Ask students *Was Wabaunsee happy to wait for a solution for the problem to arrive? Was he angry, or was he patient when he found the cause of the problem? What did he do?* Have students discuss in pairs and then share with the class.
- Give students some thinking time to decide how they would react in his situation. Ask students to raise their hands a little, midway, or all the way up to show if they think they could do the same as Wabaunsee.
- Have students think about a time they had to take action to solve a problem. Give them time to think and then tell a friend what happened.

TRACK 39 TB p. 234 Spelling Patterns *–ful* and *–fully*

Listen and write. Then check your answers.

- With books closed, write the words *hopeful* and *hopefully* on the board. Ask students what kinds of words they are (adjective and adverb) and have students repeat them. Ask what they notice about the *l*s. (one at the end of the adjective, two in the adverb)
- Play the first part of the audio and have students repeat each word. Check pronunciation to make sure students are not stressing the *–ful/–fully* syllables. Then have them open their books. Play the first part of the audio again and have them complete as many words as they can.
- Play the second part of the audio for students to check their spelling and complete any missing words. Have students underline *ful* and circle *fully*. Remind students about the different spelling of the words—one *l* in the adjectives, two *l*s in the adverbs (because we add *ly* to make an adverb). Have them read the words aloud.
- Have students look back at the reading to find more words of the same type and write them down. Invite students to read them aloud. Then have them write all the words from the lesson in a table, with the *-ful* words on one side and *-fully* words on the other. Encourage them to write matching adjectives /adverbs in the table, e.g. *beautiful/beautifully; hopeful/hopefully.*

Answers

1 beautiful 2 useful 3 grateful 4 hopefully 5 carefully

In the reading: peaceful; powerful; helpful; thoughtfully; thankfully

Cool Down

Play *How Many Letters?* (see TB p. 26) with words from the spelling pattern section.

Practice **Resource Bank:** Spelling Printout
Student's App: Reading Practice; Spelling Pattern Practice

Think Together

Lesson Objectives

- to make connections between the readings
- to explore the key concept: How do you use water every day?
- to reflect on the unit and provide personal thoughts and opinions

Warm Up

Have students look back at the VTR image on pp. 104–105 and ask *Do you now have any new ideas about the image? What do you think the people are doing? How will this help other people?*

Have students compare their ideas in pairs and then ask for their suggestions.

A Think and discuss. Then complete the mind map. Use ideas *from Clean Water for All*, *The New Dam*, and your own ideas.

- Project or draw the diagram on the board. Ask the class for one or two ideas and write them in the mind map on the board. Then have students continue to think of ideas and complete their diagrams in pairs or small groups. Encourage them to add more drops if they have more ideas.

Suggested Answers

need it to live / stay healthy; use it for drinking / cooking / watering crops / cleaning / taking showers; give water to animals; water trees and flowers

B Think and discuss. What changes can you make to the way you use water? Do a Three-step Interview.

- Introduce the key concept question at the top of the page: *How do you use water every day?* Give students some thinking time, then ask for suggestions, and fill one side of the board with their ideas.
- Have students discuss in groups why it might be good for them to change the way they use water. (Using less water means there is less risk of water shortages. It also uses less energy [less water to be processed/pumped to people's homes] which means less pollution.)
- Elicit one or two ideas from students of how they can use less water. Point out that this could be at home, school, or another location. Then set the class up for a Three-Step Interview cooperative learning routine (see TB p. 20).
- After students speak in their pairs, they can report back to their original group and exchange ideas.
- Ask students to share the best ideas they heard with the class.

C Think and discuss. Which of the things in B do you or your family already do?

- Have students work with a different classmate to share the things they heard in B that they already do to use less water. Do they do the same or different things? Also ask them to choose something new they can try at home (if appropriate) or at school to use less water.

My Reading Journal

Find five words in this unit that are interesting or new to you.

This activity encourages students to reflect on what they enjoy learning.

Ask students to remember new or interesting words from the unit. Explain that these could be words that they like the sound of, or that are fun or challenging to pronounce. Or they could be words that have an important or interesting meaning. Elicit one or two examples, then have students look back over the unit and complete the list of five new words (or more, if they want). Ask the class for some examples of the words they chose and why they chose them. Then have students choose one of their words, write it on paper in bubble letters and illustrate it with the things they imagine when they see or hear that word. Display all the bubble words on the wall.

Imagine you are standing in the rain after a long drought. Draw yourself and write how you feel.

This activity encourages students to provide a personal, imaginative, and reflective response to the reading. Check the meaning of *drought* with students (a long time with no rain).

Give students some thinking time to decide what they would do and how they would feel. You could do do a visualization activity to prompt ideas, e.g. *You are standing in the rain. It is the first time it has rained for months. You can feel the rain in your hair, running down your cheeks, You hold out your hands. What does it feel like? You stick your tongue out. What can you taste? What can you hear? What can you smell? How does the rain make you feel?* Then have them draw, write and share their ideas with a friend.

Cool Down

Have students leave their books open on p. 119 so other students can look at their drawing. Give them time to circulate around the class and look for a particularly good drawing, a fun activity for the rain, the same feeling as they described, or a feeling they didn't expect to see. After two minutes, ask students if they found any of these things.

Practice **Resource Bank:** Unit Test
Student's App: Key Concept Practice

UNIT 8

Lights, Camera, Action

Unit Overview

Themes

Movies

Actors and stunt performers

Synopsis

In this unit students will learn about different movie genres and find out about what movies can teach us and the role of different team members when making movies. They will plan and prepare a presentation to give a movie review and will plan and write a movie script using target vocabulary and grammar from the unit.

Language Book

Vocabulary
beard, director, eyebrows, eyelashes, lips, make-up, movie star, mustache, scar, studio, wig
p. 160

Explore Language
Defining Relative Clauses: *Who, That, Where*
p. 161

Global Citizenship
What can movies teach us?
animation, comedy, detective, documentary, drama, horror, musical, soundtrack, trailer
p. 162

Explore Language
Adjectives: *–ing* or *–ed*
p. 163

Take the Stage
Presentation: describing movies, making recommendations
p. 164

Write About It
A Movie Script
Text Type: features of a script
p. 165

Think It Over
Review and Reflection
p. 166

Think Together

Why do movies need a team?

p. 173

Visible Thinking

Question Starts

p. 167

Literacy Book

Fiction

Play: *Actors on Set*

Words in Context: *producer, hiring, supervisor, operator, instructions, microphone, props, shoot*

p. 171

Nonfiction

Informational Text: *Action Stars*

Words in Context: *stunt, scene, professional, martial arts, champion*

p. 168

Reading Skill

Understanding cause and effect

p. 170

Spelling Pattern

–ing

p. 169

Language and Literacy Connections

The connecting theme in Unit 8 is learning about making movies.

	Language	Literacy
Vocabulary	**Set 1:** physical characteristics and movies **Set 2:** movie genres and features	**Nonfiction:** make-up, movie star, scar(s), studio(s), wig(s) **Fiction:** make-up
Grammar	**Defining Relative Clauses:** ***Who, That, Where*** The man who is wearing sunglasses. The taxi that drove past. The café where we had lunch. **Adjectives:** ***–ing*** **or** ***–ed*** The costume was tiring. I was really tired.	**Nonfiction** The driver who was in the car is a stunt performer. Good stunt performers are always calm under pressure, organized, and well prepared. **Fiction** I have a webpage here that tells me all about it.
Skills	**Pronunciation:** /ə/	**Reading:** understanding cause and effect **Spelling Pattern:** *–ing*
International English	movie star / film star	movie star / film star; elementary/ primary

Vocabulary

Lesson Objectives

- to learn vocabulary to talk about physical characteristics and movies: *beard, director, eyebrows, eyelashes, lips, make-up, movie star, mustache, scar, studio, wig*
- to sing a song about being in a movie

Materials
Audio Tracks 87 to 90; Video

Warm Up

Ask students to imagine they are working on making a movie. Ask them to think about what their job is and what this involves. Have them discuss their ideas in pairs.

A TRACK 87 TB p. 222 **Listen and find. Who's Willis Brice?**

- Have students look at the picture on pp. 100–101 and ask *What can you see? Where are the people in the picture?* Ask if students recognize the woman with the sign that says *Studio Tour*. She's Ruby (Julio's mom) from the previous unit.
- Play the audio and have students point to the words and pictures as they listen.
- Ask the gist question *Who's Willis Brice?* and elicit the answer. Play the audio again to check.
- Remind students of the challenge at the end of Unit 7: *What's my job?* Ask *Can you answer Ruby's question now?* Play the audio again if necessary to check. (She's a studio tour guide.)

Answer
a famous movie star

B TRACK 88 TB p. 222 **Listen, say, and number the pictures in A.**

- Play the audio. Have students point to the pictures and say the words.
- Play the audio again and have students write numbers next to the pictures in the order they hear them.
- Check answers by calling out the words in random order and having students say the number.

Answers
1 *beard* 2 eyebrows 3 eyelashes 4 scar 5 lips
6 studio 7 wig 8 make-up 9 movie star
10 director 11 mustache

International English

Elicit that *movie star* is American English and *film star* is British English. Ask volunteers to make a sentence using one of the phrases.

C TRACK 89 TB p. 222 **Close your eyes. Listen, visualize, and say.**

- Prepare students for the visualization (see TB p. 21).
- Play the audio, allowing students to visualize the words as they listen.
- Have students work in pairs, taking turns to mime what they visualized and have their partner guess the word.

D Look and write.

- Draw students' attention to the Venn diagram and tell them they are going to categorize the new words into *Appearance, Making a Movie,* or *Both*.
- Refer students to the example *make-up* and elicit why it is in the middle of the Venn diagram. (It is used for people's appearance and used by actors when making a movie.)
- Give students time to complete the activity individually and then compare answers with a friend.
- Project or draw the Venn diagram on the board and invite students to come and complete one item each.

Answers
Appearance: scar; eyebrows; eyelashes; lips; beard; mustache
Making a Movie: studio; director; movie star
Both: *make-up*; wig

E TRACK 90 TB p. 222 **Listen and complete. Then watch and sing.**

- Have students look at the title of the song, *Be a Movie Star*, and ask them *What do you think movie stars need to do in their work?* Write their ideas on the board. Ask *Do you want to be a movie star? Why?*
- Play the song and allow students to listen and enjoy.
- Explain that some parts of the words are missing and they have to complete them. Ask *Can you guess what words they are?* Have students read the song and complete any words they know.
- Play the song again and have students check their answers and complete any they missed. Then check answers as a class.
- Play the song video and have students watch and sing along. Play the song video again and have students point to the appropriate parts of the face when they hear the physical characteristics words.

Answers
1 *movie star* 2 studio 3 director 4 make-up
5 beard 6 wig 7 eyebrows 8 eyelashes

Cool Down

Play *Simon Says* (see TB p. 27) with the physical characteristics vocabulary from A. Use *Simon says touch your …* (beard, eyelashes, etc.) or *Simon says put on your …* (wig, make-up) as the prompts.

Practice **Student's App:** Vocabulary Practice; Song Video

Explore Language

Lesson Objectives

- to learn how to use defining relative clauses with *who*, *that*, and *where*
- to practice vocabulary about physical characteristics and movies

Materials

Audio Tracks 91 and 92

Warm Up

Ask students to imagine they see a movie star in the street. Ask *What do you do?* Elicit all their ideas (say hello, wave, ask for an autograph, just look, follow him/her, ask questions, take a picture) and write them on the board. Have students discuss in pairs which ones they think they would do.

A TRACK 91 TB p. 222 **Listen and read. Who does Sam think the man in sunglasses is?**

- Have students look at the pictures on p. 102. Ask *What can you see? Where are the children? What do you think they are talking about? Who do you think the person in sunglasses is?* Play the audio and have students follow the story.
- Ask the comprehension question *Who does Sam think the man in sunglasses is?* Elicit the answer.

Answer

Willis Brice, the famous movie star

B Look at A. Complete.

- Write or project the table onto the board.
- Have students discuss and complete the grammar table themselves in pairs using the story.
- Check answers on the board. Discuss the word order and subject of each sentence together, but let your class guide the discussion. If you feel that students need more guidance, the **ETB** provides a differentiation activity to help you support students as they explore the grammar table.
- Tell students that words like *who*, *that*, and *where* are called relative pronouns and that they appear at the start of a defining relative clause. Say *Do you know what job the relative clause does?* Have students look at the sentences in the table and discuss ideas in pairs. Then elicit or explain that defining relative clauses give more information to help us understand which person, thing, or place we're talking about.
- Have students look at the Grammar tip *Look*. Ask them to say the *who* sentence in the grammar table using *that* (*The man that is wearing sunglasses*), and tell them that this option is also correct.

Answers

that; where; we

C **Think and discuss. Then choose.**

- Have students look at the sentences in C. Give them some thinking time and encourage them to look at the table in B, the story, in A, and the *Look* tip to help them. Then have students discuss their answers with a partner.
- Read the sentences and have students call out the words they chose. Check everyone agrees and confirm the answers.

Answers

1 that/who 2 that 3 where

D TRACK 92 TB p. 222 **Listen and say.**

- Play the audio and have students listen and repeat. (See TB p. 23 for ideas on how to vary the drill.)

E **Read and choose.**

- Tell students they are going to choose the correct relative pronoun for each sentence. Refer students to the example. Ask *Why do we use "who" in this sentence?* (It's about a person.)
- Have students complete the activity. Check answers and ask if everyone agrees.

Answers

1 *who* 2 that 3 where 4 who 5 where

F **Play *True or False*. Write and say.**

- Tell students they are going to write true and false sentences using the activities in the box. Write three example sentences about you on the board and have students guess if they are true or false: *The moon is the place where I went on vacation last year. Australia is a country where I'd love to live. A movie that I really enjoyed was* Dracula.
- Have students write at least three sentences. Tell them at least one must be false.
- Invite a pair of students to read the example dialogue, then have students take turns reading their sentences to a partner. Their partner should guess if each sentence is true or false, and then students should confirm whether their partner was correct. Tell students to make a note of how many they guessed correctly. Who had the most correct guesses?

Cool Down

Play *Running Sentences* (see TB p. 26) with key sentences from this lesson; for example, *I'll show you the house where I was born. / This is the book that I really enjoyed. / The man who is wearing sunglasses is a famous actor.*

Practice **Resource Bank:** Grammar Printout
Student's App: Grammar Practice

Global Citizenship

Lesson Objectives

- to learn vocabulary for talking about movie genres: *animation, comedy, detective, documentary, drama, horror, musical, soundtrack, trailer*
- to explore what movies can teach us
- to practice listening for gist and details

Materials

Audio Tracks 93 and 95; Audio Track H; a world map (D)

Opening Question

Ask students the opening question: *What can movies teach us?* Give students time to think, then elicit opinions.

A TRACK 93 TB p. 223 **Listen to Meg and Eric talk about movies. Which movie have they both seen?**

- Have students look at p. 104 and say what they can see. Tell students they will hear a conversation about choosing a movie to watch. Ask students *Do you think it will be easy for the two friends to decide? Why?*
- Play the audio and have students point to the pictures and words as they listen.
- Ask them the comprehension question *Which movie have they both seen?* and elicit the answer. Play the audio again to check.
- Ask students if they can remember the names of all the movies mentioned in the dialogue (*Frozen, We Bought a Zoo, Mamma Mia!*, and *Penguins of Madagascar*). Ask *Has anyone seen any of these movies?* And, if so, *Did you like it?*

Answer

Mamma Mia!

B TRACK 94 TB p. 223 **Listen, say, and number the pictures in A.**

- Play the audio and have students point to the pictures and say the words.
- Play the audio again and have students write numbers next to the words in the order they hear them.
- Write or project the answers onto the board.

Answers

1 *detective* 2 trailer 3 soundtrack 4 comedy
5 horror 6 drama 7 animation 8 musical
9 documentary

TRACK H TB p. 223 **Visualization**

The TTL has a visualization audio track for this vocabulary set. (See TB p. 21.)

C Read and write.

- Tell students they will write the correct words next to the definitions. Refer students to the example definition and answer. Ask why *documentary* is correct here (a documentary is based on real facts, not an invented story).
- Have students complete the activity and then compare answers. Check answers as a class.

Answers

1 *documentary* 2 comedy 3 soundtrack 4 detective
5 horror 6 musical

D TRACK 95 TB p. 223 **Now listen to Deepa and Eric. Who chooses the movies for the festival and for the school club?**

- To generate interest, have students look at the two pictures and notice where each child is from. Ask students *Where are these countries?* Use a map to find them.
- Have students look at the pictures and ask them *What can you see? What do you think the boy is doing?* Ask if they have ever done something similar.
- Listening for gist: play the audio and have students listen for the answer to the gist question *Who chooses the movies for the festival and for the school club?* Have students compare their ideas with a partner, and then elicit the answers.

Answers

Children choose for the festival, and the club members choose for the school club.

E Listen again and choose.

- Listening for details: have students look at the statements and ask them if they think they can choose the correct answer.
- Play the audio and have students check their answers and circle any they missed. Check answers.

Answers

1 *Adults and children* 2 more than one
3 a documentary 4 week 5 on the internet 6 write

Discussion Questions

- Draw students' attention to the discussion questions: *What kind of movies do you like? Why? How can movies connect people?* Have students discuss the questions in pairs (see ETB).
- Return to the opening question to ask again: *What can movies teach us?* Have students think about what Deepa and Eric talked about, then ask *What do you think you have learned from movies?* and give students time to think. Have them discuss with a friend and then elicit suggestions. Make a list of the suggestions on the board. Ask students *Should we always believe what we see in the movies?* (No—a lot of it is invented!)

Cool Down

Play *Backs to the Board* in pairs (see TB p. 25).

Practice **Student's App:** Vocabulary Practice; Listening Practice

Explore Language

Lesson Objectives

- to learn how to use adjectives with *–ing* or *–ed*

Materials

Audio Tracks 96 and 97

Warm Up

Ask students *Which movie star would you most like to meet? What question would you ask him or her?* Have them tell a friend and then take suggestions from the class. Does the class have a favorite movie star?

A TRACK 96 TB p. 223 **Listen and read. Who was frightened during the movie *The Warrior in the Desert?***

- Ask students *Who can you see in the picture? Where are they?* Ask what they think the boy is going to ask the movie star.
- Play the audio and have students follow the dialogue. Ask if their prediction was correct.
- Ask the gist question *Who was scared during the movie* The Warrior in the Desert? Elicit answers, then ask some additional questions; for example, *Did Willis Brice like making the movie?* (no)

Answer

Willis Brice, the movie star

B **Look at A. Complete.**

- Write or project the table onto the board.
- Have students discuss and complete the table in pairs using the dialogue.
- Check answers on the board. Have students identify the subject as well as the role adjectives play in each sentence, but let your class guide the discussion. If you feel that students need more support, use the notes in the **ETB**.

Answers

boring; bored; frightening

C **Think and discuss. Then choose.**

- Give students some time to read the sentences and think about their answers. Encourage them to use the table in B and the dialogue in A to help them. Then have them compare their ideas with a friend.
- Read the sentences and answer options and have students raise their hands to show the option they chose. Confirm answers.
- Refer students to the Grammar tip *Look*. Write on the board *I feel* __________ *because English is* __________. Ask students for their suggestions for how to complete this sentence.

Answers

1 *–ed* 2 *–ing*

Practice **Resource Bank:** Grammar Printout
Student's App: Grammar Practice

D TRACK 97 TB p. 223 **Listen and say.**

- Play the audio and have students listen and repeat. For ideas on how to vary the drill, see TB p. 23.

E **Read and choose.**

- Tell students they are going to choose the correct adjective for each sentence. Refer them to the example and ask why *bored* is correct (*–ed* adjectives describe how we feel, *–ing* adjectives describe the qualities of something).
- Have students complete the activity individually. Check the answers as a class and write or project them onto the board for everyone to see.

Answers

1 *bored* 2 amazing 3 annoyed 4 disgusting
5 excited 6 tiring

F **Play *What's My Adjective?* Choose, write, and say.**

- Tell students they are going to play a game. First, check the meaning of the words in the box by having students mime feeling this way.
- Then write two incomplete sentences on the board. One sentence should be missing an *–ed* adjective and one missing an *–ing* adjective. Have students guess the missing adjective; for example, *My friend gave me a present yesterday. I was really …* (surprised). *Once when I was a kid, I called my teacher "Mom"! It was so …* (embarrassing)*!*
- Have students write sentences using *–ed* or *–ing* adjectives using words from the box. Tell them they can write the complete sentence if they wish. Divide the class into pairs. Have students read the beginning of their sentences to each other and have their partner guess the adjective. Remind them not to let their partner see what they have written! At the end, find out who had the most correct guesses.

Cool Down

Play *Pass the Whisper!* (see TB p. 26) with some of the sentences from this lesson.

Take the Stage

Lesson Objectives

- to prepare and give a presentation making recommendations about a movie
- to recognize and reproduce words with /ə/

Materials
Video; Audio Track 98

Warm Up

Ask students to tell a friend what the last movie was that they saw. Say *Did you like it? Why or why not?* Ask for some answers from the class.

A TB p. 239 **Watch and listen. Did Anya enjoy *Inside Out?***

- Tell students they are going to watch a video of a girl talking about one of her favorite movies. Ask students *Have you seen the movie* Inside Out? *Did you like it?* Ask the class to collaborate to make a brief description of what the movie is about, and write their ideas on the board.
- Introduce the gist question *Did Anya enjoy watching* Inside Out? Play the video and have students raise their hands when they know the answer. Check answers, then play the video again and ask if students want to add anything to the description on the board.
- Ask questions to check comprehension; for example, *How many times has Anya seen the movie?* (many times) Then play the video again and ask students to notice Anya's body language and voice as she tells the story of the movie, and whether she uses the past or present tense.

Answer
Yes, she did.

B Watch again. Check (✔) the sentences you hear.

- Have students read the sentences.
- Play the video and have students complete the activity individually. Read the sentences and have students raise their hands for the ones they checked.
- Read the checked phrases again and have students categorize them into introduction, middle (the description of the movie, or end (her recommendations). (Introduction: 1, 2, 3; Middle: 4, 6, 7; End: 8, 9)

Answers
1; 2; 3; 4; 6; 7; 8; 9

Pronunciation schwa /ə/

TRACK 98 TB p. 223 **Listen and say.**

- Write *again* on the board and underline the first syllable. Say the word and have students repeat it. Point out the pronunciation of the first syllable—the short, weak sound /ə/—and have students repeat the word a few times to get the feel for the short sound.
- Read the words aloud, then play the audio and have students repeat the words, with particular care to make the short /ə/ sound accurately (i.e. weak and unstressed). Repeat if students need more practice.
- Say *These words are used in the video. What other words do you know have the same sound?* Have students work in pairs to think of other words they know with the schwa (e.g. *about*). Write the words on the board and drill them for pronunciation.

Suggested Answers
/ə/ fam**ou**s, th**e**, import**a**nt, com**e**dy

C Plan. Think about a movie you've seen. Then complete.

- Tell students they are going to plan their own presentation about a movie they have seen. Project or show the graphic organizer in C and elicit that setting = place; stars = actors; characters = people/animals in the movie.
- To give an example, choose a movie you like that you think students will also know and elicit information about it to complete the plan; e.g. for the movie *Moana, Setting: Somewhere in the Pacific Ocean—a small tropical island. / Stars: famous actors and a young girl (for the voices) / Characters: a young girl who wants to save her island, a famous hero who helps her, a giant crab who wants to stop them,* and so on.
- Now have students choose a movie they have seen and complete the information in the graphic organizer.

D Prepare your presentation. Use your ideas from C and phrases from B.

- Play the video again as a model and remind students to watch with their own presentation in mind.
- Write some example presentation notes about the movie you spoke about in C. Use your plan and the students' suggestions to build up the notes on the board.
- Now have students write presentation notes for the movie they chose. Remind them to adapt phrases from B to fit their movie (i.e. keep the part in pink and change the rest of the phrase). Encourage them to use the simple present when describing the story.

E Practice with a friend. Then share with your class.

- Now have students practice their presentation with a friend. Remind them that it is important to look at the audience and speak clearly. Encourage them to gradually look at their notes less often as they practice.
- Invite volunteers to come to the front of the classroom to give their presentation. Have the audience give a round of applause after each presentation.

Cool Down

Play *Word Tennis* in teams (see TB p. 27). Teams take turns to say a word with /ə/ in it. Each student in a team must say a word, but teams can confer first.

Practice **Student's App:** Speaking Skills Practice; Speaking Video

Write About It

Lesson Objectives

- to plan and write a movie script
- to identify and practice using features of a movie script

Materials

(Optional) Challenge, Standard, and Support writing printouts from the Resource Bank, one per student (C and D)

Warm Up

Ask students to imagine they are writing a story for a horror movie. Ask them to decide two characters, a setting, and a beginning for their story. Do a Think, Pair, Share routine to generate ideas (see TB p. 20).

A Read the script. Circle the setting, character names, and acting directions.

- Have students scan the script quickly and see if this scary story is similar to any of their ideas on the board. Ask some comprehension questions and have students read again to find the answers: *Who are the characters, and where are they?* (a brother and sister in the forest) *Why do they want to go back to camp?* (to have dinner)
- Check students understand *acting directions* (the acting directions are in parentheses and say how the characters do or say things, not what they do or say).
- Have students find and circle the setting, character names, and acting directions.
- Ask students to read the text a line at a time and for the others to raise their hands when any of the features are mentioned.
- Draw students' attention to the colon that appears after the character names and remind them that this is the way character names are always presented in a script (they will be familiar with this from looking at play scripts).

Answers

Setting: In a forest
Characters: Adam a boy (8 years old), and Lorna his sister (11 years old)
Lorna: (calling) Adam! Where are you? I know you're hiding, but you can come out now. The game is over!
Adam: I'm here! I had the best hiding place!
Lorna: Yes, you did, but it's a long way back to the camp. Come on, dinner will be ready soon.
Adam: Good. I'm really hungry. What's wrong, Lorna?
Lorna: (nervous) I don't know where we are on the map.
Adam: Are we lost? I'm scared. It's really dark now.
Lorna: Don't worry, I have a flashlight here in my bag.
Adam: Oh! What's that? It looks like a building.
Lorna: I don't know. Let's go closer.

B Complete the next part of the script.

- Tell students they are going to read the next part of the script from A and fill in the blanks using the words from the box. Refer them to the example in number 1—*setting* is the place, and this one is in a forest. Have students complete the rest of the blanks and compare with a friend.
- Project the script onto the board, elicit the answers, and write them in the script. Alternately, read the script aloud and have students raise their hands to say the answer for each blank.

Answers

1 *Setting* 2 Characters 3 knocks at door 4 Adam
5 Lorna 6 scared

C Plan. Imagine the final part of the script. Then answer the questions.

- Tell students they are going to plan the next part in the script. Have them read the questions. Give sample answers and ask students if they think it makes a good story; for example, *What happens next? They find their way home. Who are the other characters? Their mom and dad. What happens in the end? They have dinner.*
- Give students some time to think about the questions and then put them in small groups and have them do an Option Explosion routine to generate ideas (see TB p. 21). After they have come up with some initial ideas, encourage them to go further and think of some really unexpected plot lines.
- Have students choose some ideas they like and complete their plans individually. Hand out the Challenge printouts at this point.
- Ask for some suggestions from the class for each question.

D Write the final part of the script.

- Tell students to use their plan to write the final part of the script. Elicit from students what they will include in it (the character names, what they say, and some acting directions to show how they say or do things).
- Have students write a rough draft of their script in their notebooks.
- Have students self-correct or exchange their work with a friend and peer-correct. You can put a checklist of points for students to look out for on the board (e.g. spelling; capital letters; colons; inclusion of setting, character names, and acting directions).
- Have students correct any mistakes and write their final script neatly on paper. Alternatively, hand out the Support and Standard printouts from the Resource Bank.

Cool Down

Invite some students to read their scripts aloud. Have the other students listen and act out the scripts.

Practice Student's App: Writing Practice

Think It Over

Lesson Objectives

- to review what has been learned in the unit
- to reflect on the unit and their own progress
- to think about learning strategies and how to continue learning at home

Warm Up

Write the vocabulary for appearances on one side of the board and for movie genres on the other, with all the vowels taken out. Remind students what the two categories are and have them decide what the words are in pairs. Have students complete a word each on the board.

Read the questions and draw or write your answers.

- Give students time to think about and discuss activities in the unit before they complete each question. Explain that they can choose to either write a few words or sentences or to draw a picture. Allowing students to make a personal response will help them retain knowledge and engage with the learning points.

What did I do?

- Give students a few minutes to look back through the unit at the different activities they did. Ask questions about the unit or write questions on the board for students to discuss in pairs or small groups; for example, *What did you write about? What people did you meet? Where did you hear about a movie festival?*
- Encourage students to identify something in the unit that they found challenging or something that was particularly memorable for them, but tell them not to choose their favorite activity yet. Students can draw or write about their chosen activity.

What did I learn?

- Have students talk to a partner about what they remember from the unit—stories, words, phrases, people, kinds of movies.
- Ask questions about the unit to help students to think about what they learned; for example, *What did you learn about movies? What did you learn about writing a movie script? What did you learn about making recommendations? What else did you learn?*
- Encourage students to draw a picture or write sentences about their learning outcomes.
- Once students have written their statements or drawn their picture, have them talk to a friend about what they think they learned.

What was my favorite part?

- Have students look back through the unit and decide what they enjoyed the most. Tell them it can be an activity they found fun, a text they enjoyed reading, a favorite character, or a favorite action. They should try to choose just one and draw a picture or write about it.
- Explain that when we like something, it is often easier to learn.

How well did I do?

- Ask students to color in the number of movie clapboards that best expresses how well they think they learned the unit content. Ask *What do you understand? What do you need to practice more?* Encourage students to look back through the unit to see how much they remember, what they did well, and what they found difficult.

What can I do next?

- Brainstorm ideas with the class about what they can do to continue to learn (e.g. practice saying words with the /ə/ sound, watch a movie and think about what they can learn from it).
- Draw students' attention to the *What Can I Do Next?* box. Encourage students to think about what they can do at home to improve their English. Have them suggest some verbs that they can use (e.g. play, practice, watch, sing) and write the verbs in their books. Students can look back at the previous units to get more ideas. Encourage students to suggest their own ideas for different activities they can do.
- Have students choose several activities that they would like to do and write them in their notebooks. They can then share their ideas with a partner.

Looking Forward

Draw students' attention to the character at the bottom of the page. Ask *Who's this?* and elicit what they remember about him. (Willis Brice, the movie star, was on the movie set in the Vocabulary lesson on p. 100, walking down the street in Explore Language 1 on p. 102, and talking to Ray about the movie *The Warrior in the Desert* in Explore Language 2 on p. 106). Ask students *What competition do you think he might be judging?* Elicit suggestions and predictions about Unit 9. Point out that they will find out in the first lesson of the next unit.

Put It Together

To further review and recycle the language in Units 7 and 8, play the game, *Half a Crossword*, on pp. 112–113. See TB p. 209 for teaching notes.

Practice **Resource Bank:** Unit Test
Student's App: Vocabulary and Grammar Review

Get Ready to Read

Lesson Objectives

- to activate prior knowledge about movies
- to encourage students to observe and interpret through a Question Starts VTR
- to preview the reading skill of understanding cause and effect

Materials

Ball (WU); (optional) VTR printout from the Resource Bank (A, B, C)

Warm Up

Play *Pass the Ball* (see TB p. 26) and have students say the names of their favorite movies and why they like them.

Question Starts

A Think about the picture. Then brainstorm questions. Write a list.

Students are going to do a Question Starts VTR to explore the illustration of scenes in a movie studio.

- Ask students *What can you see in the picture?* Have students look at the picture for a minute and then elicit suggestions. If they don't know a word in English, ask them to describe what they see so you can provide the word.
- Draw students' attention to the question words. Ask *What questions would you like to ask about the picture?*
- Give students a few minutes to write questions in their notebooks, based on the prompts.
- Encourage students to raise their hands to suggest questions. Write all suggestions on the board, helping students correct their questions when needed.

B Look at your list from A. Which questions seem the most interesting? Discuss them with the class.

- Ask students to look at their list of questions individually and identify the ones they would most like to know the answers to.
- Tell students that they are going to practice negotiation skills by working as a group to decide which three questions they want to ask. Have students work in groups of three to review the questions and discuss possible answers. This will help them decide which questions they think are the most interesting. Have students write the questions in the books. Then discuss them in as a class and decide on the most interesting questions.
- Remind students to respect each other's thoughts and opinions, and encourage them to say if they hear a particularly interesting question from a classmate. Let your class lead the discussion as much as possible.

Here's an example of this part of the routine.

Teacher: Which questions seem the most interesting? What do you really want to know?
Student A: What's in that box?
Teacher: That's a good question. What do you think?
Student A: Maybe props or costumes.
Student B: It could be equipment for the Foley artist.
Teacher: Good. What other questions do you have?
Student C: Why is that background green and that background purple?
Student D: Good question!
Student E: I think green is good for the camera. It's easy to see the actors.

C What new ideas or questions do you have now? Talk about your ideas with your partner.

- Encourage students to use the picture to think about ideas and questions related to making movies globally. Encourage students to think beyond this picture, but tell them they can use their previous questions as a starting point. Refer students to the example questions and give them a couple of minutes to think of their own questions. Then have students share their questions in pairs and discuss any possible answers. Encourage them to be as creative as possible.

Transition

Ask students if they have ever seen a movie with a scene that is similar to the one in the picture. Ask *What was the movie about? What happened in it?*

D Think and discuss. Do you think it's dangerous to make a movie? Why or why not?

- Have students discuss the question in small groups. They might discuss genre, stunt actors, and digital effects, but don't prompt them too much at this stage. They will find out more about the topic in the next reading.

E Think and discuss. Look at the picture. What do you think caused this scene?

This activity previews the reading skill of understanding cause and effect.

- Project the picture onto the board or have students look at it in their books. Ask *What can you see?* and elicit suggestions.
- Ask students what event in the movie they think caused this scene. Have students continue the discussion in pairs.
- Invite pairs to share their ideas and have the class vote for the one they like best.

Now read **Action Stars**

Nonfiction: *Action Stars—* Informational Text

Lesson Objectives

- to read an informational text about stunt performers
- to make a personal connection to the reading

Materials
Audio Tracks 40 and 41; Video

Warm Up

Play *Mime It!* (see TB p. 26) with some of the action verbs from the reading: *jump, fall, dive, swim, do karate, ride a horse, crash a car, ride a motorcycle, do gymnastics, fight!*

TRACK 40 TB p. 234 Reading Approach

First Reading: Engage with the Text

- Have students look at the title and look quickly at the photos. Ask students *What do you think the reading is about?*
- Ask students to close their books. Play the video or audio, but pause it after each stunt and ask students to rate the stunt from 1 to 10 (with 10 being the most difficult).

TRACK 41 TB p. 234 Words in Context

- Play the audio and have students repeat the words.
- Play the video again and tell students to **use pictures/ actions/events in the video to help establish the meaning of the new words** (see TB p. 22). Have them discuss their ideas with a partner, using L1 if necessary.
- Then bring the class together and use these discussion points to confirm the meanings.

stunt (p. 122) Have students read the whole page. Ask *Was it a real accident?* (no) *Where do we see people doing stunts?* (in movies) Elicit examples from the reading/video.

scene (p. 122) Have students recall what they saw in the video. Ask *What is a scene part of?* (a movie) *Is a scene set in one place or a lot of places?* (one place)

professional (p. 124) Ask *Do you think the stunt people do this as a hobby?* (No—as a job. It takes many years of hard work to be a professional.)

martial arts (p. 124) Have students notice the rest of the sentence that comes after the word. Ask *What's the example of martial arts?* (karate) *What other martial arts do you know?* Elicit ideas.

champion (p. 126) Have students notice the words before *champion*, and the sentence after. Ask *Do you think a champion is good at what he does?* (yes, he has won awards) *What do you think a world champion is?* (someone who is the best in the world)

International English

Elicit that *movie star* and *train car* are American English and *film star* and *train carriage* are British English. Have students point to the train car in the picture (behind the engine).

Second Reading: Analyze the Text and Features

- Have students read the text individually without the audio. To focus them, ask them to think about which is the most dangerous stunt and which is the most exciting while they read. You can return to this in the Cool Down.
- Discuss the questions in the blue boxes.
  - **Critical Thinking** (p. 122): *Why do movies need stunt performers?* Elicit ideas. Ask *What do you think action movies would be like without stunt performers?*
  - **Fact** (p. 125): *For their safety, stunt performers often have to wear protective clothing.* Look at the picture on p. 123 and ask *How is the protective clothing keeping the stunt performer safe?* (It stops the fire from burning his/her skin.)
  - **Fact** (p. 124): *It takes at least a year of training to become good at each of these sports!* Have students count the skills a stunt person needs and say how long it would take to get good at all these things. Ask what can happen if the stunt person is not good at something he/ she needs to do.
  - **Critical Thinking** (p. 125): *Movie stars are often not allowed to do their own stunts. Why?* Ask students *Do you think movie stars are trained in gymnastics, driving, karate, and so on? What could happen if they are not trained?* Ask students for their ideas. Students might also mention that often the actors are also too important to the movie to be allowed to do stunts—if they are injured, they may not be able to keep filming.
  - **Personalization** (p. 127): *What movie stunts do you remember?* Give students some thinking time and a minute to discuss with a partner any stunts they remember from movies or TV shows.

Third Reading: Interact with the Text

- Have students work in pairs to look at each photo in the reading and decide on a suitable caption for it. To do this, they should not only look at what's going on in the photo, but also re-read that part of the reading and underline any key words that will help them to identify the main ideas.

Cool Down

Elicit all the stunts from the lesson and list them on the board. Take a vote to find out which one students think is the most dangerous stunt and which is the most exciting. Ask them which movie from the reading they would most like to see and have them discuss in pairs.

Practice **Student's App:** Nonfiction Video

Explore the Reading

Lesson Objectives

- to understand and analyze *Action Stars* through reading comprehension activities
- to learn about drama through CLIL (arts and humanities): understanding attributes needed to be a stunt performer
- to recognize and reproduce spelling of words ending in *–ing*

Materials

Video; Audio Tracks 40 and 42

TRACK 40 TB p. 234 Warm Up

Elicit all the different actions students can remember from the reading (e.g. *fall from a building, dive, swim, do karate, ride a horse, fight*) and write them on the board. Play the video again and have students say if all their ideas were mentioned and count how many others they didn't remember.

A Read and write *True* or *False*.

- Before students open their books, find out what they remember from the reading. Have students discuss the following questions in small groups. Ask *Who does all the dangerous things in movies?* (stunt doubles) *What kinds of things do they do?* (jumping from a helicopter, fighting, car crashes, etc.) *Why don't actors do stunts?* (It's too dangerous.) *How long does it take to learn to be a stunt performer?* (years)
- Refer students to the first sentence in A and elicit the answer. Ask students why it is false (p. 123—*A stunt performer takes the place of the main actor during the risky scenes.*)
- Have students complete the activity individually and compare their answers with a friend.
- Check the answers and ask if everyone agrees. Ask students to justify a false answer with something from the reading.

Answers

1 False 2 False 3 True 4 True 5 False 6 True

B Think and write. What did you already know about stunt performers? What did you learn?

- Project or draw the graphic organizer on the board. Choose a confident student and elicit one thing they already knew about stunt people (e.g. *It's dangerous!*) and one thing they learned (e.g. *Yakima Canutt was one of the first stunt performers*). Write these on the board and then have students continue to complete the infographic with their own ideas.

C Think and discuss. Imagine a movie director calls you. She needs a stunt performer in the studio immediately. Are you the right person for the job? Why or why not?

This activity connects the topic of the reading to students' own lives and draws on the CLIL drama objective of understanding the attributes needed to be a stunt performer.

- Tell students they need to think about the skills and attributes a stunt performer needs. Elicit a couple of ideas, then have students work in small groups to add to the list.
- Give students some thinking time to decide which attributes they have and whether they think they'd make a good stunt performer and then have them discuss their answers in pairs. Point out the prompts in the book. You could also write some additional prompts on the board, e.g. *I can … so I think …; I'm not good at … so I don't think …; I know how to … If the stunt was … I could … I think I'm the right person because …*

TRACK 42 TB p. 234 Spelling Pattern *–ing*

Listen and write. Then check your answers.

- With books closed, write *swimming* on the board. Have students repeat it. Underline *–ing* and tell students they'll hear and see some more words ending with *–ing*.
- Play the first part of the audio and have students repeat each word. Make sure students are not putting the stress on the *–ing* syllable. Then have them open their books. Play the first part of the audio again and have them complete as many of the words as they can.
- Play the second part of the audio for students to check their spelling and complete any words they missed. Have them read the words aloud.
- Have students look back at the reading to find more words with *–ing* and write them down. Have them write all the *–ing* words from the lesson in a word cloud.

Answers

1 lightning 2 melting 3 getting 4 spring
5 carrying

In the reading: missing; screaming; clothing; during; something; falling; building; hanging; fighting; training; diving; swimming; riding; driving; working; speeding; wearing; doing; turning; avoiding; exciting; amazing

Cool Down

Have students work in pairs to write a short poem using some of the -ing words. Give your own example first, e.g.

Last night, I watched an action movie.
In bed, I was dreaming
That my house was turning,
And I was falling,
I woke up screaming!
Tonight, I'll watch a comedy.

Practice **Resource Bank:** Spelling Printout
Student's App: Reading Practice; Spelling Pattern Practice

Get Ready to Read

Lesson Objectives

- to practice the reading skill of understanding cause and effect
- to activate prior knowledge about jobs in the movie industry

Materials

Large sheets of paper, one per group (C); small cards, some with causes written on, some blank (CD)

Warm Up

Test students' memories about *The New Dam* (which features in A) by playing *Stand up, Sit Down* (see TB p. 27). If a sentence is false, ask them to say why. Suggested sentences: *The people in the village didn't like fish.* (False, they ate fish from the river.) *Wabaunsee was the chief of the village.* (False, he asked the chief questions.) *The dam was at the town of Sugar Lake.* (False, it was at the town of Kingstown.) *The mayor didn't want to help the villagers.* (True.) *Wabaunsee found a solution to the problem.* (True.) *He built the new dam on his own.* (False, a lot of people worked together to build the dam.) *Everyone had enough water after the new dam was built.* (True.)

A Think and answer. Look at the reading *The New Dam* in Unit 7 again. Which dam caused each effect? Write *Old* or *New*.

This lesson practices the reading skill of understanding cause and effect.

- Ask students *What can you see in the images? Do they come from the beginning or the end of the reading? Which one shows the old dam? Which one shows the new dam?*
- Elicit why the first sentence belongs to the old dam. (The dam in Kingstown completely stopped the water, so it didn't go into the river or ponds.) Have students continue the activity individually and then compare with a friend.
- Check answers.
- Refer students to the skills box about cause and effect. Ask students *What was the cause of the drought?* (the old dam) *What was the effect?* (There was no water in the river or ponds.) *What was the effect of the drought on the village?* (no fish and no crops) Ask students how being able to identify cause and effect helps them to understand the story. They might mention it helps them to understand the main plot line better, because they can see why something happened. You could take this further by discussing how cause and effect often drives the plot line. (If the people of Kingstown hadn't build their dam, Wabaunsee's village wouldn't have had a problem, Wabaunsee probably wouldn't have met the engineer, and it would have been a very different story …)

Answers

a *Old* b New c Old d Old e New f New

B Read, think, and draw. Read the situation below. What are some possible effects of this cause?

- First ask students what they can see in the picture and ask them to say what they think is happening. Have them read the dialogue below and ask if it confirms or changes their ideas.
- Draw a quick example on the board of one stick figure giving another stick figure an award (a little stick figure on a plinth!). Ask students what your effect is. (Sam wins an award for her wonderful movie.)
- Have students draw an effect that follows the cause given, and then share their ideas with friends around them. Ask students *Did you have similar or different ideas?* Ask if any students would like to show and explain their picture to the class.

C Think and discuss. How many different people does it take to make a movie? How many jobs can you think of? What are they?

- Ask students first to say who they think the most important people are to make a movie— elicit *actors* and *director* and maybe *camera operator.* Write these on the board.
- Have students work in small groups to think of the different people in different jobs who are needed to make a movie. You could have them do a Round Robin to generate ideas (see TB p. 20), then nominate a scribe to write them on a large sheet of paper. Help with vocabulary, as needed.
- Have each group say say how many jobs they thought of. Ask the group who found the most to share their list. The others listen and write down any they didn't think of.
- Ask *What would happen if we didn't have all of these people. Could we still make a movie?* Have students discuss in pairs.

Cool Down

Prepare some cards with causes such as *forgetting to do homework, eating three pieces of cake,* and *staying up late.* Give small groups a set of cards with causes and the same number of blank cards. Have students take a card and write a possible effect on a different card. Students can then swap cards with another group and match the causes and effects.

Now read **Actors on Set!**

Fiction: *Actors on Set—Play*

Lesson Objectives

- to read a play about making a movie for the first time
- to make a personal connection to the reading

Materials
Audio Tracks 43 and 44

Warm Up

Ask *What would you like to make a movie about?* Have them brainstorm and write a list of their ideas on the board. Take a vote for the best idea.

TRACK 43 TB p. 234 **Reading Approach**

First Reading: Engage with the Text

- Play the audio while students follow along in their books. Ask *Would you like to work with Sam on making a movie?* Ask students if there are any jobs in the reading that they didn't mention at the end of the previous lesson.

TRACK 44 TB p. 235 **Words in Context**

- Play the audio and have students repeat the words.
- Have students race to find the words in the play.
- Remind students they can **use the sentence or paragraph before and the next words or sentence to guess the meaning of the new words** (see TB p. 22). Have them discuss their ideas with a partner.
- Then bring the class together and use these discussion points to confirm the meanings.

producer (p. 130) Have students read the sentence and the one before it. Ask *What do you think producers do? What does Sam do in the play?* (Producers are a kind of leader for making a movie. They choose a script, arrange financing, and hire all the other people needed to make the movie.)

hiring (p. 130) Have students find the word and read the sentence that follows. Elicit that *hiring* is a verb and here it means to give someone a job (in this case the job of director).

supervisor (p. 131) Ask students to find what the script supervisor does (in charge of the script). Ask *Does the supervisor write the script?* (No, Sam emails the script to him.)

operator (p. 131) Ask students to identify a word that means the same as camera operator. (cameraperson) Ask *Who is going to be the camera operator?* (Rachel) *What will she do?* (film the movie)

instructions (p. 131) Have students find the sentence *Listen to Mike's instructions.* Ask them to look in the lines before and find another phrase that tells us what Mike will do (tell the camera operator what to film). Elicit other examples of instructions, e.g. a teacher telling the class what to do, a recipe (telling you how to cook).

microphone (p. 132) Have students read the sentences with the word and the one after. Ask *What does a microphone do?* (records sound) *Who else might use a microphone?* (singer, journalist)

props (p. 133) Ask students to guess which of the students in the picture is the props master (the one with the plant pot). Ask *If a scene is set in a classroom, what props might you need?*

shoot (p. 133) Have students read the sentence and the one after. Elicit that *shoot* is a verb. Can they figure out what Sam is ready to do? (make the movie) Ask *What will they use to shoot?* (the camera)

International English

Elicit that *elementary* is American English and *primary* is British English. Ask *Are you elementary students?* (yes)

Second Reading: Analyze the Text and Features

- Have students read the play individually. Ask them to think about a question while they read to keep them focused, e.g. *Why don't they have actors at the end?* (All the students already have other jobs.)
- Discuss the questions in the blue boxes.
    - **Fact** (p. 132): *Some movies have thousands of crew members!* Ask students how many jobs Sam gives. (about twelve) Have students discuss in pairs why some movies need thousands of people. (Answers might include: filmed in different countries, many technical workers for special effects and animation, etc.)
    - **Personalization** (p. 133): *When you watch a movie, do you ever watch all the credits at the end?* Elicit that the *credits* is a list at the end of a movie of the people who worked on it. Have a show of hands to see who watches the credits. Ask any students who raised their hands why they do.
- Discuss the text focus: *Why does a play need* ***stage directions*** *like this?* Give students some time to think and discuss the question in pairs. Then ask for their suggestions. Say *Imagine you are playing Sam. Do you know what to do?*

Third Reading: Interact with the Text

- Have students work in groups of eight to read the play (or you can have students share a part or read two parts). Remind them to look at all the lines that have specific stage directions about what to do or how to say something and follow the instructions; for example, *(clicks on her tablet) I've emailed it to you. / (calls across the room) Nathaniel, you're the hairdresser.*

Cool Down

Ask students to decide in pairs how many people they think they really need to make a short movie. Have them decide what each person would do. Point out that one person can have more than one role in a short movie.

Explore the Reading

Lesson Objectives

- to understand and analyze *Actors on Set!* through reading comprehension activities
- to make a personal connection to the reading
- to explore the SEL competency of relationship skills by exhibiting cooperative learning and working toward group goals

Warm Up

Play *Mime It!* (see TB p. 26) with the jobs mentioned in the play *Actors on Set!* and have students identify and name each job. Have them try to remember without looking at their books first and refer them to the play only if they can't remember the name.

A Read and match the dialogue to the characters.

- Before students open their books, find out what they remember about the reading by having a team quiz. Ask *Where did Sam learn how to make a movie?* (from a webpage) *What does a director of photography do?* (tells the camera operator what to film) *Why is Jack good for the job of grip?* (He is strong and can move equipment around.) *What's missing at the end?* (actors)
- Refer students to the first sentence in A. Elicit that Jack said this. Ask students *Can you remember why?* (Sam said they needed someone to set up the lights and asked Jack how strong he was.)
- Have students look back at the play and complete the activity individually, then compare answers with a friend.
- To check answers, ask students to read aloud one sentence and matching character each and ask if everyone agrees. Encourage students to say each sentence in a tone appropriate to the character and emotions in the play.

Answers
1 f 2 d 3 c 4 b 5 e 6 a

B Think and write. What different things do these people on a movie set do?

- Refer students to the list of jobs. Elicit the tasks that a stunt performer has to do and write them on the board as an example. If necessary, refer students back to the reading *Action Stars* to remind them what a stunt performer does.
- Have students work in pairs to discuss what each of the jobs in B involves. Encourage them to do this without looking back at the reading.
- Have students complete the sentences in their books individually. Tell them they can look back at *Actors on Set!*, to check their answers or complete any jobs they missed.
- Check answers as a class.

Answers
Producer: supervises the production of the movie
Script supervisor: in charge of the script
Director of photography: tells the camera operator what to film with the camera
Boom operator: holds the microphone
Gaffer: sets up the lights
Grip: moves all the equipment around

C Think and write. How do you think James feels about Sam? What caused him to feel that way?

- Have students look back at the play and focus on James's part. Ask them if overall his part in the play is positive or negative (the language he uses is negative—*I'm not sure … / I really don't think … / You forgot …*). Ask if they think he is negative about making the movie. (yes) Then ask students how they can describe Sam—is she negative or positive? (very positive, but she needs to learn to listen!)
- Give students some time to think, then have them write down their own ideas about how James feels about Sam and why.
- Have students share their ideas in small groups. Do they all agree, or do some people have different ideas?

Suggested Answer
I think James is frustrated with Sam. Sam took charge of making the movie and didn't ask other people what they thought.

D Think and discuss. Imagine you are the producer in charge of the movie. What advice do you give to Sam and other members of the crew?

This activity draws on the SEL competency of exhibiting cooperative learning and working toward group goals.

- Ask students *Is this the first movie Sam has made?* (yes) *What's good advice for someone starting to do something new?* Elicit some possible advice to give; for example, *start small and simple and then be more ambitious / listen to people's advice and questions / ask others for their ideas / experiment and think about the results.*
- Have students work in pairs to decide on some more advice to give to Sam and the others to help them work well together to make a successful movie. Ask students for their ideas.

Cool Down

Play *Correct the Teacher* (see TB p. 25) with some of the key phrases from the play. Suggested sentences: Who made you leader?; I'm called the director, not the leader. (producer); Do you have a video camera?; Yes, on my phone.; Listen to Jack's instructions. (Mike's); We don't have any costumes. (lights); I'll get some cake. (flashlights) Find a hairbrush. We're ready to go. (shoot) Perhaps we could ask the cooking club. (drama)

Practice Student's App: Reading Practice

Think Together

Lesson Objectives

- to make connections between the readings
- to explore the key concept: Why do movies need a team?
- to reflect on the unit and provide personal thoughts and opinions

Warm Up

Have students look back at the VTR image on pp. 120–121 and ask *Do you now have any new ideas about the image? Do you have any more answers for the questions you wanted to ask about it? Do you have any new questions? Which movie jobs can you see?*

Have students compare their ideas in pairs and then ask for their suggestions.

A Look, think, and write. Look at the pictures from two different movie scenes. Which movie jobs are needed for each scene?

- Ask students how many of the jobs from the play *Actors on Set!* they can remember.
- Elicit one job needed each for each scene and then have students continue individually. Have them compare answers with a friend.
- Project the activity onto the board. Ask students for their answers and invite them to come and write them on the board.
- Introduce the key concept question at the top of the page: *Why do movies need a team?* Do a Think, Pair, Share routine (see TB p. 20), encouraging students to think about what they learned in both readings.

Suggested Answers

First image: stunt performer; director of photography; director; camera operator
Second image: director; script supervisor; director of photography; boom operator; gaffer; grip; camera operator

B Imagine you can have any job in a movie. What do you choose?

- Ask students if they can think of any other movie jobs not already mentioned (e.g. catering, assistant to actors, runner) and add them to the list on the board. Give students some thinking time. Call out the jobs and have students raise their hands for the one(s) they chose.

C Think and discuss. Why did you choose the job in B? Do a Three-Step Interview.

- Set up the class for a Three-Step Interview cooperative learning routine (see TB p. 20).
- Before students interview each other elicit the questions they will ask: *What job did you choose? Why?* Encourage them to also ask follow-up questions where appropriate, e.g. *What actors do you want to work with? What kind of movie do you want to work on? What food do you want to make?* and so on.
- Regroup the class so that all the students who asked questions first are together and all the students who answered first are together. Have students tell the others in their group what they learned about their partner's choice of job. Ask students *Were there any jobs that no one chose? Why?*

My Reading Journal

What job in a movie would you like to learn more about? How can you find out more?

This question encourages and motivates students to think about how they can continue to learn about the topic.

Ask students if they think they can already do the job they chose in the movie. Why or why not? Ask where they think they can learn more about these jobs. Have them write a sentence or two about their choice.

Example Answer

I'd like to learn more about what the gaffer does.
I could find out more by looking on the internet.

Color the stars to rate the unit. Then write a short review.

This activity encourages students to reflect on their own learning and form a personal response.

Have students color in the stars to rate how much they enjoyed this unit.

Elicit from students what information they can put in a review of the unit and write headings on the board: *the theme, the topics of the readings, what you liked and why, what you didn't like and why, was the unit good overall?*

Have students write their review, using the prompts on the board as a guide.

Have them compare their review with one or two friends. Ask if their reviews were similar or different. Invite volunteers to read their reviews to the class.

Example Answer

The theme of this unit is movies. The readings were about doing stunts and making a movie. I liked the second reading best because it was funny and I learned about different jobs in a movie. I didn't like the picture of the car crash in the first reading because it looks scary. I liked this unit because I love watching movies!

Cool Down

Play *Draw It!* (see TB p. 25) with the movie jobs from the unit.

Practice **Resource Bank:** Unit Test
Student's App: Key Concept Practice

UNIT 9

The World of Tomorrow

Unit Overview

Themes

Towns and cities

Future changes

Synopsis

In this unit students will learn about different features of cities and find out about how cities connect people and transportation of the future. They will plan and prepare a presentation about cities of the future and will write the ending of a futuristic story using target language from the unit.

Language Book

Vocabulary

clean the windows, do the laundry, empty the dishwasher, iron the clothes, mow the lawn, sweep the street, take out the trash, vacuum the carpet, wash the dishes

p. 176

Explore Language

Present Perfect: *Ever, Never,* and *Already*

p. 177

Global Citizenship

How do cities bring people together?

apartment building, bench, bridge, fountain, office building, path, railroad, rural, skyscraper, urban

p. 178

Explore Language

Present Perfect Simple and Simple Past

p. 179

Take the Stage

Presentation: making predictions, giving opinions

p. 180

Write About It

A Story

Punctuation: speech marks

p. 181

Think It Over

Review and Reflection

p. 182

Literacy Book

Think Together
How will family life change 100 years from now?
p. 189

Visible Thinking
See, Think, Wonder
p. 183

Nonfiction
Informational Text: *Fast Forward*

Words in Context: *pollute, self-driving, radar, crisscross, magnets, structures, double-decker*
p. 187

Fiction
Science Fiction: *Pinocchia*

Words in Context: *chores, in advance, client, let her down, cheerfully, heartbreaking, battery, charging*
p. 184

Reading Skill
Comparing and contrasting
p. 186

Spelling Pattern
Soft *g*
p. 188

Language and Literacy Connections

The connecting theme in Unit 9 is cities and the future.

	Language	Literacy
Vocabulary	**Set 1:** household chores **Set 2:** towns and cities	**Fiction:** do the laundry, sweep the floor, wash the dishes **Fiction:** urban
Grammar	**Present Perfect:** ***Ever, Never, Already*** Have you ever heard of it? I've never seen a mess like this before! I've already done the laundry. **Present Perfect and Simple Past** Have you ever eaten there? Yes, I have. When did you go there? I went there a few weeks ago.	**Fiction** This is one of the best robots we've ever made! I've come to collect my robot. They worked around the clock. **Nonfiction** Have you ever wondered about transportation in the future? In 2016, pilots flew a solar-powered plane around the world.
Skills	**Pronunciation:** silent *gh* 2	**Reading:** comparing and contrasting **Spelling Pattern:** soft *g*
International English	take out the trash / take out the rubbish; wash the dishes / do the washing up; I already did the laundry / I've already done the laundry; railroad/railway; apartment building / block of flats	wash the dishes / do the washing up

Vocabulary

Lesson Objectives

- to learn vocabulary for household chores: *clean the windows, do the laundry, empty the dishwasher, iron the clothes, mow the lawn, sweep the street, take out the trash, vacuum the carpet, wash the dishes*
- to sing a song about household chores

Materials
Audio Tracks 99 to 102; Video

Warm Up

Play *Simon Says* (see TB p. 27), but in this version students must do the actions you say in the style of a robot.

A TRACK 99 TB p. 223 **Listen and find. When's the movie star going to arrive?**

- Have students look at the pictures pp. 114–115 and ask *What can you see? What kind of place do you think this is? What are the people in the picture doing? What are the robots doing?* Ask students who they think the movie star in the question will be and elicit suggestions.
- Play the audio and have students point to the words and pictures as they listen. Ask *Were your predictions correct?*
- Ask the comprehension question *When is the movie star going to arrive?* Elicit the answer. Play the audio again to check.
- Remind students of the challenge at the end of Unit 8: *What competition do I judge?* Ask *Can you answer Willis Brice's question now?* Refer students to the picture if necessary. (He's going to judge a "best city" competition.)

Answer
in an hour

International English

Elicit which phrases are American English and which phrases are British English. Ask *Which do we use?* Have students mime while saying the phrases.

B TRACK 100 TB p. 223 **Listen, say, and number the pictures in A.**

- Play the audio. Have students point to the pictures and say the phrases.
- Play the audio again and have students write numbers next to the words in the order they hear them.
- Check answers and ask a few students to repeat each phrase to check pronunciation.

Answers
1 *do the laundry* 2 wash the dishes 3 take out the trash 4 mow the lawn 5 empty the dishwasher 6 sweep the street 7 clean the windows 8 vacuum the carpet 9 iron the clothes

C TRACK 101 TB p. 223 **Close your eyes. Listen, visualize, and say.**

- Prepare students for the visualization (see TB p. 21).
- Play the audio, allowing students to visualize the chores as they listen.
- Then have pairs of students take turns choosing a chore they visualized and miming it for their partner to guess.

D **Look and write.**

- Tell students they have to complete the missing part of each phrase. Refer them to the example *do the laundry*. Ask them how we know *the laundry* is the answer. (It's the only phrase from A that uses *do*.)
- Give students time to complete the activity. Encourage them to try to remember the collocations first before checking the picture dictionary on pp. 114–115.
- Check answers and write them on the board.

Answers
1 *the laundry* 2 wash 3 take out 4 mow 5 the dishwasher 6 sweep 7 windows 8 carpet 9 iron

E TRACK 102 TB p. 224 **Listen and complete. Then watch and sing.**

- Have students look at the title of the song, *Cleaning All Day Long*, and ask them *Do you think a song about cleaning will be a happy song or not?*
- Play the song once, allowing students to listen and enjoy it.
- Explain that some of the words are missing and they have to write them in. Ask *Can you guess what words they are?* Have students read the song and complete any words they know. Remind them that all of the words that they need are on pp. 114–115, so they can check their spelling.
- Play the song again and have students check their answers and complete any they missed. Then check answers as a class.
- Play the song video and have students watch and sing along. Play the song video again and have students mime doing the chores as they sing along.

Answers
1 *Sweep* 2 Vacuum 3 clean 4 Wash 5 lawn 6 iron 7 the trash

Cool Down

Play *What Was the Last Word?* with the song video (see TB p. 27) with the phrases from A.

Practice **Student's App:** Vocabulary Practice; Song Video

Explore Language

Lesson Objectives

- to learn and practice the present perfect with *ever*, *never*, and *already*
- to practice vocabulary for household chores

Materials
Audio Tracks 103 and 104

Warm Up

Tell students to imagine they have been given a personal robot. Brainstorm with students what functions they would like it to have. Write their ideas on the board.

A TRACK 103 TB p. 224 **Listen and read. Who or what is Bingo?**

- Have students look at the pictures on p. 116 and ask *What can you see? What activities can you see in the pictures?*
- Play the audio and have students follow the story.
- Ask the gist question *Who or what is Bingo?* Elicit the answer. Then ask *Is he like the personal robot you imagined?*

Answer
It's a robot.

International English

Elicit which phrase is American English and which phrase is British English. Ask *What is the difference between the two phrases?* (the verb is different) Tell students that the present perfect is used more often in British English than in American English.

B **Look at A. Complete.**

- Write or project the table onto the board.
- Have students discuss and complete the grammar table themselves in pairs using the dialogue.
- Check answers on the board. Discuss word order and verb forms, but let your class guide the discussion. If you feel that students need more guidance, the **ETB** provides a differentiation activity.
- Elicit the parts we need to make a present perfect sentence (subject, *have* + past participle). Ask *How is the question different?* (*have* comes before the subject) Ask *Do we use* ever *in questions or statements?* (questions)
- Have students look at the Grammar tip *Look*. Point to the *already* sentence in the table and ask *How can we change the word order so it still makes sense?* (I've done the laundry already.) Ask students if we can make the same change with *ever* and *never*. Have them try it out with the examples in the table and elicit that we can't.

Answers
ever; heard; never; seen; already; done

C **Think and discuss. Then choose.**

- Have students look at the sentences in C. Give students some thinking time and then have them discuss their answers with a partner.
- Read the sentences and the answer options and have students raise their hands for the options they chose. Check everyone agrees and confirm the answers.

Answers
1 up until now 2 completed activities

D TRACK 104 TB p. 224 **Listen and say.**

- Play the audio and have students listen and repeat. For ideas on how to vary the drill, see TB p. 23.

E **Read and choose.**

- Tell students they are going to choose the correct word to complete each sentence. Refer students to the example. Ask why *already* is used. (The word *twice* tells us how many times the movie has been seen and shows that it is a completed action.)
- Have students complete the sentences. Remind them to consider whether it is an experience that has been happening up until now or a completed action. Check the answers.

Answers
1 *already* 2 never 3 ever 4 already 5 already

F **Write questions. Then ask and answer. Who's more helpful?**

- Tell students they are going to complete the questions using the present perfect. Read the example question and have students stand up if their answer is *yes* and sit down if their answer is *no*.
- Elicit the past participle of the verbs in the other prompts. Have students write the questions in their notebooks and then ask and answer with their partner.
- Ask them to count how many *yes* answers they have and then tell their partner whether they are a helpful person or not, according to the key!

Answers
Questions: 1 *Have you ever ironed a shirt?* 2 Have you ever mowed the lawn? 3 Have you ever vacuumed the living room carpet? 4 Have you ever helped with the cooking? 5 Have you ever done the laundry? 6 Have you ever cleaned the windows?

Cool Down

Play *Disappearing Sentences* (see TB p. 25) with questions or sentences from this lesson.

Practice Resource Bank: Grammar Printout
Student's App: Grammar Practice

Global Citizenship

Lesson Objectives

- to learn vocabulary for talking about towns and cities: *apartment building, bench, bridge, fountain, office building, path, railroad, rural, skyscraper, urban*
- to explore how cities bring people together and provide community spaces
- to practice listening for gist and details

Materials
Audio Tracks 105 to 107; Audio Track I; a world map (D)

Opening Question

Ask students the opening question: *How do cities bring people together?* Give them time to think and then elicit opinions.

A TRACK 105 TB p. 224 **Listen to Madison talk to a friend about an interesting place in New York City. What was this place in the past?**

- Tell students they will hear two friends talking about a place to go to in New York City. Ask students *Do you know the names of any places in New York City? Have you ever been to New York? If so, where did you go?*
- Play the audio and have students point to the pictures and words as they listen.
- Ask the gist question *What was this place in the past?* and elicit the answer. Play the audio again to check.

Answer
It was a railroad.

International English

Elicit which phrases and words are American English and which are British English. Ask *Which do we use?*

B TRACK 106 TB p. 224 **Listen, say, and number the pictures in A.**

- Play the audio and have students point to the pictures and say the words.
- Play the audio again and have students write numbers next to the words in the order that they hear them.
- Check answers by having one student call out a number and nominating another student to respond.

Answers
1 *bench* 2 bridge 3 skyscraper 4 path
5 apartment building 6 office building 7 fountain
8 railroad 9 urban 10 rural

TRACK I TB p. 224 **Visualization**

The TTL has a visualization audio track for this vocabulary set. (See TB p. 21.)

C **Read and complete.**

- Refer students to the example answer. Ask why it is *office*. (It is the only word that goes with *buildings*).
- Have students complete the activity individually and then compare answers. Ask students to read a completed sentence each.

Answers
1 *office* 2 bridge 3 rural 4 urban 5 skyscrapers
6 bench

D TRACK 107 TB p. 224 **Now listen to Mariana and Liam. How do the places they talk about help their communities?**

- To generate interest, have students look at the two pictures and notice where each child is from. Ask students *Where are these countries? What do you know about them?* Use a map to find them.
- Have students look at the pictures and ask them *What can you see? Do you have something like this in your city?*
- Listening for gist: play the audio and have students listen for the answers to the gist question *How do the places they talk about help their communities?* Have students compare ideas with a friend and then elicit the answers.

Answers
Medellín, Colombia: People get along better and share experiences.
Montreal, Canada: People can relax and enjoy community events.

E **Listen again and complete.**

- Listening for details: have students look at the questions and ask them if they can complete any of the sentences.
- Play the audio and have students check their answers and complete any they missed. Check answers.

Answers
1 *2008* 2 ten 3 2,000 4 two 5 30 6 200

Discussion Questions

- Draw students' attention to the discussion questions: *What community spaces do you have? Why is your environment important?* Have students discuss the questions in small groups (see **ETB**).
- Return to the opening question to ask again: *How do cities bring people together?* Encourage students to think about all the community spaces mentioned in this lesson and ask them why people like to go there. Then ask what other events in cities bring people together (e.g. festivals, concerts, sports). Ask *Why do you think it's important to have places that bring people together?* and have students discuss ideas in pairs before sharing with the class.

Cool Down

Play *Draw It!* (see TB p. 25) with the vocabulary from this lesson.

Practice **Student's App:** Vocabulary Practice; Listening Practice

Explore Language

Lesson Objectives

- to learn how to use the present perfect and the simple past
- to practice vocabulary for towns and cities

Materials
Audio Tracks 108 and 109

Warm Up

Brainstorm students' favorite places in their city and make a list on the board. Take a vote to find the class favorite and ask *Why do you like to go there?*

A TRACK 108 TB p. 224 **Listen and read. Whose favorite place is the playground?**

- Ask students *What can you see in the picture? Who do you think the people are? What do you think they might be talking about?* Ask students if they recognize the girl with her grandpa. (It's Bea from Lesson 2 in this unit.)
- Play the audio and have students follow the dialogue. Ask if they saw or heard any of the places from their list in the Warm Up.
- Ask the gist question *Whose favorite place is the playground?* Elicit the answer.

Answer
Bea's

B Look at A. Complete.

- Write or project the table onto the board.
- Have students discuss and complete the grammar table in pairs using the dialogue.
- Check answers on the board. Discuss word order and verb forms, but let your class guide the discussion. If you feel that students need more guidance, the **ETB** provides a differentiation activity to help you support them as they explore the grammar table.
- Ask students to label each question and answer *present perfect* (in the top half of the table) or the *simple past* (in the bottom half of the table) and to underline the words that tell us what they are.
- Refer students to the Grammar tip *Watch Out* and highlight the difference between *been* and *gone*. Ask a student *Where did you go on vacation last year?* Write the student's answer on the board and have the rest of the class come up with a sentence about that student using *has been*; for example, (Student' name) *has been to France*. Then elicit why they used *has been* (because the student came back from vacation). Challenge students to make a sentence using *gone*; for example, *My mom's gone to work*. Ask *Is your mom at work now?* (yes)

Answers
have; did; went; ago

Practice **Resource Bank:** Grammar Printout
Student's App: Grammar Practice

C Think and discuss. Then choose.

- Give students time to read the questions, think about their answers, and discuss with a friend.
- Read the sentences and answer options and have students raise their hands to show the option they chose. Confirm the answers.
- Ask *Do we use time phrases with the present perfect?* (no)

Answers
1 general experiences 2 simple past

D TRACK 109 TB p. 224 **Listen and say.**

- Play the audio and have students listen and repeat. For ideas on how to vary the drill, see TB p. 23.

E Read and choose.

- Tell students they are going to choose simple past or present perfect phrases to complete sentences correctly. Refer students to the first sentence and ask if it is about a general experience or a specific event. (general experience) Ask *How do we know?* (There is no time phrase.)
- Have students complete the activity individually. Remind them to consider if it is a general experience or a specific event.
- Check answers as a class.

Answers
1 *Have you ever been* 2 took 3 Have you ever stood
4 saw

F Write questions for a survey. Use these ideas or your own. Ask and answer.

- Tell students they are going to write questions for a survey. Elicit a *Have you ever . . .?* question with see; for example, *Have you ever seen a tiger?* Write the question on the board. Have the class ask you the question, and then give your answer; for example, *Yes, I have. I saw one in London Zoo last year.* Have students think of a follow-up question with the adjective *scared*; for example, *Were you scared?* and give your answer. (e.g. *No, I wasn't. It was asleep!*)
- Elicit from students whether each question and answer used the present perfect or simple past. (Q1: present perfect; A1: present perfect and simple past; Q2: simple past; A2: simple past)
- Have students write *Have you ever . . .?* questions for their own survey. Tell them they can use the verbs in the box and the prompts given, or think of their own ideas.
- Have students ask and answer in pairs and ask follow-up questions where possible. Tell students the follow-up questions can be in the simple past. Remind them to listen to the questions and to answer using the correct verb form.

Cool Down

Play *Pass the Whisper!* (see TB p. 26) with questions from this lesson.

Take the Stage

Lesson Objectives

- to prepare and give a presentation about making predictions and giving opinions
- to recognize and reproduce words with silent *gh*

Materials
Video; Audio Track 110

Warm Up

Ask students *Which movies have you seen about the future? What are the homes and cities like in the movies? Do you think they are good places to live?* Have them discuss with a partner.

A TB p. 239 **Watch and listen. How does Otis think children will get to school in the future?**

- Tell students they are going to watch a video of a boy talking about cities in the future. Ask *Do you think Otis is excited about the future?* Play the video and elicit opinions.
- Introduce the comprehension question *How does Otis think children will get to school in the future?* Play the video again and have students raise their hands when they know the answer. Elicit the answer. Then ask some more comprehension questions; for example, *Does Otis think buildings will be taller or smaller in fifty years?* (taller)

Answer
They will fly.

B **Watch again. Check (✔) the sentences you hear.**

- Have students read the sentences.
- Play the video again and have students check the sentences they hear. Read the sentences and have students raise their hands for the ones they checked.
- Read the checked sentences again and ask students to say if they are introducing the topic (raise hands), making predictions (clap hands) or giving an opinion (fold arms). Tell students that number 6 is just a statement, so it doesn't fall into any of these categories. (Introducing the topic: 1, 2; Making predictions: 3, 4, 8, 10; Giving opinion: 9)

Answers
1; 2; 3; 4; 6; 8; 9; 10

Pronunciation Silent *gh* 2

TRACK 110 TB p. 224 **Listen and say.**

- Refer students to the words in the box and read them aloud. Ask them which letters are not pronounced (*gh*).
- Play the audio and have students repeat the words.
- Say *These words are used in the video. What other words do you know have a silent gh?* Have students say the words again and then work in pairs to try to remember any other words they know that also have a silent *gh* (e.g. *bought*). Write them on the board and drill them for pronunciation at the end.

Suggested Answers
brought, drought, flashlight, night, fight

C **Plan. Think about cities now and cities in 50 years. Then complete.**

- Tell students they are going to plan their own presentation about cities in the future.
- Draw or project the table onto the board. Do a Think, Pair, Share routine (see TB p. 20) to generate ideas for ways to complete the categories. Write students' ideas on the board.
- Have students work individually to complete the table in their books with their favorite ideas.

D **Prepare your presentation. Use your ideas from C and phrases from B.**

- Play the video again as a model and remind students to watch with their own presentation in mind.
- Have students use their ideas from C to write notes for their presentation. Remind them to adapt the phrases from B by keeping the part in blue and changing the rest of the phrase. Encourage students to include opinions to make their presentation more interesting.

E **Practice with a friend. Then share with your class.**

- Now have students practice their presentation with a friend. Encourage them to practice each part of the presentation separately so they can feel confident in one part before moving on to the next.
- Invite volunteers to come to the front of the classroom to give their presentation. Have the audience give a round of applause after each presentation.

Cool Down

Play *Correct the Teacher* (see TB p. 25) by reading the following section of Otis's presentation with some of the key words changed.

First, we already have very tall giraffes (buildings). *I think hippos* (buildings) *will get taller and taller. Also, we won't have snakes* (space) *on the ground to scare* (build) *anything, so perhaps some snakes* (buildings) *will be floating in the school* (sky).

Practice **Student's App:** Speaking Skills Practice; Speaking Video

Write About It

Lesson Objectives

- to learn how to use quotation marks
- to plan and write the ending for a story

Materials

(Optional) Challenge, Standard, and Support writing printouts from the Resource Bank, one per student (C and D)

Warm Up

Ask *What would you prefer to be able to do—fly like a bird, swim like a dolphin, run like a cheetah, or jump like a cat?* Have students discuss their ideas with a friend and then ask for some opinions from the class. Ask which of these they think will be possible in the future.

A Read the story. Underline the dialogue. When do we use quotation marks, commas, periods, and exclamation points?

- Tell students they are going to read part of a story set in the future. Have them scan the text quickly to find things that are similar to and different from their own morning routine. Elicit answers, and then ask *What helps Deema fly?* (her backpack) *Why did Stella start flying slowly?* (Her backpack was broken.)
- Check that students understand the word *dialogue* (a conversation or what people say to each other in a book, play, or movie). Have them underline all the dialogue in the story. Ask *Where do you find quotation marks?* (at the beginning and end of each new part of dialogue) Ask if the punctuation at the end of each part of dialogue (exclamation point, period, comma) is before or after the quotation marks. (before)
- Ask students to notice when a comma is used and when a period is used. Point out that a comma is used when the quotation marks are followed by phrases that tell us who was speaking, like *said Deema*. Tell students that we can also introduce the dialogue with the speaker, e.g. *Deema said, "Hurry up!"* In this case, we put a comma before the first quotation marks. Remind students that exclamation points are used when something exciting or dramatic is said.

Answers

"Goodbye, Mom!"; "Hurry up,"; "We're going to be late for school!"; "I can't fly any faster!"; "I think my backpack has broken."; "I'll go to school and get help,"; "Deema! Help!"

B Read the sentences and add the punctuation ("" ,.!).

- Tell students they are going to add punctuation to some sentences. Point out the quotation marks at the beginning and end of the line of dialogue in the example, and highlight that the end quotation marks come after the comma.
- Have students complete the punctuation in the rest of the sentences and compare with a friend.
- To check answers, project or write the sentences on the board and invite students to come and insert one piece of punctuation each. Ask if everyone agrees.

Answers

1 *"That's the office where Dad works," she said.* 2 She called, "Dad, look out your window!" 3 "See you later, Mom," she said. 4 "Oh no, I'm lost!" Stella shouted. 5 "I'm going to try and jump on the sky train," she shouted. 6 "Stella needs our help," Deema said.

C Plan. Imagine the ending of the story. Then answer the questions.

- Tell students they are going to imagine how the story in A ends. To get them thinking, do a visualization activity, pausing between sentences to give students time to imagine. Say *Imagine you are Deema. You see Stella flying off to the big city. You can hear Stella shouting. What is she saying? What do you say to Stella? What do you do? What happens next?* Have students share their ideas in pairs and invite some students to share their ideas with the class.
- Then have students work individually to answer the questions in C. Tell them they don't have to write exactly the same things as they visualized. They may have more ideas now! You can hand out the Challenge printouts at this point.

D Write the ending of the story.

- Write example answers for questions 1 and 2 on the board; for example, *What happened next? Stella stopped flying. What did Stella do and say? Stella waved her arms and said, "I'm airsick!"* Elicit from students a possible way to continue the story, using these answers; for example, *Stella suddenly stopped flying again. She waved her arms in the air like a bird. Her face was green. "I'm feeling airsick," she shouted…*
- Have students write a rough draft of their endings in their notebooks using their ideas in C. Encourage them to use a mix of punctuation.
- Have students self-correct or exchange their work with a friend and peer-correct. You can put a checklist of points for students to look out for on the board (e.g. spelling, capital letters, commas, periods, exclamation points, quotation marks).
- Have students correct any mistakes and write their final instructions neatly on paper. Alternatively, hand out the Support or Standard printouts from the Resource Bank. Allow them some time to illustrate their stories.

Cool Down

Read the beginning of the story from A and one of the endings by students and have them act out the story.

Practice **Student's App:** Writing Practice

Think It Over

Lesson Objectives

- to review what has been learned in the unit
- to reflect on the unit and their own progress
- to think about learning strategies and how to continue learning at home

Warm Up

Play *Shark* (see TB p. 26) with key vocabulary from the unit. Each time students guess correctly, ask them to make a sentence using that word.

Read the questions and draw or write your answers.

- Give students time to think about and discuss activities in the unit before they complete each question. Explain that they can choose to either write a few words or sentences or to draw a picture. Allowing students to make a personal response will help them retain knowledge and engage with the learning points.

What did I do?

- Give students a few minutes to look back through the unit at the different activities they did. Ask questions about the unit or write questions on the board for students to discuss in pairs or small groups; for example, *What did you talk about? What people did you meet? Where did you hear about libraries and underground tunnels?*
- Encourage students to identify something in the unit that they found challenging or something that was particularly memorable for them. Students can draw or write about their chosen activity.

What did I learn?

- Have students talk to a partner about what they remember from the unit—stories, words, phrases, people, different household chores.
- Ask questions about the unit to help students think about what they learned; for example, *What did you learn about the future? What did you learn about Colombia and Canada? What did you learn about writing dialogue? What else did you learn?*
- Encourage students to draw a picture or write sentences about their learning outcomes.
- Once students have written their statements or drawn their picture, have them talk to a friend about what they think they have learned. Tell them to consider what was different and what was the same.

How did I learn?

- Ask students how they learned the town and city words in the Global Citizenship lesson. Elicit ideas (e.g. by doing a visualization activity, by hearing the words in dialogue, by doing a writing activity, by using them in a discussion).
- Encourage students to think about how they learned throughout the unit; for example, how did they learn to use the present perfect?
- Encourage students to draw a picture or write about some of the activities that helped them learn. Then have them compare their answers in pairs and think about what was similar and what was different about how they learned. Ask *Do we all learn in the same way?*

How well did I do?

Ask students to color in the machine that best expresses how well they think they learned the unit content (i.e. the bigger the machine, the more they think they have learned). Ask *What do you understand? What do you need to practice more?* Encourage students to look back through the unit to see how much they remember what they did well and what they found difficult.

What can I do next?

- Brainstorm ideas with the class about what they can do to continue to learn (e.g. research technology in the future; write another story).
- Draw students' attention to the *What can I do next?* box. Encourage students to think about what they can do at home to improve their English. Have them suggest some verbs that they can use (e.g. play, practice, watch, sing) and write the verbs in their books. Students can look back at the previous units to get more ideas. Encourage students to suggest their own ideas for different activities they can do.
- Have students choose several activities that they would like to do and write them in their notebooks. They can then share their ideas with a partner.

Looking Forward

Draw students' attention to the character at the bottom of the page. Ask *Who's this?* and elicit what they remember about him. (Grandpa Elliot was with his granddaughter Bea talking about places in the town in Explore Language 2 on p. 120.) Ask students what they think he might be watching at the amusement park. Elicit suggestions and predictions about Unit 10. Point out that they will find out in the first lesson of the next unit.

Practice **Resource Bank:** Unit Test
Student's App: Vocabulary and Grammar Review

Get Ready to Read

Lesson Objectives

- to activate prior knowledge about technology
- to encourage students to observe and interpret through a See, Think, Wonder VTR
- to preview the reading skill of comparing and contrasting

Materials
(Optional) VTR printout from the Resource Bank (A, B, C)

Warm Up

Ask students to think about the future and call out topics for students to give their opinions. They should lower their hands if they think the topic will be worse in the future, fold their arms for the same, and raise their hands if they think it will be better. Suggested topics: *School / Cars / Movies / Food / Pollution / Vacations.*

See, Think, Wonder

A Look at the picture. What do you see?

Students are going to do a See, Think, Wonder VTR to explore the image of a city of the future.

- Give students a minute to look at the picture. Have them discuss in small groups or pairs. Then bring the groups together for a class discussion.

Here's an example of this part of the routine.
Teacher: What do you see?
Student A: I see a curved building.
Teacher: Tell us more about the building. What can you see?
Student A: It's glass.
Student B: It looks like a snake.

B What do you think?

- Ask students *What do you think about the picture?* Give them one minute to think silently about the picture and then share their ideas.
- Have students consider the meaning of the quotation and how it connects to the picture. Read it aloud and then have students discuss it in pairs. Ask the class for their ideas.

Here's an example of this part of the routine.
Teacher: What do you think the quotation means?
Student A: I think it means everything is a dream in science fiction because it's not real.
Student B: I think it means we should dream more, like people who write science fiction.
Student C: Why do you say that?
Student B: Because writers can make anything happen, like this putting this building here.

C What do you wonder?

- Say *I wonder why the buildings are curved.* Then ask students *What do you wonder? What questions do you have?* Give them one minute to think about the picture silently and think of questions they have.
- Have students discuss their ideas in groups or as a class.

Here's an example of this part of the routine.
Teacher: What do you wonder?
Student A: Is this a set for a science-fiction movie?
Teacher: What do you think?
Student A: Yes, because it looks like it's in the future.
Teacher: Good. What else do you wonder?
Student B: I wonder if there's an elevator to get to the top?

Transition

Ask students *Do you think that there are any robots working in this building? What do you think they do there?* Have them discuss ideas with a partner and then ask for ideas from the class.

D Think and discuss. How do we use robots today?

- Ask the class for one or two suggestions about how we use robots. Encourage them to think about robots in the home, robots in work or industry, and robots in space. Then have them continue thinking of ideas in pairs.

Suggested Answers
We use robots to make cars / put things together / carry things / clean homes.

E Think and discuss. Look at the pictures. Compare and contrast Pinocchio and Pinocchia.

This is a preview of the reading skill of comparing and contrasting.

- Have students compare and contrast the pictures in small groups. Have them present their ideas in a table or Venn diagram.

Suggested Answers
Compare: Both images are dolls / fictional characters, have big eyes, and look friendly.
Contrast: The image on the left is made of wood / is a boy / has strings; the one on the right is made of metal or plastic / is a girl / has buttons.

Now read **Pinocchia**

Fiction: *Pinocchia*—Science Fiction

Lesson Objectives

- to read a science fiction story about a robot
- to make a personal connection to the reading

Materials

Audio Tracks 45 and 46; Video; an image of Pinocchio to show students (WU)

Warm Up

Look at the first question in a blue box, on p. 138: *Do you know the story of Pinocchio?* Show students an image of Pinocchio and ask them if they know the story. Ask *Who or what is Pinocchio? Who made him? Why is he special? What happens when he lies?*

TRACK 45 TB p. 235 Reading Approach

First Reading: Engage with the Text

- Play the video on mute. Ask students to look at the faces and actions to figure out what is happening. Elicit ideas and then play it again with sound. How much of the story had students understood without the dialogue? Point out that images can help us understand new words.

TRACK 46 TB p. 235 Words in Context

- Play the audio and have students repeat the words.
- Play the video again and tell students to **use pictures/ actions/events in the video to help establish the meaning of the new words** (see TB p. 22). Have them discuss their ideas with a partner, using L1 if necessary.
- Bring the class together and use these discussion points to confirm the meanings.

chores (p. 138) Have students find the word and read the rest of the sentence. Ask *What are the examples of chores in the story?*

in advance (p. 139) Ask what helped them to understand the phrase (the second part of the sentence: giving the money before they started work). Ask *Why is this good for Beneto and Paola?* (They know they have the money for their work.)

client (p. 139) Ask *What does a client do?* (buys things from a business or shop)

let her down (p. 139) Ask if the context of what happens in the story helps them to understand the phrase. Can they think of a synonym? (disappoint).

cheerfully (p. 142) Ask how the video helped them to understand the word. (They could hear her voice when she said "Sorry, I'm late!" and see her smiling.)

heartbreaking (p. 142) Ask *How do you think Beneto and Paola feel? Why?* (They are losing someone they like very much.) Elicit how the video helped them to understand the word. (the expression on their faces)

battery (p. 143) Ask if they can guess the meaning from the context of the video. Elicit some other things that have a battery and what a battery does.

charging (p. 143) Have students identify a picture that illustrates Pinocchia's battery charging. Invite students to explain what is happening.

International English

Elicit that *wash the dishes* is American English and *do the washing up* is British English.

Second Reading: Analyze the Text and Features

- Now have students read the story silently on their own. Ask them to find examples of things that Pinocchia says or does that seem more like a real girl than a robot.
- Do a Think, Pair Share routine to discuss the questions in the blue boxes (see TB p. 20).
  - **Language Focus** (p. 139): *What does* around the clock *mean?* (all the time, day and night) Ask *Do you think Beneto and Paola worked very hard when they were making Pinocchia?* (yes)
  - **Personalization** (p. 140): *What job in the house would you like Pinocchia to do for you?* Ask students for their ideas and why.
  - **Making Connections** (p. 142): *Are Beneto and Paola happy to see Mrs. Atario this time?* Have students look at the pictures for this part of the story. Ask them *How do you think Beneto and Paola feel? Why?*
- Discuss the text focus: ***Contrasting*** *characters helps us understand them better. How has Pinocchia changed since the beginning of the story?* Ask students what differences they can see in Pinocchia's appearance and her behavior. What does this tell us about the way the character is feeling?
  - **Personalization** (p. 143): *How do you know Pinocchia has no energy? How do you feel when you have no energy?* Guide students to think about how they feel with no energy and how that helps them to recognize how Pinocchia is feeling.

Third Reading: Interact with the Text

- Have students read the story again and underline all the words that show how the characters are feeling, then discuss in pairs.

Cool Down

Ask students *Did you like this story? Why / Why not?* Have them discuss their feelings about the story in pairs.

Practice **Student's App:** Fiction Video

Explore the Reading

Lesson Objectives

- to understand and analyze *Pinocchia* through reading comprehension activities
- to revisit the SEL competency of developing relationship skills by providing help to those who need it

Materials
Video (A); Audio Track 45

Warm Up

Play the video of the story of *Pinocchia* and have students mime each household chore. Then elicit from students all the verbs for the mimes they did in order.

A Read and sequence the events from *Pinocchia*.

- Before students open their books, find out what they remember from the reading. Have them answer the following questions in small groups. *Why do Beneto and Paola make Pinocchia?* (Mrs. Atario wants a robot for her daughter.) *What does Mrs. Atario want Pinocchia to do?* (play games and do the chores) *Where was Mrs. Atario?* (on Mars) *How did Pinocchia feel in her new home?* (sad and tired) *Who was happy at the end of the story?* (Beneto, Paola, and Pinocchia)
- Refer students to the sentences in A, and elicit which one happens first. (*Mrs. Atario orders Pinocchia for Cleo's birthday.*)
- Have students complete the rest of the activity individually and compare their answers with a friend.
- Check the answers and ask if everyone agrees.

Answers
3; 5; 2; 1; 4

B Think and check (✔). Which sentence best describes the ending of the story?

- Ask students if they think sentence 1 is a good ending for the story. (No—Beneto and Paola aren't worried, because they know Pinocchia's battery is fine)
- Have students choose either sentence 2 or 3 to describe the ending and then compare answers with a friend.
- Read all the sentences and have students raise their hands for the one they chose. Ask why the others are not suitable.

Answer
3

C Think and write. Then discuss. How do you think the characters in each scene feel?

- Project the pictures onto the board or have students look at them in their books. Ask *What can you see happening in each picture? Are the pictures of scenes from the beginning, middle, or end of the story?* Elicit suggestions.
- Then ask them to look at the adjectives in the box. Read them one by one and have students act out the different emotions.
- Refer students to the first word, *proud*, and ask which picture they think it refers to (1). Ask *Why did Paola and Beneto feel proud?* Have students find something in the story to explain why they feel that way. (Pinocchia is one of the best robots they've ever made.)
- Have students continue the activity in pairs, matching the emotions to the pictures and explaining why the characters feel that way.

Answers
1 proud 2 excited 3 sad 4 disappointed 5 angry
6 surprised 7 happy

D Think and discuss. How does Pinocchia feel in this scene? Why? What do you do to make your best friend feel better if he or she feels sad?

This activity reviews the SEL competency of providing help to those who need it.

- Ask *How is Pinocchia feeling in this picture? Why does she feel like this?* Have students discuss their ideas in pairs and then elicit answers and write them on the board.
- Say *When my best friend is sad, I take some time to sit and listen to her. Then we take a walk and have ice cream! What do you do to make a friend feel better if he or she is sad?* Give students some thinking time before they discuss their answers in small groups.
- Ask if any students would like to share their ideas with the class.

Cool Down

Call out different situations from the reading and have students act out the appropriate emotion for each situation and character. For example, *Beneto and Paola have two weeks to make a robot!* (worried, determined) *Beneto and Paola finish testing Pinocchia.* (happy) *They don't find Mrs. Atario at home.* (disappointed, annoyed) *Beneto, Paola, and Pinocchia live together.* (happy)

Practice **Student's App:** Reading Practice

Get Ready to Read

Lesson Objectives

- to review and practice the reading skill of comparing and contrasting
- to activate prior knowledge about transportation
- to make a personal connection to the reading

Warm Up

Play *Who Said It?* (see TB p. 27) by reading phrases from *Pinocchia*. Ask one student for the answer and ask if the others agree. Suggested phrases: *I'd like a new robot for my daughter.* (Mrs. Atario) *This is one of the best robots we've ever made!* (Paola) *I like vacuuming the carpet.* (Pinocchia) *Look at this wonderful city.* (Beneto) *It smells delicious!* (Pinocchia) *I went on a trip to Mars.* (Mrs. Atario) *Come on, silly robot. Let's play!* (Cleo) *I've never been so disappointed.* (Mrs. Atario) *Please choose another robot.* (Beneto) *It feels great to be home.* (Pinocchia)

A Think and write. Compare and contrast Paola and Mrs. Atario.

Students are going to review and practice the reading skill of comparing and contrasting.

- Refer students to the Venn diagram in their books. Alternately, project or draw it onto the board.
- Elicit one piece of information that is true only for Paola, one that is true only for Mrs. Atario, and one that they have in common (for the middle area). Write them in the Venn diagram on the board and then have students continue the activity individually. Have them compare their answers with a friend and expand their lists if possible.
- Ask for students' ideas and complete the diagram on the board. Check if everyone agrees.
- Refer students to the skills box about comparing and contrasting. Point out that having contrasting characters is a good way to make a story interesting. You could also point out that comparing and contrasting helps us to organize information in our minds, which makes it easier to remember, and can give us new ideas about the characters and story. Comparing and contrasting is a skill we can use to help us make good decisions in all areas of our lives—not just reading! Can students think of any situations in their own life when it would be good to compare and contrast? (e.g. deciding which cell phone is the best to buy)

Suggested Answers
Both: 1 like robots; 2 are women; 3 live in the same city
Paola: 1 is kind; 2 can make robots; 3 loves Pinocchia; 4 is sad when Pinocchia leaves
Mrs. Atario: 1 doesn't think about other people; 2 is rich; 3 has a daughter; 4 gets angry at Pinocchia

B Think and discuss. Look at the pictures from *Fast Forward*. Compare and contrast the different methods of transportation.

- Refer students to the pictures of the two cars and ask for ideas to complete the two prompts on the page.
- Have students continue comparing and contrasting the cars in pairs and then ask if any pairs would like to share their ideas with the class. Did anyone have an idea that no one else spotted?

Suggested Answers
Both: 1 have four wheels; 2 are used for driving
First image: 1 has a plug/cord; 2 is small; 3 drives on the road/ground
Second image: 1 looks like a sports car; 2 maybe goes fast; 4 might fly

C Think and discuss. How do you travel from place to place?

- Have students think about all the different types of transportation they use in their lives—whether regularly or rarely. Elicit a couple of examples, e.g. *I go to school by car or bus. I catch a plane when I go on vacation.* Then have students continue to brainstorm in small groups. You could have them do a Round Robin routine to generate more ideas (see TB p. 20). Elicit some examples and write them on the board. Try to cover all the methods of transportation.

Cool Down

Give each student a slip of paper as an exit pass. Have them predict one thing they think they will learn about in the reading. They should give you the paper as they leave the classroom.

Now read **Fast Forward**

Nonfiction: *Fast Forward—* Informational Text

Lesson Objectives

- to read an informational text about transportation in the future
- to make a personal connection to the reading

Materials

Audio Tracks 47 and 48; magnets (WiC)

Warm Up

Play *Shark* (see TB p. 26) with methods of transportation in the previous lesson (C).

TRACK 47 TB p. 235 Reading Approach

First Reading: Engage with the Text

- Have students look at the pictures of the different methods of transportation and decide quickly which they think is going to be the fastest. Take a vote by a show of hands and write students' answer on the board.
- Have students read the text individually. Ask if their prediction about the fastest method of transportation was correct.

TRACK 48 TB p. 236 Words in Context

- Play the audio and have students repeat the words.
- Have students race to find the words in the reading.
- Remind students they can sometimes **use the separate parts of the words to help establish the meaning** (see TB p. 22). Have them discuss their ideas with a partner, using L1 if necessary.
- Then bring the class together and use these discussion points to confirm the meanings.

pollute (p. 146) Have students find the word and read the rest of the paragraph. Ask *What don't electric cars use?* (gas or diesel) Elicit that gas and diesel create *pollution* and that the verb is *pollute*.

self-driving (p. 146) Have students find the word and read the whole paragraph. Elicit that *we won't need drivers* helps us to understand the word. Ask *What does the word* self *at the beginning mean?* (on its own, not done by other people)

radar (p. 146) Ask them how they think radar can help avoid accidents. (It sees what's ahead in the road.)

crisscross (p. 147) Ask *What kind of word is "crisscross"?* (a verb) *What does "cross" mean?* (go from one side to the other) Ask if they think crisscross means more things or fewer things crossing. (more)

magnet (p. 147) Have students find the word and the sentence that describes what the magnets do (push away from each other so the train floats above the rails). Pass around some magnets so students can see for themselves what happens when two magnets are together.

structures (p. 147) Have students identify what the structures look like in this reading (big pipes) and point to them in the picture. Ask *Is a building a structure?* (yes)

double-decker (p. 148) Ask students what *double* means. (two of something) Ask what they think there are two of in these planes. (floors of seats)

cruise speed (p. 148) Elicit that the word *speed* tells us the phrase is about how fast something goes. Ask *Do you think the plane is going as fast as it can go?* (no—cruise speed is below that)

Second Reading: Analyze the Text and Features

- Play the audio and have students follow in their books. Ask them to lower or raise their hands to show if they would or wouldn't like to travel on each type of transportation.
- Ask some comprehension questions to check understanding, e.g. *How do you recharge an electric car?* (just plug it in)
- Use Group Time to discuss the questions in the blue boxes.
  - **Text Focus** (p. 146): *How does the author make the different ways of traveling in the future stand out?* Ask how the sections of the text are separated (they all have headings) and how we can find the names of the different methods of transportation quickly. (they are in bold)
  - **Making Connections** (p. 147): *Maglev stands for Magnetic Levitation.* Ask students to remember what a *magnet* is. Ask *What type of word is* magnetic? (an adjective) Ask *Does* levitation *mean to go up or down?* (up)
  - **Making Connections** (p. 148): *What other double-decker methods of transportation do you know?* Ask students if they have seen other types of transportation with two floors of seats (e.g. some buses and trains). Ask *Have you ever been on a double-decker bus, train, or plane?*
  - **Personalization** (p. 149): *What is the fastest method of transportation you have ever used?* Invite students to describe their experiences.

Third Reading: Interact with the Text

- Have students read the text again and write down three new things they learned. Then have them rank them from one to three, in order of interest.

Cool Down

Read aloud or display the predictions students made at the end of the previous lesson about what they would learn in the reading. Ask *Were any of the predictions correct?*

Explore the Reading

Lesson Objectives

- to understand and analyze *Fast Forward* through reading comprehension activities
- to review the reading skill of making inferences
- to practice the reading skill of comparing and contrasting
- to learn about engineering through CLIL (science): understanding the relative benefits of different methods of transportation
- to make a personal connection to the reading
- to recognize and reproduce with the soft *g* sound

Materials

Audio Tracks 47 and 49

Warm Up

TRACK 47 TB p. 235 Play *What's the Next Word?* (see TB p. 27) with the audio from the previous lesson's reading.

A Think and discuss. Read and check (✔). Which inferences can you make after reading *Fast Forward*?

- Before students open their books, find out what they remember about the reading by having a team quiz. Ask *Why don't electric cars pollute so much?* (They don't use gas or diesel.) *How will trains of the future be different?* (They won't touch the tracks; they will be faster.) *Where did a solar plane fly in 2016?* (around the world) *Where will people have holidays in the future?* (in space)
- Ask students if they remember what *infer* or *inference* means. (to look at what we can see in text or pictures and make guesses about something) Refer students to the first sentence in A. Ask if they can infer this from the reading and, if so, what part of the reading helps them infer it. (yes—p. 146, *Electric cars are quiet and they pollute less* and p. 148, *... zero gas! So, planes will probably use solar energy in the future.*) Point out that the reading doesn't specifically say *Transportation will be more environmentally friendly*, but we can make a guess that this is true from what it does say.
- Have students complete the activity and then compare answers with a friend. To check answers, ask students to read one sentence each and say yes or no. Ask if everyone agrees. For the ones that they check, ask students to find something in the text that justifies the inference.

Answers

1; 3; 4; 6

B Think and write. Find these vehicles in the reading. Label the pictures.

- Have students look at the first picture and say what type of transportation it is. (train) Ask students first to say which page they can find the information on (p. 147) and then to find the name of this type of train in the reading.
- Have students complete the activity individually. Check answer as a class.

Answers

1 Maglev train 2 Virgin Galactic plane/spaceship
3 Hyperloop 4 flying car

C Think and discuss. Compare and contrast the different methods of transportation in the reading. Which would you like to use in the future? Why?

In addition to focusing on the reading skill of comparing and contrasting, this activity draws on the CLIL engineering objective of understanding the relative benefits of different methods of transportation

- Ask students to choose any two methods of transportation and make a Venn diagram on the board. Elicit a couple of suggestions from students to compare and contrast the two methods.
- Have students work in pairs to choose two more types of transportation. Have students compare them in the same way, using a Venn diagram or a table, and decide which one they'd like to use.
- Have students share their conclusions with another pair.

TRACK 49 TB p. 236 Spelling Pattern soft *g*

Listen and write. Then check your answers.

- With books closed, write the word *danger* on the board and have students repeat it. Underline the *g* and have students repeat the sound after you in isolation. Then have them say the word again.
- Play the first part of the audio and have students repeat each word. Make sure that students are making the /dʒ/ sound and not just /ʒ/. Then have them open their books. Play the first part of the audio again and have them complete as many of the words as possible.
- Play the second part of the audio for students to check spelling and complete any missing words. Ask them what letters come after the *g* in these words (*e* or *i*). Have students read the words aloud.
- Have students look back at the reading to find more words with the same sound. Ask *Is the soft g always followed by* e *or* i? and elicit that in energy and technology is followed by a *y*. Have students read the words aloud. Invite students to read the words. Have them draw a giraffe or angelfish and write all the soft *g* words from the lesson inside.

Answers

1 danger 2 angelfish 3 giraffe 4 stage
5 emergency
In the reading: large; recharge; average; imagine; passengers; energy; engineers; Virgin; technology

Cool Down

Have students make a *Word Tree* (see TB p. 25) with the word *future* at the base.

Practice **Resource Bank:** Spelling Printout
Student's App: Reading Practice; Spelling Pattern Practice

Think Together

Lesson Objectives

- to make connections between the readings
- to explore the key concept: How will family life change 100 years from now?
- to reflect on the unit and provide personal thoughts and opinions

Warm Up

Have students look back at the VTR image on pp. 136–137 and ask *Do you now have any new ideas about the image? Do you have any answers for the questions you had about the image? Do you have any new questions?*

Have students compare their ideas in pairs and then ask for their suggestions.

A Think and discuss. Look at both readings. How will life for children change in the future?

- Ask students to look back at the readings and find the ways life will change in the future in general. Ask for their suggestions and make a list on the board.
- Give students time to think about how these factors (and others) will change life for children in the future and discuss with a partner.

B What do families do together today? What will be different 100 years from now? Do an Inside–Outside Circle and make a list.

- Have students work in pairs to brainstorm all the different family activities they do. Write some prompts on the board to guide the discussion, e.g. travel, vacations, food, houses, and entertainment.
- Then ask students to consider how these activities might change in the future. Use this activity to explore the key concept question *How will family life change 100 years from now?* Elicit a suggestion for each prompt on the board. Then give students some time to think of their own ideas.
- Set the class up to do the Inside–Outside Circle routine to share ideas about both questions (see TB p. 20).
- Give students time to discuss the topic, making sure you have students rotate and trade places to give them opportunities to ask and answer the questions with a variety of partners.
- At the end, invite each student to say a new idea they heard during the Inside–Outside Routine. Ask students *What do you think will be most different in the future?*

Suggested Answers

Today: do chores together; go on vacations to other countries/places; travel by plane/car/bus/train, eat out; go to the movies

100 Years From Now: have robots do the chores; go on vacations to space; travel by Maglev trains or spaceship; have virtual reality glasses to watch movies

Practice **Resource Bank:** Unit Test
Student's App: Key Concept Practice

C Think, draw, and write. Choose a year in the future. Draw yourself and your surroundings. Complete the sentences.

- Give an example of your own idea first: draw on the board a picture of yourself in class, projecting pictures from a smartphone-sized gadget onto the wall of the classroom. In the drawing, have two or three students using tablets to take notes. Elicit what is happening from students and what you can write about it; for example, *This is me in 2030. I'm in the classroom, and I'm using my phone as a projector!*
- Have students think about their own future—remind them they can talk about anything they want! Give time to think, draw, and write. Then have them show and talk about their drawings in small groups.

My Reading Journal

You are Beneto and Paola's client. Send them a message with an order for a new robot. What would you like your robot to do?

This question gets students to respond creatively to what they have learned.

Ask students what they would like their personal robot to do, and take suggestions from the class.

Encourage students to think imaginatively and really consider their own personal needs and wants.

Have students share their ideas with a friend.

Suggested Answer

I'd like a robot that makes cakes. You put a recipe in its mouth, open a door in its stomach and a cake comes out!

How does this unit make you feel about the future?

This question gets students to link their learning to the wider world and to reflect on their own personal response to what they have learned.

Start off by taking a class vote—ask them to raise their hands if they think the future is going to be a better world to live in, fold their arms if it is going to be the same, and lower their arms if they think it is going to be worse.

Have students write their answers and then discuss with a friend.

Cool Down

Ask students to leave their books open on their desk at the page with their drawing about the future. Have them circulate around the classroom, looking at other students' work. Ask them to look out for the most interesting, imaginative, or funniest idea. Invite a few students to say which drawings they liked and why.

UNIT 10

Use Your Senses

Unit Overview

Themes

Senses

The importance of different senses

Synopsis

In this unit students will learn about the different senses, look at whether some senses are more important than others, and learn about animals with special senses. They will plan and prepare a conversation to describe an object using different senses, and write a description using target language from the unit.

Language Book

Vocabulary

feel, hear, listen, look, see, smell, taste, touch, watch

p. 192

Explore Language

Tag Questions: *Do, Did, Be*

p. 193

Global Citizenship

Is one sense more important than another?

bitter, disgusting, flavor, hard, rough, salty, savory, smooth, soft, sour, sweet

p. 194

Explore Language

Tag Questions: *Should, Will, Have*

p. 195

Talk About It

Conversation: discussing an object

p. 196

Write About It

A Description

Sentence Building: interesting adjectives

p. 197

Think It Over

Review and Reflection

p. 198

Literacy Book

Think Together
Why are our senses so important?
p. 205

Visible Thinking
Step Inside
p. 199

Fiction
Poem: *The Wrinklecrinkle Man*
Words in Context: *barrel, saluting, justice, grudge, charge, plea, decree, case dismissed*
p. 203

Nonfiction
Informational Text: *Sense Superstore*
Words in Context: *sensitive, nerve endings, pores, prey, camouflage, ability, organ, taste buds*
p. 200

Reading Skill
Identifying literal and figurative language
p. 202

Spelling Pattern
Long e
p. 204

Language and Literacy Connections

The connecting theme in Unit 10 is exploring the world through different senses.

	Language	Literacy
Vocabulary	**Set 1:** sense verbs **Set 2:** sense adjectives	**Nonfiction:** hear, look(s), see, smell, taste, touch **Fiction:** hear, smell, taste
Grammar	**Tag Questions:** ***Do, Did, Be*** That slide looks fun, doesn't it? I touched a spider once at the zoo, didn't I? It isn't full of spiders, is it? **Tag Questions:** ***Should, Will, Have*** We should buy Mom something, shouldn't we? Mom won't like these chocolates, will she? We still haven't bought anything for Mom, have we?	**Nonfiction** You'll want to add all these super-senses to your basket, won't you? **Fiction** He isn't doing wrong, is he? This man should pay, shouldn't he?
Skills	**Pronunciation:** *gh* as /f/	**Reading:** identifying literal and figurative language **Spelling Pattern:** long e
International English	savory/savoury	honor/honour

Vocabulary

Lesson Objectives

- to learn vocabulary about the senses: *feel, hear, listen, look, see, smell, taste, touch, watch*
- to sing a song about senses

Materials
Audio Tracks 111 to 114; Video

Warm Up

Ask students *Have you ever been to an amusement park?* If they have, ask them what they saw and did there and, if not, ask what they think they could see or do there. Have them discuss in small groups.

A TRACK 111 TB p. 225 **Listen and find. Who's afraid of the dark?**

- Have students look at the pictures on pp. 126–127 and say what they can see happening and where the people are. Ask *Do you think it looks fun? Which activities do you want to do?*
- Play the audio and have students point to the words and pictures as they listen.
- Ask students the comprehension question *Who's afraid of the dark?* and elicit the answer. Play the audio again to check.
- Remind students of the challenge at the end of Unit 9: *What am I watching at the amusement park?* Ask *Can you answer Elliot's question now?* Draw students' attention to the picture Grandpa Elliot is holding of his younger self. Point out to students that they are looking for this young Elliot at the amusement park. (He's watching the juggler.)

Answer
David

B TRACK 112 TB p. 225 **Listen, say, and number the pictures in A.**

- Play the audio and have students point to the pictures and say the words.
- Play the audio again and have students write numbers next to the words in the order they hear them.
- Check answers and ask a few students to repeat each word to check pronunciation.

Answers
1 *look* 2 watch 3 see 4 hear 5 listen 6 taste 7 smell 8 touch 9 feel

C TRACK 113 TB p. 225 **Close your eyes. Listen, visualize, and say.**

- Prepare students for the visualization (see TB p. 21).
- Play the audio, allowing students to visualize the actions as they listen.
- Then have students draw what they imagined during their visualization for their partner, who then guesses the sense verb.

D **Look and write.**

- Tell students they are going to match the body parts to the sense verbs. Refer students to the example *my nose* and *smell*. Ask why they are together. (We smell with our noses.)
- Have students complete the activity by writing the other sense verbs next to the correct parts of the body. Encourage students to try to do the activity without looking before checking the words in A.
- Project or write the answers on the board for everyone to check.

Answers
1 *smell* 2 hear; listen 3 touch; feel 4 look; watch; see 5 taste

E TRACK 114 TB p. 225 **Listen and complete. Then watch and sing.**

- Have students look at the title of the song, *Use Your Senses!*, and ask *What do you think the song will be about?*
- Play the song once, allowing students to listen and enjoy it.
- Explain that some parts of the words are missing and they have to complete them. Ask *Can you guess what words they are?* Have students read the song and complete any words they know.
- Play the song again and have students check their answers and complete any they missed. Check answers as a class.
- Play the song video and have students watch and sing along. Then play the song video again and have students do actions for the senses as they hear them in the song.

Answers
1 *look* 2 hear 3 see 4 feel 5 taste 6 smell 7 touch 8 watch 9 listen

Cool Down

Play *Draw It!* (see TB p. 25) with short sentences using the sense verbs; for example, *He's listening to music. They're watching TV. She's feeling cold. He can smell a burger. They're touching the tablet.*

Practice **Student's App:** Vocabulary Practice; Song Video

Explore Language

Lesson Objectives

- to learn how to use tag questions with *do*, *did*, and *be*
- to practice sense verbs

Materials

Audio Tracks 115 and 116

Warm Up

Ask students *What are you afraid of?* Elicit as many answers as possible (e.g. spiders, bees, snakes) and write them on the board. Have everyone stand up, then read out sentences such as *I'm afraid of bees.* Have all students who agree sit down. Then say *I'm afraid of spiders* and more students sit down. Continue, substituting different animals until there are only a couple of students remaining and ask them *What are you afraid of?*

A TRACK 115 TB p. 225 **Listen and read. Who thinks the slide is scary?**

- Have students look at the picture on p. 128 and ask *What can you see? Do you want to go there?* Ask if they'd like to try any of the activities.
- Play the audio and have students follow the dialogue.
- Ask the comprehension question *Who thinks the slide is scary?* Elicit the answer, then ask *Do you think the slide looks scary or fun?*

Answer

Amit

B Look at A. Complete.

- Write or project the table onto the board.
- Have students discuss and complete the grammar table on the board using the dialogue.
- Check answers on the board. Discuss verb forms and patterns, but let your class guide the discussion. If you feel that students need more guidance, the **ETB** provides a differentiation activity.
- If students haven't noticed a pattern already, have students underline positive verbs in one color and negative verbs in a different color. Ask *What pattern do you see?* Students should see that if the main clause is positive, the tag question is negative, and if the main clause is negative, the tag question is positive. Ask *Are the verbs in the main clause and the tag question always the same?* (no; elicit or point out that if the verb is *be* in the main clause, then the tag question is also *be*, but if the main clause uses a different verb, the tag question takes *do*)
- Have students look at the Grammar tip *Watch Out*. Write on the board *I'm good at English, am not I? I'm good at English, aren't I?* and elicit which one is correct. Drill the second question and then ask students if they can make another sentence with *aren't I*; for example, *I'm tall, aren't I?*

Practice **Resource Bank:** Grammar Printout
Student's App: Grammar Practice

Answers

doesn't; is; are; didn't; don't

C Think and discuss. Then choose.

- Have students look at the sentence in C. Give them some thinking time. Then have them discuss their answer with a partner.
- Read the sentence and the different answer options and have students raise their hands for the option they chose. Confirm the answer.
- Explain that we often use tag questions to check information that we think we know is true.

Answer

1 can

D TRACK 116 TB p. 225 **Listen and say.**

- Play the audio and have students listen and repeat. For ideas on how to vary the drill, see TB p. 23.

E Think about a friend in your class. Read and complete.

- Tell students they are going to complete questions to ask a friend. Look at the first question together. If you know the name of any of the students' fathers, insert that name into the question. If not, invent any name and choose a student at random! If you get a *yes* answer, say *Yes! One correct!* Elicit the tag question for number 2. Remind students to check whether the main clause is positive or negative and to make the tag question the opposite.
- Divide the class into pairs and then have students complete the questions individually. Remind them to think about what they know about their partner to do this. If they aren't sure about something, they can guess.

Answers

1 student's own answers; *isn't it* 2 student's own answers; aren't they 3 student's own answers; don't you 4 student's own answers; is it 5 student's own answers; don't you 6 student's own answers; are you

F Look at E. Ask and answer.

- In the same pairs, have students ask and answer the tag questions. Ask students to count the number of positive answers they get.
- At the end, ask them how many correct tag questions they made.

Cool Down

Divide the class into pairs or groups of three. Read the main clause from tag-question sentences in this lesson and have students write the tag question as quickly as possible and hold it up for you to check. The first pair or group to hold up a correct question wins a point.

Global Citizenship

Lesson Objectives

- to learn sense adjectives: *bitter, disgusting, flavor, hard, rough, salty, savory, smooth, soft, sour, sweet*
- to explore whether one sense is more important than another
- to practice listening for gist and details

Materials

Audio Tracks 117 to 119; Audio Track J

Opening Question

Ask students to name the five senses and write them on the board. Ask the opening question: *Is one sense more important than another?* Give students time to think and then elicit opinions.

A TRACK 117 TB p. 225 **Listen to Jordi talk about his visit to a chocolate factory. Why couldn't he taste the chocolate?**

- Have students look at p. 130 and ask *What can you see?* Tell students they will hear a boy talking about his experience in a chocolate factory. Ask students *Have you ever visited a factory?*
- Play the audio and have students point to the words and pictures as they listen.
- Ask them the comprehension question *Why couldn't he taste the chocolate?* and elicit the answer. Play the audio again to check.

Answer

because he has a cold

International English

Ask students to notice the spelling difference between the two words. Model the pronunciation, highlighting that it is exactly the same for both words. Ask students if they can find another word on this page that has no *u* in American English but does have one in British English (*flavor*).

B TRACK 118 TB p. 225 **Listen, say, and number the pictures in A.**

- Play the audio and have students point to the pictures and say the words.
- Play the audio again and have students write numbers next to the words in the order that they hear them. Check answers.

Answers

1 *rough* 2 smooth 3 hard 4 soft 5 bitter 6 sour 7 sweet 8 salty 9 disgusting 10 flavor 11 savory

TRACK J TB p. 225 **Visualization**

The TTL has a visualization audio track for this vocabulary set. (See TB p. 21.)

C Read and complete.

- Tell students that they will complete the sentences with the new vocabulary. Refer students to the first example answer. Point out that *salty* is the only answer that makes sense with the first part of the question.
- Do number 2 as a class and then have students complete the rest of the activity individually. Check answer as a class.

Answers

1 *salty* 2 sour 3 savory 4 bitter 5 flavor 6 disgusting

D TRACK 119 TB p. 225 **Now listen to Oliver and Courtney. Who uses their sense of taste?**

- To generate interest, have students look at the two pictures and notice where each child is from. Ask students *What do you remember about these countries?*
- Have students look at the pictures and ask them *What can you see?*
- Listening for gist: play the audio and have students listen for the answer to the gist question *Who uses their sense of taste?* Have students compare ideas with a friend and then elicit the answer.

Answer

Oliver

E Listen again and answer the questions.

- Listening for details: have students look at the questions and ask them to answer as many as they can.
- Play the audio and have students check their answers and complete any they missed. Check answers.

Answers

1 *London* 2 bread 3 like he was there during the fire 4 her seat moved 5 the wind and cold snow 6 hot chocolate

Discussion Questions

- Draw students' attention to the discussion questions: *What's your favorite sense? How do experiences change using different senses?* Have students discuss the questions in small groups (see **ETB**).
- Return to the opening question to ask again: *Is one sense more important than another?* Divide the class into pairs and have them decide together. Encourage them to think of as many reasons as possible to back up their answer. Ask students to share their ideas.

Cool Down

Divide the class into groups of four. Do a Numbered Heads Together routine (see TB p. 20) Say *Name four things that are … sweet/hard/rough/salty/disgusting/soft.*

Practice **Student's App:** Vocabulary Practice; Listening Practice

Explore Language

Lesson Objectives

- to learn how to use tag questions with *should*, *will*, and *have*
- to practice using the sense adjectives

Materials
Audio Tracks 120 and 121

Warm Up

Ask students what present they last bought or gave to their mom or dad. Ask *What kinds of presents do your parents like?* Have them compare in pairs and then ask for some ideas to share with the class.

A TRACK 120 TB p. 226 **Listen and read. What do the children buy?**

- Ask students *What can you see in the picture? What do you think the boy and girl are doing?* Ask students if they recognize the boy in the pictures. (It's Amit from pp. 126–128.)
- Play the audio and have students follow the story. Ask if they saw or heard any of the items they mentioned in the discussion during the Warm Up.
- Ask the comprehension question *What did the children buy?* Elicit answers, then ask *Do you think they did the right thing?*

Answers
a scarf and chocolates

B Look at A. Complete.

- Write or project the table onto the board.
- Have students discuss and complete the grammar table in pairs using the story.
- Check answers on the board. Discuss verb forms and patterns, but let your class guide the discussion. If you feel that students need more guidance, the **ETB** provides a differentiation activity to help you support students as they explore the grammar table.
- Refer students to the Grammar tip *Remember.* If they haven't already discussed this, have students recall from the previous lesson that when the verb from the main sentence is positive, the verb in the tag question is negative and the other way around. Have students find examples of this in the table; for example, *should*, which is positive, and *shouldn't we?* which is a negative tag question.

Answers
shouldn't; will; have

C Think and discuss. Then choose.

- Give students time to read the sentence, think about their answer, and discuss with a friend.
- Read the sentence and answer options and have students raise their hands to show the option they chose. Confirm the answer.
- Ask students if the two verbs are the same in each of the sentences in the table and elicit that they are. Point out that *should*, *will*, and *have* (and other modal verbs) are like *be* from Explore Language 1 in this respect.
- Look at the sentences in the table again and ask *Do you think the children are asking for information here?* Point out that sometimes we use tag questions to ask for agreement when we already know the answer.

Answer
1 first

D TRACK 121 TB p. 226 **Listen and say.**

- Play the audio and have students listen and repeat. For ideas on how to vary the drill, see TB p. 23.

E Read and choose.

- Tell students they are going to choose the correct verbs to complete the tag questions. Refer students to the example and ask why it is *shouldn't* (positive verb, negative tag question).
- Have students complete the activity individually. Remind them to notice each time if the verb is positive or negative in the sentence and use the opposite in the tag question.
- Check answers with the class.

Answers
1 *shouldn't* 2 will 3 have 4 will 5 should 6 hasn't

F Think about your class. Read and complete. Then ask and answer.

- Tell students they are going to make some sentences about their classmates, and then check if they were right using tag questions.
- Look at the example together. Then personalize it and ask someone in the class—for example, *(Luis), you can speak three languages, can't you?*—and have the student answer honestly. If necessary, do another example with the class.
- Have students complete the sentences about people in their class.
- Students could write the tag questions for these sentences in their notebooks. Then have them circulate, ask their questions, and also answer any questions directed to them from other students. Tell them to make a note of how many *yes* answers they get. Find out who had the most *yes* answers and knows their classmates the best.

Cool Down

Play *Running Sentences* (see TB p. 26) using tag questions from this lesson.

Practice **Resource Bank:** Grammar Printout
Student's App: Grammar Practice

Talk About It

Lesson Objectives

- to prepare and practice a conversation describing an object
- to recognize and reproduce words with *gh* as /f/

Materials
Video; Audio Track 122; variety of items of different materials in a bag, e.g. a scarf, an eraser, a key, a phone, a stone, an action figure (WU)

Warm Up

Invite students to come to the front of the classroom and reach into a bag with various objects inside. Have them close their eyes, hold up an object, and try to guess what it is. If they guess correctly, ask them how they knew. Remove that object from the bag and continue with other volunteers.

A TB p. 239 **Watch and listen. What sound can Natalia hear?**

- Tell students they are going to watch a video of three friends playing a guessing game. Ask *Which object do you think is most difficult to guess?* Play the video, then elicit ideas.
- Introduce the comprehension question *What sound can Natalia hear?* Elicit the answer, then play the video again to check and have students raise their hands when they hear the answer.

Answer
the ocean

B Watch again. Check (✔) the sentences or questions you hear.

- Have students read the sentences and questions.
- Play the video and have students complete the activity. Read the sentences/questions and have students raise their hands for the ones they checked.
- Have students identify which sentences contain adjectives and which contain nouns. Point out that we can say it *feels/tastes/smells* + adjective, but that it *smells/sounds/feels like* + noun.

Answers
1; 2; 3; 5; 7; 8; 9

Pronunciation *gh* as /f/

TRACK 122 TB p. 226 **Listen and say.**

- Write *rough* on the board. Say the word, underline the *gh*, and ask students what the pronunciation of these letters is (/f/ in this word). Have students repeat the word.
- Play the audio and have students repeat the words. Ask students if *gh* is always pronounced /f/ (no). Ask them if they can remember words where it isn't pronounced at all. (*although*, *through*, or *thought*, *bright*)
- Say *These words are used in the video. What other words do you know have the same sound?* Have students say the words again and then work in pairs to try to remember any other words they know that also have *gh* pronounced as /f/ (e.g. *cough*, *tough*). Write the words on the board and drill them for pronunciation at the end.

C Plan. Choose an object. Think of adjectives to describe it. Complete.

- Tell students they are going to plan their own conversation in which they describe an object.
- Draw or project the graphic organizer onto the board. Show students one of the objects you had in your bag in the Warm Up and elicit information about it to complete the diagram; for example, object: *scarf*; taste: *none*; feel: *soft, warm*; smell: *new wool*; sound: *quiet*; look: *long, bright colors, red, green, blue.*
- Have students choose an object they have with them and complete the graphic organizer.

D Prepare notes for your conversation. Use your ideas from C and phrases from B.

- Play the video again as a model and remind students to watch with their own conversation in mind.
- Have students work in pairs to prepare notes for their conversation using the two objects from their plans. Remind them to adapt the questions and sentences from B to fit their objects (i.e. keep the part in blue and change the rest of the phrase as necessary). Point out they can also use other verbs, e.g. *What does it smell like? What can you see?* Encourage them to talk about as many different senses as is appropriate for the objects.

E Practice with a friend.

- Have students practice their conversation as many times as they need to. Encourage them to gradually look at their notes less often to make the conversation more fluid. If you feel students are ready, have students have a conversation with a new partner. Provide praise and help as necessary.

Cool Down

Play a variation of *I Spy* (see TB p. 26). Have students use the language from B to give the clues, e.g. *I spy with my little eye something that feels / sounds like / tastes … .*

Practice Student's App: Speaking Skills Practice; Speaking Video

Write About It

Lesson Objectives

- to plan and write a description
- to learn how to use adjectives to make a piece of writing interesting

Materials

(Optional) Challenge, Standard, and Support writing printouts from the Resource Bank, one per student (C and D)

Warm Up

Ask students to think about their favorite place to go on vacation or on the weekend and explain to a friend why they like to go there. Ask if anyone would like to share their ideas with the class.

A Read the description. Circle the adjectives.

- Have students scan the text and ask *Do you know a place like this? Where?* Ask some comprehension questions about the description; e.g. *Where is the beach?* (on an island) *How do you get there?* (by ferry)
- Read the first paragraph aloud and have students raise their hands every time you say an adjective. Have students circle these adjectives in their book. Then have them continue the activity individually.
- Have students compare with a friend before you check answers as a class.

Answers

My favorite place is a small, quiet beach on an island with smooth, soft, white sand. The name of the island is Carrim Island. To get there, you have to take a ferry from our town.

The beach on Carrim Island has a lot of tiny, pink shells near the sea—they make a crunchy sound when you walk across them. I love it at the beach when the sun is warm and the water is cool.

The best time to visit Carrim Island is in the spring. Then, along the paths leading to the beach, you can see beautiful flowers all around. When you touch their feathery leaves, they smell sweet, like coconut. There are always birds here, flying around, singing to each other in the sky. You can even collect and cook some seaweed. Make sure it smells fresh—it will taste delicious but very salty!

B Look at A. Write the adjectives from the description that tell us about these things.

- Tell students they are going to organize the adjectives from A into categories. Look at the example together and elicit the other adjectives that refer to how something feels (check understanding of *feathery*—feels like a bird's feathers).
- Have students complete the rest of the activity individually.
- Have students compare answers in pairs, then check answers as a class.

Practice **Student's App:** Writing Practice

Answers

1 *smooth*; soft; feathery; warm, cool 2 small; white; tiny; pink; beautiful 3 sweet; fresh 4 quiet; crunchy 5 delicious; salty

C Plan. Think about a favorite place. Then use adjectives to describe it.

- Tell students they are going to plan a description about a favorite place—they can use the place they mentioned in the Warm Up if they wish.
- Do a visualization activity. Ask students to imagine they are at their favorite place. Say *What can you see? What can you smell? What can you hear? Stretch out your hand. What can you feel? Open your mouth. What can you taste?* Pause after each question to give students time to imagine.
- Have students share what they visualized in pairs.
- Then have students use their ideas from the visualization and discussion to complete the bubbles with adjectives: refer them to the categories in B. Encourage them to write two or more adjectives for each bubble. You can hand out the Challenge printouts at this point.
- While they are planning, draw or project the bubbles onto the board and write your own adjectives to describe a favorite place.

D Write a description of your favorite place.

- Draw students' attention to your plan on the board and elicit a first paragraph. Tell them what the place is and then decide as a class how to put the information together into a description. Write the paragraph on the board.
- Have students write a rough draft of their own description in their notebooks. Remind them that they can use the text in A as a model, and the adjectives in B, and encourage them to write about all five senses.
- Have students self-correct or exchange their work with a friend to peer-correct. You can put a checklist of points for students to look out for on the board (e.g. spelling, capital letters, punctuation, use of adjectives).
- Have students correct any mistakes and write their final instructions neatly on paper. Alternatively, hand out the Support and Standard printouts from the Resource Bank. Give students time to illustrate their descriptions.

Cool Down

Put students into small groups and have them share their favorite place descriptions with each other. Tell students to write down one thing they liked about each description they read.

Think It Over

Lesson Objectives

- to review what has been learned in the unit
- to reflect on the unit and students' own progress
- to think about learning strategies and how to continue learning at home

Warm Up

Play *Physical Spelling* (see TB p. 26) with key vocabulary from pp. 126–127 and p. 130. Each time students guess a word correctly, have them say a sentence with that word.

Read the questions and draw or write your answers.

- Give students time to think about and discuss activities in the unit before they complete each question. Explain that they can choose to either write a few words or sentences or to draw a picture. Allowing students to make a personal response will help them retain knowledge and engage with the learning points.

What did I do?

- Give students a few minutes to look back through the unit at the different activities they did. Ask questions about the unit or write questions on the board for students to discuss in pairs or small groups; for example, *What did you sing about? What did you find out about Amit? Where did you hear about an exhibition and a movie?*
- Encourage students to identify something in the unit that they found challenging or something that was particularly memorable for them, but tell them not to choose their favorite activity yet. Students can draw or write about their chosen activity.

What did I learn?

- Have students talk to a partner about what they remember from the unit—stories, words, phrases, people, words for describing things using the senses.
- Ask questions about the unit to help students think about what they learned; for example, *Did you learn any new words that you didn't know before? What did you learn about the senses? What did you learn about writing a description? What else did you learn?*
- Have students draw a picture or write sentences about their learning outcomes. Then have them talk to a friend about what they think they can do.
- Ask students what they think they have learned during the course of the year. Highlight the progress they have made and encourage them to be proud of their progress in English.

What was my favorite part?

- Have students look back through the unit and decide what they enjoyed the most. Tell them it can be an activity they found fun, a text they enjoyed reading, a favorite character, or a favorite action. They should try to choose just one and draw a picture or write about it.
- Remind them that when we like something, it is often easier to learn.

How well did I learn?

- Tell students to color the ice cream that best expresses how well they have learned the unit content. Ask *What do you understand? What do you need to practice more?* Encourage students to look back through the unit to see how much they remember, what they did well, and what they found difficult.

What can I do next?

- Brainstorm ideas with the class about what they can do to continue to learn (e.g. practice describing objects or places, watch the videos again).
- Encourage students to think about what they can do at home to improve their English. Have them suggest some verbs that they can use (e.g. play, practice, watch, sing) and write the verbs in their books. Students can look back at the previous units to get more ideas. Encourage students to suggest their own ideas for different activities they can do.
- Have students choose several activities that they would like to do and write them in their notebooks. They can then share their ideas with a partner.

Reflection

Draw students' attention to the characters at the bottom of the page. Ask *Can you remember their names? What do you remember about them?* Have students discuss what they remember about the characters in pairs. Then have students look at all the different units in the book and say which unit was their favorite.

Put It Together

To further review and recycle the language in Units 9 and 10, play the game, *Keep Talking!*, on pp. 138–139. See TB p. 210 for teaching notes.

Play 2

To further review and recycle the language in Units 6–10, have students practice and perform the play, *The Mystery of the Missing Ring*, on pp. 142–143. See TB p. 212 for teaching notes.

Practice **Resource Bank:** Unit Test; End-of-year Test
Student's App: Vocabulary and Grammar Review

Literacy

Get Ready to Read

Lesson Objectives

- to activate prior knowledge about the senses
- to encourage students to observe and interpret through a Step Inside VTR

Materials

(Optional) VTR printout from the Resource Bank (A, B, C)

Warm Up

Write the following questions on the board and have students discuss them in pairs:

What's the best music you've heard this week? What's the nicest food you've tasted this week? What's the most comfortable place you've been in this week? What's the most beautiful thing you've seen this week? What's your favorite smell?

Step Inside

A Look at the picture. Choose a person or thing. What can they smell? What can they taste? What can they see?

Students are going to do a Step Inside VTR to explore the picture of the people eating.

- Ask *What can you see in the picture?* Elicit suggestions. (people eating, bowls of soup, bread, ice cream, fruit, tables, a band, instruments, a cell phone, a book)
- Choose one person or object in the picture and ask students questions about him/her/it, eliciting answers; for example, *The bowl of soup—what do you think it can smell?* (the fire, the people at the table) *What can it see?* (the lamp) *What do you think it can taste?* (soup, tomatoes, vegetables, the ladle)
- Then have students work in pairs and discuss another person or thing the picture, asking the same questions. Remind them it doesn't have to be a person!

Here's an example of this part of the routine.
Student A: This spoon can see the woman's mouth!
Student B: It can smell and taste ice cream!
Student A: Strawberry ice cream!

B What do you think they believe?

- Ask students to imagine what the people and things in the picture are thinking.
- Say *I think the boy reading believes no-one can see him. What does your person or thing believe?*
- Give students time to think about the person or thing they have chosen, then have students discuss their ideas in pairs or small groups, and then as a class.

Here's an example of this part of the routine.
Teacher: What does your thing or person believe?
Student A: It thinks the ice cream is very cold!
Teacher: OK, What else does it believe?
Student B: The woman's mouth is scary!
Teacher: Why do you think that?
Student B: She has lots of teeth!

C What do you think they care about?

- Ask students to imagine what is important to the people or things in the picture. Give an example. Then have students think and discuss in pairs. Elicit ideas and encourage students to give reasons.

Here's an example of this part of the routine.
Teacher: What does your person or thing care about?
Student A: I think the boy under the table cares about his book.
Teacher: What makes you say that?
Student A: He's hiding under the table so that he can read, so I think it must be a really good story!
Teacher: Good. (Student B) What does your person or thing care about?
Student B: This spoon cares about making people happy. It gives them ice cream to eat!

Transition

Ask students if everything they hear, see, feel, taste, and smell around them is nice and pleasant. Are there any things they would like to stop hearing, for example? Give students some thinking time and then take some suggestions from the class.

D Think and discuss. What are our five senses? How do our senses help us?

- Elicit the five senses from the class. Ask students *How do our senses help us? How can they help us find good things and avoid dangerous things?* Have them discuss their ideas with a friend. Ask for suggestions from the class and make two lists on the board to show how our senses can help us find good things and avoid bad things.

E Think, and make a list. Then discuss. How many words describing the senses can you think of?

- Have students work in pairs to brainstorm a list of adjectives relating to the senses. Invite pairs to share ideas and write them on the board. Who found the most words?
- Ask students which of the words on the board are specific to one sense, e.g. *tasty, delicious, disgusting, sour, sweet* all relate to *taste*. Some may describe more than one sense. Have students make a sense poster to categorize the words—draw pictures for each of the senses and write the words inside, e.g. *tasty* inside a picture of a mouth. Display the posters on the wall.

Now read **Sense Superstore**

Nonfiction: *Sense Superstore—* Informational Text

Lesson Objectives

- to read an informational text about super senses
- to make a personal connection to the reading

Materials

Audio Tracks 50 and 51; Video

Warm Up

Divide the class into small groups and do an animal quiz. Possible questions: *What's the fastest land animal?* (cheetah) *What's the largest animal in the world?* (blue whale) *What's the tallest animal?* (giraffe) *What's the longest snake?* (python/anaconda) *What's the largest cat?* (tiger)

TRACK 50 TB p. 236 Reading Approach

First Reading: Engage with the Text

- Before reading, have students look at p. 154 and answer the question in a pink box together: *What senses do animals have that are different from human senses?* Ask students if they know of animals that have a better or different sense from humans. (dogs have a better sense of smell; birds have much better sight)
- Play the video (or audio) and have students point to the part of the body related to each sense talked about. After each section, ask students *Would you like to have that super sense?*
- Then look at the Words in Context.

TRACK 51 TB p. 236 Words in Context

- Play the audio and have students repeat the words.
- Have students race to find the words in the reading.
- Remind students to **use the words around the new words and the type of word to guess their meaning** (see TB p. 22). Have them discuss their ideas with a partner, using L1 if necessary.
- Then bring the class together and use these discussion points to confirm the meanings.

sensitive (p. 154) Ask *What kind of word is this?* (an adjective) *Do you think it means the senses are very good or very bad?* (good)

nerve endings (p. 154) Elicit that nerve endings help the mole to touch with its nose. Have students point to where they think the nerve endings are in the picture (the word *endings* provides a clue). Ask students to suggest a place where we have nerve endings (e.g. our fingertips).

pores (p. 154) Ask *What words in this sentence tell you what pores are?* (small holes) *Where are a shark's pores?* (on its head) Have students point out the pores in the picture.

prey (p. 154) Ask *What do sharks want to find when they're swimming in the sea?* (food) *Which words in this sentence tell you what "prey" is?* (wants to eat) *What food do sharks eat?* (other animals/fish)

camouflage (p. 155) Have students find the word and read the sentence before it. Ask *Why are wolves hard to spot?* (They are difficult to see against the background.) *Do you know other animals that have this appearance that makes them hard to spot?* (snakes, leopards, chameleons, octopuses)

ability (p. 155) Ask *Do you think the beetle can find fire?* (yes) Elicit that we could replace *has the ability* with *can.*

organ (p. 157) *Where is the Jacobson organ?* (in the snake's mouth) *What does it do?* (helps the snake to smell) *Do we use the same organ to smell?* (no) Elicit that an organ is a special body part.

taste buds (p. 157) Elicit the meaning of *taste* and encourage students to guess what taste buds are in this context. Ask *Where are our taste buds?* (on our tongue)

Second Reading: Analyze the Text and Features

- Play the audio and have students follow in their books.
- Ask some comprehension questions to check understanding: *What does ultraviolet light help a reindeer see?* (wolves) *What do elephants use infrasonic sound for?* (to stay in touch or communicate with family)
- Discuss the questions in the pink boxes using Think, Pair, Share (see TB p. 20).
  - **Fact** (p. 156): Scientists believe that elephants can hear storms as far as 240 km. away! Ask *Why are elephants are so much better at hearing the storms than us?* (The storms make low noises, which we can't hear and which travel a long way.)
  - **Making Connections** (p. 157): Some people have highly developed senses. What jobs could they do? Give students some thinking time to imagine what jobs people with highly developed senses could do. (Possible answers: Someone with a highly developed sense of smell could make perfume, sight could be an artist, taste could be a chef, touch could be a surgeon, and hearing could be a musician.)

Third Reading: Interact with the Text

- Have students work in pairs to create their own fictional super animal, including three of the super senses from the reading. Have them draw and label a picture of their animal and then share it with another pair.

Cool Down

Elicit all the animals with super senses and make a list on the board. Take a vote for which animal students would like to be and then ask individuals why they voted for their animal.

Practice **Student's App:** Nonfiction Video

Explore the Reading

Lesson Objectives

- to understand and analyze *Sense Superstore* through reading comprehension activities
- to learn about biology through CLIL (science): understanding different animal senses

Materials
Video; Audio Track 50

TRACK 50 TB p. 236 **Warm Up**
Read descriptions of different animals with super senses and ask students to mime being that animal when they know what it is; for example, *I have a special organ in the roof of my mouth, and I use it to smell things.* (snake) *I make noises humans can't hear, and I listen to the echoes to find my way around.* (bat) *I can taste all over my body—ten times better than humans!* (catfish) *I can talk to my mom long distance without a phone!* (elephant) *The wolves think I can't see them, but I can.* (reindeer) *I lay my eggs in burnt wood, so I'm great at finding fires.* (fire-chaser beetle) *My nose is incredibly sensitive!* (star-nosed mole) Play the video or audio again for students to check their answers.

A Read and complete the table.

- Before students open their books, find out what they remember from the reading. Have students answer the following questions in pairs. Ask *What different super senses does the reading talk about?* (super touch/sight/hearing/smell/taste) *Which animals make sounds we can't hear?* (elephants and bats) *Why does a shark use electroreception?* (to get food / find prey) *Where do catfish live?* (at the bottom of rivers and lakes)
- Draw or project the table in A onto the board. Complete the first row of the table with the class as an example. Have them remember or find the super sense *electroreception* in the text to fill in the Animal and Use cells.
- Have students complete the activity individually and compare their answers with a friend.
- Check answers as a class. Ask if everyone agrees.

Answers
Sense: *Electroreception*; Infrared; Echolocation; Infrasonic *Ultraviolet*; Taste buds
Animal: Shark; Fire-chaser beetle; Bat; *Elephant*; Reindeer; *Catfish*
Use: Find animals to eat; *Find a fire and lay eggs; Hunt and find their way in the dark;* Communicate; See predators against the snow; Find food particles in the water

B Think and write. Look at the ways the animals use their senses. Now think about your own senses. Which sense would you like to improve? Why?

- Give your own example first: *I'd like to improve my sense of taste, because I love food! Imagine being like a catfish—I could pick up an apple and taste it with my hands!*
- Have students choose one of the senses and say why they would like to improve it. Allow some time for students to think and write their sentences. Then have students share ideas with a friend.
- Ask if any students would like to share their ideas with the class.

C Think and discuss. You have $80 to spend. Which of the animal senses do you buy? What will you use it for?

- Call out the names of the super senses and have students scan the text and call out the price as soon as they find it. Ask *Can I buy echolocation, Jacobson's organ, and extra taste buds with $80?* (yes—total $70) *Can I buy nerve endings, ultraviolet, and infrared?* (no—total $95)
- Have students work in pairs to decide which combination of super senses they want to buy for their $80 and then compare their ideas with another pair. Remind them to say what they will use the senses for.
- Ask if any students made the same choices and if anyone would like to share their ideas with the class.

D Think and discuss. Answer the questions in your own words. Use facts from *Sense Superstore*.

This activity explore the CLIL science objective of understanding animals' senses.

- Have students look at question 1. Elicit what they remember about the star-nosed mole from memory. Have them re-read the text if necessary. Then without looking at the text, have them answer the question. Guide them to explain in their own words. Write a version of the answer on the board as an example. Have students do questions 2 and 3 in pairs in their notebooks.
- Check answers as a class and have students notice the different ways their classmates have phrased their answers.

Suggested Answers
1 It has very sensitive tentacles on its nose, with more than 100,000 nerve endings.
2 It senses chemicals in the air. The Jacobson's organ tells the snake what those chemicals mean.
3 It has 100,000 taste buds all over its body.

Cool Down

Play *Disappearing Words* (see TB p. 25) with some of the key words from the reading.

Practice **Student's App:** Reading Practice

Get Ready to Read

Lesson Objectives

- to practice the reading skill of identifying literal and figurative language
- to activate prior knowledge about smells, sounds, and emotions
- to make a personal connection to the reading

Materials

(Optional) a book of simple poems (WU); large sheet of paper (CD)

Warm Up

Ask students if they know any poems by heart. Invite students to recite poems they know in their own language. Alternately, read some poems to the class, including the Cinquain poems from Unit 1. Ask *Which poems do you like? Why do you like them?*

A Read and match. What do you think these sentences mean?

Students are going to practice the reading skill of identifying literal and figurative language

- Point out these sentences all use comparisons to create vivid images (language you might find in a poem). Refer students to the first sentence and check the meaning of *couch*. Ask *If someone sits on the couch all day, what kind of person do you think they are—energetic or lazy?* Have them decide on which meaning matches the sentence and explain why. (Someone who sits on the couch all day is lazy.)
- Have students continue the activity in pairs and then check answers. Ask students to explain why these sentences mean the same thing each time.
- Refer students to the skills box about figurative and literal language. Tell students that things can be described in a literal (or straightforward) way or things can be described in a figurative (or metaphorical) way, for example, by comparing something to something else.
- Read some sentences from both columns in A and ask students to say if they use figurative or literal language. Give students a minute to think about why a writer might use figurative language like this (to paint a picture of the character or setting for the reader, to create interest and encourage the reader to want to read on).

Answers

1 c 2 a 3 e 4 d 5 b

B Read and write. Read these lines from *The Wrinklecrinkle Man*. What do you think they mean? Try to write them in literal language.

- Refer students to the first sentence. Ask *Do you think he is old or young? Why?* Work together to write a literal sentence; for example, *Lived an old man.*
- Have students continue the activity in pairs and then invite them to share their literal suggestions and explain why they think each sentence means that. Ask if anyone has anything different.

Suggested Answers

1 Lived an old man … 2 He's made me very angry.
3 The old man stood proudly. 4 I am very excited.

C Think and discuss. What are some of your favorite smells and sounds? How do they make you feel?

- Tell students what your favorite smells and sounds are and how they make you feel, e.g. *I love the smell of flowers after rain. They make me feel like hopeful.* Elicit possible sentences for a favorite sound. Write these on the board to provide students with an example.
- Give students some time to think about their own favorite smells and sounds, then have students discuss their ideas with a friend. Ask students if they would like to share their ideas with the class.

Cool Down

Show students the title of poem *The Wrinklecrinkle Man* and the picture on p. 160. Ask students what they think the poem will be about. Elicit ideas and write them on a large sheet of paper to look at in the next lesson.

Now read **The Wrinklecrinkle Man**

Fiction: *The Wrinklecrinkle Man*—Poem

Lesson Objectives

- to read a poem related to the senses
- to make a personal connection to the reading

Materials
Audio Tracks 52 and 53

Warm Up

Tell students they are going to read a poem and elicit anything they remember about the genre (e.g. rhyme, rhythm, stanzas, etc).

TRACK 52 TB p. 236 Reading Approach

First Reading: Engage with the Text

- Have students sit in a circle around you. Give students a minute to look at the pictures, then ask them what they think the setting of the poem is. Read the poem aloud, using facial expressions, gestures, and sound effects to convey meaning. Alternately, play the audio and have students follow in their books.
- Then look at the Words in Context.

TRACK 53 TB p. 237 Words in Context

- Play the audio and have students repeat the words.
- Have students race to find the words in the poem.
- Review different strategies for figuring out the meaning of new words (see TB p. 22). Have students discuss the Words in Context ideas with a partner.
- Then bring the class together and use these discussion points to confirm the meanings.

barrel (p. 160) Have students identify the word in the picture. Ask what they think the barrel is made from? (wood)

saluting (p. 161) Have students find the word and read the following sentence. Ask what word helps us to figure out what he was doing. Elicit that *saluting* is a verb so it must be an action we do when we say *hello* (waving). Point out that the picture confirms this.

justice (p. 163) Ask them *What's Dominic's problem, and what does he want? What is justice for him?* (He wants the wrinklecrinkle man to pay for smelling his bread, so justice for him is to get some money.)

grudge (p. 163) Ask *What does it mean that Dominic wouldn't drop his grudge?* (He refused to forget his problem with the wrinklecrinkle man.)

charge (p. 163) Ask students *Who is making the charge?* (Dominic) *In a court, what is a charge?* (a complaint that one person has about another person)

plea (p. 163) Have students find the wrinklecrinkle man's answer on the next page. Ask *What is a plea in a court?* (saying if you did something wrong or not)

decree (p. 164) Ask *What does the judge do when she says "I do decree"?* (She makes her decision.)

case dismissed (p. 165) Ask students which words give us a clue as to what *case dismissed* means ("you are free"). Ask *When the case is dismissed, do they have to come back again?* (No, it's the end of the case.)

International English

Model the pronunciation of *honor/honour*, pointing out that it is the same for both words; it is just the spelling that is different.

Second Reading: Analyze the Text and Features

- Give students some time to read the poem silently. Ask a question to check understanding: *Does the judge think Dominic's problem is real?* (no)
- Discuss the questions in the pink boxes in pairs.
  - **Critical Thinking** (p. 160): *Why do you think the wrinklecrinkle man used these materials to build his house?* Students might say that he doesn't have much money, or that he likes simple things that he can find himself.
  - **Text Focus** (p. 162): *What kind of character is Dominic?* Ask students *Do you like the character of Dominic the baker?* Ask if they can think of any adjectives to describe him.
  - **Language Focus** (p. 164): *What does* with a straight face *mean? Do you have a similar phrase in your language?* If students are struggling, encourage them to think about what our face looks like when we smile—is it straight? Ask *Why did the judge have a straight face?* (She didn't want to show she had a funny idea.)
  - **Personalization** (p. 165): *What do you think of the judge's decision?* Ask students to vote on whether the judge's decision was a good or bad one. Then elicit reasons.
- Discuss the text focus: *Which line repeats in the poem? What effect does this have on you?* Give students some time to think and then discuss their ideas in groups.

Third Reading: Interact with the Text

- Put students into five groups and assign two stanzas to each group. Have them practice reading and acting out their stanzas. Then put the whole poem together by having each group read their stanzas in turn. Encourage everyone to join in with the repeated line.

Cool Down

Read out the predictions students made at the end of the previous lesson. How many of them were correct?

Explore the Reading

Lesson Objectives

- to understand and analyze *The Wrinklecrinkle Man* through reading comprehension activities
- to explore the SEL competency of responsible decision-making by becoming self-reflective and self-evaluative
- to make a personal connection to the reading
- to recognize and reproduce words with long e

Materials
Audio Tracks 52 and 54

TRACK 52 TB p. 236 Warm Up

Play *What's the Next Word?* (see TB p. 27) with the recording of the poem from the previous lesson.

A Read and answer.

- Before students open their books, find out what they remember about the poem. Give them four answers and have them work in pairs to write possible questions for the answers, e.g. 1 *happy, friendly* (What was the wrinklecrinkle man like?) 2 *He was a baker.* (What was Dominic's job?) 3 *court* (Where did Dominic take the Wrinklecrinkle Man? / Where did they decide the problem? / Where was the judge?) 4 *the judge* (Who made a decision? / Who said "I do decree"? / Who was in court?)
- With books open, do question 1 together as an example. Elicit that we should use literal language here, not figurative.
- Have students continue the activity individually, initially from memory and then looking back at the poem to check. Have them compare answers with a friend. Then check answers as a class.

Answers
1 He lives in Wobblewell. 2 He says hello to people. 3 Smelling his bread. 4 The wrinklecrinkle man doesn't owe any money. 5 So Dominic can hear the sound of the coins. 6 He goes free.

B Think, write, and discuss. Why do you think the author wrote *The Wrinklecrinkle Man*?

- Establish with the students that while the poem is fun it also has a message.
- Have students discuss in pairs why the author wrote the poem and what the message is.
- Have them share their ideas with the class.

Suggested Answers
The author wrote the poem to make people laugh and for the fun of creating a town with funny characters. He/she also wanted to give a message about the way we behave toward people—if we are not kind and are greedy, our actions can turn against us and we get nothing.

C Think and discuss. Imagine the judge orders you to pay for your senses and you only have enough money for one sense. Which sense do you think is the most useful?

- This activity draws on the SEL competency of being self-reflective and self-evaluative to make good decisions, encouraging students to consider themselves and their own needs.
- Tell students one opinion and ask them if they agree; for example, *I think the sense of taste is most important, because I love food.* Give students time to think about their own answers and then complete the sentence, saying which sense and why.
- Have students circulate to ask and answer the question. Encourage them to give reasons and to listen to each other's answers. Tell them to keep a tally of the senses mentioned. Invite students to share some of the most interesting answers they heard. Then have them write the results of their tally in a bar chart.

TRACK 54 TB p. 237 Spelling Pattern long e

Listen and write. Then check your answers.

- With books closed, write the word *cheese* on the board and underline the ee. Say the word and ask what the sound of these letters is (**/iː/**) and have students repeat it.
- Play the first part of the audio and have students repeat each word. Then have them open their books. Play the first part of the audio again and have them complete as many of the words as they can.
- Play the second part of the audio for students to check their spelling and complete any missing words. Have them underline the long e in each word and read the words aloud. Ask students what letters can make the this sound (in this activity, *e*, *ee* and *ea*). Have students notice that in *details* and *pretend*, the long e is at the end of a syllable.
- Have students look back at the reading to find more words with the long e sound and write them down. Invite them to read a word from their list, helping with pronunciation as necessary. Point out that the *ey* in *money* also makes the long e. Have them write all the long e words from the lesson in a word cloud.

Answers
1 repeat 2 details 3 knee 4 pretend 5 cheese
In the reading: sea; be; green; he; streets; see; free; seeing; 3 (three); fee; she; me; plea; breathe; sweet; stealing; decree; money

Cool Down

Play *Physical Spelling* (see TB p. 26) with words from the Spelling Pattern activity in this lesson.

Practice **Resource Bank:** Spelling Printout
Student's App: Reading Practice; Spelling Pattern Practice

Think Together

Lesson Objectives

- to make connections between the readings
- to explore the key concept: Why are our senses so important?
- to reflect on the unit and provide personal thoughts and opinions

Materials

(Optional) Candy or fruit (B)

Warm Up

Have students look back at the VTR image on pp. 152–153 and ask *Do you now have any new ideas about the image? What senses are the people in the picture using? Which do you think are most important in this picture?*

Have students discuss ideas in pairs and then ask them to share their ideas with the class.

A Complete the table with examples from *Sense Superstore* and *The Wrinklecrinkle Man*.

- Refer students to first row in the table and ask half the class to find an example of sight in *Sense Superstore* and the other half to find an example of sight in *The Wrinklecrinkle Man*.
- Have students complete the rest of the table individually and then compare with a friend. Check answers with the class.

Suggested Answers

Sight: ultraviolet light (SS); seeing the sun; waving to / saluting people he sees (TWM)
Hearing: echolocation (SS); the sound of the coins; jingles, a sparrow's tune; the judge listens (TWM)
Touch: moles have sensitive nerve endings (SS); the judge scratches her chin; the old man holds his purse (TWM)
Smell: Jacobson's organ (SS); the smell of bread (TWM)
Taste: catfish have 100,000 taste buds (SS); the taste of bread (TWM)

B Think and write. Sit quietly. What can you see? What can you hear? What can you smell? What can you feel or touch? What can you taste? Do a Think, Pair, Share.

- If possible, take students somewhere outside to do this activity. Alternatively, bring in some candy or fruit, hand one item to each student, and have them focus on this.
- Tell students to sit quietly, as if for a visualization but with eyes open, and to use their senses to answer the questions: *What can you see? What can you hear? What can you smell? What can you feel or touch? What can you taste?* Have them do this for a short time initially and elicit one or two ideas, e.g. *I can smell lemons.* Then give them another minute or two to concentrate on their senses. If you have given them candy or fruit, tell them they will have to do *taste* last!
- Have students share what they saw, heard, smelled, touched, and tasted in pairs. Then have them work together to answer the questions in B.
- Have pairs share their ideas for each question with another pair.

C Complete the Y chart with your information from B. Then share with the class.

- Have students copy the chart into their notebooks and complete it with their sensory experiences from B. Encourage them to use similes to describe their experience, e.g. *the bird sounds like a flute, the candy sounds like footsteps in my mouth.*
- Invite students to share what they "sensed" with the class. Ask students if their experience was the same as all the other students in the class and if they enjoyed the activity.
- Introduce the key concept question *Why are our senses so important?* on the board. and have students discuss it in small groups. Encourage them to draw on everything they have learned through the unit as well as the ideas discussed in this lesson. Invite students to share ideas with the class.

My Reading Journal

What did you find surprising in the unit? Why?

This question encourages students to reflect on their own learning and form a personal response.

Have students look back at the unit and find one surprising thing and write down what it was and why it was surprising.

Suggested Answer

I didn't know that fire-chaser beetles existed. They are really strange!

How did you do? What was one thing that you did well during the unit that you used to find difficult?

This question encourages students to reflect on the learning process and their own strengths and the progress that they have made.

Ask students to look back at all the different activities in the unit (including the readings) and find one thing that they think they do better now than before.

Have students write their answers and then share ideas in pairs.

Congratulate students on the progress they have made this year. Remind them that they can now read, understand, and analyze long texts in English, so they should be proud of themselves!

Cool Down

Have students work in pairs or groups to write a short poem about their sense experiences, using the similes they wrote in C. They could also include similes for the other senses; smell and taste. Tell them that the poem doesn't have to rhyme. Ask for volunteers to read their poems to the class.

Practice **Resource Bank:** Unit Test; End-of-year Test
Student's App: Key Concept Practice

Give a Reason!

Lesson Objectives

- to review vocabulary from Units 1 and 2, focusing on types of art, describing art, experiments, and time
- to review grammar from Units 1 and 2, focusing on quantifiers, future predictions, and future plans
- to practice communication and fluency skills

Materials

Spinner and Counters printout from the Resource Bank (one counter per player)

Warm Up

Ask students *Why do you learn English?* Elicit as many reasons as possible using *because,* and make a list on the board. Ask *What do you think is the most important reason?*

How to Play

- Note: to save time, download and cut out the spinner and counters before the lesson. Ensure you have one spinner per group and one counter for each student.
- Students are going to play a game in which they move around a board and make sentences giving reasons. Go through the instructions on the **Language Book** page. More detailed instructions on how to play are given below.
- Students play in small groups of three or four. They only need one book between them to play. Have students write their name at the top of one of the points charts on p. 34 or p. 35. Give each student a counter. Students should color their counter to match their points chart.
- Students take turns spinning the spinner and moving around the board, placing their counter. When they stop on a square, they must read what it says aloud (so everyone can hear rather than trying to read upside down!). Then they have to think of a reason to continue the sentence, and they must use the words given. If there are alternates (e.g. *coming/going*), they only need to use one of these words.
- Each time they produce a correct sentence, students can color in another square on their points chart in whatever color they want. Encourage students to listen carefully to the other players' sentences to decide if they're correct or not.
- Before students start playing the game, write an example on the board: *I can't go to English class today, because … (going to).* Elicit various possible reasons using the beginning of the sentence and the words *going to* in the continuation; for example, … *because I'm going to see the dentist. / because I'm going to play soccer for the school. / because my parents are going to take me to Australia!*

Here is an example:

Student A: Four. One, two, three, four. We won't have a picnic today because … *going to.* OK. We won't have a picnic today because it's going to rain.

Student B: Good answer. Color a square.

Student C: OK. My turn. Three. One, two, three. I don't like that painting because … *too* or *enough*. Hmm. I don't like that painting because it's too dark.

- Encourage students to listen carefully to the other players' sentences to decide if they're correct or not. Students keep going around the board until one player reaches 20 points.

Answers

Students' own answers

Playtime Practice

At the end of the game, encourage other students to also contribute ideas for squares they didn't land on. Can anyone make a correct sentence for all the squares?

Cool Down

Write some long words from Units 1 and 2 randomly on the board. Have students categorize them according to the stress pattern. They could do this in pairs or teams and race to finish first. Have students say the words aloud to check answers. Suggested words: 1st syllable stress: *homework, something, measure, collage, landscape, background, decade, minute*; 2nd syllable stress: *remember, important, expensive, opinion, photography, experiment, thermometer, millennium.*

Race Around the Galaxy

Lesson Objectives

- to review vocabulary from Units 3 and 4, focusing on emotions, friendships, space, and Mars
- to review grammar from Units 3 and 4, focusing on first conditionals (statements and questions) and modal verbs
- to practice communication and fluency skills

Materials

Spinner and Counters printout from the Resource Bank (one counter per player)

Warm Up

Play *Board Race* with the word *space* (see TB p. 25).

How to Play

- Note: to save time, download and cut out the spinner and counters before the lesson. Ensure you have one spinner per group and one counter for each student.
- Students are going to play a board game where they move around the board and answer questions. They may move forward or miss a turn. Go through the instructions on the **Language Book** page. More detailed instructions on how to play are given below.
- Students play in groups of three or four. They only need one book between them to play. Each student has a counter. Students should color their counter a different color from those of the other players.
- Students take turns spinning the spinner and moving around the board, placing their counter. When they stop on a square, they must answer the question or follow the instructions. If they answer correctly, they move forward one square and the next player goes (only one question or move per turn). If they don't answer correctly, they stay on that square. Encourage students to listen carefully to the other players' sentences to decide if they're correct or not.
- If students land on the tail of a shooting star, they follow it forward to the square where the star is. If they land on the tail of a comet, they follow it back to the square where the comet is.
- The winner is the first person to go over the finish line.
- Before students start playing the game, write an example on the board: *You've passed astronaut training. How do you feel?* Elicit possible emotions to answer the question. Encourage students to make full sentences; for example, *I feel nervous. I feel excited.*

Here is an example:

Student A: Four. One, two, three, four. *What's this?* Oh, yes—it's a sand dune!

Student B: That's right! Move forward one space.

Student C: OK. My turn. Three. One, two, three. *You make a friend at the space station, but you have to speak Russian. How do you feel?* Hmm. Well, I feel fine, because I studied Russian before I came to the space station!

Suggested Answers

1 Russian/science 2 proud 3 (linked to 7) 4 sand dune 5 Mars 6 The solar system is part of a galaxy. 7 (go down to 3) 8 nervous/confident/calm/relaxed 9 (linked to 17) 10 (linked to 2) 11 crater 12 rocks 13 calm 14 (go forward 1 space) 15 (linked to 19) 16 (miss a turn) 17 (linked to 9) 18 Earth 19 (linked to 15) 20 iron 21 astronomer 22 (linked to 11) 23 observatory 24 telescope 25 nervous/lonely/proud/calm 26 (go back 3 spaces) 27 Students' own answers 28 embarrassed/calm

Playtime Practice

There are several blank squares on the board. Have students work as a group to write extra questions to hand to another group. When they stop on a blank square, they read and answer one of these questions.

Cool Down

Have students turn their books over and say as many of the questions and answers as they can. This can be played as a team game with teams taking turns and winning points for correct sentences until they can't remember any more. Then have them check their books and see what they missed.

The Great Outdoors

Lesson Objectives

- to review vocabulary from Units 5 and 6, focusing on Vikings, trade and travel, actions and survival, and camping equipment
- to review grammar from Units 5 and 6, focusing on *used to* (statements and questions) and the present perfect (questions and statements)
- to practice communication and fluency skills

Warm Up

Give students two minutes to do a drawing of a typical Viking. Ask them to think about what he/she is wearing, carrying, and doing. Have them compare their pictures with friends and see if they are similar. Ask students *What was similar about your pictures? What was different?*

How to Play

- Students are going to play a spot-the-differences game with pictures of Vikings and modern families camping. They describe their picture to their partner or ask questions to find the differences.
- Students play in pairs. Designate each student a letter, either A or B. Each student should only look at one side of the double page, so students who are A must look at the pictures on p. 86 and cover p. 87, and students who are B must look at the pictures on p. 87 and cover p. 86.
- Students look first at the picture of the Vikings. Students take turns describing something in their picture or asking about their partner's picture. When they find something different, they circle it in their picture.
- When they finish the Viking pictures, then they look at the other picture of the modern families camping and follow the same procedure to find the differences. Point out that there are seven differences to find in total.
- Before students start playing the game, write the sentence and question beginnings on the board and elicit possible ways to complete them; for example. *Did your Viking family use to …* (send messages by horse)*? In this picture, the Viking family used to …* (grow vegetables). *The modern family in my picture has …* (washed some clothes). *Has your modern family …* (eaten pizza)*?*

Here is an example:

Student A: OK. Did your Viking family use to send messages by horse?
Student B: No, they didn't. My Viking family used to send messages by bird. That's one difference! OK, my turn. In my picture, the Viking family used to wash clothes in the river.
Student A: Yes, my Viking family used to wash clothes in the river, too. No difference.

- When a pair think they have found all the differences, they should compare open their books and compare pictures.

Answers

1 In picture A, the Viking family used to build their shelter from wood. In picture B, they used to build it from leaves.
2 In picture A, the Viking father used to send messages by horse. In picture B, he used to send messages by bird.
3 In picture A, the Viking family used to grow wheat. In picture B, they used to grow vegetables.
4 In picture A, the modern family has put up one big tent. In picture B, they have put up two small tents.
5 In picture A, the modern father has sent a message on his cell phone. In picture B, he has sent a message on his tablet.
6 In picture A, the modern family has eaten pizza. In picture B, they haven't eaten the pizza.
7 In picture A, the modern family has drunk three bottles of water. In picture B, they have drunk one bottle of water.

Playtime Practice

When students have finished playing the game, have them play *Kim's Game*. With books closed, they should try to remember everything they can from the different pictures and write a list in their notebooks. Then they compare the picture to their list to see how much they remembered and what they missed. Who remembered the most?

Cool Down

Play *Disappearing Words* (see TB p. 25) with key vocabulary from Units 5 and 6.

Half a Crossword

Lesson Objectives

- to review vocabulary from Units 7 and 8, focusing on the water cycle, water, physical characteristics, movies, movie genres, and movie features
- to review grammar from Units 7 and 8, focusing on gerunds as subjects, prepositions after adjectives, defining relative clauses, and adjectives with *–ed* or *–ing*
- to practice communication and fluency skills

Warm Up

Do a short general-knowledge quiz about famous things, people, and places using relative clauses. Possible questions: *What are the countries where the Vikings came from?* (Denmark, Norway, Sweden) *What is the country that has the largest area?* (Russia) *Name the swimmer who has won the most Olympic medals.* (Michael Phelps, 28 medals) *What is the animal that moves the slowest?* (sloth) *What's the name of the scientist who invented the theory of relativity?* (Albert Einstein) *What is the name of the country where you can see the Taj Mahal?* (India)

How to Play

- Students are going to complete a crossword where they have half the answers and have to explain them to a partner in order to complete the puzzle. Go through the instructions on the **Language Book** page. More detailed instructions on how to play are given below.
- Students play in pairs. Designate each student a letter, either A or B. Each student should only look at one side of the double page, so if they are A, they must look at p. 112 and cover p. 113, and if they are B, they must look at p. 113 and cover p. 112.
- Before they start, refer students to the prompts on each page and explain they can use these to make definitions for the words in their crossword. Do an example, by writing the word *musical* on the board. Elicit a possible definition using one of the prompts, e.g. *It's a movie that has songs.* Ask why we use *that* (it's a thing). Then have students look at the complete words in their crossword and write clues, or definitions, in their notebooks.
- Have students take turns asking each other for the definitions of the missing words; for example, *What's 9 Down? / What's 8 Across?* (write *down* with a down arrow and *across* with a right-pointing arrow on the board). To start, Student A asks for a definition, Student B gives the definition, and Student A guesses the word. If it is correct, Student B confirms.

Here is an example:

Student A: What's 5 Across?
Student B: 5 Across … Ah, OK. This is a type of movie that makes you laugh.
Student A: Oh, yes. Comedy—C-O-M-E-D-Y, right?
Student B: Right! OK, what's 12 Down?
Student A: That's difficult to explain … OK, let's try. It's something that a movie star in a horror movie has on his face.
Student B: Oh … wait a minute … It's a … scar! S-C-A-R.

Answers

Across: 2 famous 5 comedy 7 pond 8 bucket 11 movie star 13 director 14 faucet 15 interested 16 wig
Down: 1 studio 3 sound track 4 reservoir 6 excited 9 frightening 10 afraid 12 scar

Playtime Practice

When the crosswords are completed have students take turns miming or using sound effects to explain the words for their partner can guess.

Cool Down

Give definitions of other key words from Units 7 and 8 for students to guess. This can be played as a team game for points. Suggested clues: *It's a wall that you build to stop a river.* (dam) *It's a type of movie with a lot of singing in it.* (musical) *It's a small, man-made river where some people live on boats.* (canal) *It's a person who investigates crimes.* (detective) *It's the hair around your eyes.* (eyelashes) *You feel this if you don't get any sleep.* (tired) *It's a type of movie that makes you feel scared.* (horror) *It's a thing that happens when it hasn't rained for a very long time.* (drought) *It's a word to describe food that you really don't like.* (disgusting) *It's a place that cleans water so that people can use it.* (water plant)

Keep Talking!

Lesson Objectives

- to review vocabulary from Units 9 and 10, focusing on household chores, towns and cities, sense verbs, and sense adjectives
- to review grammar from Units 9 and 10, focusing on present perfect (with *ever*, *never*, and *already*), and present perfect and simple past
- to practice communication and fluency skills

Materials

Spinner and Counters printout from the Resource Bank (one counter per player)

Warm Up

Play a game of *Change Places* (see TB p. 25). Suggested questions: *Have you ever been to another country? Do you like the taste of chocolate ice cream? Are you afraid of touching a spider? Have you ever seen an elephant? Do you like listening to classical music? Have you helped with the housework this week? Do you like the smell of coffee? Have you ever lost your cell phone?*

How to Play

- Note: to save time, download and cut out the spinner and counters before the lesson. Ensure you have one spinner per group and one counter for each student.
- Students are going to play a board game where they move around the board and answer a question or complete a sentence. Go through the instructions on the **Language Book** page. More detailed instructions on how to play are given below.
- Students play in groups of three or four, with one book between them. Each student has a counter. Students should color their counter a different color from those of other players.
- Students take turns spinning the spinner and moving around the board, placing their counter. Every square has a question to answer or a sentence to complete. If the student can answer the question or complete the sentence, he/she moves the counter forward two spaces. If the student can't answer the question or complete the sentence, he/she moves the counter back three spaces. After that, the next person in the group continues. Remind students to listen carefully to each other to judge whether an answer or sentence is correct.
- The winner is the first person to reach the end of the board.
- Before students start playing, write some sample questions on the board; for example, *Have you ever climbed a mountain? I've already seen … What's he doing?* (show an image of an activity from the book, e.g. Mr. Sim on p. 28) *When was the last time you sang a song?* Elicit the possible answers for the questions and check the use of the verb forms.

Here is an example:

Student A: Three. One, two, three. *When did you last get a big surprise? Why?* Let me think … Oh—this morning! I got my math test, and I got a good grade. I thought it was going to be terrible! I was really surprised!

Student B: Good answer! Move forward two spaces.

Student C: OK. My turn. Five. One, two, three, four, five. *What's he doing?* Oh … I can't remember how to say it. No, sorry. I don't know.

Student A: Bad luck. He's mowing the lawn. You have to move back three spaces.

Answers

Students' own answers for the questions. The pictures as follows:
square 8 He's mowing the lawn; square 10 fountain; square 13 skyscraper; square 17 railroad; square 21 She's taking out the trash; square 24 path; square 28 on a bench

Playtime Practice

When the game is finished, have students look through the rest of the book to find images of activities and ask each other questions in pairs using *Have you ever …?* or *What's/are he/she/they doing?*

Cool Down

Have students choose two or three questions from the game to ask to all their other friends in the class. Have them mingle, ask, and answer. At the end, ask if they found out any interesting information about their friends.

Time Traveler

Materials
Audio Track 123; simple props: desks together to make a bed, a thick coat as an astronaut's suit, a ruler and a big book (or a tray) as a sword and shield, a woolen garment to be weaving, a plastic bowl and cup

Warm Up

Write these periods of time on the board: the time of the dinosaurs, the time of the pyramids, the time of the Silk Road, or the time of the beginning of space travel. Have students discuss in pairs and then vote on which one they would most like to visit.

Teacher's Notes

Setting: Lucy's home; a spaceship; a Viking village; an Egyptian field.

Synopsis: Lucy travels through time and space and meets an astronaut, a Viking boy, and an Egyptian girl and her mom before she finds herself back in her bedroom, waking up for school!

TRACK 123 TB p. 226 Listen and Engage

- Tell students the title of the play and check understanding of *time traveler.* Elicit what they think the play will be about. Then have them look at pp. 140–141. Ask *How many characters are there?* (seven, plus the narrator)
- Play the audio and have students follow and find how many places Lucy visits in the play. Have them find and point to Lucy, an astronaut, a Viking, and an Egyptian girl. Ask students how they think Lucy feels at different points in the play. What gives them a clue?
- Remind students that the sentences in light blue are the stage directions—they help the actors know what to do.

Interact

- Play the audio again and encourage students to invent some actions, e.g. thinking hard, floating around, closing eyes, and counting to ten.
- Then play the audio for students to repeat each line—first with no actions and then with actions. Encourage them to listen and copy the intonation, pronunciation, and emotion in the voices.

Practice and Prepare

- Tell students they are going to practice the play so that they can perform it in front of an audience—you can decide whether they perform to another class or to parents.
- Divide the class into groups of eight. Give students in each group a number from one to eight. Tell students that this time, all number ones are the narrator, all twos are Lucy, all threes are Mom, all fours are the astronaut, and so on. Students who don't wish to act can have behind-the-scenes roles, e.g. director, stage manager (responsible for all props and everything needed for the play), costume director, make-up artist, scenery painter, prop designer, camera operator. They can be involved in organizing and creating simple props, scenery, invitations and programs while the others are rehearsing.
- Play the audio and have students mime their character's actions. Remind them to look at the stage directions and narrator lines when deciding what to do and encourage other students to make suggestions. Give the groups time to practice their parts while reading from their books.
- If you can, allow students ten minutes to practice the play every day—the more times students practice, the better their performance will be. When they have memorized their lines, have them incorporate simple props into their performance. You can suggest the props listed above, or encourage students who are not acting to make the props.

Perform

- Invite parents or other classes to the performance. You may wish to use the school auditorium for this. An end-of-term performance can be a good way to show what students have been learning.
- Give some students the responsibility of welcoming the audience and showing them to their seats, and give others the role of introducing the play.
- Stand at the side of the stage and prompt any students who forget their lines. Alternately, give this role to a confident student!
- Make sure students know that if they have fun and enjoy the performance, the audience will enjoy it, too!

Cool Down

After the performance, congratulate students and ask them if they enjoyed performing the play. Review all the different things they had to do to prepare (e.g. practicing the lines, thinking of actions for the characters, creating the props and scenery). Ask students to work in pairs to put the things in order from what they found most difficult to what they found easiest. Invite pairs to share their answers and encourage them to give reasons.

The Mystery of the Missing Ring

Materials

Audio Track 124; simple props: cell phones, a broom, a mop or even a tennis racket as a metal detector, two plastic cups for binoculars, a chair to climb onto, a toy car (or something of similar size), and a key ring (with no keys)

Warm Up

Tell students they are going to read a story that involves a ring, a hammock, a tree, and a bird. Write these items on the board and have students work in pairs to imagine what the story of the play might be. Elicit ideas.

Teacher's Notes

Setting: Detective Du Pree's desk; the road to Lady Richmond's house; Lady Richmond's garden; and Lady Richmond's kitchen.

Synopsis: Lady Richmond thinks her ring has been stolen. Detective Du Pree goes to investigate and meets a little boy with a toy car, a man with a metal detector, a gardener, and a little girl and her dad. Together they help solve the mystery of the missing ring, and Lady Richmond and her cook invite them into the kitchen to celebrate.

TRACK 124 TB p. 226 Listen and Engage

- Have students read the title of the play and look at the pictures. Ask *What do you think it will be about? How many characters are there?* (eight)
- Play the audio and have students follow and listen for the objects the detective finds. Have them point to the pictures of the detective, the gardener, and the machine for finding metal. Ask how they think Lady Richmond feels at the beginning and at the end of the play.

Interact

- Play the audio again and encourage students to invent some actions, e.g. crawling along the ground, using a metal detector, mowing the lawn.
- Play the audio again, pausing to have students repeat each line—first with no actions and then with actions. Encourage them to focus on pronunciation, intonation, and the expression in the characters' voices.

Practice and Prepare

- Tell students they are going to practice the play so that they can perform it in front of an audience.
- Divide the class into groups of eight and give each student a number from one to eight. Tell students that this time, all number ones are Lady Richmond; all twos are the detective; all threes are the little boy, and so on. Remind students that everyone should say the last line in the play. Students who don't wish to act can have behind-the-scenes roles and be involved in organizing and creating simple props, scenery, invitations and programs while the others are rehearsing.
- Play the audio and have students mime their character's actions and think about how their character is feeling. Remind them to look at the stage directions for clues. Give the groups time to practice their parts, while reading from their books. Encourage them to listen to each other and help with pronunciation and intonation, as well as suggestions for actions.
- If you can, allow students ten minutes to practice the play every day. When they have memorized their lines, have them incorporate simple props into their performance. You can suggest the props listed above, or encourage students who are not acting in the play to to make their own props.

Perform

- Invite parents or other classes to the performance. You may wish to use the school auditorium for this. An end-of-term/-year performance can be a good way to show what students have learned during the year.
- Give some students the responsibility of welcoming the audience and showing them to their seats, and give others the role of introducing the play.
- Stand at the side of the stage and prompt any students who have forgotten their lines. Alternatively, give this role to a confident student!
- Make sure students know that if they have fun and enjoy the performance, the audience will enjoy it, too!

Cool Down

After the performance, congratulate students and ask them if they enjoyed performing the play. Review all the different things they had to do to prepare (e.g. practicing the lines, thinking of actions for the characters, creating the props and scenery). Ask students what they liked doing best and what they would like to try in the future.

Audio Scripts

Language Book

Language Review

TRACK 1

Language Review

A Listen and write. Where's Lucas?

1 **Min:** Hi, everyone! Can you all hear me?
Everyone: Yes, Min!
Min: Let's see. The play starts at two o'clock. It's noon now, so we have two more hours.

2 **Min:** Mariam, what are you doing here?
Mariam: Hi, Min, I have my project to show, but I think I'm early.
Min: Never mind! You can put your project there.

3 **Min:** OK, is everyone here now? We should have one more rehearsal. Everyone has to know what to do.

4 **Min:** Stand on the stage, please, everyone.

5 **Min:** Where's Ruben?
Ruben: I'm here! Sorry I'm late!

6 **Min:** That's OK. Stand with the fish. Wait, everyone's in their costume. Where's yours?

7 **Ruben:** Oh, no! I think I left it backstage, Min.
Min: OK, well, go and get it.
Ruben: Sorry!

8 **Min:** OK. Let's start the play at the beginning. Oh, no! Lucas, are you OK? Where are you?
Lucas: I'm OK! I'm here, Min, under the curtain!

TRACK 2

Language Review

B Read and complete the dialogue. Then listen and check.

Mr. Paul: Good morning, Ruben! Are you enjoying the day?
Ruben: Yes, thank you! I'm waiting for our play to start.
Mr. Paul: Hello, girls. What are you doing?
Mariam: We're selling tickets for the play.
Mr. Paul: Oh, look at Lucas! What's he doing?
Min: He's playing a game with a plastic fish.
Mariam: But he isn't using a stick. He's catching the fish with his hook!

TRACK 3

Unit 1, Vocabulary

A Listen and find. What does Lucas add to some artwork?

Jan: Look, Lucas. There's Poppy. She's painting … something. What is it?
Lucas: Maybe a landscape? Is it of those trees, Jan?
Jan: Oh, it's a still life. Yes—it's that vase of flowers.
Lucas: Oh!
Jan: Hey, what's that hanging from the tree?
Lucas: It's a mobile! It's really cool! Let's go and look at that big sculpture. Is it made of glass?
Jan: No, it's made of ice.
Lucas: Ooh, this looks interesting. Excuse me, what are you making?
Bob: I'm making a collage out of things people have in their pockets.
Lucas: I have a bus ticket in my pocket. Can I add it to your collage?
Bob: Sure.
Jan: Come on, Lucas. Let's go look at that installation.
Miss Clay: OK, everyone, it's time to go back to school. Do you all have your bus tickets?
Lucas: Oh, no! Miss Clay … I don't have mine.
Miss Clay: Where is it?
Lucas: Umm … it's in the collage.
Miss Clay: Oh, Lucas!

Unit 1

TRACK 4

Unit 1, Vocabulary

B Listen, say, and number the pictures in A.

1 sculpture
2 portrait
3 landscape
4 still life
5 collage
6 installation
7 mobile
8 mural
9 sketch
10 photography

TRACK 5

Unit 1, Vocabulary

C Close your eyes. Listen, visualize, and say.

Sculpture. Mime making a sculpture. What's it made of? Say *sculpture*.
Portrait. You are painting a portrait. Whose face are you painting? Say *portrait*.
Landscape. You're looking at a beautiful landscape. What can you see? Say *landscape*.
Still life. Imagine a still-life painting. What's in it? What colors can you see? Say *still life*.
Collage. You are making a collage. What objects do you like best in your collage? Say *collage*.
Installation. You are walking through an installation. What can you see, feel, and hear? Say *installation*.
Mobile. Imagine a mobile moving in the wind. What can you hear? Say *mobile*.
Mural. Mime painting a mural. Where is it? What are you painting? Say *mural*.
Sketch. Mime drawing a sketch. What are you looking at? Say *sketch*.
Photography. Take my picture. Click! Does it look like me? Say *photography*.

TRACK 6

Unit 1, Vocabulary

E Listen and complete. Then watch and sing.

Art Is for Everyone

There's art all around us, just look and you'll see
Art is for everyone, for you and for me.

Let's make some art, it's fun and it's free
We can use a camera to do photography.
A sculpture, a collage—anything you make
What will you use, how long will it take?

A mural is easy, it's big and it's tall
We'll draw a sketch first, then paint it on the wall.
Let's paint a picture—what will it be?
A still life, a landscape, or a portrait of me?

TRACK 7

Unit 1, Explore Language

A Listen and read. Who's Larry drawing?

Larry: Miss Clay, this is my grandpa.
Miss Clay: I see, Larry. Does he have any hair?
Larry: Well, he doesn't have a lot of hair. He only has a little hair here at his ears.
Miss Clay: What color is his hair?
Larry: Most of his hair is white. Just this little bit is brown.
Miss Clay: Welcome to our art gallery! All the paintings are by our students. Now, I know a few parents and grandparents … Ah, you're Larry's grandpa!
Grandpa: Yes, I am. But how did you know?
Miss Clay: You look just like the portrait Larry drew!

TRACK 8

Unit 1, Explore Language

D Listen and say.

1 He only has a little hair.
2 There are a few people here.
3 Are all the children's pictures on the walls?
4 Most of my pictures are portraits.

TRACK 9

Unit 1, Global Citizenship

A Listen to Jane talk to her art teacher about shadow boxes. Why do people make shadow boxes?

Jane: Do you know that in Japan they have a traditional paper art called origami? I read it in a book.

Teacher: Yes, all over the world people use paper for different kinds of art. For example, picture books tell a story. Another way to tell a story is to make a shadow box.
Jane: A shadow box? What's that?
Teacher: I'll show you one I made.
Jane: Wow! It's amazing. It's very detailed. There are so many small things to look at. How did you make it?
Teacher: Well, first I made a sketch of the complete picture. I drew different trees on a lot of pieces of paper. The trees go in the background. And in front of the trees, for the foreground, I cut out a rabbit and another big tree.
Jane: I like the pale blue sky. It looks almost white.
Teacher: Yes, look what happens when I hold my picture up to this lamp.
Jane: I can see the dark shadows of the tree and the rabbit! I'd love to learn how to make a shadow box.
Teacher: It isn't difficult to make a simple one, with just a few pieces of paper. I'll teach you and you can tell your own story!

TRACK 10
Unit 1, Global Citizenship
B Listen, say, and number the pictures in A.
1 simple
2 detailed
3 foreground
4 background
5 dark
6 light
7 shadow
8 bright
9 pale

TRACK A
Unit 1, Global Citizenship
Close your eyes. Listen, visualize, and say.
Simple. Imagine a simple drawing of the sun. Can you draw it? Say *simple*.
Detailed. Imagine a very detailed pattern. What kinds of things can you see? Say *detailed*.
Foreground. Imagine a landscape with some animals in the foreground. What animals are they? Say *foreground*.
Background. Imagine a house with mountains in the background. Are the mountains near or far? Say *background*.
Dark. You are in a dark room. What can you see and hear? Say *dark*.
Light. Mime opening the curtains in the morning. Is it light or dark? Say *light*.
Shadow. You are standing with the sun behind you. Is your shadow long or short? Say *shadow*.
Bright. You are wearing a bright T-shirt. Do you like the color? Say *bright*.
Pale. You want to make a pale color with paint. Do you need lots of white paint or black paint? Say *pale*.

TRACK 11
Unit 1, Global Citizenship
D Now listen to Yoko and Juan. Why do people make these artworks?
Yoko: This is my origami bird. It's very simple to make. Origami is a Japanese word. It means to fold paper. Origami is a traditional Japanese art. We don't all learn to make origami at school, but most of us learn it from our parents. We take a piece of paper and fold it into different shapes to make flowers and animals like fish or birds. You can also glue lots of shapes together to make big sculptures. I like doing origami; it's relaxing. During the summer, at our Star Festival, we make lots of origami stars and hang them up.
Juan: Look at my decoration. I used bright yellow paper to make it. Paper cutting is a tradition in Mexico, where I'm from. It started long ago. First, you fold a big piece of paper into squares. Do it a few times. Then, draw and cut out patterns on the paper. Open the paper, and look at the pattern! My pattern is very simple, but a lot of artists use very thin, soft paper and special tools to make beautiful, detailed pictures. Paper cutting is a good way to express yourself. We usually hang the patterns to make decorations for festivals. We use different colors for different festivals.

TRACK 12
Unit 1, Explore Language
A Listen and read. Which picture do Larry and Poppy like best?
Larry: Which picture is best? This one's too dark, I think, and this one's too light.
Poppy: Let's try it in black and white. That's better.
Larry: But the house is too far away. It's not close enough to see the details.
Poppy: You're right. It isn't big enough. Can we make it a bit bigger?
Larry: But not too big … There! Do you think it's good enough for the photography competition?
Poppy: Yes, it's perfect!

TRACK 13
Unit 1, Explore Language
D Listen and say.
1 This one's too dark.
2 They're big enough.
3 I'm not too young.
4 You aren't old enough.

TRACK 14
Unit 1, Talk About It
Pronunciation. Listen and say.
Silent *gh* I
bright light right

Unit 2

TRACK 15
Unit 2, Vocabulary
A Listen and find. Which ball bounces the highest?
Poppy: Right. Pour some water into each glass. Then put them in the sun. Now, which color glass has the hottest water, black or white? I need a thermometer. Oh!
Hugo: Oops, sorry, Poppy and Ahmed. We're doing an experiment.
Poppy: That's OK, Hugo. Ahmed, do you know what they're doing?
Ahmed: They want to find out how high different balls can bounce.
Poppy: Oh, I see! And why are they putting an egg and some salt in the bowl of water?
Ahmed: They want to see what happens. Look, that egg is floating!
Poppy: That's amazing! Oh, dear. There goes the other ball.
Ahmed: Look, Poppy, the golf ball bounced the highest—even higher than Hugo's head!
Poppy: Wow! And what's Ben making?
Ahmed: It's a scale. He wants to measure the weight of that sugar.
Poppy: What's that boy doing at the counter, Ahmed?
Ahmed: He's measuring its length. It looks about two meters long.
Poppy: Oh, no. Look at Mr. Sim's book!
Ahmed: There's always something exciting happening in Science Club!

TRACK 16
Unit 2, Vocabulary
B Listen, say, and number the pictures in A.
1 scale (British English: scales)
2 length
3 width
4 height
5 weight
6 experiment
7 thermometer
8 measure
9 pour
10 float

TRACK 17
Unit 2, Vocabulary
C Close your eyes. Listen, visualize, and say.
Scale. You are going on a plane. Put your suitcase on a scale. What is the weight of your suitcase? Say *scale*.
Length. Imagine a long string from your desk to the classroom door. How long is it? Say *length*.
Width. Measure the short side of your desk. How wide is it? Say *width*.
Height. Measure your height. Are you taller than your friend? Say *height*.
Weight. Imagine you are holding a tomato in one hand and bag of sugar in the other hand. Which object feels heavier? Say *weight*.
Experiment. Mime doing a science experiment. What are you doing? What can you see? Say *experiment*.

Thermometer. You have a thermometer. Take your temperature. Say *thermometer.*
Measure. Mime measuring your foot. How long is it? Say *measure.*
Pour. You are pouring yourself a glass of fruit juice. What does it sound like? Which fruit can you smell? Say *pour.*
Float. You are floating on your back in a swimming pool. How does it feel? Say *float.*

TRACK 18

Unit 2, Vocabulary

E Listen and complete. Then watch and sing.

Measure It!

What's the length of a crocodile?
What's the height of the tallest tree?
What's the weight of a hippo on a scale?
Is it heavier than you and me?

Measure it,
Measure it.
Then you'll know for sure.
Do an experiment to help you find out more!

How hot is it in the sunshine today?
What does the thermometer show?
What's the width of the widest bridge in the world?
What's the answer? I don't know!

TRACK 19

Unit 2, Explore Language

A Listen and read. What are the students measuring?

Ben: Oh, look, Ahmed. There are balloons on the table. We're going to do a science experiment!
Teacher: That's right, Ben. It's an experiment with air. What am I going to do now?
Ahmed: You're going to make a hole in a balloon.
Teacher: That's right. What will happen next?
Ben: I think the stick will go down at one end.
Ahmed: No, I think it won't move at all.
Ben: Look! One balloon is heavier than the other.
Ahmed: Air has weight!
Teacher: Right! The experiment was to measure the weight of air, without using a scale.

TRACK 20

Unit 2, Explore Language

D Listen and say.

1 We're going to do a science experiment.
2 Do you think we'll be on time?
3 Look at those clouds. It's going to rain soon.
4 Let's have a race to the end of the street. It'll be fun!

TRACK 21

Unit 2, Global Citizenship

A Listen to Anton talk to his dad about time. When did people first use clocks?

Dad: Anton, are you ready? It's almost time for school.
Anton: Don't worry, Dad, I'm ready. And look at the clock. I still have five minutes ... What did people do before they had clocks? How did they plan or make arrangements?
Dad: Hmm ... I don't know.
Anton: I'm going to look it up. How did people tell the time before they had clocks? For hundreds of years, people used the sun, candles, water, or sand clocks to tell the time.
Dad: Look, it says they couldn't measure seconds, minutes, or hours; they only knew when it was day or night.
Anton: And then, look, they figured out that a minute was 60 seconds, an hour was 60 minutes, and a day was 24 hours. But when did they first use clocks?
Dad: Let me see. Ah, nearly a millennium ago. That's a thousand years. This says the oldest clock is about 700 years old. That's from the 14th century. And this clock made a sound every hour. Later, clocks started to show minutes and seconds.
Anton: Did people have calendars showing all the days of the week and months of the year?
Dad: Hmm ... Oh, yes, they did, but they used the sun and the moon to know the date.
Anton: Oh, look! I can't believe we spent five minutes talking about time! I have to go! Bye!

TRACK 22

Unit 2, Global Citizenship

B Listen, say, and number the pictures in A.

1 calendar
2 millennium
3 century
4 decade
5 year
6 month
7 hour
8 minute
9 second

TRACK B

Unit 2, Global Citizenship

Close your eyes. Listen, visualize, and say.

Calendar. There's a calendar on your wall. What picture is on the calendar? Say *calendar.*
Millennium. Imagine you are living in the past millennium. What does your house look like? Say *millennium.*
Century. Imagine you are living in the 19th century, exactly 200 years ago. What clothes are you wearing? Say *century.*
Decade. Travel back in time a decade ago. What technology did people have? Say *decade.*
Year. Think of your birthday last year. How old were you? Say *year.*
Month. Imagine your favorite month. Is it hot or cold? Say *month.*
Hour. Imagine closing your eyes for an hour. Does it feel like a long time? Say *hour.*
Minute. Close your eyes for a minute. How do you know when a minute is over? Say *minute.*
Second. Close your eyes and count five seconds. Then open your eyes. Say *second.*

TRACK 23

Unit 2, Global Citizenship

D Now listen to Salma and Markus. Which clock is older?

Salma: About 4,000 years ago, the Egyptians used the sun to tell the time. Last week, I made a similar sun clock in my yard. It's called a sundial. First, you have to find a sunny place. Put a stick in the ground. Every hour, see where the shadow of the stick is pointing. Put a stone there. It took me a few days to complete the clock with 12 stones, one for 7 o'clock in the morning, then 8 o'clock, 9 o'clock, all the way to 7 o'clock in the evening. Time goes very slowly when you are watching the time!
Markus: I'm from Germany, where cuckoo clocks come from. People started making them almost 300 years ago. It doesn't look like a clock. It looks like a little house with windows and a door, and detailed trees and leaves on the front. There is a small toy cuckoo inside—cuckoos are birds—and there are also little toy people in the house. At 1 o'clock, 2 o'clock, and all through the day, the cuckoo comes out and sings the correct number of times, "Cuckoo!" or "Cuckoo, cuckoo!" Then the people come out and dance. The cuckoo and the people will be here again in ten minutes at 3 o'clock. Ten minutes feels like a really long time to wait!

TRACK 24

Unit 2, Explore Language

A Listen and read. When are the children going to start their project?

Amelia: We have to find time to do our science project. What are you doing on Saturday?
Ben: I'm playing soccer in the morning.
Amelia: My parents are taking us to the circus in the afternoon.
Muna: Let's do it at lunchtime on Saturday.
Ben: I don't know. How long is it going to take?
Mr. Sim: You aren't doing anything in the rest of this lesson. Start it now and finish it on Saturday.
Muna: Yes, Mr. Sim.
Ben: What's our project about?
Amelia: How to use time in the best way!

TRACK 25

Unit 2, Explore Language

D Listen and say.

1 What are you doing on Saturday?
2 I'm having lunch with my cousin.
3 Are you running in the marathon next weekend?
4 No, I'm not, but my dad's running in it.

TRACK 26

Unit 2, Take the Stage

Pronunciation. Listen and say.

Word Stress 1
something important homework
remember

Unit 3

TRACK 27

Unit 3, Vocabulary

A Listen and find. Did Dani have a good day?

Frank: Hi, Dani! What's wrong? You look stressed.
Dani: Hi Frank! I don't want to be late for class! Sorry I'm late, Mr. Sim … Oh, no.
Mr. Sim: Pick up your things, Dani, and please sit down.
Dani: I'm so embarrassed.
Hana: Aren't you hungry today, Dani?
Dani: I dropped my lunchbox, and it's under Mr. Sim's table.
Hana: So that's why you look so upset! Here, have one of my sandwiches.
Dani: Oh, thank you, Hana! That's so kind of you. I'm very grateful. Do you want to play soccer, Frank?
Frank: Sorry, I'm going to play a video game.
Hana: Hey, Dani! You look lonely. Come and sit with me and Amit! I'm really nervous about the science test in the next class, but you seem very relaxed, Dani!
Dani: Yes, I am. I like science. I'll help you, Hana.
Hana: I feel calm now, Dani!
Mr. Sim: Here are your test scores. Dani, you got 20 out of 20! Well done!
Mom: Hello, Dani! How was school?
Dani: Oh … it was fine!

TRACK 28

Unit 3, Vocabulary

B Listen, say, and number the pictures in A.

1 proud
2 nervous
3 lonely
4 upset
5 calm
6 relaxed
7 embarrassed
8 stressed
9 confident
10 grateful

TRACK 29

Unit 3, Vocabulary

C Close your eyes. Listen, visualize, and say.

Proud. Think about the last time you felt proud of yourself. What made you feel proud? Say *proud*.
Nervous. You're going to travel alone tomorrow. Are you nervous? Say *nervous*.
Lonely. All your friends are busy and there's nobody to talk to. What do you do? Say *lonely*.
Upset. Your friend was not kind to you. What do you say to your friend? Say *upset*.
Calm. You are alone in a dark house. You hear a noise. Try to stay calm. Say *calm*.
Relaxed. You are sitting in the sun, feeling relaxed. What are you thinking about? Say *relaxed*.
Embarrassed. Think about the last time you felt embarrassed about something. What happened? Say *embarrassed*.
Stressed. Imagine you are very stressed. What does it feel like? Say *stressed*.
Confident. You studied hard for the test. Do you feel confident? Say *confident*.
Grateful. You feel grateful. Why? What are you grateful for? Say *grateful*.

TRACK 30

Unit 3, Vocabulary

E Listen and complete. Then watch and sing.

You'll Be Fine

Do you ever feel nervous before a test?
Do you feel so tired that you just want
to rest?
Do you feel confident, relaxed, or stressed?
Or are you just grateful that you do
your best?

Just take one day at a time.
Stay calm, and you'll be fine.

What do you get embarrassed about?
What do you do that makes you feel proud?
When something goes wrong, do you
get mad?
Are you upset or angry or just very sad?

TRACK 31

Unit 3, Explore Language

A Listen and read. How does Lizzie feel about her trip?

Hana: Are you nervous about your trip to New York?
Lizzie: No, not at all! I'm excited, Hana.
Hana: Don't forget a map! If you don't know where you're going, you'll get lost. Then you'll be upset.
Lizzie: Don't worry. If I get lost, I'll stay calm. People will help me if I ask for directions.
Hana: You'll be lonely there.
Lizzie: Well, if I'm lonely, I'll call you. If you don't answer, then I'll be upset!

TRACK 32

Unit 3, Explore Language

D Listen and say.

1 If I get lost, I'll stay calm.
2 The teacher will be stressed if we're late for class.
3 I'll be upset if you forget my party.
4 If the children talk to the new student, he won't be lonely.

TRACK 33

Unit 3, Global Citizenship

A Listen to Paula talk to her mom about friendship. Who's Kari?

Paula: I'm meeting a lot of new people here, but I don't want to forget my best friends from my old school.
Mom: Well, I have a friend who lives in another country—we still email each other every month.
Paula: Oh! How did you meet her?
Mom: Kari was a new girl at our school. She looked lonely, so I decided to make friends with her. I sat next to her and we started to talk. We immediately got along well, and we became really good friends after that. Of course, we sometimes didn't get along—usually about silly things—but we were never angry for long. One of us always said, "Sorry!" But one time, we didn't speak to each other for about two weeks!
Paula: Why did you have a falling out?
Mom: I told her a secret. I said, "Kari, promise me you won't tell anybody else. I got a zero on my English writing test." Kari said, "Don't worry, I promise I won't tell anyone." But the next day, she told her brother when he did badly on an English test …
Paula: That's not good. A good friend never breaks a promise.
Mom: That's true. But remember, good friends also forgive each other.

TRACK 34

Unit 3, Global Citizenship

B Listen, say, and number the pictures in A.

1 forgive
2 make a promise
3 laugh at
4 make friends with
5 break a promise
6 get along well with (British English: get on well with)
7 have a falling out with (British English: fall out with)
8 keep in touch with
9 tell a secret

TRACK C

Unit 3, Global Citizenship

Close your eyes. Listen, visualize, and say.

Forgive. You lost your friend's favorite book. Your friend isn't angry and says, "I forgive you." How do you feel? Say *forgive*.
Make a promise. Your friend is moving to another city. Make a promise to write to your friend every week. Say *make a promise*.
Laugh at. Imagine people are laughing at you. How do you feel? Say *laugh at*.
Make friends with. There's a new student in class. Smile and say hello. Say *make friends with*.
Break a promise. Your friend breaks a promise to you. Are you upset, annoyed, or angry? Say *break a promise*.
Get along well with. Think about your friends. What kinds of things do you do or talk about together? Say *get along well with*.
Have a falling out with. You feel sad because you had a falling out with your friend. You want to be friends again. What do you say? Say *have a falling out with*.
Keep in touch with. Your best friend moves to another country. How do you keep in touch? Say *keep in touch with*.
Tell a secret. Mime telling a secret. Do you speak loudly or quietly? Say *tell a secret*.

TRACK 35

Unit 3, Global Citizenship

D Now listen to Carla and Sem. Where did they meet their friends?

Carla: Paula, Maria, and I met on our first day at school, when I was five. We started chatting and found out that we all liked the same things! We became best friends, and we were always together. But then Paula's dad got a new job in another city and her family went to live there. I miss her a lot, but luckily I've still got Maria. We love talking to Paula online. We send each other photos and videos, too. We live far from each other now, but I think we'll always be friends and keep in touch with each other.

Sem: I left my home country, Namibia, when I was six, and I came to the US. I was really nervous about speaking English because my English wasn't good. I thought, If I make mistakes, everybody will laugh at me and make fun of me. But I wasn't lonely because my classmates were very friendly. I soon made lots of friends. They helped me learn the language. They also helped me learn about their country and the way people do things here. This country is my home now. One day, if you have to leave your country and live here, I'll help you make it your home, too.

TRACK 36

Unit 3, Explore Language

A Listen and read. Does Amit tell Lizzie's secret?

Dani: Hey, Amit, it says here, "Best friends tell each other everything." Do you think that's true?

Amit: I don't know … hmm! Maybe? … If it is true, I'll tell *you* a secret.

Dani: OK.

Amit: Yesterday, Lizzie told me …

Dani: Wait, Amit. You can't tell me Lizzie's secret. How will Lizzie feel if you break a promise?

Amit: Angry, I guess.

Dani: Right! And if Lizzie is angry, how will you feel?

Amit: Oh … upset! Really upset!

Dani: So, if someone tells you a secret, what will you do?

Amit: I won't tell anyone. Not even my best friend! But I can tell you *my* secrets.

TRACK 37

Unit 3, Explore Language

D Listen and say.

1 How will Lizzie feel if you break your promise?
2 If it rains tomorrow, will we still have a picnic?
3 How will I know if your train is late?
4 What will your teacher do if you are late for school?

TRACK 38

Unit 3, Take the Stage

Pronunciation. Listen and say.

Silent *l*

half walk talks

Unit 4

TRACK 39

Unit 4, Vocabulary

A Listen and find. What does Amit want to be?

Alfie: Look at all the stars, Diana! I wonder how many there are.

Diana: Ask Amit's uncle. He's an astronomer. He works in the observatory, that building with the round top. Amit's there now. They're looking at the sky through a telescope. It makes things that are far away look much closer! I wonder what Amit and his uncle can see …

Amit: One day I want to be an astronomer like you, Uncle, and study the stars. Look how many there are.

Uncle: That's the Milky Way, Amit.

Amit: And what's that?

Uncle: It's a galaxy. A galaxy is a group of many, many stars. Like the sun—that's a star. In every galaxy, there are solar systems. Our solar system is part of the galaxy called the Milky Way. It has eight planets, including the Earth.

Amit: What else is in our galaxy?

Uncle: Apart from the sun, there are more than 200 billion stars.

Amit: Two hundred billion! … Oh, I can see a spaceship flying up there!

Uncle: It's carrying astronauts. They're traveling to the space station, to do experiments in space.

Amit: Wow! That's what I want to be.

TRACK 40

Unit 4, Vocabulary

B Listen, say, and number the pictures in A.

1 astronaut
2 telescope
3 observatory
4 comet
5 shooting star
6 planet
7 spaceship
8 astronomer
9 galaxy
10 solar system

TRACK 41

Unit 4, Vocabulary

C Close your eyes. Listen, visualize, and say.

Astronaut. You're an astronaut. Act out walking on the Moon. Say *astronaut*.
Telescope. Mime looking at space through a telescope. What can you see? Say *telescope*.
Observatory. Imagine an observatory. What shape is it? Say *observatory*.
Comet. Imagine a comet in the night sky. What can you see? Say *comet*.
Shooting star. Imagine you are a shooting star. Mime moving through the sky. Say *shooting star*.
Planet. You see a planet. Mime the shape of a planet. Say *planet*.
Spaceship. You are in a spaceship. Mime moving around. Say *spaceship*.
Astronomer. You are an astronomer. Mime studying the stars. Say *astronomer*.
Galaxy. Imagine you are a star in a galaxy. How does it feel up in the sky? Say *galaxy*.
Solar system. You are the sun in our solar system. How do you feel? Say *solar system*.

TRACK 42

Unit 4, Vocabulary

E Listen and complete. Then watch and sing.

The Astronomer's Song

I live on Earth, and look into space
At the planets in our galaxy
My feet on the ground, and my head in the clouds
Working in the observatory

Looking through my telescope
When the stars in the sky shine bright
Hoping to see a shooting star
Or a comet in the night.

A spaceship travels way up high
An astronaut inside.
He's on his way to the space station
Leaving Earth behind.

TRACK 43

Unit 4, Explore Language

A Listen and read. Why does Alfie want to go to the gym?

Diana: Do astronauts have to learn another language? I'm not very good at languages …

Astronaut: You mustn't give up! You will get better! To work at the International Space Station, an astronaut has to speak Russian.

Alfie: I have a question. Do you have to be very fit?

Astronaut: Yes, you do. You don't have to be good at sport—just fit and strong. Any more questions?

Alfie: No, thank you—I must go to the gym and start getting fit.

TRACK 44

Unit 4, Explore Language

D Listen and say.

1 An astronaut has to speak Russian.
2 Sam doesn't have to finish his project today.
3 I must remember to take my library book back.
4 You mustn't be late for school.

TRACK 45

Unit 4, Global Citizenship

A Listen to an astronaut talk about Mars. What do people call this planet?

Now I'd like to talk to you about the planet Mars. It's called the Red Planet, and that's because the soil on Mars has a lot of iron in it. That iron makes the soil look red. Here are some pictures of Mars. You see, there are mountains and sand dunes, just like our planet, Earth. Sand dunes are these hills made only of sand. And this is a photo of an ice cap. Ice caps are mountains made of ice. Now, do you know who took these pictures? Well, scientists sent satellites up into space to take them. They also sent robots to Mars to help them do experiments and study the soil there. They found out that long ago, there was water on Mars. Today, that water is ice. This means that the climate changed completely. If we study Mars, perhaps we will learn how to stop climate change on Earth. And that's something we have to do.

TRACK 46

Unit 4, Global Citizenship

B Listen, say, and number the pictures in A.

1 Mars
2 Earth
3 ice cap
4 crater
5 iron
6 rock
7 sand dune
8 satellite
9 soil

TRACK D

Unit 4, Global Citizenship

Close your eyes. Listen, visualize, and say.

Mars. Mime walking on Mars. What color is the ground? Say *Mars*.
Earth. You are in space, looking at Earth. What can you see? Say *Earth*.
Ice cap. Imagine you are on an ice cap. How does it feel? Say *ice cap*.
Crater. Imagine you're standing in a crater. Is the ground higher or lower around you? Say *crater*.
Iron. You're holding a big, old iron key. How does it feel? Say *iron*.
Rock. You are standing on a rock in the sea. What can you see around you? Say *rock*.
Sand dune. Mime walking up a sand dune. Is it difficult? Say *sand dune*.
Satellite. Look up at a satellite in the sky. What can you see? Say *satellite*.
Soil. You're planting a flower. Dig your fingers in the soil. Is it dry or wet? Say *soil*.

TRACK 47

Unit 4, Global Citizenship

D Now listen to Max and Lily. Do they talk about plants, experiments, or machines?

Max: In September 2015, an astronaut took 2 kg. of seeds to the International Space Station. Six months later, he brought them back to Earth to do an experiment. Our school got two packets of seeds—a red packet and a blue packet. Only one packet came from space—we didn't know which one. We planted all the seeds in the same soil, and after five weeks, they were the same height. Later we found out that the red packet came from space, but it didn't make a difference to the seeds! This means that one day, perhaps astronauts can grow food in space.
Lily: I always thought astronauts went into space because they wanted to float around a spaceship! But my week at space camp taught me how important experiments in space are and how they can help us on Earth. Some astronauts came to talk to us, and one talked about different space experiments. For example, he said that in the 1960s scientists started inventing a special machine so that astronauts always had clean water to drink. Today we use similar machines in factories and even in our homes. It's just one of the many ways that space exploration helps us in our everyday lives.

TRACK 48

Unit 4, Explore Language

A Listen and read. What do the children want to use the mirror for?

Freya: Let's use this old mirror, Alfie. It looks like a window.
Alfie: I'm not sure. It might be too heavy. Oh, no, Freya! It was too heavy.
Freya: We should clean up the glass. We shouldn't leave it here.
Alfie: I know! Let's make a door.
Freya: Hmm. It might not be wide enough.
Alfie: You're right. It isn't wide enough.
Freya: You look so funny! Oh, no, it's starting to rain.
Alfie: I think I might just stay in here!

TRACK 49

Unit 4, Explore language

D Listen and say.

1 It might be too heavy.
2 I might not stay up late tonight.
3 You should clean your room.
4 We shouldn't wait to start our homework.

TRACK 50

Unit 4, Talk About It

Pronunciation. Listen and say.

Word Stress 2
interesting different listening

Unit 5

TRACK 51

Unit 5, Vocabulary

A Listen and find. When did the Vikings arrive in England?

Freya: The Vikings came from the countries we now call Denmark, Norway, and Sweden. In around 700 AD, they built and sailed boats to lots of places, such as England and Ireland, and went to live there.
Oliver: Where are we, Freya? I can see houses and crops growing in the fields ...
Freya: We're in a Viking village! We have to look like Vikings. Here, Oliver, hold this in your hand.
Oliver: It's a very long knife, and it's heavy.
Freya: It's a Viking sword. Hold this shield in front of you. If people fight with you, their swords won't hurt you. Put this helmet on your head. Now you look like a real Viking warrior!
Oliver: But I don't want to fight! What's in that big building?
Freya: That's a house, Oliver. Everyone lives in one room. Mmm, someone's cooking a stew for dinner. It smells good.
Oliver: We're all going to sleep in one room? I don't think I like it here, Freya. Let's take one of their boats and sail back to the 21st century!
Freya: What an exciting dream! I want to find out more about the Vikings now.

TRACK 52

Unit 5, Vocabulary

B Listen, say, and number the pictures in A.

1 crops
2 stew
3 hunt
4 village
5 weave
6 warrior
7 fight
8 helmet
9 sword
10 shield

TRACK 53

Unit 5, Vocabulary

C Close your eyes. Listen, visualize, and say.

Crops. You're standing in a field of crops. What colors can you see? Say *crops*.
Stew. Make a stew. What does it smell and taste like? Say *stew*.
Hunt. A lion is hunting a deer. How does it hunt? Say *hunt*.
Village. You live in a village. Are there any stores? Say *village*.
Weave. Mime weaving a carpet. What color is it? Say *weave*.
Warrior. You are a Viking warrior. What clothes are you wearing? Say *warrior*.
Fight. Imagine a tiger fighting a bear. Who wins? Say *fight*.
Helmet. Imagine you are wearing an iron helmet. How does it feel? Say *helmet*.
Sword. Mime holding a sword. Is it heavy? Say *sword*.
Shield. Design your own shield. What pictures or words are on it? Say *shield*.

TRACK 54

Unit 5, Vocabulary

E Listen and choose. Then watch and sing.

The Viking Life

Take some wool,
Weave a shirt,
Make some pants,
Or a skirt.

Oh! Life is so exciting!
When you live like a Viking!

Grow some crops,
Milk a cow,
Hunt some animals,
We'll show you how.

Hold a sword,
And a shield.
Be a warrior,
Fight in the field.

TRACK 55

Unit 5, Explore Language

A Listen and read. What did Viking children do in their free time?

Freya: Halima, this Living Museum is awesome! Did you know Vikings used to weave their own clothes from wool?

Halima: Wow! It was a hard life. The children used to work, too! How terrible!

Freya: Yes. But look, in their free time they used to swim, go ice-skating, and play ball games.

Halima: Just like us, Freya!

Freya: There was just one difference. It says here, Viking children didn't use to go to school.

Halima: Really? Then perhaps it wasn't so terrible after all!

TRACK 56

Unit 5, Explore Language

D Listen and say.

1 The children used to work, too!
2 People didn't use to have TV.
3 I didn't use to like vegetables.
4 My grandmother used to have long, fair hair.

TRACK 57

Unit 5, Global Citizenship

A Listen to Becky talk to her mom. Name three things the Vikings traded for spices, silk, and pottery.

Becky: That's a lovely scarf, Mom. Is it made of silk?

Mom: Yes, it is. It's from Turkey.

Becky: Ah! Silk is something the Vikings brought back with them from Turkey. They used to travel there to find new places to trade and farm. They brought lots of things back to Europe, like pottery and spices to cook with.

Mom: You know a lot about the Vikings, Becky.

Becky: Yes, we're studying the Vikings in History.

Mom: What kinds of things did they trade for the spices, silk, and pottery?

Becky: They traded wood. Many Vikings lived near forests, so they cut down trees to trade. They also sold wool from their sheep and fur from the animals they hunted. Oh, and the leather from the animals' skins. They had a lot of fish and honey to sell, too. They paid with big, heavy coins. They put the coins on a scale to make sure they got the right price.

Mom: Isn't that interesting? Today we have so many different ways to trade, but one thing is still the same. We buy and sell things just like people did so many years ago.

TRACK 58

Unit 5, Global Citizenship

B Listen, say, and number the pictures in A.

1 fur
2 silk
3 spices
4 wheat
5 pottery
6 wood
7 leather
8 necklace
9 jewelry
10 coins
11 honey

TRACK E

Unit 5, Global Citizenship

Close your eyes. Listen, visualize, and say.

Fur. Touch the fur of a puppy. How does it feel? Say *fur.*

Silk. You are wearing a silk scarf. Touch it. Say *silk.*

Spices. Add some spices to your food. What can you smell? Say *spices.*

Wheat. Grow some wheat. What color is it? Say *wheat.*

Pottery. Mime making pottery. How does it feel? Say *pottery.*

Wood. Mime cutting down a tree. What does the wood smell like? Say *wood.*

Leather. You've got a leather bag. How does it feel? Say *leather.*

Necklace. You buy a silver necklace. Who is it for? Say *necklace.*

Jewelry. You have a box full of jewelry. What colors do you see? Say *jewelry.*

Coins. You have three coins in your hand. How do they feel? Say *coins.*

Honey. You have a jar of honey. Smell it. Say *honey.*

TRACK 59

Unit 5, Global Citizenship

D Now listen to Ari and Jing. How did the two groups of people travel?

Ari: Here in New Zealand, we don't have any Viking history—they didn't travel this far. Our explorers and traders were the Maori people. The Maoris were very good at building canoes. For about a thousand years, before they sailed to New Zealand, they explored many of the islands in the Pacific Ocean. The sun and the stars helped them find their way as they paddled their canoes. As they were sailing, they studied the movements of birds and whales and figured out where land was. It's amazing to learn about the skills that these groups of explorers had, so many centuries ago.

Jing: Did you know that people were using paper money before the 1st century? Chinese explorers around 618 BC started using paper money to trade with because they found coins too heavy to carry on their travels. Around that time, Chinese explorers were sailing across the seas to Egypt and Syria, where they traded their beautiful Chinese pottery for glass, carpets, and plants. They often traveled on huge ships called junks, which could carry up to 700 passengers at a time, along with leather and silk to trade, too. In fact, some of these ships were so big that they couldn't sail too close to the land. Instead, traders and passengers jumped into small boats to get there.

TRACK 60

Unit 5, Explore Language

A Listen and read. Why is Freya glad that she wasn't a Viking?

Halima: How did people use to travel in Viking times?

Jennifer: They used to build long, thin ships so that they could sail up narrow rivers. Some longships could carry about 120 Vikings.

Halima: Did they use to sleep on the ships?

Jennifer: Yes, they did. They made sleeping bags out of sealskins.

Freya: What did they use to eat?

Jennifer: They couldn't carry fresh food with them, so they used to dry fish, and that lasted for a long time.

Halima: Dried fish—every day!

Freya: I'm glad I wasn't a Viking.

TRACK 61

Unit 5, Explore Language

D Listen and say.

1 What did they use to eat? Dried fish.
2 Did you and your brother use to fight? No, we didn't.
3 Did you use to ride a bike to school? Yes, I did.
4 What kinds of books did you use to read? Adventure books.

TRACK 62

Unit 5, Talk About It

Pronunciation. Listen and say.

/s/ see
/z/ cards
/s/ see soccer interested
/z/ cards these easy

Unit 6

TRACK 63

Unit 6, Vocabulary

A Listen and find. What was David looking for in the tree?

Dee: On today's show, David is with a team on a desert island! Can they survive there for a week? Let's talk to their leader, Jennifer.

Jennifer: Hello Dee. Well, Alex and Naima are going to sleep in a tent. They're just putting it up now. Ethan's going to sleep in a hammock. He's hanging it between two trees. Ned and Patrick are building a shelter out of wood and leaves.

Dee: And where's David?

Jennifer: He's over there. He went to look for some fruit. Hmm. I can see monkeys in that tree …

Alex: Yes, but David's very brave. He isn't scared of monkeys.

Jennifer: Then why is he crawling along the ground, Alex?

Alex: Oh no. Jennifer, look! The monkeys are throwing mangoes at him!

Ethan: Poor David! He wanted to help us find some mangoes for lunch. But it looks like the monkeys found them first!

TRACK 64

Unit 6, Vocabulary

B Listen, say, and number the pictures in A.

1 crawl
2 swing
3 dive
4 put up
5 tent
6 build
7 survive
8 hammock
9 rope
10 shelter

TRACK 65

Unit 6, Vocabulary

C Close your eyes. Listen, visualize, and say.

Crawl. Imagine crawling along the floor. How does it feel? Say *crawl*.
Swing. You're swinging from a tree. How high are you? Say *swing*.
Dive. Imagine diving into a pool of water. How does the water feel? Say *dive*.
Put up. Mime putting up a hammock. Is it difficult? Say *put up*.
Tent. Imagine sleeping in a tent. What can you hear? Say *tent*.
Build. Imagine building a house. What does it look like? Say *build*.
Survive. Imagine you have to survive in the desert for a week. What will you eat and drink? Say *survive*.
Hammock. You're sleeping in a hammock. Can you feel the sun on your face? Say *hammock*.
Rope. Mime pulling a long rope. What's at the end of the rope? Say *rope*.
Shelter. Imagine finding a shelter in the forest. What is it made of? Say *shelter*.

TRACK 66

Unit 6, Vocabulary

E Listen and complete. Then watch and sing.

Desert Island Fun

We can survive on a desert island.
It will be such fun!
We can put up a hammock
Between two trees.
Or a tent in the sun.

We can find some wood and build a boat.
We can dive into the sea.
If we're lucky, we will catch some fish.
Oh, how happy we will be!

We can swing on a rope,
kick a coconut
Down from the highest tree.
We can pick up leaves, and sticks and stones,
Build a shelter for you and me.

TRACK 67

Unit 6, Explore Language

A Listen and read. What do the children want to cook for dinner?

David: It's going to be fun sleeping outside tonight! Have you ever slept under the stars?
Alex: No, I haven't.
Naima: Yes, I have. And Ethan has, too!
David: Has he ever put up a hammock?
Alex: No, he hasn't. I hope he's put it up well!
David: What are you kids going to cook for dinner?
Naima: Well, Lara and Jim are fishing right now ...
David: And have Lara and Jim ever caught a fish?
Naima: No, they haven't, but I hope they've caught one for dinner tonight!

TRACK 68

Unit 6, Explore Language

D Listen and say.

1 Have you ever slept under the stars? Yes, I have.
2 Have you and your friends ever put up a tent? No, we haven't.
3 Has your father ever run a race? Yes, he has.
4 Has Lena ever eaten insects? No, she hasn't.

TRACK 69

Unit 6, Global Citizenship

A Listen to Ryan and his friend Josh talk about camping equipment. What are they going to bring home?

Ryan: You're going to love the camp, Josh. I'm really excited about going again. Do you want help with your packing?
Josh: Oh thanks, Ryan.
Ryan: I'll carry the tent. It's going to be cold at night. Have you packed a warm sleeping bag? You'll need it.
Josh: Yes, I have. What else should we take?
Ryan: A flashlight will be useful to see in the dark. And bug spray will help to keep away mosquitoes and other insects. We'll need matches to start a fire. Oh, and a fishing rod to catch fish for dinner!
Mom: Don't forget sunscreen. It can be very sunny, even in the forest. And if you get lost, a compass will help you find your way. Oh, and rope to make a clothesline.
Ryan: We aren't going to do any laundry at camp.
Josh: Yeah, we're going to bring our dirty clothes home to wash!

TRACK 70

Unit 6, Global Citizenship

B Listen, say, and number the pictures in A.

1 flashlight (British English: torch)
2 binoculars
3 first aid kit
4 sunscreen (British English: sun cream)
5 mosquito net
6 bug spray (British English: insect repellent)
7 matches
8 fishing rod
9 sleeping bag
10 compass

TRACK F

Unit 6, Global Citizenship

Close your eyes. Listen, visualize, and say.

Flashlight. Imagine it's dark. Turn on your flashlight. What can you see? Say *flashlight*.
Binoculars. Mime looking through some binoculars. What can you see? Say *binoculars*.
First aid kit. You've cut your finger. Open your first aid kit. Say *first aid kit*.
Sunscreen. Put sunscreen on your skin. How does it feel? Say *sunscreen*.
Mosquito net. Imagine you're in bed with a mosquito net over it. Can you hear buzzing? Say *mosquito net*.
Bug spray. There are mosquitoes flying around. Put bug spray on your arms. Say *bug spray*.
Matches. You're making a fire. Light it with a match. Say *matches*.
Fishing rod. You are fishing. Mime holding your fishing rod. What have you caught? Say *fishing rod*.
Sleeping bag. Imagine you're in bed in a sleeping bag. How do you feel? Say *sleeping bag*.
Compass. You are lost. Use a compass to find your way. Say *compass*.

TRACK 71

Unit 6, Global Citizenship

D Now listen to Ryan and Hailey. Which object did they both learn to live without on their trips?

Ryan: The last time I went to an adventure camp, our class learned a lot about the outdoors and also about working together as a team. It was called Survive in the Wild. Putting up a tent is easier with someone else! It's also quicker if you divide tasks. While some of us collected wood for the fire, the others got the food ready to cook. We learned how to make a fire without matches. We also learned how to find water under the ground and which plants and berries were safe to eat. I really enjoyed being outdoors—I didn't even miss my cell phone!
Hailey: Last summer I spent a day in the country with my family and our friends. Everyone got a map with different places marked on it. Our task was to work as a team to find our way to all the places. Together, we figured out the quickest and easiest way. We crawled through long grass and helped each other climb over rocks. Now, I know how to read a map and use a compass. People usually use their phones to get directions. But a phone can't always help you if you get lost on a mountain.

TRACK 72

Unit 6, Explore Language

A Listen and read. Is David's pet dangerous?

David: Thank you for inviting me on your program, Dee! Don't worry about my pet snake. It's traveled everywhere with me, and it hasn't bitten anyone!
Dee: Umm ... Right.
David: I've traveled to a lot of dangerous places, you know. But I haven't traveled to the North Pole—that's my next trip!

Dee: Yes … How have you survived with huge wild animals around?
David: I'm not afraid of them. I've learned that if you're confident, everything will be fine. Aaaahhh! There's a mouse crawling across the floor!
Dee: But you aren't afraid of huge animals …
David: No, but I've always been terrified of tiny ones!

TRACK 73
Unit 6, Explore Language
D Listen and say.
1 I've traveled to a lot of dangerous places.
2 We haven't visited China.
3 He hasn't swum in the sea.
4 They've built a boat.

TRACK 74
Unit 6, Talk About It
Pronunciation. Listen and say.
ph as **/f/**
Sophie photo elephants

Unit 7

TRACK 75
Unit 7, Vocabulary
A Listen and find. Where does all the water we don't drink go back to?
David: Oh, no! It's raining … again! Why does it have to rain?
Julio: Ooh, I know, Dad! It rains because the water in our lakes and rivers slowly goes into the air and makes it wet. That then becomes rain … I think?
Ruby: That's right, Julio.
David: Well, I still hate rain. I think it should never rain!
Ruby: But, David, we're really lucky it rains! Rain gives us water.
Julio: Huh? Mom, this water in my glass, is … rain?
Ruby: That's right! When it rains, we can collect the water in big, special lakes called reservoirs or in deep holes in the ground called wells. That water then flows through pipes in the ground that go …
Julio: Here, to our house?
Ruby: Not yet! First it goes to a water plant so we can clean the water. Then it flows back through pipes into our homes.
Julio: And then what happens to the water we don't drink, when we take a shower or flush the toilet?
Ruby: Well, that water flows into a drain outside the house, to another water plant. We clean the water again and it flows back into the rivers.
Julio: Oh, I see! Ready to start all over again!
Ruby: That's right.
Julio: Wow! Rain is awesome!
David: You know, Julio, Ruby—you're right! I'll never complain about the rain again!
Ruby and Julio: Me neither!

TRACK 76
Unit 7, Vocabulary
B Listen, say, and number the pictures in A.
1 pipe
2 well
3 pond
4 water plant
5 reservoir
6 drain
7 faucet (British English: tap)
8 flush
9 flow

TRACK 77
Unit 7, Vocabulary
C Close your eyes. Listen, visualize, and say.
Pipe. Put your ear next to a water pipe. Can you hear anything? Say *pipe*.
Well. Look into a well. What does it look like in there? Say *well*.
Pond. You're standing by a pond. What's in it? Say *pond*.
Water plant. You are at a water plant. Is it a big place? Say *water plant*.
Reservoir. Imagine a reservoir. What's in it? Say *reservoir*.
Drain. Imagine a drain. Where is it? Say *drain*.
Faucet. Turn on the faucet. What happens? Say *faucet*.
Flush. Mime flushing the toilet. What sound does it make? Say *flush*.
Flow. Watch a river flowing. What does it sound like? Say *flow*.

TRACK 78
Unit 7, Vocabulary
E Listen and complete. Then watch and sing.
Where Does the Water Go?

Listen to the sound of the falling rain
As into the river it flows.
Into the river, the lake, and pond
And into the ground it goes.

Where does the water go?
If you turn on the faucet, water will flow!
It will flow, flow down the drain
On the way to the river again.

Along the pipes to the water plant
Where they make it safe and clean.
Next time you drink a glass of water,
Think about where it's been!

TRACK 79
Unit 7, Explore Language
A Listen and read. What does Julio choose to do in the end?
Broadcaster: Remember! Saving water is important. Washing fruit is necessary, of course, but don't leave the faucet on! It wastes water. Saving water while you brush your teeth is also a good idea. So turn off the faucet! Think before having a bath. Bathing is relaxing, but taking a shower uses less water.
Julio: I think I'll just watch TV instead. Watching TV doesn't use *any* water!

TRACK 80
Unit 7, Explore Language
D Listen and say.
1 Saving water is important.
2 Drinking water is good for you.
3 Reading comics is fun.
4 Playing basketball is my favorite activity.

TRACK 81
Unit 7, Global Citizenship
A Listen to Tarek talk to his uncle about the Aswan High Dam. When did building start on the dam?
Tarek: Uncle Ziad, I have to find out about the Aswan High Dam for my homework. My teacher says some people think building it was good, and some people think it was bad. Do you know anything about it?
Uncle: I know a little … let me think … so, I know that it's the biggest and the most important dam in Egypt. I think building started in about 1960? Yes, that's right, and then it took ten years to finish. And I know it was good for farmers, like me. You see, before we had the dam, the Nile used to flood every year. There was too much water in the river, and it used to pour over the riverbanks and destroy the crops. Now, the dam stops the water in a reservoir. They use it to make electricity, and, I remember, they built canals to carry the water to different areas. So, we can use the water in the reservoir to irrigate our crops, helping them grow. That means we can grow them even in a drought, when there's no rain.
Tarek: Great! So, what about the bad things?
Uncle: Well … many people lost their homes when they built the reservoir and … wait a minute. Tarek, did you say this is your homework?
Tarek: Yes …
Uncle: Hmm … How about you look up the rest? Then you can tell me all about it.
Tarek: OK, Uncle.

TRACK 82
Unit 7, Global Citizenship
B Listen, say, and number the pictures in A.
1 flood
2 dam
3 banks
4 canal
5 drought
6 irrigate
7 bucket
8 hose (British English: hosepipe)

TRACK G
Unit 7, Global Citizenship
Close your eyes. Listen, visualize, and say.
Flood. Imagine a flood in your street. How do you get to school? Say *flood*.
Dam. Think about a dam. What can you hear? Say *dam*.
Banks. Mime jumping from one bank of a river to the other. Don't fall in the river. Say *banks*.

Canal. Imagine a canal in a city. What can you see on the water, and on the banks? Say *canal*.
Drought. Imagine a drought. What does the ground look like? Say *drought*.
Irrigate. You are a farmer, irrigating your crops. Touch the soil. How does it feel? Say *irrigate*.
Bucket. Mime pouring water into a bucket. Carry it. How does it feel? Say *bucket*.
Hose. Mime using a hose in the garden. Is it fun? Say *hose*.

TRACK 83

Unit 7, Global Citizenship

D Now listen to Mesi and Tarek. Are the water inventions still in use today?

Mesi: In my geography lesson we're learning about a boy named William Kamkwamba. He's from Malawi, in Africa, like me. When William was 14, he saw a picture of a windmill in a book in the library, and it gave him an idea. He decided to design and build his own windmill for his village. He used it to make electricity and get water from the ground. He built the windmill out of wood, old metal, and car parts. It was a big success, and now many people in different countries use William's windmill to irrigate their crops.

Tarek: The River Nile is very important for Egyptians. We need its water for growing crops, for fishing, and for transportation, too. Long ago, Egyptian farmers thought of a clever way to bring the water up from the river to their lands. They built a *shaduf*. Some farmers still use it, but my uncle doesn't. He uses a modern electric machine. When he turns on the machine, water flows from the river to the fields. He uses the machine once a week in summer and every two weeks in winter. This way, we can grow crops to feed many people in Egypt, even in times of drought.

TRACK 84

Unit 7, Explore Language

A Listen and read. Does the man like living on a houseboat?

Julio: Look at that boat, Mom! It looks like a house.

Ruby: You're right, it does!

Julio: Excuse me, do you live here?

Man: Yes, I do. This canal is famous for houseboats.

Julio: Ooh! I want to live on a houseboat. It looks so fun! Do you like it?

Man: Yes. At first, it was difficult to move around in such a small space! But I'm good at it now.

Ruby: And you never get bored with life on the canal?

Man: No. There's always lots to see and do on the water, and when I get tired of living in one place, I can just move away!

Julio: Wow!

TRACK 85

Unit 7, Explore Language

D Listen and say.

1 This canal is famous for houseboats.
2 We're tired of waiting.
3 I'm not very good at playing chess.
4 Jaime is very proud of his mom.

TRACK 86

Unit 7, Take the Stage

Pronunciation. Listen and say.

/dʒ/ huge
/g/ garden
/dʒ/ huge large age
/g/ garden green grass

Unit 8

TRACK 87

Unit 8, Vocabulary

A Listen and find. Who's Willis Brice?

Ruby: Welcome to our studio tour! Today they're making an adventure movie right here in the studio!

Leo: Excuse me, Ruby. Is that Willis Brice, the famous movie star?

Ruby: Yes, Leo. In this movie he's going to be a sailor. The sailor is a really bad guy.

Sam: Look at that scar on the side of his head! What happened to him?

Ruby: It isn't a real scar, Sam. It's just make-up. He doesn't usually have a scar—or a mustache!

Sam: Who's that lady with the long eyelashes and the bright red lips?

Ruby: That's Cheryl Street.

Leo: But her hair is usually short and brown.

Ruby: Yes. That red hair isn't her real hair. She's wearing a wig!

Director: Hello, visitors, are you enjoying the tour? Oh, there you are, Willis. Your costume looks amazing. I love that scar, too. You look like a real bad guy. Come on, we're ready to film you now.

Man: But I'm not a bad guy. I'm not even an actor. My scar is real. I'm just here for the tour!

TRACK 88

Unit 8, Vocabulary

B Listen, say, and number the pictures in A.

1 beard
2 eyebrows
3 eyelashes
4 scar
5 lips
6 studio
7 wig
8 make-up
9 movie star (British English: film star)
10 director
11 mustache

TRACK 89

Unit 8, Vocabulary

C Close your eyes. Listen, visualize, and say.

Beard. Imagine you have a long beard. Touch it. How does it feel? Say *beard*.
Eyebrows. Touch your eyebrows. How do they feel? Say *eyebrows*.
Eyelashes. Touch your eyelashes. How do they feel? Say *eyelashes*.
Scar. Imagine you have a scar. Show where it is with your finger. Say *scar*.
Lips. Feel your lips. Draw around them with your finger. How do they feel? Say *lips*.
Studio. Imagine you are in a movie studio. What can you see? Say *studio*.
Wig. You are wearing a wig. What color is it? Say *wig*.
Make-up. Mime putting on make-up. Where are you putting it? Say *make-up*.
Movie star. You are a famous movie star. What kind of movies are you in? Say *movie star*.
Director. You are a director. Sit in your director's chair. Say *director*.
Mustache. Imagine you have a mustache. Touch it. How does it feel? Say *mustache*.

TRACK 90

Unit 8, Vocabulary

E Listen and complete. Then watch and sing.

Be a Movie Star

Be a movie star, on the movie screen.
Come to the studio, and see what I mean.
Meet the director. Try and get a part.
They're doing the make-up now. Are you ready to start?

What kind of movie will it be?
An adventure or a mystery?
What character will you play?
Can you really be someone else for a day?

Put on a beard, wear a wig
Paint your eyebrows really big.
Make your eyelashes curly and long.
Color them black or blue or blonde.

TRACK 91

Unit 8, Explore Language

A Listen and read. Who does Sam think the man in sunglasses is?

Sam: Do you see that man over there, Leo? He's going past the café where we had lunch. Isn't it Willis Brice?

Leo: What man? Where?

Sam: Over there! The man who's wearing sunglasses.

Leo: Oh, yeah! I think it is.

Sam: Come on! I've never talked to a famous movie star! Quick!

Leo: I don't think you're going to talk to one today either, Sam. Willis Brice is in the taxi that drove past!

TRACK 92

Unit 8, Explore Language

D Listen and say.

1 He's the man who's wearing sunglasses.
2 The woman that lives here is a famous actor.
3 This is the office where my dad works.
4 Japan is a country that I'd love to visit one day.

TRACK 93

Unit 8, Global Citizenship

A Listen to Meg and Eric talk about movies. Which movie have they both seen?

Eric: What shall we do now? Do you want to watch a DVD?

Meg: Sure. Which movie should we watch? What about *Frozen*?

Eric: Is it a documentary about Antarctica?

Meg: No, silly! It's an animation about a lonely girl named Elsa … It made me feel so sad.

Eric: I don't want to feel sad …

Meg: Well, this looks good, *We Bought a Zoo*. It's a drama about a family that wants to have a zoo and how difficult it is. It sounds interesting.

Eric: Yes, it does. Or what about this—*Mamma Mia!*? All my favorite songs are on that soundtrack.

Meg: Yes, that movie has some great music. But we've both seen *Mamma Mia!* How about a comedy, something really funny?

Eric: *Penguins of Madagascar* is a comedy. Let's watch the trailer. Then we'll know if it's really funny.

Meg: It sure is funny!

TRACK 94

Unit 8, Global Citizenship

B Listen, say, and number the pictures in A.

1 detective
2 trailer
3 soundtrack
4 comedy
5 horror
6 drama
7 animation
8 musical
9 documentary

TRACK H

Unit 8, Global Citizenship

Close your eyes. Listen, visualize, and say.

Detective. You're a detective in a movie. What are you wearing? Say *detective*.
Trailer. Watch a trailer of a new movie. What do you think the movie will be like? Say *trailer*.
Soundtrack. Listen to a soundtrack. What's your favorite song? Say *soundtrack*.
Comedy. You're watching a comedy. Are you laughing or do you feel sad? Say *comedy*.
Horror. You're watching a horror film. What sounds can you hear? Say *horror*.
Drama. You're watching a drama. What's happening? Say *drama*.
Animation. You're making an animation movie. Who are the characters? Say *animation*.
Musical. Watch a musical. Sing along to one of the songs. Say *musical*.
Documentary. You're going to make a documentary. What is it going to be about? Say *documentary*.

TRACK 95

Unit 8, Global Citizenship

D Now listen to Deepa and Eric. Who chooses the movies for the festival and for the school club?

Deepa: Every year, children in my city, Delhi, have the chance to take part in an unusual festival. The Chinh India Kids Film Festival only shows movies for or made by children. Anyone can see the movies, but only kids can choose the movies that they show at the festival. Last year I saw lots of different kinds of movies, but my favorite was a documentary that some children made. It was about the relationship between kids from the city and kids from the country. It's always interesting to see what other children think of important subjects like this. That's what I love most about this festival.

Eric: I'm from Brighton, in the UK, and last year, my school started a film club. Once a week after school, one of the classrooms becomes a cinema! To find films to watch, we read reviews on the internet. After watching a film, we always talk about our opinions. We say what we learned and ask and answer questions about it. When we get home, we write an online review. The film club has given me the chance to watch lots of different kinds of films. My favorites are dramas and animations because they make me think about the world in different ways.

TRACK 96

Unit 8, Explore Language

A Listen and read. Who was frightened during the movie *The Warrior in the Desert*?

Ray: Excuse me, Mr. Brice, can you sign this?

Brice: Of course! Ah! This is my warrior movie. We made this movie in the desert. The costume was very hot and tiring to wear.

Ray: Oh. But … was it exciting? Being a warrior in a movie?

Brice: No, it was boring actually. There was a lot of waiting around every day. I was very bored. And the desert at night was frightening. It was dark and there were snakes. So, do you want to be an actor, like me, when you're older?

Ray: Um … yes. But maybe not a desert warrior!

TRACK 97

Unit 8, Explore Language

D Listen and say.

1 I was really tired.
2 The food was disgusting.
3 I'm surprised to see you here!
4 I love exciting movies.

TRACK 98

Unit 8, Take the Stage

Pronunciation. Listen and say.

Schwa /ə/
again afraid adults

Unit 9

TRACK 99

Unit 9, Vocabulary

A Listen and find. When's the movie star going to arrive?

Brice: This is Willis Brice! I'm on my way to see your beautiful city! Is everything ready, Mayor Anika?

Anika: Hello, Mr. Brice … A special machine is just vacuuming the red carpet to get it nice and clean for you to walk on. There are machines cleaning the windows, too, so they will all be nice and shiny. I'm near the kitchen now. It's very busy in there. A machine is washing the dishes. Oops!

Brice: What happened?

Anika: Oh, a robot is emptying the dishwasher, and there was a very small accident. But it's all fine! The washing machines are doing the laundry—the staff has clean uniforms, and we have lovely clean white tablecloths for you.

Man: Hey! Be careful!

Brice: What was that?

Anika: It's a machine. It's sweeping the streets to get them clean. But it nearly swept someone away, too. But don't worry, it's all fine! …

Man: Wait, stop!

Brice: What's going on, Anika?

Anika: Oh, nothing to worry about, Mr. Brice! The machine mowing the lawn is working a bit too hard … but it's all …

Brice: I know! It's all fine! Well, I can't wait to see the results! I'll be there in an hour.

TRACK 100

Unit 9, Vocabulary

B Listen, say, and number the pictures in A.

1 do the laundry
2 wash the dishes (British English: do the washing up)
3 take out the trash (British English: take out the rubbish)
4 mow the lawn
5 empty the dishwasher
6 sweep the street
7 clean the windows
8 vacuum the carpet
9 iron the clothes

TRACK 101

Unit 9, Vocabulary

C Close your eyes. Listen, visualize, and say.

Do the laundry. Mime watching the washing machine doing the laundry. Are your clothes going around and around? Say *do the laundry*.
Wash the dishes. Imagine you are washing the dishes. How do your hands feel? Say *wash the dishes*.
Take out the trash. Mime carrying a bag of trash. Is it heavy? Say *take out the trash*.
Mow the lawn. Somebody is mowing the lawn outside. What does it smell like? Say *mow the lawn*.

Empty the dishwasher. Imagine emptying the dishwasher. What clean things are you taking out of the dishwasher? Say *empty the dishwasher.*
Sweep the street. Listen! Somebody is sweeping the street. What noise can you hear? Say *sweep the street.*
Clean the windows. Mime cleaning the windows. What can you see outside? Say *clean the windows.*
Vacuum the carpet. You're vacuuming a dirty carpet. What noise does the vacuum cleaner make? Say *vacuum the carpet.*
Iron the clothes. Mime ironing the clothes. Is the iron hot or cold? Say *iron the clothes.*

TRACK 102

Unit 9, Vocabulary
E Listen and complete. Then watch and sing.
Cleaning All Day Long

Sweep the streets and wash the floors.
Vacuum the carpet. Clean the windows and doors.
Wash the dishes. Mow the lawn, too.
Oh me, oh my, there's so much to do!

Cleaning, cleaning, all day long.
There isn't much time to sing this song!
It's tiring work. You know what I mean?
But the town looks nice when it's neat and clean!

Are the clothes all dry? Then iron them flat.
Take out the trash. Don't forget that!
Everything has to look clean and new.
Oh me, oh my, there's so much to do!

TRACK 103

Unit 9, Explore Language
A Listen and read. Who or what is Bingo?
Anika: What are you looking at, Bea?
Bea: My grandpa's invented a robot to get Willis Brice's hotel room ready. Have you ever heard of it? It's called Bingo. Look. Let's see what it's done.
Anika: Oh, no!
Bea: I've never seen a mess like this before!
Bingo: Hello! This is Bingo. I've already done the laundry, I've washed the dishes, and I've cleaned the windows.
Bea: And the yard …?
Bingo: Done! I've vacuumed the lawn already, and I've mowed the carpet, too.

TRACK 104

Unit 9, Explore Language
D Listen and say.
1 Have you ever heard of it?
2 I've already done my homework.
3 I've never stayed up all night.
4 I've visited England already, but I've never visited Ireland.

TRACK 105

Unit 9, Global Citizenship
A Listen to Madison talk to a friend about an interesting place in New York City. What was this place in the past?
Friend: The city is so noisy. Where can we go to relax?
Madison: I'll take you to the High Line! It's an old railroad, high above the streets. Imagine walking for miles through the middle of New York City—without ever touching the ground! They've changed the old railroad where trains used to go into a path that you can walk along. You forget that you are in an urban area, because it feels so rural with all the trees, flowers, grass, and plants on either side of the tracks.
Friend: It sounds lovely.
Madison: There are benches to sit on, and in summer you'll feel nice and cool. You can sit by the fountain and listen to the sound of the water. There's a great view of New York's tall skyscrapers, and you can even see the apartment building where I live. It's a nice place for people to meet and relax and look at all the murals.
Friend: I can't wait to see it. Let's go!

TRACK 106

Unit 9, Global Citizenship
B Listen, say, and number the pictures in A.
1 bench
2 bridge
3 skyscraper
4 path
5 apartment building (British English: block of flats)
6 office building
7 fountain
8 railroad (British English: railway)
9 urban
10 rural

TRACK 1

Unit 9, Global Citizenship
Close your eyes. Listen, visualize, and say.
Bench. You see a bench in the park. Sit on it and look around. Say *bench.*
Bridge. You're standing on a bridge. Look over the edge. What can you see? Say *bridge.*
Skyscraper. Stand next to a skyscraper and look up. Can you see the top? Say *skyscraper.*
Path. Walk along a path. Where does the path take you? Say *path.*
Apartment building. You live in an apartment building. Which floor do you live on? Say *apartment building.*
Office building. Your office is on the top floor of an office building. Go up to your office in the elevator. Say *office building.*
Fountain. You're standing near a fountain. Can you feel the water? Say *fountain.*
Railroad. Imagine you are on a train on the railroad. What sound does the train make? Say *railroad.*
Urban. Imagine an urban park. What are you doing in it? Say *urban.*
Rural. Imagine a rural place. What can you see and hear? Say *rural.*

TRACK 107

Unit 9, Global Citizenship
D Now listen to Mariana and Liam. How do the places they talk about help their communities?
Mariana: I'm from Medellín, Colombia. In my city, between 2008 and 2011, they built ten fantastic libraries. They have beautiful green parks around them that make you feel like you're in a rural area. We call them library parks. All the people who live in the community around a library park had a chance to decide on the design and even the books! A library park is a place where you can go to learn things and relax, too. Every day, between 1,000 and 2,000 people use the library parks. These wonderful places have really helped people in the community get along better and share experiences.
Liam: Did you know that here in Montreal, Canada, there's an underground city? It's been here for years. That's why some people call Montreal two cities in one! The underground city has over 30 kilometers of tunnels. You can walk underground from one end to the other! In the tunnels, there are more than 200 restaurants, 1,700 shops, and 30 movie theaters. You can sit and relax on a bench in the public squares, enjoy lots of community events, and there is always a lot of art to look at. It really is a complete city!

TRACK 108

Unit 9, Explore Language
A Listen and read. Whose favorite place is the playground?
Bea: Isn't it great that we won the prize for the best city on the planet? Willis Brice really liked our floating restaurant. Have you ever eaten there, Grandpa Elliot?
Elliot: Yes, I have. It's my favorite restaurant.
Bea: When did you go there?
Elliot: I went there a few weeks ago for my friend's goodbye party. He's gone to live on Mars!
Bea: Wow! Down there's my favorite place—the indoor playground. I've been there lots of times.
Elliot: Well, I've never been there.
Bea: Why not?
Elliot: It wasn't here 50 years ago when I was your age!

TRACK 109

Unit 9, Explore Language
D Listen and say.
1 Have you ever eaten there? Yes, I have.
2 I traveled to New York last year.
3 Have you ever been to Australia? No, we haven't.
4 I visited my grandma two days ago.

TRACK 110

Unit 9, Take the Stage
Pronunciation. Listen and say.
Silent *gh* 2
although through thought

Unit 10

TRACK 111
Unit 10, Vocabulary
A Listen and find. Who's afraid of the dark?

Elliot: Come on, Freya! Let's go and watch Willis Brice juggle.
Freya: He's great, isn't he, Elliot?
Man: You've won some binoculars! Look through them.
Amit: I can see … a butterfly on a flower! Now I'll try to win a prize for you, Poppy. Would you like that toy bear?
Poppy: Yes, please, Amit. You've won it! Thank you! It feels so soft.
Mr. Sim: Hey, what's that sound, Jennifer? Listen.
Jennifer: Oh, yes, I can hear it, Mr. Sim. It's the music from those horses going up and down! I'm going to go for a ride.
David: I don't think I like this train, Ruby. It's too dark in this tunnel. It's scary. Ugh! Something touched my face. What is it?
Ruby: It's just my scarf blowing in the wind, David. Oh, I'm glad that ride is over. It was really frightening! Mmm, I can smell hot chocolate. Shall we have some, David?
David: Yes, good idea. Mmm. It tastes delicious. It's just what we needed after that scary ride.

TRACK 112
Unit 10, Vocabulary
B Listen, say, and number the pictures in A.

1 look
2 watch
3 see
4 hear
5 listen
6 taste
7 smell
8 touch
9 feel

TRACK 113
Unit 10, Vocabulary
C Close your eyes. Listen, visualize, and say.

Look. Choose something to look at. Point at it. What are you looking at? Say *look*.
Watch. Watch a program on TV. What are you watching? Say *watch*.
See. Imagine you are in a dark forest. What can you see? Say *see*.
Hear. You're in the jungle. Make the sounds you can hear. Say *hear*.
Listen. Listen to your favorite song. Sing along to it. Say *listen*.
Taste. Mime eating a lemon. What does it taste like? Say *taste*.
Smell. Imagine someone is cooking your favorite food. What does it smell like? Say *smell*.
Touch. Imagine a kitten. Touch its fur. Say *touch*.
Feel. You're now holding the kitten. What does its fur feel like? Say *feel*.

TRACK 114
Unit 10, Vocabulary
E Listen and complete. Then watch and sing.

Use Your Senses!

There are colors everywhere, every flower, every tree.
Use your eyes, look around and you will see.
There are sounds all around, far away and very near.
Use your ears, listen closely
and you'll hear.

Can you hear the sound of a telephone ring?
Can you see the color of the sky?
Can you feel how soft a baby's skin is?
Can you taste the apples in this pie?

Can you smell the fresh green grass that's mowed?
Can you touch a butterfly's wing?
Do you like to watch a bird as it flies?
Do you like to listen to it sing?

TRACK 115
Unit 10, Explore Language
A Listen and read. Who thinks the slide is scary?

Poppy: That slide on the huge ear looks fun, doesn't it? Listen to the people screaming.
Amit: It's too scary for me. Let's go into that tunnel!
Poppy: The tunnel through the huge nose? It isn't full of spiders, is it?
Amit: I don't know. You aren't afraid of spiders, are you? I'm not. I touched one once at the zoo, didn't I?
Poppy: Then you won't be afraid of the one that's crawling towards you …
Amit: Aaaaagh!
Poppy: But you like spiders, don't you? You aren't scared of them!

TRACK 116
Unit 10, Explore Language
D Listen and say.

1 That slide looks fun, doesn't it?
2 They aren't hungry, are they?
3 We heard this music on the radio, didn't we?
4 It's scary, isn't it?

TRACK 117
Unit 10, Global Citizenship
A Listen to Jordi talk about his visit to a chocolate factory. Why couldn't he taste the chocolate?

Dad: Hi, Jordi! How was your class trip to the chocolate factory?
Jordi: it was so interesting! We learned how they make chocolate in different flavors, and we met a woman who is a chocolate taster!
Dad: What a fantastic job!
Jordi: Not always! Some chocolate is burnt, and that makes it taste bitter, like strong coffee.
Dad: OK, but it's difficult to believe it doesn't always taste nice! How much chocolate does she taste in a day?
Jordi: A lot! This is how she tastes it. First, she puts a small piece in her mouth. She has to think about how it feels on her tongue. Does it feel rough, like sand, or smooth, like silk? Is it soft or hard? Does it taste sweet, like sugar, or does it have salt in it? Then, after each piece of chocolate, she waits 30 seconds and drinks plain warm water to clean her mouth.
Dad: Oh, interesting.
Jordi: And did you know there is a chemical in chocolate that makes us feel happy?
Dad: Yes, that's amazing, isn't it! Did you eat a lot of chocolate there?
Jordi: Yes, but I couldn't taste it, because I have a cold. I still felt happy, though!

TRACK 118
Unit 10, Global Citizenship
B Listen, say, and number the pictures in A.

1 rough
2 smooth
3 hard
4 soft
5 bitter
6 sour
7 sweet
8 salty
9 disgusting
10 flavor
11 savory (British English: savoury)

TRACK J
Unit 10, Global Citizenship
Close your eyes. Listen, visualize, and say.

Rough. Feel a piece of wood from a tree. Be careful, it's rough. Say *rough*.
Smooth. Feel the shell of an egg. Is it smooth? Say *smooth*.
Hard. Imagine a rock. Can you break it, or is it too hard? Say *hard*.
Soft. Touch the feathers of a baby chicken. They're soft. Say *soft*.
Bitter. Mime drinking black coffee, without sugar. It's bitter. Say *bitter*.
Sour. Mime eating a piece of lemon. Is it sour? Say *sour*.
Sweet. Mime eating strawberry ice cream. What does it taste like? Is it sweet? Say *sweet*.
Salty. Add some salt to your chips. Do they taste salty? Say *salty*.
Disgusting. Mime smelling disgusting food that has gone bad. What does it smell like? Say *disgusting*.
Flavor. You are in an ice cream shop. Which flavor do you choose? Say *flavor*.
Savory. Make a savory crepe with cheese. Which do you prefer—savory or sweet crepes? Say *savory*.

TRACK 119
Unit 10, Global Citizenship
D Now listen to Oliver and Courtney. Who uses their sense of taste?

Oliver: I'm from the UK, and I went with my class to a fascinating exhibition at the Museum of London. It was all about the Great Fire of London in 1666. This was a big fire that burned down more than

13,000 homes and lasted for four days. At the exhibition, there was a really clever installation. While you're watching a film about the fire, there are lots of sounds and smells. The fire started in a bakery, and you can smell the bread and hear the fire burning and taste the smoke in the air! I've seen lots of paintings about the Great Fire of London, but it's still difficult to imagine. However, at the exhibition, I felt like I was right in the middle of the city, during the fire. It really helped me understand what it was like. It's a brilliant way to learn about history!

Courtney: I just saw a movie called *The Polar Express* in a 4DX movie theater. That means while you're watching the movie, you can also experience different senses. Your seat moves, and you feel as if you're on the train as it moves through the landscape. You can hear the sound of the wheels on the railroad and you can feel the wind blowing on your face. You can feel the cold snow falling on you, and there's one part of the movie where the characters have a cup of hot chocolate. You can actually smell the sweet hot chocolate! I don't think watching movies will ever be the same after this one!

TRACK 120

Unit 10, Explore Language

A Listen and read. What do the children buy?

Amit: We should buy Mom something, shouldn't we?

Priyah: Yes, Amit. Feel this scarf. It's so soft, isn't it? I'm going to buy it.

Amit: For Mom?

Priyah: No, for me! Mom won't like these chocolates, will she? She prefers bitter or spicy chocolates. These will be too sweet.

Amit: Mmm, but they smell good, don't they? I think I'll buy some for me.

Priyah: There! We've bought two really nice things.

Amit: But, Priyah, we still haven't bought anything for Mom, have we?

TRACK 121

Unit 10, Explore Language

D Listen and say.

1 We should buy Mom something, shouldn't we?
2 You haven't forgotten, have you?
3 It won't rain, will it?
4 He hasn't gone, has he?

TRACK 122

Unit 10, Talk About It

Pronunciation. Listen and say.

gh as **/f/**

rough laugh enough

Play 1 Units 1–5

TRACK 123

Time Traveler

Lucy: I'm too tired to watch TV, Mom. I'm going to bed.

Mom: Good night, Lucy!

Narrator: Lucy's lying in bed, thinking aloud.

Lucy: Our science lesson was interesting today … I can't stop thinking about the moon and the planets, the stars in the galaxy … I wonder what it's like in space.

Narrator: She falls asleep. Suddenly, she wakes up.

Lucy: Oh! Where am I? Is this a plane? It's flying so fast … Aaah! Who are you?

Astronaut: I'm an astronaut! How did you get into my spaceship?

Lucy: This is a spaceship?

Astronaut: Yes, we're going to the space station to do some experiments. Look. That's Mars over there. See the craters and the red soil?

Lucy: But why are we floating around?

Astronaut: That's what happens in space! Don't be nervous.

Lucy: But I want to go back to Earth!

Astronaut: Well, if you close your eyes and count to ten, you might find yourself back at home.

Narrator: Lucy closes her eyes and counts to herself.

Lucy: Phew! I'm glad I'm back on Earth.

Narrator: She looks around in surprise.

Lucy: But where's this village? Who are these people? Excuse me, who are you and what are you doing?

Viking boy: I'm a Viking warrior! Do you want to fight with me? You must use a sword and a shield, then. Hold them in front of you. If you're nervous, you won't be a good warrior. You have to be confident and proud.

Lucy: But I'm not a warrior! I'm just a ten-year-old girl.

Viking boy: You might get along well with my sister then.

Viking girl: Hello. Come and help me. I'm weaving a dress.

Lucy: Umm … What century are we in?

Viking girl: It's the 10th century.

Lucy: The 10th century! How did this happen? Perhaps if I close my eyes and count to ten again, I'll go back home …

Narrator: Lucy closes her eyes and counts to herself.

Lucy: Where am I now? Excuse me, which country am I in and what are you doing?

Egyptian girl: This is Egypt and I'm picking some crops. It's time for dinner. I can tell by the sun. Come to my home. My mother is making a stew.

Narrator: Lucy goes with the Egyptian girl to her house.

Egyptian mom: Hello! Would you like some dinner? Here's a bowl. I'll pour you some water, too.

Lucy: Thank you. I'm very grateful. Now I feel relaxed. I think I'll just lie down here for a while.

Narrator: Lucy lies down and falls asleep.

Mom: Lucy! Wake up! You have to go to school. You mustn't be late!

Lucy: Am I at home?

Mom: Of course you're at home, where you should be!

Lucy: Phew, it was only a dream! But what an adventure!

Play 2 Units 6–10

TRACK 124

The Mystery of the Missing Ring

Lady Richmond: Hello, my name's Lady Richmond. Is this Detective Du Pree?

Detective: Yes, it is. Has something happened?

Lady Richmond: Yes, someone has taken my very expensive ring!

Detective: When did you last see it?

Lady Richmond: I saw it when I was putting on my make-up and my wig yesterday. It was lying next to my false eyelashes. Now it's gone.

Detective: Can you describe it to me please, Lady Richmond?

Lady Richmond: Yes, it's made of gold, and it has a white diamond in the middle.

Detective: I'll be there very soon. Don't worry, we'll find your ring, I'm sure. Excuse me, this is the right way to Lady Richmond's house, isn't it?

Little boy: Yes, just follow this path through the trees. It's the big house behind the pond with the fountain in the middle.

Detective: Thank you. Umm … excuse me, what are you doing? Have you lost something?

Man: No, I'm looking for metal. This is a metal detector. It's a machine that helps you find things under the ground. There. Did you hear that sound? Look, it's an old coin.

Detective: Aha! So you're a kind of detective like me. I'm also looking for something. I'm trying to solve a mystery. Lady Richmond has lost her ring.

Man: If it's made of metal, my machine will find it.

Detective: It's made of gold!

Man: Well, that should be easy to find. If I find it, I'll give it to you.

Detective: Thank you. Hello! Is this Lady Richmond's house?

Gardener: Yes, it is.

Detective: What were you doing early this morning? Did you see anybody come to the house?

Gardener: This morning I took out the trash, and then I swept the leaves. I filled a bucket with water from the faucet and watered the flowers. No, I didn't see anybody.

Little girl: You're Detective Du Pree, aren't you?

Detective: That's right.
Dad: Can I borrow your binoculars please, Detective?
Detective: Sure. What are you looking at?
Dad: Can you see that little boy over there, lying in a hammock? He's crying.
Little girl: He was swinging very high. Perhaps he's frightened.
Gardener: What's the matter?
Little girl: I was lying in my hammock, playing with my new metal car. Then a big bird flew down and took it!
Gardener: Aha, those birds are famous for collecting shiny objects. They love things made of metal, and bright, hard objects.
Detective: Really? You've given me an idea. Let's put up a ladder and climb the tree.
Little boy: It's my toy car! Thank you!
Detective: And this is Lady Richmond's ring!
Lady Richmond: My ring! You've found it! Thank you. Come into the kitchen.
Cook: The gardener brought me fresh pineapples from the greenhouse this morning.
Lady Richmond: I think we should celebrate with some delicious sweet fruit, shouldn't we?
Everyone: Yes, please!

Literacy Book

Literacy Review

TRACK 1

Literacy Review, Fiction, *Thump!*
Chris: I dropped my shovel and took a drink of water. Even though it was still morning, it was already hot in the desert. A scorpion climbed over the sand to see what was going on. I pushed it away with my boot. "We'll never find it!" I sighed.
Dad: Don't give up now, Chris.
Chris: said Dad. I'm so tired.
Dad: But the map says we are in the right place. Look!
Chris: Dad pointed at the map. We were standing on the place marked with a big X. The prize was here. "All right, I guess I can dig for a little longer," I sighed.
Dad: Well done, son.
Chris: said Dad. We started digging again. "How much do you think it's worth?" I asked. Dad shrugged.
Dad: Enough to buy a new house. How does that sound?
Chris: I was about to answer when my shovel hit something with a loud thump!

TRACK 2

Literacy Review, Spelling Patterns, final *ough* and *ight*
Listen and repeat. Then complete the words with *ough* or *ight*.
1 knight
2 cough
3 night
4 dough
5 delight
6 tonight
7 rough
8 light
9 tough
10 fight
11 though
12 enough
Now check your answers.
1 knight, k-n-i-g-h-t, knight
2 cough, c-o-u-g-h, cough
3 night, n-i-g-h-t, night
4 dough, d-o-u-g-h, dough
5 delight, d-e-l-i-g-h-t, delight
6 tonight, t-o-n-i-g-h-t, tonight
7 rough, r-o-u-g-h, rough
8 light, l-i-g-h-t, light
9 tough, t-o-u-g-h, tough
10 fight, f-i-g-h-t, fight
11 though, t-h-o-u-g-h, though
12 enough, e-n-o-u-g-h, enough

TRACK 3

Literacy Review, Nonfiction, *Whale Valley*
Whale Skeletons
In the middle of the Egyptian desert lies Wadi Al-Hitan, also known as Whale Valley. Usually, a dry desert is a strange place to find whales, but this valley is home to the skeletons of more than 400 whales. The whale skeletons are from 40 million years ago, when water covered this land.
An Important Story
The skeletons of these whales tell an important story. The skeletons show that these whales once had back legs and feet. But the back legs on the skeletons are tiny. This means that the whales were changing from land animals to sea animals. The whales didn't need their legs anymore. Their legs were becoming smaller and smaller. Today, of course, whales don't have legs or feet at all.
A World Heritage Site
Whale Valley has a large number of whale skeletons, and the dry desert air has preserved them well. This makes it an important place for science. In 2005, UNESCO named the area a World Heritage Site, protecting it for years to come.

TRACK 4

Literacy Review, Spelling Patterns, *–ar* and *–or*
Listen and repeat. Then complete the words with *ar* or *or*.
1 storm
2 alarm
3 fork
4 polar
5 cartoon
6 artist
7 torn
8 star
9 shark
10 sport
11 torch
12 world
Now check your answers.
1 storm, s-t-o-r-m, storm
2 alarm, a-l-a-r-m, alarm
3 fork, f-o-r-k, fork
4 polar, p-o-l-a-r, polar
5 cartoon, c-a-r-t-o-o-n, cartoon
6 artist, a-r-t-i-s-t, artist
7 torn, t-o-r-n, torn
8 star, s-t-a-r, star
9 shark, s-h-a-r-k, shark
10 sport, s-p-o-r-t, sport
11 torch, t-o-r-c-h, torch
12 world, w-o-r-l-d, world

Unit 1

TRACK 5

Unit 1, Fiction, *True Colors*
Mrs. Blanche: Hello, Emil!
Narrator: says the owner of the shop, Mrs. Blanche.
Mrs. Blanche: Have you run out of paint again?
Emil: You know me too well!
Narrator: Emil says from across the store.
Emil: I used the last of it this morning. What's this?
Narrator: Emil wonders.
Emil: It's called True Colors …
Mrs. Blanche: Interesting choice, Emil. There are so many colors and you picked this one.
Narrator: Mrs. Blanche says.
Mrs. Blanche: You should be careful with it. It's the last one.
Emil: This still life isn't good enough!
Narrator: Emil says angrily.
Emil: The fruit and vegetables look real but they're too boring.

Narrator: He decides to start a new painting with his new paint. There are a lot of things he could paint, but what?
Emil: My croissant!
Narrator: Emil thinks.
Emil is almost finished. Then he sees something odd. His new painting is … real!
Emil: What is True Colors made of?
Narrator: He wonders. Emil can't stop painting with his new paint. He even fixes his bike!
Emil: This is amazing!
Narrator: he exclaims. Emil loves painting with True Colors. He paints a bee. Will it come to life, too?
Emil: Oh, no! I didn't want that to happen!
Narrator: Emil says.
Emil: Wait, I can fix it! I can make it better.
Woman: Wow! Thanks!
Narrator: says the woman. Emil is happy that he can help people with True Colors. Who else can he help?
Old man: (Taxi! Taxi! Taxi! Oh, taxi, hello!) You're so kind!
Narrator: says the old man.
Emil: Watch out!
Narrator: cries Emil. He saves the day with his True Colors.
Emil: Helping people is so much fun!
Narrator: Emil says. He wants to help more, but … there's only enough paint left for something small. Emil starts to walk home slowly.
When he gets home, he sees his neighbors. They can't get in their apartment.
Mrs. Durand: I told you to take the key!
Narrator: Mrs. Durand says.
Mr. Durand: I thought you had it!
Narrator: her husband replies.
Emil: Excuse me. Is that your key?
Narrator: asks Emil quietly.
Mr. Durand: It is!
Narrator: Mr. Durand says.
Mr. Durand: Thank you so much! Why don't you join us for some delicious onion soup?
Narrator: Mr. Durand asks. Emil can't say no!
Mrs. Durand: So, you're a painter.
Narrator: Mrs. Durand says.
Mrs. Durand: Can you show us a few of your paintings after dinner?
Narrator: Emil is worried. What if his neighbors don't like them?
Emil: OK.
Narrator: he says nervously.
Mrs. Durand: We think your paintings are wonderful!
Narrator: says Mrs. Durand.
Mrs. Durand: And so does Lucy!
Emil: Thank you!
Narrator: Emil says, smiling.
Emil: I guess they aren't so bad after all.
Mr. Durand: Can you paint Lucy's portrait for us?
Narrator: asks Mr. Durand.
Emil: I'd love to!

TRACK 6
Unit 1, *True Colors*, Words in Context
Find these words in the reading. What do you think they mean?
owner
run out of
choice
croissant
exclaims

TRACK 7
Unit 1, Nonfiction, *My Guide to Photography*
Narrator: Huan Chen, 12, has won many awards for her photos and has 16,000 followers online. Here are her tips to help you become a better photographer.
Huan Chen: *Tip Number 1: Fill Your Frame*
In photography, the shape of the photograph is important. Photographers call this the "frame." I like to fill my frame with only one thing and I only include a few elements in the photo. This keeps it simple. Imagine you're taking a photo of an insect. Move closer so that the insect is in the foreground and it fills up the whole frame.
I do the same thing with portraits of people. I zoom in close with my camera. I make sure that the person's face is the most important element, with not too much background. This is a portrait of my brother.
Tip Number 2: Choose Your Format
Photos can be horizontal or vertical. This is called the "format." Most of the time, I take horizontal photos. This format looks nice with wide landscapes. It's also more comfortable to hold a camera horizontally. But a vertical format works better for portraits and tall objects, like trees.
Tip Number 3: Follow the "Rule of Thirds"
Imagine your photo divided into nine squares. Make sure that the most important elements in your photo line up with the edges of the squares. See how the butterfly in this photo is right on the lines?
I think this makes my photos look more interesting. Without the Rule of Thirds, the butterfly would be in the middle, and that would look boring!
Tip Number 4: Remember to Focus!
Have you ever seen a photo where some parts are blurry and other parts are clear? This is called the "focus." You can choose which parts of your photo are in focus (clear) or out of focus (blurry). Sometimes I like to experiment with my focus. First, I focus on something in the foreground. Then, I focus on something in the background. These are two photos of a cat on a fence. I posted the first one. What do you think?
Tip Number 5: Be Yourself!
Remember, you're the photographer! Your camera or smartphone is your tool. Have fun with it and find your own unique style.

TRACK 8
Unit 1, *My Guide to Photography*, Words in Context
Find these words in the reading. What do you think they mean?
frame
elements
zoom in
horizontal
vertical

TRACK 9
Unit 1, Spelling Pattern, final *ent*
Listen and write. Then check your answers.
1 present
2 intelligent
3 parent
4 ingredient
5 invent
Now check your answers.
1 present, p-r-e-s-e-n-t, present
2 intelligent, i-n-t-e-l-l-i-g-e-n-t, intelligent
3 parent, p-a-r-e-n-t, parent
4 ingredient, i-n-g-r-e-d-i-e-n-t, ingredient
5 invent, i-n-v-e-n-t, invent

Unit 2

TRACK 10
Unit 2, Fiction, *A World Without Time*
Narrator: In the town of Undergroundia, a loud noise woke Ooleck the inventor. He looked out of his bedroom window. In the giant cave outside, workers were fixing the road with a steamroller.
Ooleck: Working time already?
Narrator: Ooleck grumbled. He was sure it was still sleeping time.
But that was the problem. Undergroundians spent their whole lives underground. There was no sun or moon. There was no way of telling if it was day or night. Undergroundians didn't have a way to tell time.
Ooleck: Time to get up.
Narrator: Ooleck called to his wife, Zeena.
Ooleck: We're late.
Zeena: How can you tell?
Narrator: asked Zeena.
Ooleck: Exactly! Everyone in Undergroundia either gets up early or late, or they never wake up at all. I need to invent a way of measuring time! Then everyone can do things properly.
Zeena: Good idea.
Narrator: said Zeena. In his workshop, Ooleck sat down at his desk and began brainstorming. He worked and scribbled, and still couldn't come up with an answer. Then the candle on his desk burned down and it went dark. Ooleck lit another candle.
Ooleck: That's the sixth candle I've burned down trying to solve this problem.
Narrator: he grumbled to Zeena.
Ooleck: When I invented the tooth scraper, that only took one candle.

Zeena: But remember when you invented the two-wheeled cycle, it took fifteen.
Narrator: said Zeena.
Ooleck: Six candles … one candle … fifteen candles,
Narrator: thought Ooleck, rubbing his chin. Ooleck rubbed his chin some more. The hairs on his chin suddenly gave him an idea.
Ooleck: I know! We can measure time by counting how long it takes for a beard to grow! We can pay a man to stand in the town square and measure the length of his beard.
Zeena: Don't be so silly. What other ideas do you have?
Narrator: asked Zeena.
Ooleck: We can measure time by how long it takes a cup of tea to cool down. We can call it tea time.
Zeena: Silly.
Ooleck: How about we get someone to cycle around Undergroundia? Each time he finishes we call it one cycle. We work for ten cycles and sleep for ten cycles.
Zeena: Silly.
Ooleck: I still can't solve it.
Narrator: Ooleck sighed, reaching for another candle.
Ooleck: That's another candle almost burned down. It's taken seven candles so far.
Zeena: You'll figure it out.
Narrator: said Zeena.
Zeena: The answer is probably right under your nose.

TRACK 11

Unit 2, *A World Without Time*, Words in Context
Find these words in the reading. What do you think they mean?
grumbled
underground
scribbled
cool down
sighed
figure it out

TRACK 12

Unit 2, Spelling Pattern, final *le*
Listen and write. Then check your answers.
1 handle
2 whale
3 trouble
4 purple
5 castle
Now check your answers.
1 handle, h-a-n-d-l-e, handle
2 whale, w-h-a-l-e, whale
3 trouble, t-r-o-u-b-l-e, trouble
4 purple, p-u-r-p-l-e, purple
5 castle, c-a-s-t-l-e, castle

TRACK 13

Unit 2, Nonfiction, *Timelines*
Timelines are a way of showing the passing of time. They show time information in a way that makes it easy to see. They show us what important events happened and when they happened.
Timelines can also show how things change over time and help us predict how things are going to change.
We can make a timeline that measures the history of life on Earth starting with 3.8 billion years ago.
3.8 billion years ago. First life on Earth appears.
530 million years ago. Sea life appears.
475 million years ago. Land plants grow.
370 million years ago. Amphibians appear.
320 million years ago. Reptiles appear.
225 to 65 million years ago. Dinosaurs roam the Earth.
55 million years ago. Early primates appear.
14 million years ago. Big apes appear.
200,000 years ago. Human beings appear.
Timelines can show how inventions change over centuries. Just look at the bike timeline above. Bikes in the past were very different.
1816. Draisine. The rider sat on the wooden frame and moved the bike by running along the ground.
1867. Boneshaker. These bikes were the first to have pedals. Riding them was extremely bumpy, so they were called Boneshakers.
1871. High Wheeler. This bike also had a nickname, "the Penny Farthing."
1885. Safety bikes. These had a chain, two wheels the same size, and a shape we still recognize today.
1920s. Children's bikes. In this decade, bike makers started to make smaller bikes for kids.
1970s. Mountain bikes and BMX bikes. Mountain bikes were designed for riding off-road. BMX bikes were designed for racing and stunt riding.
1990s. Electric bikes. These have motors so riders don't have to pedal.
2010s. Smart bikes. These have features like GPS navigation, lights for night riding, and an alarm system built into the handlebars.
We can even have a timeline about telling time!
2000s BCE. Sundials. The Egyptians used sundials to measure the day.
500s CE. Candles. The Chinese used candles with marks on them to tell the time.
1300s. Mechanical clocks. The Italians invented these.
1950s. Atomic clocks. These can measure the exact length of a second!
1970s. Digital clocks. Clocks with glowing numbers became popular.
2010s. Smartwatches. These clocks are small computers! They can play music, send text messages, run apps, and tell time.
There are many different timelines. Timelines like these help us to see how things have changed, and visualize how they will change. What will come next?

TRACK 14

Unit 2, *Timelines*, Words in Context
Find these words in the reading. What do you think they mean?
apes
extremely
chain
sundials
mechanical

Unit 3

TRACK 15

Unit 3, Nonfiction, *A Friendly Message*
This is the true story of Amanda Moore, a 10-year-old student in California, USA. Amanda wrote a note in Spanish. In English it reads:
"Hello, Rafael. Would you like to sit with me today? Look for me and I will show you where I sit. We can color or simply tell scary stories. Thank you for your time."
Amanda wrote this for Rafael Anaya, a new student in her class. He moved from Mexico to the USA and he didn't speak much English. He was lonely and he often got upset when he couldn't understand the teacher. Amanda saw this and decided to make friends with him, but there was one problem. She didn't speak any Spanish, so she had to find a different way to communicate with Rafael.
Amanda used her smartphone and an app called Google Translate to write her message. She typed it into the app in English and clicked on "Translate to Spanish." Then she copied the message in Spanish on a piece of paper and gave it to Rafael. He felt really happy because he had a new friend. "No one has given me a letter before," Rafael explained in Spanish. "Amanda will be my friend forever."
Paloma Elementary School, where the children study, gave Amanda an award for being kind and she was Student of the Month. Rafael's and Amanda's parents were also there when Amanda received her award. They got a chance to meet.
"Amanda did a lovely thing. It's wonderful," Rafael's mom said. She explained that Rafael used to feel really nervous about going to school, so she was grateful to Amanda for helping him feel less nervous.
Amanda's mom was very proud of her daughter and she talked about all the messages people sent her. "I've received 1,600 personal Facebook messages from people all across the world just saying gracias," she said. She also said she didn't need a translator to explain what that word means.
The story of Amanda and Rafael shows us that nothing can stop a friendship from growing. Two people who don't speak the same language can still communicate. So, be nice to new classmates and make friends with them. Amanda didn't let anything stop her from making a new friend. Don't let anything stop you. You'll find a way to communicate if you want to!

TRACK 16
Unit 3, *A Friendly Message*, Words in Context
Find these words in the reading. What do you think they mean?
communicate
translate
typed
award
personal
friendship

TRACK 17
Unit 3, Spelling Pattern, final *ed*
Listen and write. Then check your answers.
1 waited
2 annoyed
3 decided
4 recognized
5 slipped
6 hugged
Now check your answers.
1 waited, w-a-i-t-e-d, waited
2 annoyed, a-n-n-o-y-e-d, annoyed
3 decided, d-e-c-i-d-e-d, decided
4 recognized, r-e-c-o-g-n-i-z-e-d, recognized
5 slipped, s-l-i-p-p-e-d, slipped
6 hugged, h-u-g-g-e-d, hugged

TRACK 18
Unit 3, Fiction, *Trust Me*
Narrator: Maria and Luana's friendship started when they were toddlers. The two girls grew up together, sharing their toys and secrets, and always looking out for each other. At school, Maria gets along well with everyone. She's a great student.
Maria: So, what's the capital of China?
Narrator: Maria asks the class before the geography test.
Luis: Beijing!
Narrator: Luis shouts.
Maria: That's right. And the capital of Peru?
Narrator: Maria asks again. No one remembers the answer.
Maria: Luana, do you know?
Narrator: Maria asks.
Luana: Umm … Sorry, what? I'm studying, too.
Narrator: says Luana.
Elena: "No, you're not, Luana. You're reading a storybook!"
Narrator: Elena says.
Luana: Hey! Give that back!
Narrator: shouts Luana, a little embarrassed.
Teacher: What's going on?
Narrator: asks the teacher. After the test …
Maria: Don't worry, Luana. If you study a bit more next time, you'll do a lot better.
Narrator: Maria says and makes Luana a promise.
Maria: Let's go swimming tomorrow at the Blue Waterfalls. We'll have a lot of fun!
Luana: Yippee!
Narrator: Luana shouts. It's a long walk to the Blue Waterfalls, but not a boring one. Luana always has entertaining stories to tell.
Luana: Did you know I once saw a wolf in the forest?
Narrator: Luana tells Maria.
Maria: Really? What happened?
Luana: I was going to visit my grandmother. On the way, I stopped to pick flowers for her. Suddenly, a big wolf appeared out of nowhere.
Maria: Wow! Were you scared?
Luana: Of course not. So, the wolf …
Maria: What color was its fur?
Luana: Uh … Well, I think … um … gray … or black? Oh, it doesn't matter! So, I sang a song and I made friends with the wolf. And …
Maria: Luana?
Narrator: Maria whispers.
Luana: Wait. I haven't finished my story.
Narrator: Luana says.
Maria: I know but …
Narrator: Maria insists.
Luana: Shhhh …
Narrator: Too late.
Maria: If we run, will we get away?
Narrator: Maria asks.
Luana: No, bears run faster than us.
Narrator: Luana replies.
Maria: If we climb up a tree, will it reach us?
Narrator: Maria asks.
Luana: Yes, bears are better at climbing than us.
Narrator: Luana replies.
Maria: So, what do we do, Luana?
Narrator: Maria cries.
Luana: Just lie down and don't move.
Narrator: Luana whispers.
Luana: Trust me.
Maria: I can't believe it! It worked! You're a genius, Luana!
Narrator: Maria says.
Luana: You know, I can protect you from anything.
Narrator: Luana says.
Maria: I know.
Narrator: Maria replies.
Maria: Aaaaaah! It's back!
Luana: That's just a rock!
Maria: I owe you one.
Narrator: Maria says.
Luana: Nah, best friends always help each other.
Narrator: Luana replies.
Luana: Look! We're here!

TRACK 19
Unit 3, *Trust Me*, Words in Context
Find these words in the reading. What do you think they mean?
toddlers
capital
entertaining
trust
genius

Unit 4

TRACK 20
Unit 4, Fiction, *Hope You Like Fish*
Narrator: The launch pad, just before dawn. The rocket stands tall. Steam comes from the engines.
Mission control: Check. Check. Check. Check.
Narrator: Mission control checks everything. Mars 11 is ready to blast into space.
But there is a problem. Two of the astronauts on board the spaceship are not happy.
Marfusha: I can't believe they're sending us into space with these guys again.
Katyusha: Worst day ever.
Ham: Hey, what did we do wrong?
Marfusha: Remember the last time?
Katyusha: You landed us in totally the wrong place. You were reading the map upside down.
Enos: I guess maybe we got distracted.
Ham: It could happen to anybody.
Marfusha: Shhh!
Mission control: Get ready for launch. Good luck astronauts, this mission is very important.
Narrator: The countdown begins.
Mission control: 5, 4, 3, 2, 1. Blast off!
Narrator: Fire blasts from the rocket engines. The rocket shakes and roars. It lifts off towards the sky. It is loud. It is scary.
Enos: What's the mission again?
Marfusha: To land on Mars and collect rocks, remember?
Katyusha: We're exploring new worlds for science.
Marfusha: It's a two-year mission.
Ham: Oh yeah, right. Mars. Two years? That's a long time.
Ham: I've changed my mind!
Marfusha & Katyusha: Sit down!
Narrator: Soon, Mars 11 is up in space. From up there, the Earth looks beautiful. Marfusha turns off the rockets. The astronauts take off their safety belts and float in zero gravity.
Enos: Wow, it looks like a long way down.
Ham: Are you sure Mars is this way?
Marfusha: Of course. The rabbits are in charge.
Narrator: The spaceship flies towards the red planet. Marfusha moves the controls.
Marfusha: Mission control, we're on course for the planet Mars.
Enos: I'm hungry. Snack time!
Ham: Hey, that's not fair! Where's my space snack?
Enos: I didn't bring you one.
Narrator: The two chimps chase each other around the tiny spaceship. They only have one thing on their minds: food.
Marfusha: This isn't the time for a space snack!
Enos: Give that back!

Katyusha: You must sit down. You're going to cause an accident.
All: Oh, no!
Narrator: The spaceship drops like a stone. It zooms back towards Earth. It is out of control.
Marfusha, Katyusha, Enos, Ham: Aaaaah!
Narrator: Later, back down on Earth … The spaceship floats in the middle of the ocean. There is nothing else in sight. The astronauts are a long way from home. It might be a while before mission control finds them. There's time to catch something tasty for dinner.
Marfusha: You chimps shouldn't think about food all the time!
Katyusha: Never go up in space with chimps.
Ham: We said we were sorry.
Marfusha: Never, ever.
Enos: We hope you like fish …

TRACK 21

Unit 4, *Hope You Like Fish*, Words in Context
Find these words in the reading. What do you think they mean?
launch
mission control
blast
gravity
in sight

TRACK 22

Unit 4, Spelling Pattern, long *i*
Listen and write. Then check your answers.
1 library
2 lion
3 quiet
4 grind
5 migrate
Now check your answers.
1 library, l-i-b-r-a-r-y, library
2 lion, l-i-o-n, lion
3 quiet, q-u-i-e-t, quiet
4 grind, g-r-i-n-d, grind
5 migrate, m-i-g-r-a-t-e, migrate

TRACK 23

Unit 4, Nonfiction, *First Man in Space*
On April 12, 1961, an astronaut squeezed into a tiny space capsule and got ready for launch. The name of the space capsule was Vostok 1, and the name of the astronaut was Yuri Gagarin… the first man to go into space.
Yuri Gagarin was born in 1934 in a small farming village in Russia.
While his parents worked on the farm, Gagarin's older sister looked after him.
When he was in high school, Gagarin joined a flying club and learned to fly. Later, he went to an air force school and became a fighter pilot.
In 1960, 20 air force pilots were chosen for a secret mission to put the first human into space. Gagarin was one of them.
The 20 astronauts had to go through a lot of tough training. They had to learn to survive on their own. To help keep in shape, they played sports. Gagarin did everything well. He often had a smile on his face. Gagarin's skills and upbeat attitude made him the best man to explore space.
Space exploration was very dangerous. Before putting a human on board, the Vostok capsule was tested many times. Several launches failed.
On the day of the launch, Gagarin was calm as he waited for blast-off. He even asked for some music on the radio.
At last, at 6:07 a.m., the control room pressed the ignition button. As Vostok 1 blasted off into space, control said "LIFT OFF! We wish you a good flight."
Gagarin answered by saying Poyekhali! which is Russian for "Let's go!"
Eleven minutes later, at 6:18, Yuri Gagarin became the first man to enter space. From the small windows of Vostok 1, Gagarin looked down on planet Earth. "I can see clouds. I can see everything. It's beautiful," said Gagarin.
When Vostok 1 returned to Earth, Gagarin parachuted down. He landed in a field near Smelovka in Russia where he met some surprised people. "I am a friend," he quickly said.
Soon, Gagarin was one of the most famous people in the world. Everywhere he went people treated him as a hero for his bravery and threw him big parades. Gagarin earned many medals and awards. He got a lot of mail from fans and had streets named after him.
Today, near the place where he was born, there is a town called Gagarin with a statue of him. Everyone will remember the first human in space. He was the astronaut with the famous smile.

TRACK 24

Unit 4, *First Man in Space*, Words in Context
Find these words in the reading. What do you think they mean?
capsule
attitude
failed
pressed
parachuted
hero

Unit 5

TRACK 25

Unit 5, Nonfiction, *The Silk Road*
These days, there are big planes and ships to take goods from one side of the world to the other. But in the past, it wasn't that easy to trade with people in faraway places. So how did people do it? They used to trade on the Silk Road.
What was the Silk Road?
The Silk Road wasn't really a road made of silk. It was a 4,000-mile network of land and sea routes. These routes connected to create a path from Eastern Europe to China.
Merchants used to travel on the Silk Road to trade goods such as tea, furs, and pottery. But the most valuable goods were spices and silk from China. That's why it's called the Silk Road. Spices were important because they preserved food to make it last longer. Silk was light and it used to be as valuable as gold.
How did people travel on the Silk Road?
Much of the Silk Road was across desert, so many merchants used camels to carry their goods. They also used horses. It was safer to travel in a big group, or caravan, because there were a lot of thieves along the Silk Road. Some merchants even had guards to protect them and their goods. Others took a different route every time they made the trip.
Why was the Silk Road important?
The Silk Road wasn't just a route for people to buy and sell goods. At a time when there were no planes, phones, or computers, it helped people from distant places keep in touch. The traders met new cultures, exchanged ideas, and spread inventions across the world.
Paper is a good example of this. At first, traders brought the idea west from the Arab world on the Silk Road. Then, Europeans learned how to make paper, too. The same thing happened with the printing press, which was invented in China.
People traveled on the Silk Road from 200 BCE until the 1400s. Sailing then became more popular because it was safer and faster. In 2014, the Silk Road became a UNESCO World Heritage Site because it helped different cultures build peace and understanding.

TRACK 26

Unit 5, *The Silk Road*, Words in Context
Find these words in the reading. What do you think they mean?
goods
faraway
network
routes
merchants
preserved
thieves

TRACK 27

Unit 5, Fiction, *Sinbad's First Voyage*
Sinbad: My father used to be a wealthy merchant. He traded jewelry and spices on the Silk Road. When he died, he left me all his money, but I wasted it.
One day, I woke up penniless and alone. All I had left was my father's dagger.
Male friend: See you around, Sinbad.
Sinbad: A man I knew, Maruf, told me there was work in the port.
I met rich merchants and saw the beautiful things they traded. I wanted to be one of them, but how?
In those days, it used to cost 20 gold coins to get a place on a ship. I worked hard and saved my money.

Finally, the day came when I boarded *The Rose*. The ship took me to wonderful places around the world.
I traded pottery for spices, and silk for wheat. I saw amazing animals. I met people in villages who spoke languages I didn't understand. The world was my oyster.
One day, we were surprised to arrive at a desert island. It wasn't on the map …
We camped on the beach. But that night, something woke us up.
The ground was shaking.

Male sailor: Earthquake! To the ship!
Sinbad: But it wasn't an earthquake …
Male sailor: It's a whale!
Sinbad: I felt my body hit the sea. I sank deeper and deeper. I had no strength left to swim to the surface. I was too weak.
I thought I was dead, but somehow, I held on to a piece of wood. I woke up on a beach.
I looked around and I saw a stranger walking towards me.
I didn't know him but he had the most beautiful horse in the world!
From its saddle, I could tell the horse belonged to someone rich and important.
I thought my troubles were over, but …
I was wrong.
It's the whale again!
Where's my dagger? Take that!
I lost my father's dagger, but the beautiful horse was safe. I closed my eyes and saw my father smiling at me.
Prince Zayn: A thousand thanks. I'm Prince Zayn, the King's eldest son. This is the King's favorite horse.
Sinbad: I knew it! It's a pleasure to meet you, sir.
Prince Zayn: I'm sure the King would like to thank you for saving the horse's life. Follow me.
Sinbad: I stayed at the palace and worked for the King for almost a year. Finally, I came home a wealthy man, rich in knowledge.
Ali: The end?
Sinbad: Well, that was my first voyage. I went on many more, but let's keep those for another time.

TRACK 28

Unit 5, *Sinbad's First Voyage*, Words in Context
Find these words in the reading. What do you think they mean?
wealthy
penniless
boarded
sank
strength
stranger
troubles

TRACK 29

Unit 5, Spelling Pattern, soft *c*
Listen and write. Then check your answers.
1 face
2 pencil
3 medicine
4 science
5 prince
Now check your answers.
1 face, f-a-c-e, face
2 pencil, p-e-n-c-i-l, pencil
3 medicine, m-e-d-i-c-i-n-e, medicine
4 science, s-c-i-e-n-c-e, science
5 prince, p-r-i-n-c-e, prince

Unit 6

TRACK 30

Unit 6, Nonfiction, *SOS*
Narrator: Mrs. Collins stopped on the trail and searched the wilderness. She looked at her cell phone and shook her head.
Joe: What's wrong?
Narrator: asked Joe.
Mrs. Collins: I'm afraid we're lost, and my phone isn't working.
Narrator: said Mrs. Collins.
Micaela: Really?
Narrator: said Micaela.
Mrs. Collins: No, not really.
Narrator: Mrs. Collins laughed.
Mrs. Collins: But let's pretend we really need to call for help to survive. I'm giving you ten minutes to each think of an idea, starting now.
Narrator: Micaela's Idea
Micaela: Use a whistle. A whistle is a really good way of getting attention. Whistles are light and easy to carry. You can attach a whistle to a strap on your backpack.
Three loud blasts on the whistle is the call for help that most people will know.
Narrator: Joe's Idea
Joe: Use a mirror. The reflection from a mirror can travel a very long distance. You can get the attention of planes and boats.
Some hiking mirrors have a sight that helps you aim the mirror at your target, or the spot you are pointing at.
If the mirror doesn't have a sight, start by shining the reflection onto your hand or finger. Then move your finger to the target. Then take away your finger and wiggle the mirror back and forth slowly.
Narrator: Mia's Idea
Mia: The international signal for help is the letters SOS. There are many ways to send that message.
Build a big SOS by putting rocks or branches on the ground. If you are in snow, stamp the letters in the snow and fill them with something dark. If you are on a beach, write the letters in the sand.
Use Morse code to spell out SOS. In Morse code, the letters of the alphabet are made with dots and dashes. SOS is written like this: dot, dot, dot, dash, dash, dash, dot, dot, dot.
At night, use a flashlight to make your dots and dashes. Hold the dashes a little longer than the dots. Then continue repeating that pattern.
Narrator: Yuki's Idea
Yuki: When you need help, you want to be seen.
Make a bright flag. You can use the rain cover from a tent. You can use a brightly colored jacket or any other piece of clothing. Put up the flag somewhere out in the open.
You can also use a flag to spell SOS in Morse code. For a dot, hold your flag on your right side. For a dash, hold your flag to the left.
Mrs. Collins: Good job, those are all good ideas. Hopefully I have some SOS for you.
Narrator: said Mrs. Collins.
Joe: SOS?
Narrator: asked Joe. Mrs. Collins smiled and handed out snack bars.
Mrs. Collins: Stuff Our Stomachs!

TRACK 31

Unit 6, *SOS*, Words in Context
Find these words in the reading. What do you think they mean?
wilderness
pretend
attention
attach
reflection
target
dots and dashes

TRACK 32

Unit 6, Spelling Pattern, initial *st*
Listen and write. Then check your answers.
1 storm
2 strong
3 striped
4 straight
5 stairs
Now check your answers.
1 storm, s-t-o-r-m, storm
2 strong, s-t-r-o-n-g, strong
3 striped, s-t-r-i-p-e-d, striped
4 straight, s-t-r-a-i-g-h-t, straight
5 stairs, s-t-a-i-r-s, stairs

TRACK 33

Unit 6, Fiction, *Panic or Calm?*
Narrator: Alex pushed on the door. It was locked, she couldn't get in. She rang the doorbell.
Alex: Where was Mom?
Narrator: The house was empty and her cell phone was dead. Then, the whole street went dark. Every light in the city died. It was a power outage. Alex's heart began to beat fast. She suddenly felt scared.
Panic.
Narrator: Alex's head started spinning. She had to find Mom. Before she knew it, her legs were moving. They seemed to have a mind of their own.
Alex ran into the street. She looked right and left in the darkness. She chose left and ran towards the stores downtown.
Alex: Maybe Mom is there!
Calm.
Alex: What do I do?

Narrator: thought Alex. She could hear Mrs. Bryson, her teacher, ask,
Mrs. Bryson: Have you ever wanted to panic? Don't! Spell out STOP: 'S–T–O–P.'"
Alex: S means "sit down."
Narrator: remembered Alex. She sat down in the backyard and took a deep breath.
Alex: It's only a power outage.
Narrator: she said.
Alex: I can handle this. I can do this. T. Think. Where is Mom?
Narrator: Alex wondered. She remembered Mom saying something about the car being fixed at the repair shop. Mom had to take the bus.
Panic.
Narrator: The streets were full of people going home after work. A few stores had emergency lights. Alex searched the faces in the crowd for Mom. In the shadows, the faces looked cold and mean.
Alex: Where is she?
Narrator: Alex had no idea. She began to cry. Then she felt a hand on her shoulder. It was Mrs. Bryson, her teacher.
Mrs. Bryson: Alex, are you OK? What are you doing here all alone?
Calm.
Alex: O. Observe.
Narrator: thought Alex. That meant look. She looked around the backyard. In the darkness, Alex saw the potted plant.
Alex: Of course! The hiding place for the spare key!
Panic.
Mrs. Bryson: Let's get you home.
Narrator: said Mrs. Bryson. As they walked back up the street, a bus stopped. Mom got off and was very surprised to see Alex with her teacher.
Mom: I'm so sorry I'm late.
Narrator: Mom gasped.
Mom: Is everything alright?
Narrator: Alex blushed.
Alex: No, I was so scared!
Mrs. Bryson: I don't think Alex has remembered my stop lesson.
Narrator: Mrs. Bryson laughed.
Calm.
Alex: P. Plan!
Narrator: Alex made a plan. She decided to stay at home. She would be safe there. She opened the door with the key. She locked it behind her. She found a flashlight. Then, she heard a key in the lock. The door opened.
Mom: Oh, thank goodness!
Narrator: exclaimed Mom.
Mom: I was worried about you in the power outage. My bus was stuck in traffic and your phone was off. Have you been all right?
Narrator: Alex smiled.
Alex: I've been fine.

TRACK 34

Unit 6, *Panic or Calm?* Words in Context
Find these words in the reading. What do you think they mean?
locked
power outage (British English: power cut)
handle this
spare
gasped
blushed
stuck

Unit 7

TRACK 35

Unit 7, Nonfiction, *Clean Water for All*
Having clean water is extremely important to our health. Doctors say we need to drink about six glasses of water a day. However, in many places clean drinking water isn't easy to get.
Some really clever inventions can help with this problem. Here are four of them.
Water Billboard
Lima, Peru has very little rain, but it is very humid. Because it's near the Pacific Ocean, there's a lot of water in the air. Engineers at the city's University of Engineering and Technology invented the Water Billboard to turn air into clean water.
It looks like an advertising billboard, but it can produce 96 liters of clean water a day. Hot, humid air goes through the billboard where five condensers cool it down. The vapor in the air turns into liquid water, and the water then flows through a filter into a tank at the base of the billboard. People get the water from a simple faucet.
Lifestraw
Drinking water from rivers, lakes, or ponds is safe with Lifestraw. It looks like a thick straw and it actually works like one. You place it in the water and suck. As the water flows through the straw, a filter stops the dangerous bacteria. The water that comes out is clean to drink.
People like Lifestraw because it's practical. When they go hiking, they don't need to carry heavy bottles of water. One Lifestraw lets you clean up to 1,000 liters of dirty water and it only weighs 57 grams.
Eliodomestico
Italian designer Gabriele Diamanti invented Eliodomestico, a solar-powered sterilizing system, to make seawater drinkable and take out the salt.
In the morning, seawater is poured into the boiler pot on the top of the device. All day the sun heats the boiler pot and turns the seawater into steam. Pressure inside the boiler pot pushes the steam through a pipe to the clay pot. When the steam meets the metal lid on the clay pot, it condenses, turning the steam into drinkable water. Eliodomestico can distill up to 10 liters of water a day for families.
Cycloclean
Cycloclean is a Japanese invention. You cycle to a river, lake, or pond and put a filter in the dirty water. You pedal the bike to power a pump. The pump pulls the water up into the filter. The water flows through the filter and up into a box with more filters on the back of the bike. It comes out clean and safe to drink.
The inventors of Cycloclean designed it for times of emergency, like droughts and earthquakes, when people have to travel long distances to get water.
Thanks to hard-working scientists and inventors, more people will have safe, clean water in the future.

TRACK 36

Unit 7, *Clean Water for All*, Words in Context
Find these words in the reading. What do you think they mean?
humid
advertising
vapor (British English: vapour)
bacteria
practical
steam
pump

TRACK 37

Unit 7, Fiction, *The New Dam*
Narrator: The peaceful villagers of Powatawomi respected River Kalamazoo. It gave them drinking water and fish. When the ice melted in spring, it became powerful and sometimes flooded the fields.
But now it was barely a creek!
Wabaunsee: Where's the river we once knew?
Narrator: Wabaunsee asked the chief.
Wabaunsee: There isn't enough water for the salmon or for us to irrigate our crops. No fish and no crops mean no food.
Chief: The rain will come.
Narrator: said the chief.
Chief: Be patient.
Narrator: Wabaunsee was tired of being patient.
Wabaunsee: Waiting for the rain isn't helpful.
Narrator: he argued.
Wabaunsee: It isn't a drought. Something's wrong. I'm going to find out what it is!
Narrator: Early the next morning, Wabaunsee left the village. He rode north, up the river. He rode for hours Finally, he reached a town.
Wabaunsee: What's that in the river?
Narrator: Wabaunsee cried.
Wabaunsee: "They're stopping the water with that wall!"
Mayor: We built this dam—'the wall' as you call it—because we need it.
Narrator: the mayor of Kingstown said.
Engineer: Now we can direct the water toward our fields and we have a lake for swimming and boating.
Narrator: explained the engineer.

Wabaunsee: But there's no water left for us.
Narrator: Wabaunsee insisted.
Mayor: Sorry, but we're busy.
Narrator: said the mayor.
Mayor: Let us know if you have a better idea …
Narrator: Wabaunsee explained the dam to the chief and village elders. They understood that River Kalamazoo was important to the people of Kingstown, but it didn't belong to them.
Chief: We have to share what nature gives us.
Narrator: the chief said.
Chief: "Everything is connected."
Wabaunsee's friend: The frog doesn't drink up the pond in which it lives.
Narrator: Wabaunsee's friend said.
Wabaunsee: You've given me an idea!
Narrator: exclaimed Wabaunsee.
Wabaunsee: There's a river animal that'll help us!
Narrator: At Kingstown the next day, Wabaunsee explained his idea.
Wabaunsee: Beavers!
Narrator: Wabaunsee began.
Wabaunsee: They build dams with sticks and mud for food and protection. But the river still flows through them. Your dam stops the river because it's made of stone.
Narrator: The engineer listened thoughtfully.
Engineer: But a wooden dam won't hold.
Narrator: he said.
Engineer: The river is too strong in spring.
Narrator: After weeks of discussion … the two men finally found a solution.
Wabaunsee: We can build a wooden gate at the base of the dam.
Narrator: said Wabaunsee.
Engineer: We can lift it when there's no rain to let more water through. Or close it in spring so your village doesn't flood.
Narrator: the engineer added. It took them months to build the new dam. Thankfully, it was a big success! River Kalamazoo flowed past the village and the salmon returned. The villagers could fish again and irrigate their crops. There was food for everyone to share.

TRACK 38

Unit 7, *The New Dam*, Words in Context
Find these words in the reading. What do you think they mean?
respected
powerful
creek
salmon
direct
hold

TRACK 39

Unit 7, Spelling Patterns, final *ful* and *fully*
Listen and write. Then check your answers.
1 beautiful
2 useful
3 grateful
4 hopefully
5 carefully

Now check your answers.
1 beautiful, b-e-a-u-t-i-f-u-l, beautiful
2 useful, u-s-e-f-u-l, useful
3 grateful, g-r-a-t-e-f-u-l, grateful
4 hopefully, h-o-p-e-f-u-l-l-y, hopefully
5 carefully, c-a-r-e-f-u-l-l-y, carefully

Unit 8

TRACK 40

Unit 8, Nonfiction, *Action Stars*
The red sports car speeds through busy city streets, just missing trucks and buses. People run screaming. Then, all of a sudden, the car flips, rolls over, and crashes.
People gather around the scene of the crash. The door of the car opens, and the driver climbs out. She gives everyone a wave. The crowd cheers and claps.
Why isn't anyone scared? Because this is a movie set. The driver who was in the car is a stunt performer. The car crash was a carefully planned action scene.
When movies have dangerous scenes or parts that need a lot of action, they often use stunt men and women. Sometimes known as a stunt double, a stunt performer takes the place of the main actor during the risky scenes.
A stunt might be something like falling from a building, hanging from a helicopter, or fighting.
To become a professional stunt person requires many years of hard work and training.
Stunt performers learn skills in gymnastics, high diving, falling, swimming, horseback riding, driving, and martial arts such as karate. They must also spend a lot of time in movie studios, on movie sets, and in front of cameras before they can perform their first stunt.
Good stunt performers are always calm under pressure, organized, and well prepared. The stunt has to be exactly right or the stunt person might get injured.
Stunt performers are also actors. They watch the main actors and learn how to move like them and sometimes say their lines. Often they wear wigs and make-up—even fake scars—to look like the main actors.
One of the first stunt performers was Yakima Canutt. Canutt was a world champion rodeo rider. He won many awards before he started working in movies.
In a famous scene from an old movie, Canutt jumped from one horse to another. He fell off the horse, but still hung on while the horses ran. Then he disappeared between the wheels of the speeding coach!
Some actors can also perform stunts. Jackie Chan is an actor who is well-known for doing his own stunts. Before he became an actor, Chan was a stunt coordinator for many years. He planned stunts and fight scenes. In the movie Shanghai Noon, he planned and performed many stunts. He ran and jumped from train car to train car while the train moved. Then he jumped from the top of the train engine!
While stunt people get to do exciting things like jump motorcycles and hang from horses, danger is never far away. So, the next time you see an amazing stunt in a trailer or a movie, stop and think about all the training and hard work it took the stunt person to make it happen.

TRACK 41

Unit 8, *Action Stars*, Words in Context
Find these words in the reading. What do you think they mean?
stunt
scene
professional
martial arts
champion

TRACK 42

Unit 8, Spelling Pattern, final *ing*
Listen and write. Then check your answers.
1 lightning
2 melting
3 getting
4 spring
5 carrying

Now check your answers.
1 lightning, l-i-g-h-t-n-i-n-g, lightning
2 melting, m-e-l-t-i-n-g, melting
3 getting, g-e-t-t-i-n-g, getting
4 spring, s-p-r-i-n-g, spring
5 carrying, c-a-r-r-y-i-n-g, carrying

TRACK 43

Unit 8, Fiction, *Actors on Set!*
Sam: I've got a script. Now let's make a movie. I can't wait to get started. Come on, James.
James: Who made you leader?
Sam: I did. Anyway, in a movie I'm called the producer, not the leader. I'm hiring you as director. Your job is to direct the filming of the movie.
James: Have you ever made a movie before?
Sam: No, but I've got a webpage here that tells me all about it. First, we'll need a script supervisor. Hey, Rick! Want to be in the movie?
Rick: Sure.
Sam: You're in charge of the script. There! I've emailed it to you. Mike, I'm making you director of photography.
Mike: OK. But what do I do?
Sam: You tell the camera operator what to film with the camera. Rachel, do you have a video camera?
Rachel: Yes, on my phone.
Sam: Good, you're the cameraperson. Listen to Mike's instructions.
James: Are you sure we really need all these people?
Sam: Of course. It says right here on the webpage. Now we want a boom operator.
James: A what?
Sam: A boom operator holds the microphone.

James: But the microphone is built into Rachel's phone. It records the sounds as well as the pictures.
Sam: Sarah. Drop your math book. You're wanted on set. You're the boom operator.
Sarah: OK.
Sam: Emma, you're our gaffer.
James: A gaffer?
Sam: The person in charge of setting up the lights.
James: We don't have any lights.
Emma: I'll get some flashlights.
Sam: Jack. How strong are you?
Jack: Pretty strong, I guess.
Sam: Good, you can stop writing. You're the grip. You're in charge of moving all the equipment around.
James: I really don't think …
Sam: James, a proper movie needs all the right people. Stop arguing. Now we need a set designer to build the set, a props master to take care of the props, a make-up artist, and a costume designer.
James: You forgot a hairdresser.
Sam: Good point. Nathaniel, you're the hairdresser. Find a hairbrush. OK. We're ready to shoot. Actors on set, please! Actors! Actors?
James: There are no actors. There's no one left.
Sam: How did this happen?
James: Don't ask me, you're the producer, remember? But perhaps we could ask the drama club to help us out …

TRACK 44

Unit 8, *Actors on Set!* Words in Context
Find these words in the reading. What do you think they mean?
producer
hiring
supervisor
operator
instructions
microphone
props
shoot

Unit 9

TRACK 45

Unit 9, Fiction, *Pinocchia*
Paola: Ready for lunch?
Narrator: Paola asked.
Paola: I'm almost finished with this.
Narrator: she added.
Beneto: Yes, I'm starving.
Narrator: Beneto said.
Beneto: That's really good, Paola …
Mrs. Atario: Good morning, Beneto. Hello, Paola!
Narrator: Mrs. Atario said.
Mrs. Atario: I'm here because I'd like a new robot for my daughter, Cleo. It's her birthday in two weeks. The robot must like playing games. It must also do chores—you know, sweep the floor, do the laundry, wash the dishes.
Narrator: Mrs. Atario always paid in advance, giving Beneto all the money before they started work. She was Beneto and Paola's best client. Two weeks weren't enough to make a robot, but they couldn't let her down.
They worked around the clock to finish Mrs. Atario's robot…
…and they did!
Beneto: Ta-da!
Narrator: Beneto cried.
Paola: Her name's Pinocchia!
Narrator: Paola shouted. Before taking Pinocchia to Mrs. Atario, they tested her.
Beneto: Hello, Pinocchia. How are you?
Narrator: asked Beneto.
Pinocchia: Very well, thank you.
Narrator: answered Pinocchia.
Beneto: What do you like to do?
Pinocchia: I like vacuuming the carpet.
Paola: This is one of the best robots we've ever made!
Narrator: cried Paola.
The next day, Beneto took Pinocchia to Mrs. Atario's apartment.
Beneto: Look at this wonderful city, Pinocchia!
Narrator: Beneto shouted. They waited to see Mrs. Atario, but no one was there.
Beneto: Come on, Pinocchia. Let's go home.
Narrator: said Beneto.
Beneto: Still no news from Mrs. Atario.
Narrator: Beneto said.
Paola: I'm sure she'll be in contact soon.
Narrator: replied Paola.
Pinocchia: I love this movie!
Narrator: Pinocchia said.
Pinocchia: What a great story!
Narrator: Pinocchia cried.
Pinocchia: It smells delicious!
Narrator: Pinocchia exclaimed. As the months went by, Beneto, Paola, and Pinocchia became a family.
Mrs. Atario: Sorry, I'm late!
Narrator: Mrs. Atario said cheerfully.
Beneto: Late?
Narrator: said Beneto.
Paola: Where have you been, Mrs. Atario?
Narrator: asked Paola.
Mrs. Atario: We went on a trip to Mars. My uncle was sick … nothing serious. Anyway, I've come to collect my robot!
Narrator: said Mrs. Atario. She grabbed Pinocchia. It was heartbreaking, but there was nothing Beneto and Paola could do. Pinocchia had to go.
At her new home, Pinocchia was unhappy. Mrs. Atario and Cleo didn't love her.
Cleo: Come on, silly robot. Let's play!
Narrator: Cleo demanded. When Pinocchia was unhappy, she didn't have any energy. She couldn't play with Cleo and she couldn't do the chores well.
Mrs. Atario: This is ridiculous!
Narrator: cried Mrs. Atario while Pinocchia's battery was charging.
Mrs. Atario: I paid good money for this robot and this is what I get! You're going back to the lab, Pinocchia!
I've never been so disappointed, Beneto. This robot of yours doesn't work. Something's wrong with her energy levels.
Narrator: Mrs Atario explained.
Beneto: Let me see.
Narrator: said Beneto. He took a closer look.
Beneto: You're right, Mrs Atario. Pinocchia's battery is no good.
Narrator: Beneto said.
Beneto: Please choose another robot from the shelf.
Narrator: he added.
Paola: Welcome back, Pinocchia! We missed you!
Narrator: Paola said.
Pinocchia: It feels great to be home!
Narrator: Pinocchia said.

TRACK 46

Unit 9, *Pinocchia*, Words in Context
Find these words in the reading. What do you think they mean?
chores
in advance
client
let her down
cheerfully
heartbreaking
battery
charging

TRACK 47

Unit 9, Nonfiction, *Fast Forward*
Have you ever wondered about transportation in the future? What will cars, trains, and planes look like, and how fast will they travel? Let's see what's new in transportation today and what we can expect by the end of this century.

Cars

In many big cities, people are now driving electric cars. They look like normal cars, but they don't use gas or diesel. They have an electric motor and a large battery. To recharge the battery, the owner just plugs in the car. Electric cars are quiet and they pollute less.
Soon, we won't drive cars. There will be cars but they won't need drivers! Self-driving cars will have computers with maps and radar to avoid accidents. Scientists are also developing flying cars. People will park them high up in the air outside their apartments or office buildings.

Trains

These days, high-speed trains crisscross Asia and Europe and can reach an average speed of 250 to 300 kilometers per hour! A high-speed train is so powerful because there's a motor in each car.
Many trains in the future will be Maglev trains. In some places, people are already using them. These trains don't touch the track. They float on air because the magnets on the rail and the train push away from each other. Scientists predict they'll soon reach speeds of over 500 kilometers per hour and link cities that are thousands

of kilometers apart. Another idea is the Hyperloop. Imagine a modern subway with structures like big pipes. Inside them there will be capsules for passengers that will travel faster than planes travel today.

Planes

One of the biggest planes in the world is the Airbus A380. It's a double-decker and it's as long as eight buses! These planes fly over oceans and continents at a cruise speed of 900 kilometers per hour. More than 500 passengers and thousands of suitcases can travel on an A380.

Designers have already developed planes that use energy from the sun. In 2016, pilots Bertrand Piccard and André Borschberg flew a solar-powered plane around the world. It took them 505 days and zero gas! So, planes will probably use solar energy in the future.

Engineers also think space travel will be possible by 2050. Virgin Galactic is already working on planes that will take tourists in a spaceship to space!

Individual Transportation

As well as electric bikes, scooters, and skateboards, inventors are developing other more efficient ways of traveling as an individual. Have you ever seen anyone on a Segway? That's one type of individual transportation that people use in some urban areas today. In the future, we may go to school or work on floating skateboards or in flying suits!

Traveling is definitely faster and safer thanks to technology, and there are a lot of great ideas for the future.

TRACK 48

Unit 9, *Fast Forward*, Words in Context

Find these words in the reading. What do you think they mean?

pollute
self-driving
radar
crisscross
magnets
structures
double-decker

TRACK 49

Unit 9, Spelling Pattern, soft *g*

Listen and write. Then check your answers.

1 danger
2 angelfish
3 giraffe
4 stage
5 emergency

Now check your answers.

1 danger, d-a-n-g-e-r, danger
2 angelfish, a-n-g-e-l-f-i-s-h, angelfish
3 giraffe, g-i-r-a-f-f-e, giraffe
4 stage, s-t-a-g-e, stage
5 emergency, e-m-e-r-g-e-n-c-y, emergency

Unit 10

TRACK 50

Unit 10, Nonfiction, *Sense Superstore*

Welcome to the Sense Superstore! The best place for amazing senses. Sight, smell, taste, hearing, and touch, we have it all! This month only—20% off all sensational animal senses.

Super Touch

Nerve endings

The nose of the star-nosed mole has an incredible sense of touch.

Around the nose of this mole are 22 little tentacles. These tentacles are very sensitive and have more than 100,000 nerve endings— many more than a human hand. They help the mole sense things in the ground without needing to see.

Electroreception

When living things move, they give off small amounts of electricity.

Thanks to special pores, or small holes, on its head, the shark can feel that electricity as it travels through the water. It uses this electroreception to find prey it wants to eat.

Super Sight

Ultraviolet

To find anything that is hard to spot, use amazing reindeer sight.

In the Arctic, the camouflage of a wolf's white fur doesn't work on a reindeer. The reindeer's eyes can see ultraviolet light— light that is not visible to the human eye. Using ultraviolet sight, the wolf looks black against the snow.

Infrared

The fire-chaser beetle has the ability to find fire. This beetle looks for places with forest fires, where it can lay its eggs safely in burnt wood.

The fire-chaser beetle has 70 sensors on its body that detect infrared radiation— the invisible rays of heat from fire. This means the beetle can sense fire from great distances—scientists believe more than 100 km. away!

Super Hearing

Infrasonic

Infrasonic sound is low sound that is lower than humans can hear. But elephants can hear it.

Elephants are well known for their powerful hearing and use infrasonic sound to communicate with each other. Elephants in the same family stay in touch through infrasonic sound even when they are far away.

Echolocation

As they fly, bats make sounds which the human ear cannot hear.

These sounds echo, or bounce off of objects. The bat listens to these echoes and measures how long it takes for the sound to bounce back. That way, it can hunt and find its way in the dark.

Super Smell

Jacobson's Organ

In the roof of a snake's mouth is the Jacobson's organ—a super-smelling tool. When a snake flicks its tongue in and out, it senses chemicals in the air. The tongue passes this information on to the Jacobson's organ. The snake can then tell where the smell is coming from, and what is making the smell.

Super Taste

Taste buds

A catfish has 100,000 taste buds all over its body (compared with a human's 10,000). Catfish live in muddy water at the bottom of rivers and lakes. They use their extraordinary sense of taste to find the tiny particles of food in the water they need to survive.

We're sure you'll want to add all these super senses to your basket, won't you?

TRACK 51

Unit 10, *Sense Superstore*, Words in Context

Find these words in the reading. What do you think they mean?

sensitive
nerve endings
pores
prey
camouflage
ability
organ
taste buds

TRACK 52

Unit 10, Fiction, *The Wrinklecrinkle Man*

In the town of Wobblewell, hanging over the sea,
Lived a wrinklecrinkle man, as plain as plain can be.
His home came from sticks the sea washed to shore,
With green bottles for windows, and a barrel for a door.
Each day he roamed the streets, saluting passers-by,
"Hello to you," he called in joy, followed with "Goodbye!"
The townspeople laughed and smiled, they all liked him you see,
The wrinklecrinkle man, from Wobblewell by the sea.
All but Dominic the baker, who grumbled behind his back,
"Every day he walks past my shop, and never buys a snack.
But sticks his nose up in the air, and smells my bread for free,
That wrinklecrinkle man, from Wobblewell by the sea."
"This can't go on," said Dominic, "He's got me seeing red.
He should pay $3 if he wants to smell my bread!"

"It's true he doesn't taste it. That costs a larger fee.
But smelling is a pleasure you just can't have for free."
The townspeople all shook their heads, "He isn't doing wrong, is he,
The wrinklecrinkle man, from Wobblewell by the sea?"
The baker brought the man to court, to stand before the judge.
Dominic wanted justice done, and wouldn't drop his grudge.
"This man should pay to smell my bread, Your Honor, shouldn't he,
This wrinklecrinkle man, from Wobblewell by the sea?"
The judge, she listened carefully, and then she listened some more,
"In all my years, sitting here, I've never heard this before.
To this baker's serious charge, tell me, what is your plea?
Oh wrinklecrinkle man, from Wobblewell by the sea."
The man puffed out his chest, standing straight and strong,
"It's true, Your Honor, I breathe in bread, but surely there's no wrong?
The sweet smell of bread, a sparrow's tune, the sun all belong to me,"
Said the wrinklecrinkle man, from Wobblewell by the sea.
The judge then scratched her chin while weighing the case,
"I do believe you owe the baker," she said with a straight face.
"For stealing smells, you must pay the price, I do decree,
Oh wrinklecrinkle man, from Wobblewell by the sea."
The old man held his purse, though the coins inside were few,
"Now shake the coins," ordered the judge. "That's what you must do."
The old man did as he was told and shook the coins loudly,
That wrinklecrinkle man, from Wobblewell by the sea.
"Now Dominic, this man's coins, can you hear their jingle?"
"Oh yes, I can," said Dominic, "My skin is all a-tingle!"
"Good, well, the price for smelling your bread
Is the sound of his money!" the judge then said.
"Now off you go, case dismissed, once more you are free,
Oh wrinklecrinkle man, from Wobblewell by the sea."

TRACK 53

Unit 10, *The Wrinklecrinkle Man*, Words in Context

Find these words in the reading. What do you think they mean?

barrel
saluting
justice
grudge
charge
plea
decree
case dismissed

TRACK 54

Unit 10, Spelling Pattern, long *e*

Listen and write. Then check your answers.

1 repeat
2 details
3 knee
4 pretend
5 cheese

Now check your answers.

1 repeat, r-e-p-e-a-t, repeat
2 details, d-e-t-a-i-l-s, details
3 knee, k-n-e-e, knee
4 pretend, p-r-e-t-e-n-d, pretend
5 cheese, c-h-e-e-s-e, cheese

Video Scripts

Language Book

The video scripts for the songs in the **Language Book** are exactly the same as for the audio scripts and the text on the page. Please refer to the relevant unit in the Audio Scripts on TB pp. 213–227.

Unit 1

CONVERSATION

I Love This Painting!

Stephen: Hi, Otis! Come in.
Otis: Wow, Stephen, you have a lot of art in your home!
Stephen: What do you think of this picture? Do you like it?
Otis: Not really. I think the colors are too bright.
Stephen: I disagree. I think it's fantastic! I kind of like that picture, too. It's really detailed.
Otis: I don't mind it. I like the trees in the foreground. Oh! I really like that picture.
Stephen: It's OK, I guess. I think it's too dark. It isn't light enough.
Otis: But this is my favorite.
Stephen: You're right. It's very good.
Otis: I'm sure the artist is very famous. Why are you laughing? Do you know who it is?
Stephen: Yes, I do. But he's not famous. Not yet! It's me! I painted it last week in art class!
Otis: Wow, Stephen! You're really good. Maybe you will be famous one day!

Unit 2

PRESENTATION

More Time, Please

Lewis: Today I'm going to talk about something very important. Time. It's part of our everyday lives.
Do you ever feel there isn't enough time to do all the things you want to do?
I think it's very important to plan your time. Here are some tips.
I find that the best thing to do is to make a list every day. Always do the things you have to do first, and then the things you want to do! So, my advice is do your homework first. Then you can have fun, talk to your friends, or play sports!
Something else to remember is don't make your list too long. Don't plan every minute. You can't do everything in one day.
My next tip is about taking time for yourself. Don't forget that doing nothing can be good for you, too. Your brain needs to have a rest sometimes.
Finally, try to do two things at the same time, if you can. For example, I practiced this presentation as I cleaned my room last night! Thank you for listening.

Unit 3

PRESENTATION

My Friend

Rania: Today I want to introduce you to my best friend Suyin. She's ten and a half, like me, and she's as tall as me. We always walk to school together. Our parents are friends too. We met when we were tiny babies! Our birthdays are in the same month, December. So we often celebrate together. Suyin is kind and helpful. She always talks to you if you feel lonely or upset. If you tell her a secret, she won't tell anyone else. We have the same interests and hobbies: modern dance, cooking, and watching movies. She likes reading, and so do I. We both enjoy playing the guitar, although she's better at it than me! There's only one difference between us. Suyin loves playing sports, but I don't!
I hope we'll always be best friends.

Unit 4

CONVERSATION

What Do You Know About Space?

Anya: We need to choose a planet for our science presentation.
Natalia: Why don't we talk about Jupiter? It sounds really interesting.
Anya: Oh, I love Jupiter! Did you know it's the largest planet in the solar system? We can look for information on the internet. Let's ask Mom for help.
Natalia: How should we organize our presentation?
Anya: Let's choose three different headings: size, appearance, and fun facts.
Natalia: That sounds good. I'll make some notes about size and appearance. And, can you find any fun facts?
Anya: Sure. It might be a good idea to make a mobile of the planets.
Natalia: Ooh. That's an excellent idea!
Anya: Listen to this. Earth and Jupiter are very different, except for one thing. They both have bad storms.
Natalia: Really? That's interesting!
Anya: And also, scientists sent the spaceship Juno to Jupiter in 2011. It took five years to arrive there!
Natalia: Five years! That is a fun fact. We should print out a picture of Juno.
Anya: I'll look for one. I think people are really going to enjoy listening to our presentation.

Unit 5

CONVERSATION

Let's Trade

Stephen: Hey, Lewis, I see you're collecting World Cup soccer cards, too.
Lewis: Yes, I am. Do you have anything to trade?
Stephen: Sure. I have two of these. I'm interested in your Argentinian players. I don't have any in my collection. If I give you a card, will you give me one of yours?
Lewis: One of my Argentinian players? No, that's not a good trade. I was lucky to get them. They aren't easy to find, but I know you really want one. I'll give you one of them for five of your cards.
Stephen: Five! That's too many. I'll give you three.
Lewis: OK, that's a deal.

Unit 6

CONVERSATION

An Adventurous Gift

Rania: We need to decide on a present for Sophie. Her family's going on a trip to the jungle, remember? Why don't we get her something for that?
Otis: What about a diary? She loves writing. She can write about her adventures. What do you think?
Rania: I think that sounds good. What about you?
Natalia: I suggest a really long cotton scarf. She can use it to keep mosquitoes away or to keep the sun off her head. What do you think?
Lewis: Hmm, I was thinking of a useful object like a small flashlight.
Rania: I'm not sure. It's useful, but it's not a fun present. Why don't we buy her a photo album? I know she wants to take photos of elephants and tigers.
Otis: That's true. She'll like that, and it will be useful at the same time.
Rania: So, we agree we want to get her something that she will like and that will be useful. Is that right?
Natalia: Yes. So which idea do you think we should buy?
Lewis: Let's look for a photo album.
Rania: I agree. I think that's best.
Otis: Let's take a photo to put in the album! Say "cheese"!

Unit 7

PRESENTATION

What Do You See?

Stephen: Look at these two pictures. Both are about people using water. In the first picture, I can see a woman watering a huge garden with a hose. There is green grass and some trees, and in the background of the picture there is a large pond. In the other picture, two boys are using soap and water to wash a car. It looks like they're having fun. Another similarity between these two pictures is the weather. It's a warm day in both pictures, and the people are wearing summer clothes. One difference is their age. In the first picture, there is an adult, but in the other picture, there are children. They might be brothers of about eight and ten.
I think both people are enjoying what they are doing. My favorite picture is the second one. I think washing the car is fun to do with friends and family. Both pictures show people doing jobs which make them happy.

Unit 8

PRESENTATION

My Favorite Movie

Anya: I want to tell you about a movie I've seen again and again, and enjoyed every time. It's called *Inside Out*. It's an animation, so it stars some famous actors' voices as the different characters.
It's set in the imagination of a young girl, Riley. At the beginning of the movie, Riley's very happy. Her life is wonderful. And then when she's 11 years old, her family goes to live in a new city, and suddenly she has lots of different feelings. The other characters are all feelings, like happy and sad. These feelings all fight with each other. At different times, different feelings are stronger, and they make her feel happy, then sad, then angry, then afraid. But in the end, they learn that all feelings are important and they learn to work together, so there's a happy ending.
I thought the movie had a lot of important messages about family and friends. Although the movie is for children, I recommend it to adults as well, because it will really help them to understand how children feel and that all feelings are OK—good or bad.

Unit 9

PRESENTATION

My City of the Future

Otis: Let's think about cities in 50 years, when we're adults. What will they look like? How will they change? Here are my ideas. First, we already have very tall buildings. I think buildings will get taller and taller. Also, we won't have space on the ground to build anything, so perhaps some buildings will be floating in the sky. To get to them, we'll probably all use private flying machines, although it might be a bit dangerous to fly through a storm.
Second, today we have moving paths in airports. I think in 50 years we'll have moving paths everywhere so that we won't have to walk at all. We'll just stand on the path and it will transport us around town. Long ago, people thought a car without a driver was an impossible idea. As we know, we already have cars like this. One day, I'm sure we'll have planes without drivers, too. Children will fly to school! In my opinion, that will be the best thing of all!
We don't know exactly how life will change in the future, but one thing is certain, in 50 years, cities will look very different.

Unit 10

CONVERSATION

What Is It?

Anya: Natalia, it's your turn to guess the mystery object. What does it feel like?
Natalia: It feels cold and hard. It's rough on the outside, and it's smooth on the inside.
Anya: Good. Now hold it next to your ear. Listen. What can you hear?
Natalia: Oh, it's making me laugh. I can hear the sound of the ocean! Is it a shell?
Anya: Yes, it is! Well done! OK, now it's Stephen's turn. Stephen, hold this bag up to your nose. That's it. Now, what can you smell?
Stephen: It smells … sweet, like ice cream.
Anya: Right. Now look at the object but don't show Natalia. Have you looked at it long enough? OK. Can you describe it?
Stephen: It's long, thin, and black … a kind of plant. A plant that smells like ice cream.
Natalia: It's vanilla!
Anya: Yes, that's right! Now here's another object. Don't show it to anyone else. Can you describe it? What does it feel like?
Stephen: It's kind of hard and smooth, with a little rough part at one end. It has a hole in it at the top.
Anya: What's it made of?
Stephen: It's cold; it's made of metal. It's something we all need, for doors, bikes, windows …
Natalia: Is it a key?
Stephen: Yes, it is!
Anya: Great!

Literacy Book

The video scripts for the **Literacy Book** reading texts are exactly the same as for the audio scripts and the pages of the book.

Unit 1

NONFICTION
My Guide to Photography
Audio Track 7 TB p. 228

Unit 2

FICTION
A World Without Time
Audio Track 10 TB p. 228

Unit 3

FICTION
Trust Me
Audio Track 18 TB p. 230

Unit 4

NONFICTION
The First Man in Space
Audio Track 23 TB p. 231

Unit 5

NONFICTION
The Silk Road
Audio Track 25 TB p. 231

Unit 6

NONFICTION
SOS
Audio Track 30 TB p. 232

Unit 7

FICTION
The New Dam
Audio Track 37 TB p. 233

Unit 8

NONFICTION
Action Stars
Audio Track 40 TB p. 234

Unit 9

FICTION
Pinocchia
Audio Track 45 TB p. 235

Unit 10

NONFICTION
Sense Superstore
Audio Track 50 TB p. 236